Paper F7

Financial Reporting

EXAM KIT

December 2014 – June 2015

PUBLISHING

British Library Cataloguing-in-Publication Data

A catalogue record for this book is available from the British Library.

Published by:

Kaplan Publishing UK

Unit 2 The Business Centre

Molly Millar's Lane

Wokingham

Berkshire

RG41 2QZ

ISBN: 978–1–78415–047–1

© Kaplan Financial Limited, 2014

Printed and bound in Great Britain

Acknowledgements

The past ACCA examination questions are the copyright of the Association of Chartered Certified Accountants. The original answers to the questions from June 1994 onwards were produced by the examiners themselves and have been adapted by Kaplan Publishing.

We are grateful to the Chartered Institute of Management Accountants and the Institute of Chartered Accountants in England and Wales for permission to reproduce past examination questions. The answers have been prepared by Kaplan Publishing.

CONTENTS

Section

Key features in this edition

In addition to providing a wide ranging bank of real past exam questions, we have also included in this edition:

- An analysis of all of the recent examination papers.

- Paper specific information.

- Our recommended approach to make your revision for this particular subject as effective as possible. This includes step by step guidance on how best to use our Kaplan material (Complete text, pocket notes and exam kit) at this stage in your studies.

- Enhanced tutorial answers packed with specific key answer tips, technical tutorial notes and exam technique tips from our experienced tutors.

- Complementary online resources including full tutor debriefs and question assistance to point you in the right direction when you get stuck.

You will find a wealth of other resources to help you with your studies on the following sites:

www.mykaplan.co.uk

www.kaplan-exam-tips.com

www.accaglobal.com/students/

Quality and accuracy are of the utmost importance to us so if you spot an error in any of our products, please send an email to mykaplanreporting@kaplan.com with full details, or follow the link to the feedback form in MyKaplan.

Our Quality Co-ordinator will work with our technical team to verify the error and take action to ensure it is corrected in future editions.

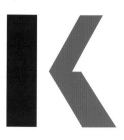

Kaplan Publishing are constantly finding new ways to make a difference to your studies and our exciting online resources really do offer something different to students looking for exam success.

This book comes with free MyKaplan online resources so that you can study anytime, anywhere

Having purchased this book, you have access to the following online study materials:

CONTENT	ACCA (including FFA,FAB,FMA)		FIA (excluding FFA,FAB,FMA)	
	Text	Kit	Text	Kit
iPaper version of the book	✓	✓	✓	✓
Interactive electronic version of the book	✓			
Progress tests with instant answers	✓			
Material updates	✓	✓	✓	✓
Latest official ACCA exam questions*		✓		
Extra question assistance using the signpost icon*		✓		
Timed questions with an online tutor debrief using the clock icon*		✓		
Interim assessment including questions and answers	✓		✓	
Technical articles	✓	✓	✓	✓

* Excludes F1, F2, F3, FFA, FAB, FMA

How to access your online resources

Kaplan Financial students will already have a MyKaplan account and these extra resources will be available to you online. You do not need to register again, as this process was completed when you enrolled. If you are having problems accessing online materials, please ask your course administrator.

If you are already a registered MyKaplan user go to www.MyKaplan.co.uk and log in. Select the 'add a book' feature and enter the ISBN number of this book and the unique pass key at the bottom of this card. Then click 'finished' or 'add another book'. You may add as many books as you have purchased from this screen.

If you purchased through Kaplan Flexible Learning or via the Kaplan Publishing website you will automatically receive an e-mail invitation to MyKaplan. Please register your details using this email to gain access to your content. If you do not receive the e-mail or book content, please contact Kaplan Flexible Learning.

If you are a new MyKaplan user register at www.MyKaplan.co.uk and click on the link contained in the email we sent you to activate your account. Then select the 'add a book' feature, enter the ISBN number of this book and the unique pass key at the bottom of this card. Then click 'finished' or 'add another book'.

Your Code and Information

This code can only be used once for the registration of one book online. This registration and your online content will expire when the final sittings for the examinations covered by this book have taken place. Please allow one hour from the time you submit your book details for us to process your request.

Please scratch the film to access your MyKaplan code.

Please be aware that this code is case-sensitive and you will need to include the dashes within the passcode, but not when entering the ISBN. For further technical support, please visit www.MyKaplan.co.uk

KAPLAN PUBLISHING

INDEX TO QUESTIONS AND ANSWERS

INTRODUCTION

Following the revised exam format, and the addition of *IAS 41 Agriculture,* many of the previous ACCA exam questions within this kit have been adapted to reflect updated standards, and the revised exam format. If changed in any way from the original version, whether due to updates in the IFRSs or due to changes in exam format, this is indicated in the end column of the index below with the mark *(A).*

The specimen paper is included at the end of the kit.

KEY TO THE INDEX

PAPER ENHANCEMENTS

We have added the following enhancements to the answers in this exam kit:

Key answer tips

All answers include key answer tips to help your understanding of each question.

Tutorial note

All answers include more tutorial notes to explain some of the technical points in more detail.

Top tutor tips

For selected questions, we 'walk through the answer' giving guidance on how to approach the questions with helpful 'tips from a top tutor', together with technical tutor notes.

These answers are indicated with the 'footsteps' icon in the index.

ONLINE ENHANCEMENTS

 Timed question with Online tutor debrief

For selected questions, we recommend that they are to be completed in full exam conditions (i.e. properly timed in a closed book environment).

In addition to the examiner's technical answer, enhanced with key answer tips and tutorial notes in this exam kit, online you can find an answer debrief by a top tutor that:

* works through the question in full

* points out how to approach the question

* how to ensure that the easy marks are obtained as quickly as possible, and

* emphasises how to tackle exam questions and exam technique.

These questions are indicated with the 'clock' icon in the index.

 Online question assistance

Have you ever looked at a question and not know where to start, or got stuck part way through?

For selected questions, we have produced 'Online question assistance' offering different levels of guidance, such as:

* ensuring that you understand the question requirements fully, highlighting key terms and the meaning of the verbs used

* how to read the question proactively, with knowledge of the requirements, to identify the topic areas covered

* assessing the detail content of the question body, pointing out key information and explaining why it is important

* help in devising a plan of attack

With this assistance, you should then be able to attempt your answer confident that you know what is expected of you.

These questions are indicated with the 'signpost' icon in the index.

Online question enhancements and answer debriefs will be available on MyKaplan at:

www.MyKaplan.co.uk

PREPARATION OF SINGLE COMPANY FINANCIAL STATEMENTS

BUSINESS COMBINATIONS

ANALYSING FINANCIAL STATEMENTS AND STATEMENTS OF CASH FLOWS

ANALYSIS OF PAST EXAM PAPERS

The table below summarises the key topics that have been tested in the F7 examinations to date. It is important to note that the format of the exam has been changed, and the specimen column highlights that a much wider range of topics will now be examined following the introduction of multiple choice questions.

	Jun 09	Dec 09	Jun 10	Dec 10	Jun 11	Dec 11	Jun 12	Dec 12	Jun 13	Dec 13	Specimen 14
Group financial statements											
Consolidated statement of profit or loss and other comprehensive income		✓			✓			✓			✓
Consolidated statement of financial position	✓		✓			✓	✓		✓		✓
Consolidated P/L and SFP				✓						✓	
Associates	✓	✓	✓			✓	✓	✓			✓
Non-group financial statements											
From trial balance	✓	✓	✓	✓	✓	✓	✓	✓	✓	✓	✓
Redraft											
Statement of changes in equity				✓	✓		✓	✓	✓		✓
Statement of cash flows	✓	✓	✓		✓	✓	✓		✓	✓	✓
Performance appraisal											
Ratios					✓			✓			✓
Mixed transactional											
IASB Framework		✓			✓		✓	✓	✓	✓	✓
Accounting principles / substance			✓							✓	✓
Not for profit/specialised entities											✓
IAS 2											
IAS 8				✓				✓			✓
IAS 10	✓										
IAS 11					✓			✓			
IAS 12											✓
IAS 16	✓	✓						✓	✓	✓	✓
IAS 17										✓	✓
IAS 18										✓	✓
IAS 20								✓			
IAS 23		✓									
IAS 32/IAS 39/IFRS 7/IFRS 9						✓					✓
IAS 33		✓			✓						✓
IAS 36							✓		✓		✓
IAS 37						✓		✓		✓	✓
IAS 38		✓									✓
IAS 40											
IAS 41											✓
IFRS 5				✓					✓		
IFRS 13											

EXAM TECHNIQUE

- Use the allocated **15 minutes reading and planning time** at the beginning of the exam:
  - read the questions and examination requirements carefully, and
  - begin planning your answers.

  See the Paper Specific Information for advice on how to use this time for this paper.

- **Divide the time** you spend on questions in proportion to the marks on offer:
  - there are 1.8 minutes available per mark in the examination
  - within that, try to allow time at the end of each question to review your answer and address any obvious issues

  Whatever happens, always keep your eye on the clock and **do not over run on any part of any question!**

- If you **get completely stuck** with a question:
  - leave space in your answer book, and
  - **return to it later.**

- Stick to the question and **tailor your answer** to what you are asked.
  - pay particular attention to the verbs in the question.

- If you do not understand what a question is asking, **state your assumptions**.

  Even if you do not answer in precisely the way the examiner hoped, you should be given some credit, if your assumptions are reasonable.

- You should do everything you can to make things easy for the marker.

  The marker will find it easier to identify the points you have made if your **answers are legible**.

- **Written questions**:

  Your answer should have:
  - a clear structure
  - a brief introduction, a main section and a conclusion.

  Be concise.

  It is better to write a little about a lot of different points than a great deal about one or two points.

- **Computations**:

  It is essential to include all your workings in your answers.

  Many computational questions require the use of a standard format:

  e.g. statement of profit or loss and other comprehensive income, statement of financial position and statement of cash flow.

  Be sure you know these formats thoroughly before the exam and use the layouts that you see in the answers given in this book and in model answers.

- **Multiple-choice questions**:

  Decide whether you want to attempt these at the start of the exam or at the end.

  No credit for workings will be given in these questions; the answers will either be correct (2 marks) or incorrect (0 marks).

  Read the question carefully, as the alternative answer choices will be given based on common mistakes that could be made in attempting the question.

PAPER SPECIFIC INFORMATION

THE EXAM

FORMAT OF THE EXAM

The exam will be in **TWO sections**, and will be a mix of narrative and computational answers. Section A will be 20 multiple choice questions, each worth 2 marks. Section B will consist of two 15 mark questions and one 30 mark question.

		Number of marks
Section A:	Twenty 2-mark multiple choice questions	40
Section B:		
Question 1:	Any area of the syllabus	15
Question 2:	Any area of the syllabus	15
Question 3:	Single company or group preparation of financial statements	30
		_____
		100
		_____

Total time allowed: 3 hours plus 15 minutes reading and planning time.

Note that:

- The F7 will have both a discursive and computational element. The multiple choice questions will therefore include a mix of calculation-based and explanations-based questions.

- There is likely to be a longer discussion element in either question 1 or 2 of section B.

- Question 3 will require the preparation of a set of financial statements, either for an individual company or group.

PASS MARK

The pass mark for all ACCA Qualification examination papers is 50%.

READING AND PLANNING TIME

Remember that all three hour paper based examinations have an additional 15 minutes reading and planning time.

ACCA GUIDANCE

ACCA guidance on the use of this time is as follows:

This additional time is allowed at the beginning of the examination to allow candidates to read the questions and to begin planning their answers before they start to write in their answer books.

This time should be used to ensure that all the information and, in particular, the exam requirements are properly read and understood.

During this time, candidates may only annotate their question paper. They may not write anything in their answer booklets until told to do so by the invigilator.

KAPLAN GUIDANCE

As all questions are compulsory, there are no decisions to be made about choice of questions, other than in which order you would like to tackle them.

Therefore, in relation to F7, we recommend that you take the following approach with your reading and planning time:

- **Use the planning time to make notes on the large questions.** This will involve noting where items should go in the financial statements, or the double entries needed based on adjustments given in the narrative.

- **Write down** on the question paper next to the mark allocation **the amount of time you should spend on each part.** Do this for each part of every question.

- **Decide the order** in which you think you will attempt each question:

  This is a personal choice and you have time on the revision phase to try out different approaches, for example, if you sit mock exams.

  A common approach is to tackle the multiple choice questions first, so they are out of the way and dealt with.

  Others may prefer to tackle the longest questions first, as they will take longer than the individual questions in section A.

  Whatever your approach, you must make sure that you leave enough time to attempt all questions fully and be very strict with yourself in timing each question.

- For each question in turn, read the requirements and then the detail of the question carefully.

  Always read the requirement first as this enables you to **focus on the detail of the question with the specific task in mind**.

  For computational questions:

  Highlight key numbers / information and key words in the question, scribble notes to yourself on the question paper to remember key points in your answer.

  Jot down proformas required if applicable.

  For multiple choice questions:

  Read the question extremely carefully. All of the choices given are likely to be potential answers people could get if one or more errors are made, so take your time on these.

  For longer questions:

  Spot the easy marks to be gained in a question and parts which can be performed independently of the rest of the question. For example laying out basic proformas correctly, answer written elements not related to the scenario etc.

  Make sure that you do these parts first when you tackle the question.

  Don't go overboard in terms of planning time on any one question – you need a good measure of the whole paper and a plan for all of the questions at the end of the 15 minutes.

  By covering all questions you can often help yourself as you may find that facts in one question may remind you of things you should put into your answer relating to a different question.

- With your plan of attack in mind, **start answering your chosen section** with your plan to hand, as soon as you are allowed to start.

 Always keep your eye on the clock and do not over run on any part of any question!

DETAILED SYLLABUS

The detailed syllabus and study guide written by the ACCA can be found at:

www.accaglobal.com/students/

KAPLAN'S RECOMMENDED REVISION APPROACH

QUESTION PRACTICE IS THE KEY TO SUCCESS

Success in professional examinations relies upon you acquiring a firm grasp of the required knowledge at the tuition phase. In order to be able to do the questions, knowledge is essential.

However, the difference between success and failure often hinges on your exam technique on the day and making the most of the revision phase of your studies.

The **Kaplan complete text** is the starting point, designed to provide the underpinning knowledge to tackle all questions. However, in the revision phase, pouring over text books is not the answer.

Kaplan Online knowledge check tests help you consolidate your knowledge and understanding and are a useful tool to check whether you can remember key topic areas.

Kaplan pocket notes are designed to help you quickly revise a topic area, however you then need to practice questions. There is a need to progress to full exam standard questions as soon as possible, and to tie your exam technique and technical knowledge together.

The importance of question practice cannot be over-emphasised.

The recommended approach below is designed by expert tutors in the field, in conjunction with their knowledge of the examiner and their recent real exams.

The approach taken for the fundamental papers is to revise by topic area.

You need to practice as many questions as possible in the time you have left.

OUR AIM

Our aim is to get you to the stage where you can attempt exam standard questions confidently, to time, in a closed book environment, with no supplementary help (i.e. to simulate the real examination experience).

Practising your exam technique on real past examination questions, in timed conditions, is also vitally important for you to assess your progress and identify areas of weakness that may need more attention in the final run up to the examination.

In order to achieve this we recognise that initially you may feel the need to practice some questions with open book help and exceed the required time.

The approach below shows you which questions you should use to build up to coping with exam standard question practice, and references to the sources of information available should you need to revisit a topic area in more detail.

Remember that in the real examination, all you have to do is:

- attempt all questions required by the exam

- only spend the allotted time on each question, and

- get them at least 50% right!

Try and practice this approach on every question you attempt from now to the real exam.

Previously, the exam format meant that students were able to attempt some form of 'question spotting' as there were three large topic areas. Following the introduction of multiple choice questions, this will no longer be the case and to pass F7, students will need to understand information from the wide range of topics across the syllabus.

EXAMINER COMMENTS

We have included some of the examiners comments to the examination questions in this kit for you to see the main pitfalls that students fall into with regard to technical content.

However, too many times in the general section of the report, the examiner comments that students had failed due to:

- 'misallocation of time'

- 'running out of time' and

- showing signs of 'spending too much time on an earlier question and clearly rushing the answer to a subsequent question'.

Good exam technique is vital.

THE KAPLAN PAPER F7 REVISION PLAN

Stage 1: Assess areas of strengths and weaknesses

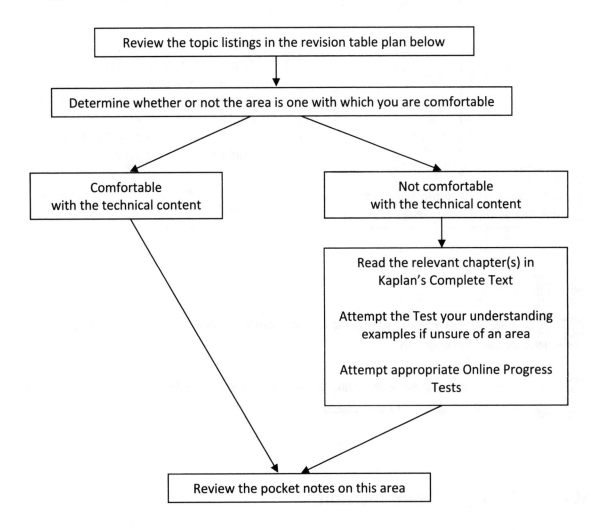

Stage 2: Practice questions

Follow the order of revision of topics as recommended in the revision table plan below and attempt the questions in the order suggested.

Try to avoid referring to text books and notes and the model answer until you have completed your attempt.

Try to answer the question in the allotted time.

Review your attempt with the model answer and assess how much of the answer you achieved in the allocated exam time.

Fill in the self-assessment box below and decide on your best course of action.

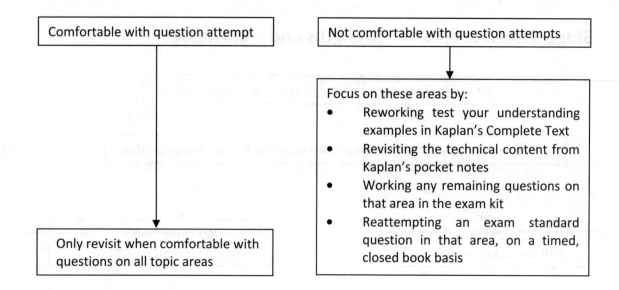

| Comfortable with question attempt | Not comfortable with question attempts |

Focus on these areas by:
- Reworking test your understanding examples in Kaplan's Complete Text
- Revisiting the technical content from Kaplan's pocket notes
- Working any remaining questions on that area in the exam kit
- Reattempting an exam standard question in that area, on a timed, closed book basis

Only revisit when comfortable with questions on all topic areas

Note that:

 The 'footsteps questions' give guidance on exam techniques and how you should have approached the question.

 The 'clock questions' have an online debrief where a tutor talks you through the exam technique and approach to that question and works the question in full.

Stage 3: Final pre-exam revision

We recommend that you **attempt at least one three hour mock examination** containing a set of previously unseen exam standard questions.

It is important that you get a feel for the breadth of coverage of a real exam without advanced knowledge of the topic areas covered – just as you will expect to see on the real exam day.

Ideally this mock should be sat in timed, closed book, real exam conditions and could be:

- a mock examination offered by your tuition provider, and/or

- the specimen paper in the back of this exam kit, and/or

- the last real examination paper (available shortly afterwards on Kaplan EN-gage with 'enhanced walk through answers' and a full 'tutor debrief').

KAPLAN'S DETAILED REVISION PLAN

Topic	Complete Text Chapter	Pocket note Chapter	Questions to attempt	Tutor guidance	Date attempted	Self assessment
Consolidated statement of financial position	17 / 19	17 / 19	176 177 178 182 184 187	Practice the Kaplan 5 working approach. Ensure you get the easy marks available in the question from adding the parent and subsidiary assets and liabilities together.		
Consolidated statement of profit or loss and other comprehensive income	18 / 19	18 / 19	179 181 183 186	Watch the dates carefully – is there a mid-year acquisition? If so you have to time apportion the subsidiary company results when adding the parent and subsidiary together.		
Consolidated statement of profit or loss and other comprehensive income and statement of financial position			176 180 188	Set up your proformas first and get the easy marks by adding the parent and subsidiary results together – then complete the 5 standard statement of financial position workings before moving on to complete the statement of profit or loss and other comprehensive income.		

Topic	Complete Text Chapter	Pocket note Chapter	Questions to attempt	Tutor guidance	Date attempted	Self assessment
Accounting standards:						
Non-current assets (IAS 16, IAS 38, IAS 40, IFRS 5)	2	2	147 152 155 157-158 1-6	Be clear on initial recognition rules and subsequent measurement for PPE, intangible assets and investment properties. Ensure you understand how to deal with assets held for sale.		
IAS 23	2	2	159 7	Ensure you know the definition of borrowing costs at the 3 recognition and 2 derecognition criteria.		
IAS 36	4	4	150 14-16	Learn the impairment test proforma and the cash generating unit write down rules.		
IAS 17	8	8	142 42-45	Be sure you can identify the differences between an operating and a finance lease.		
IAS 37	12	12	145 149 71, 72	For IAS 37 the recognition rules are very clear – learn the 3 recognition rules.		
IAS 10	12	12	106 73	Learn the differences between adjusting and non-adjusting events.		
IAS 2 / IAS 11	11	11	141, 144, 151 59-62, 66-68	The measurement of inventory is key and plenty of practice on construction contracts is recommended.		

Topic	Complete Text Chapter	Pocket note Chapter	Questions to attempt	Tutor guidance	Date attempted	Self assessment
IAS 32/39/IFRS 7/IFRS 9	10	10	52-55, 156	Amortised cost is the core area of financial liabilities here. Make sure you can deal with loans issued at a discount & redeemed at a premium. You will also need an awareness of the categories of financial asset in accordance with IFRS 9 and the accounting treatment for them.		
IAS 18	9	9	143 153 48-50	Learn the rules associated with revenue recognition for the sale of goods and provision of services and the specific exam scenario treatment such as sale and repurchase agreements and agency sales.		
IAS 8	7	7	144 151 36-38	Learn the recognition criteria for the 3 areas.		
IAS 12	13	13	76-78	Learn the definition of a temporary difference and practice its application.		
IAS 33	14	14	148 160 80-83	Learn the formula and apply to share issues.		
Framework	6/7	6/7	141 - 143	Learn the key definitions and be able to apply them to various		

Topic	Complete Text Chapter	Pocket note Chapter	Questions to attempt	Tutor guidance	Date attempted	Self assessment
			153 22-28	standards		
Preparation of individual company financial statements	1	1	161 165 167 169 173	You have to learn the accounting standards examinable first and then apply your knowledge to these recommended questions.		
Statement of cash flows	15	15	191 192 198 200	Learn the proforma. Start with calculations on 148, 149 and 156 before moving on to analysing cash flows in 154 and 158		
Ratio interpretation	20	20	189 193 197	Learn the ratio calculations and practice identifying where you pull the information for the formula out of the financial statements.		

Note that not all of the questions are referred to in the programme above. We have recommended an approach to build up from the basic to exam standard questions.

The remaining questions are available in the kit for extra practice for those who require more questions on some areas.

Technical update

IAS 41 AGRICULTURE

IAS 41 Agriculture is a new addition to the F7 syllabus, and covers biological assets, biological transformation, agricultural activity and agricultural produce.

1   Biological assets

These are living plants or animals. These should initially be recognised as fair value less any estimated 'point of sale' costs.

They should be revalued to fair value less point of sale costs at year end, with any gain or loss being taken to the statement of profit or loss.

If no fair value model exists, these should be held at the cost model.

2   Biological transformation

This is the processes of growth, degeneration, production and procreation causing changes in a biological asset. These will lead to the fair value gains or losses during the period.

3   Agricultural activity

This is the management of the biological transformation of biological assets for sale, into agricultural produce.

4   Agricultural produce

At the date of harvest, this should be recognised and measured at fair value less estimated costs to sell. After the produce has been harvested, IAS 41 ceases to apply, and agricultural produce becomes an item of inventory. Fair value at the point of harvest is taken as cost for the point of IAS 2 Inventories, which is applied from then onwards.

Section A

OBJECTIVE TEST QUESTIONS

CONCEPTUAL FRAMEWORK/INTERNATIONAL FINANCIAL REPORTING STANDARDS

1   IAS 16 *Property, Plant and Equipment* requires an asset to be measured at cost on its original recognition in the financial statements.

EW used its own staff, assisted by contractors when required, to construct a new warehouse for its own use. Which ONE of the following costs would NOT be included in attributable costs of the non-current asset?

A   Clearance of the site prior to work commencing

B   Professional surveyors' fees for managing the construction work

C   EW's own staff wages for time spent working on the construction

D   An allocation of EW's administration costs, based on EW staff time spent on the construction as a percentage of the total staff time

2   On 1 July 20X4, Experimenter opened a chemical reprocessing plant. The plant was due to be active for five years until 30 June 20X9, when it would be decommissioned. At 1 July 20X4, the costs of decommissioning the plant were estimated to be $4 million in 5 years time. The company considers that a discount rate of 12% is appropriate for the calculation of a present value, and the discount factor at 12% for Year 5 is 0.567.

What is the total charge to the statement of profit or loss (depreciation and finance charge) in respect of the decommissioning for the year ended 30 June 20X5?

A $453,600

B $725,760

C $800,000

D $2,268,000

3 An entity purchased property for $6 million on 1 July 20X3. The value of the land was $1 million and the buildings $5 million. The expected life of the building was 50 years and its residual value nil. On 30 June 20X5 the property was revalued to $7 million (land $1.24 million, buildings $5.76 million). On 30 June 20X7, the property was sold for $6.8 million.

What is the gain on disposal of the property that would be reported in the statement of profit or loss for the year to 30 June 20X7?

A   Gain $40,000

B   Loss $200,000

C   Gain $1,000,000

D   Gain $1,240,000

4 A manufacturing entity receives a grant of $1m to purchase a machine on 1 January 20X3. The grant will be repayable if the company sells the asset within 4 years, which it does not intend to do. The asset has a useful life of 5 years.

What is the deferred income liability balance at 30 June 20X3?

A $900,000

B $800,000

C $875,000

D $750,000

5 On 1 January 20X1, Sty Ltd received $1m from the local government on the condition that they employ at least 100 staff each year for the next 4 years. On this date, it was virtually certain that Sty would meet these requirements. However, due to an economic downturn and reduced consumer demand, on 1 January 20X2, Sty no longer needed to employ any more staff and the conditions of the grant required full repayment.

What should be recorded in the financial statements on 1 January 20X2?

A   Reduce deferred income balance by $750,000

B   Reduce deferred income by $750,000 and recognise a loss in the financial statements of $250,000

C   Reduce deferred income by $1,000,000

D   Reduce deferred income by $1,000,000 and a gain in the financial statements of $250,000

6 **Which one of the following properties would be classified as an investment property?**

A   A stately home used for executive training but which is no longer required and is now being held for resale

B   Purchased land for investment potential. Planning permission has not been obtained for building construction of any kind

C   A new office building used by an insurance entity as its head office which was purchased specifically in the centre of a major city in order to exploit its capital gains potential

D   A property that has been leased out under a finance lease

7 An entity has the following loan finance in place during the year:

$1 million of 6% loan finance

$2 million of 8% loan finance

It constructed a new factory which cost $600,000 and this was funded out of the existing loan finance. The factory took 8 months to complete.

To the nearest thousand, what borrowing costs should be capitalised?

A $44,000

B $29,000

C $28,000

D $20,000

8   Which of the following statements is correct?

Statement 1: If the revaluation model is used for property, plant and equipment, revaluations must subsequently be made with sufficient regularity to ensure that the carrying amount does not differ materially from the fair value at each reporting date.

Statement 2: When an item of property, plant and equipment is revalued, there is no requirement that the entire class of assets to which the item belongs must be revalued.

A   Statement 1 only is correct

B   Statement 2 only is correct

C   Both statements are correct

D   Neither statement is correct

9   Which ONE of the following CANNOT be recognised as an intangible non-current asset in GHK's statement of financial position at 30 September 20X1?

A   GHK spent $132,000 developing a new type of product. Testing proved that the product was successful in June 20X1 but management worried that it would be too expensive to fund. The finances to complete the project came from a cash injection from a benefactor received in November 20X1.

B   GHK purchased a subsidiary during the year. During the fair value exercise, it was found that the subsidiary had a brand name with an estimated value of $50,000, but was not recognised by the subsidiary as it was internally generated.

C   GHK purchased a brand name from a competitor on 1 November 20X0, for $65,000.

D   GHK spent $21,000 during the year on the development of a new product, after management concluded it would be viable in November 20X0. The product is being launched on the market on 1 December 20X1 and is expected to be profitable.

10   Which ONE of the following could be classified as development expenditure in M's statement of financial position as at 31 March 20Y0 according to IAS 38 *Intangible Assets*?

A $120,000 spent on developing a prototype and testing a new type of propulsion system for trains. The project needs further work on it as the propulsion system is currently not viable

B   A payment of $50,000 to a local university's engineering faculty to research new environmentally friendly building techniques

C $35,000 spent on consumer testing a new type of electric bicycle. The project is near completion and the product will probably be launched in the next twelve months. As this project is first of its kind for M it is expected to make a loss

D $65,000 spent on developing a special type of new packaging for a new energy efficient light bulb. The packaging is expected to be used by M for many years and is expected to reduce M's distribution costs by $35,000 a year

11   Which of the following factors is a reason why key staff are unable to be capitalised as an intangible asset by an entity?

(i)   They do not provide expected future economic benefits

(ii)   They cannot be controlled by an entity

(iii)   Their value cannot be measured reliably

(iv)   They are not separable from the business as a whole

A   All of them

B   (ii), (iii) and (iv)

C   (ii) and (iv)

D   (ii) and (iii)

12   Amco Plc carries out research and development. In the year ended 30 June 20X5, Amco incurred costs in relation to project X of $750,000. These were incurred at the same amount each month up to 30 April 20X5, when the project was completed. The product produced by the project went on sale from 31 May 20X5

The project had been confirmed as feasible on 1 January 20X5, and the product produced by the project was expected to have a useful life of five years. Amortisation is charged on a monthly basis.

What is the carrying value of the development expenditure asset as at 30 June 20X5?

A $295,000

B $725,000

C $300,000

D $nil

13 Sybil Ltd has acquired a subsidiary Basil in the current year.

Basil has a brand which has been reliably valued by Sybil at $500,000, and a customer list which Sybil has been unable to value.

Which ONE of these describes how Sybil should treat these intangible assets of Basil in their consolidated Financial Statements?

A   They should be included in goodwill.

B   The brand should be capitalised as a separate intangible, whereas the customer list should be included within goodwill.

C   Both the brand and the customer list should be capitalised as separate intangibles.

D   The customer list should be capitalised as a separate intangible, whereas the brand should be included within goodwill.

The following information is to be used for questions 14 and 15.

A division of a company has the following balances in its financial statements:

Goodwill	$700,000
Plant	$950,000
Property	$2,300,000
Intangibles	$800,000
Other net assets	$430,000

Following a period of losses, the recoverable amount of the division is deemed to be $4 million. A recent valuation of the building showed that the building has a market value of $2.5 million. The other net assets are made up of cash and receivables, and are at their recoverable amount. The company uses the cost model for valuing property, plant and equipment.

---

14 To the nearest thousand, what is the balance on property following the impairment review?

A $2,300,000

B $2,500,000

C $2,027,000

D $1,776,000

15 To the nearest thousand, what is the balance on plant following the impairment review?

A $862,000

B $837,000

C $689,000

D $261,000

16   A vehicle was involved in an accident exactly halfway through the year. The asset cost $10,000 and had a remaining life of 10 years at the start of the year. Following the accident, the expected present value of cash flows associated with the asset was $3,400 and the fair value less costs to sell was $6,500.

What is the recoverable amount of the asset following the accident?

A $6,500

B $9,500

C $3,000

D $3,400

17   BN has an asset that was classified as held for sale at 31 March 20X2. The asset had a carrying value of $900 and a fair value of $800. The cost of disposal was estimated to be $50.

According to IFRS 5 *Non-current Assets Held for Sale and Discontinued Operations*, which ONE of the following values should be used for the asset in BN's statement of financial position as at 31 March 20X2?

A $750

B $800

C $850

D $900

18   **According to IFRS 5 Non-current Assets Held for Sale and Discontinued Operations which of the following relate to the criteria for an asset held for sale?**

(i)   Available for immediate sale in its present condition

(ii)   Sale is highly probable

(iii)   The sale is expected to be completed within the next month

(iv)   A reasonable price has been set

A   All of the above

B   (i), (ii) and (iii)

C   (i), (ii) and (iv)

D   (ii), (iii) and (iv)

19   **According to IFRS 5 Non-current Assets Held for Sale and Discontinued Operations which of the following amounts in respect of a discontinued operation must be shown on the face of the statement of profit or loss?**

(i)   Revenues

(ii)   Gross profit

(iii)   Profit after tax

(iv)   Profit from operations

A   All of the above

B   (iii) only

C   (iii) and (iv)

D   (iv) only

20   Total Co has the following two lines of business that have been disposed of in the year:

Sector X operated in Country A. Total Co has no other operations in Country A, and Country A made up 0.5% of the total revenue of Total Co.

Sector Y operated in the same country as the Total Co head office. It produced a different item from the other parts of total Co, and this item contributed 10% of the total revenue of Total Co

Which of these Sectors, if any, should be disclosed as a discontinued operation in the current year?

A   Sector X is discontinued, Sector Y is not

B   Sector Y is discontinued, Sector X is not

C   Both Sector X and Sector Y are discontinued

D   Neither Sector X nor Sector Y are discontinued

21   **What is the primary reason why discontinued operations presented separately within financial statements?**

A   To show an accurate valuation of the business

B   To enhance the predictive nature of financial statements

C   To make the financial statements easier to understand

D   So the financial statements are verifiable

22   **Which one of the following gives the best description of the objectives of financial statements as set out by the International Accounting Standards Board's (IASB)** *The Conceptual Framework for Financial Reporting***?**

A   To fairly present the financial position and performance of an enterprise

B   To fairly present the financial position, performance and changes in financial position of an enterprise

C   To provide information about the financial position and performance of an enterprise that is useful to a wide range of users in making economic decisions

D   To provide information about the financial position, performance and changes in financial position of an enterprise that is useful to a wide range of users in making economic decisions

23 The IASB's *The Conceptual Framework for Financial Reporting* defines a liability as:

A an amount owed to another entity

B a present obligation arising as a result of past events, the settlement of which is expected to result in an outflow of economic benefits

C expenditure that has been incurred but not yet charged to the statement of profit or loss

D an obligation that may arise in the future

24 The IASB's *The Conceptual Framework for Financial Reporting* lists two fundamental qualitative characteristics of financial statements, one of which is faithful representation.

Which ONE of the following is NOT a characteristic of faithful representation?

A Completeness

B Neutrality

C Free from error

D Prudence

25 The IASB's *The Conceptual Framework for Financial Reporting* identifies qualitative characteristics of financial statements.

(i) Relevance

(ii) Reliability

(iii) Faithful representation

(iv) Comparability

Which of the above characteristics are NOT fundamental qualitative characteristics according to the IASB's *The Conceptual Framework for Financial Reporting*?

A (i) and (ii)

B (i) and (iii)

C (iii) and (iv)

D (ii) and (iv)

26 **Under the current structure of regulatory bodies, which of the bodies listed below acts as the overall supervisory body?**

A IFRS Interpretations Committee

B International Accounting Standards Board

C IFRS Advisory Council

D IFRS Foundation

27 **Which of the bodies listed below is responsible for reviewing International Accounting Standards and issuing guidance on their application?**

A   IFRS Interpretations Committee

B   International Accounting Standards Board

C   IFRS Advisory Council

D   IFRS Foundation

28 **Which ONE of the following is an example of following the principle of faithful representation?**

A   Showing finance lease payments as a rent expense

B   Bering prudent by recording the entire amount of a convertible loan as a liability

C   Recording the future payments under an operating lease as a long-term liability

D   Recording a sale and repurchase transaction with a bank as a loan rather than a sale

29 **The 2010 Conceptual Framework for Financial Reporting defines a liability as:**

A   An amount that needs to be paid arising from a past transaction.

B   A present obligation of an entity arising from a past event, the settlement of which is expected to result in an outflow of economic benefits. It must be capable of reliable measurement.

C   A present obligation of an entity arising from a past event, the settlement of which is expected to result in an outflow of economic benefits.

D   An outflow of economic benefits for any reason provided that it can be reliably measured.

30 **Which of the following criteria need to be satisfied in order for an item to be recognised in the financial statements?**

(i)   It meets the definition of an element of the financial statements

(ii)   It is probable that future economic benefits will flow to or from the enterprise

(iii)   It is certain that future economic benefits will flow to or from the enterprise

(iv)   The item has a cost or value

(v)   The item has a cost or value that can be reliably measured

A   (i), (ii) and (v)

B   (i), (iii) and (v)

C   (i), (ii) and (iv)

D   (i), (iii) and (iv)

31   **Which of the following best defines information that is relevant to the users of financial information?**

A   Information that is free from material error, bias and is a faithful representation

B   Information that has been prudently prepared

C   Information that is comparable from one period to the next

D   Information that influences the decisions of users

32   **Which of the following is most representative of the accounting framework used under IFRS?**

A   It is a rules-based framework

B   It is a principles-based framework

C   It is a legal obligation

D   It is based on fundamental ethical principles

33   **Which ONE of the following is not a likely advantage of the global harmonisation of accounting standards?**

A   Greater comparability between different firms

B   Greater ease for preparing consolidated financial statements

C   Easier for large international accounting firms

D   Greater compatibility with legal systems

34   **Which of the following are advantages of applying a principles-based framework of accounting rather than a rules-based framework?**

(i)   It avoids 'fire-fighting', where standards are developed in responses to specific problems as they arise

(ii)   It allows preparers and auditors to deal with complex transactions which may not be specifically covered by an accounting standard

(iii)   Principles-based standards are thought to be harder to circumvent

(iv)   A set of rules is given which attempts to cover every eventuality

(v)   Accounting standards can be developed in relation to agreed principles

A   All of the above

B   (i), (iii) and (v) only

C   (i), (ii) and (v) only

D   (i), (ii), (iii) and (v) only

35 **According to IAS 8, how should a material error in the previous financial reporting period be accounted for in the current period?**

A   By making an adjustment in the financial statements of the current period through the statement of profit or loss, and disclosing the nature of the error in a note

B   By making an adjustment in the financial statements of the current period as a movement on reserves, and disclosing the nature of the error in a note

C   By restating the comparative amounts for the previous period at their correct value, and disclosing the nature of the error in a note

D   By restating the comparative amounts for the previous period at their correct value, but without the requirement for a disclosure of the nature of the error in a note

36 **Which ONE of the following statements regarding IFRS 13 is not true?**

A   Level 1 inputs are likely to be used without adjustment

B   Level 3 inputs are based on the best information available to market participants and are therefore regarded as providing the most reliable evidence of fair value

C   Level 2 inputs may include quoted prices for similar (but not identical) assets and liabilities in active markets

D   Level 1 inputs comprise quoted prices in active markets for identical assets and liabilities at the reporting date

37 During its 20X6 accounting year, DL made the following changes.

Which ONE of these changes would be classified as 'a change in accounting policy' as determined by IAS 8 *Accounting Policies, Changes in Accounting Estimates and Errors*?

A   Increased the allowance for irrecoverable receivables for 20X6 from 5% to 10% of outstanding debts

B   Changed the method of valuing inventory from FIFO to average cost

C   Changed the depreciation of plant and equipment from straight line depreciation to reducing balance depreciation

D   Changed the useful economic life of its motor vehicles from six years to four years

38 **When can a change in accounting policy be made by an entity?**

(i)   If the change is required by an IFRS

(ii)   If the company thinks a new accounting policy would be easier to report

(iii) If a new accounting policy would show more favourable results

(iv)   If a new accounting policy results in a more reliable and relevant presentation of events or transactions

A   In any of the above circumstances

B   (i), (ii) and (iv) only

C   (i) and (iv) only

D   In none of the above circumstances

39   The following are possible methods of measuring assets and liabilities other than historical cost:

(i)   Current cost

(ii)   Realisable value

(iii) Present value

(iv)   Replacement cost

According to the IASB's *Conceptual Framework for Financial Reporting* (Framework) which of the measurement bases above can be used by an entity for measuring assets and liabilities shown in its statement of financial position?

A   (i) and (ii)

B   (i), (ii) and (iii)

C   (ii) and (iii)

D   (i), (ii) (iii) and (iv)

40   **Which ONE of the following statements is true about historical cost accounts in times of rising prices?**

A   Profits will be overstated and assets will be understated

B   The asset values will be overstated

C   Unrecognised gains will be recorded incorrectly

D   Depreciation will be overstated

41   **Which ONE of the following concepts aims to ensure that excess dividends aren't paid in times of changing prices?**

A   Going concern

B   Prudence

C   Substance over form

D   Capital maintenance

42   Z entered into a finance lease agreement on 1 November 20X2. The lease was for five years, the fair value of the asset acquired was $45,000 and the interest rate implicit in the lease was 7%. The annual payment was $10,975 in arrears.

What is the amount to be shown within non-current liabilities at 31 October 20X3?

A $27,212

B $28,802

C $37,175

D $36,407

43 HP entered into an operating lease for a machine on 1 July 20X7 with the following terms:

- three years non-cancellable lease
- 6 months rent free period from commencement
- rent of $12,000 per annum payable at $1,000 a month from month 6 onwards
- machine useful life 15 years.

What the amount that should be charged to HP's statement of profit or loss for the year to 31 December 20X7?

A $12,000

B $5,000

C $6,000

D $Nil

44 Rabbit plc has 2 options to acquire a new machine with an estimated useful life of 6 years. It can buy it today, the 1st January 20X3 at a cash price of $100,000 or it can lease the asset under the following agreement:

- An initial payment of $13,760 will be payable straight away
- 5 further annual payments of $20,000 will be due, beginning on 1st Jan 20X3
- The interest rate implicit in the lease is 8%

If Rabbit decides to lease the asset, what will be recorded in its financial statements at the y/e 31 December 20X4 in respect of the lease liability?

	Finance cost	Non-current liability	Current liability
A	4,123	35,662	20,000
B	5,299	51,539	20,000
C	5,312	51,712	20,000
D	5,851	43,709	15,281

45 Squirrel Ltd enters into an operating lease contract on the 1st July 20X5 to lease an item of office equipment for 3 years. The equipment has an expected useful life of 6 years and if bought outright would cost $50,000. The original lease agreement stated that the annual lease payments were to be $10,000 per annum commencing on 30th June 20X6. Squirrel Ltd has managed to negotiate a "lease holiday" and will pay nothing for the first year.

What will appear in the financial statements of Squirrel Ltd for the year ended 30th June 20X6?

	Statement of profit or loss expense	Statement of financial position
A	10,000	Accrual 10,000
B	3,333	Accrual 3,333
C	6,667	Accrual 6,667
D	Nil	Nil

46 On 1st January 20X4 Badger plc entered into a lease agreement to lease an item of machinery for 4 years with rentals of $210,000 payable annually in arrears. The asset has a useful life of 5 years and at the end of the lease term legal ownership will pass to Badger plc. The fair value of the asset at the inception of the lease was $635,000 and the interest rate implicit in the lease is 12.2%. For the year ended 31st December 20X4 Badger plc has accounted for this lease as an operating lease and recorded the payment of $210,000 as an operating expense. This treatment was discovered during 20X5.

In accordance with IAS 17 what will the adjustment to retained earnings b/fwd be?

A $5,530 debit

B $132,530 credit

C $210,000 debit

D $Nil

47 Owl Ltd leases an asset under a finance lease. The lease has a primary period of 5 years and a secondary period of 2 years during which a nominal rental will be payable. The asset has an estimated useful life of 6 years and a current cash value of $89,000. The present value of the minimum lease payments is $87,000.

According to the provisions of IAS 17, what will the carrying value of the asset be in Owl's statement of financial position at the end of the second year of the lease?

A $62,143

B $52,200

C $59,333

D $58,000

48 **IAS 18 *Revenue Recognition* sets out criteria for the recognition of revenue from the sale of goods.**

Which ONE of the following is NOT a criterion specified by IAS 18 for recognising revenue from the sale of goods?

A   The seller no longer retains any influence or control over the goods

B   The cost to the seller can be measured reliably

C   The buyer has paid for the goods

D   The significant risks and rewards of ownership have been transferred to the buyer

49   On 31 March 20X7, DT received an order from a new customer, XX, for products with a sales value of $900,000. XX enclosed a deposit with the order of $90,000.

On 31 March 20X7, DT had not completed credit referencing of XX and had not despatched any goods. DT is considering the following possible entries for this transaction in its financial statements for the year ended 31 March 20X7:

(i)   include $900,000 in statement of profit or loss revenue for the year

(ii)   include $90,000 in statement of profit or loss revenue for the year

(iii)   do not include anything in statement of profit or loss revenue for the year

(iv)   create a trade receivable for $810,000

(v)   create a deferred income liability for $90,000.

According to IAS 18 *Revenue Recognition*, how should DT record this transaction in its financial statements for the year ended 31 March 20X7?

A   (i) and (iv)

B   (ii) and (v)

C   (iii) and (iv)

D   (iii) and (v)

50   On 1 July 20X6, Sideshow sold a piece of property for $2 million and leased it back under a 5 year operating lease, paying $150,000 a year. The sale value and rentals were at the market value. The carrying value of the property on 1 January was $1,600,000 and it had a remaining useful life of 20 years.

What entries would be made in Sideshow's statement of profit or loss for the year ended 31 December 20X6?

A   Profit on disposal of $400,000, rent expense of $150,000

B   Profit on disposal of $400,000, rent expense of $75,000

C   Profit on disposal of $440,000, depreciation expense of $40,000, rent expense of $75,000

D   Depreciation expense of 80,000, profit on disposal of $480,000, rent expense of $75,000

51   Mango sold an item of maturing inventory to a bank on 1 January 20X3 for $500,000. At this date the inventory had cost $200,000 to produce but had a fair value of $900,000, which was expected to increase over the next 3 years. At the end of 3 years, Mango have the option to repurchase the inventory at $665,000, giving an effective interest rate of 10%.

What items should be recorded in the statement of profit or loss for the year ended 31 December 20X3?

A   Revenue $500,000, cost of sales $200,000

B   Profit on disposal $300,000

C   Deferred income $500,000

D   Finance cost $50,000

52   An entity issues 3,000 convertible bonds at the start of year 1 at par. They have a three year term and a face value of $1,000 per bond. Interest is payable annually in arrears at 7% per annum. Each bond is convertible at any time up to maturity into 250 common shares. When the bonds are issued, the prevailing market interest rate for similar debt without conversion options is 9%. The relevant discount factors are shown below.

Discount factors	7%	9%
Year 1	0.933	0.914
Year 2	0.871	0.837
Year 3	0.813	0.766

How is this initially recorded between the debt and equity elements?

	Debt element	Equity element
A	$2,988,570	$ 11,430
B	$2,829,570	$170,430
C	$528,570	$2,471,430
D	$3,000,000	$Nil

53   Viking issues $100,000 5% loan notes on 1 January 20X4, incurring issue costs of $3,000. These loan notes are redeemable at a premium, meaning that the effective rate of interest is 8% per annum.

What is the finance cost to be shown in the statement of profit or loss for the year ended 31 December 20X5?

A $8,240

B $7,981

C $7,760

D $8,000

54   For a debt investment to be held under amortised cost, it must pass two tests. One of these is the contractual cash flow characteristics test.

What is the other test which must be passed?

A   The business model test

B   The amortised cost test

C   The fair value test

D   The purchase agreement test

55   What is the default classification for an equity investment?

A   Fair value through profit or loss

B   Fair value through other comprehensive income

C   Amortised cost

D   Net proceeds

56 ABC Plc purchased 10,000 shares, to be held for long term investment purposes, and making the election to use the alternative treatment under IFRS 9, on 1 September 20X4, at a cost of $3.50 each. Transaction costs associated with the purchase were $500.

At 31 December 20X4, the shares are trading at $4.50 each.

What is the gain to be recognised on these shares for the year ended 31 December 20X4?

A $10,000

B $45,000

C $9,500

D $35,000

57 DEF Plc has purchased an investment of 15,000 shares on 1 August 20X6 at a cost of $6.50 each. DEF intend to sell these shares in the short term, and are holding them for trading purposes. Transaction costs on the purchase amounted to $1,500.

As at the year end 30 September 20X6, these shares are now worth $7.75 each.

What is the gain on this investment during the year ended 30 September 20X6, and where in the Financial Statements will it be recognised?

A $18,750 in Other Comprehensive Income

B $18,750 in Profit or Loss

C $17,250 in Other Comprehensive Income

D $17,250 in Profit or Loss

58 **For which category of financial instruments are transaction costs excluded from the initial value, and instead expensed to profit or loss?**

A   Financial Liabilities at amortised cost

B   Financial Assets at fair value through profit or loss

C   Financial Assets at fair value through other comprehensive income

D   Financial Assets at amortised cost

59 CN started a three-year contract to build a new university campus on 1 April 20X4. The contract had a fixed price of $90 million. CN incurred costs to 31 March 20X5 of $77 million and estimated that a further $33 million would need to be spent to complete the contract.

CN uses the work certified basis for measuring the stage of completion of construction contracts. At 31 March 20X5, a surveyor valued the work completed to date at $63 million.

What figures should be shown in the statement of profit or loss for the year ended 31 March 20X5?

	Revenue	Cost of sales
A	$63 million	$77 million
B	$63 million	$83 million
C	$57 million	$77 million
D	$69 million	$83 million

60 BL started a contract on 1 November 20X4. The contract was scheduled to run for two years and has a sales value of $40 million.

At 31 October 20X5, the following details were obtained from BL's records:

	$m
Costs incurred to date	16
Estimated costs to completion	18
Percentage complete at 31 October 20X5	45%

Applying IAS 11 *Construction Contracts*, how much revenue and cost of sales should BL recognise in its statement of profit or loss for the year ended 31 October 20X5?

	Revenue	*Cost of sales*
A	$40 million	$15.3 million
B	$40 million	$34 million
C	$18 million	$16 million
D	$18 million	$15.3 million

61 Malik is a construction company, recognising contract profits earned based on work certified as a proportion of total contract value. The following information relates to one of its long-term contracts as at 31 May 2014, Malik's year-end.

Contract price $200,000

Costs incurred to date $130,000

Estimated cost to complete $20,000

Invoiced to customer $120,000

Work certified to date $180,000

In the year to 31 May 2013 Malik had recognised revenue of $60,000 and profit of $15,000 in respect of this contract.

What profit should appear in Malik's Statement of Profit or Loss as at 31 May 2014 in respect of this contract?

A $15,000

B $50,000

C $45,000

D $30,000

62 Oscar is a construction company. The following information relates to one of its contracts as at 31 March 2014, Oscar's year-end.

Contract price $200,000

Costs incurred to date $90,000

Estimated cost to complete $60,000

Profit earned to date $30,000

Invoiced to customer $80,000

Payment received from customer $65,000

What amount should appear on Oscar's statement of financial position as at 31 March 2014 in respect of gross amounts due From customer?

A $40,000

B $120,000

C $110,000

D $55,000

63 **Which of the following items are included in the calculation of amounts due from/to customers in the Statement of Financial Position in relation to construction contracts?**

(i)   Total costs incurred

(ii)   Amounts invoiced to customers

(iii)   Amounts received from customers

(iv)   Recognised profits/ losses

A   All of them

B   (i), (iii) and (iv)

C   (i) and (iv)

D   (i), (ii) and (iv)

64 Ratten commenced a construction contract in the year ended 30 September 20X4. The contract price was agreed at $1.5m, and the total expected costs of the contract have been confirmed as $800,000.

The following figures were correctly recognised in the profit or loss account for the year ended 30 September 20X4:

	$000
Revenue	450
Cost of Sales	(240)
Profit	**210**

The following figures are also relevant in relation to this contract:

	X4	X5
	$000	$000
Costs incurred to date	325	575
Work certified to date	450	1,050

Ratten recognises profit on its construction contracts on a work certified basis.

What should be the cost of sales figure for Ratten in its Profit or Loss account for the year ended 30 September 20X5?

A $320,000

B $250,000

C $560,000

D   240,000

65   Hansel has commenced a construction contract in the current year.

The original contract price was agreed at $4.5m. Costs had been originally estimated at $3.75m

There was a design problem with the contract, and therefore additional costs of $820,000 were incurred. The customer has agreed to reimburse $650,000 of these costs.

As the contract is delayed, a penalty of $150,000 will be incurred by Hansel.

What is the total profit/(loss) expected on this construction contract?

A $750,000 profit

B $580,000 profit

C $220,000 loss

D $430,000 profit

66   IAS 2 *Inventories* specifies expenses that should be included in year-end inventory values. These could include:

(i)   marketing and selling overhead

(ii)   variable production overhead

(iii)   general management overhead

(iv)   factory management overhead allocated to production

(v)   cost of delivering raw materials to the factory

(vi)   abnormal increase in overhead charges caused by unusually low production levels due to the exceptionally hot weather.

Which THREE of the above are allowable by IAS 2 as expenses that should be included in the cost of finished goods inventories?

A   (i), (iii) and (v)

B   (i), (ii) and (vi)

C   (ii), (iv) and (v)

D   (iii), (iv) and (vi)

67   Neville has only two items of inventory on hand at its reporting date.

Item 1 – Materials costing $24,000 bought for processing and assembly for a customer under a 'one off' order which is expected to produce a high profit margin. Since buying this material, the cost price has fallen to $20,000.

Item 2 – A machine constructed for another customer for a contracted price of $36,000. This has recently been completed at a cost of $33,600. It has now been discovered that, in order to meet certain health and safety regulations, modifications at an extra cost of $8,400 will be required. The customer has agreed to meet half the extra cost.

What should be the total value of these two items of inventory in the statement of financial position?

A $53,600

B $51,800

C $51,600

D $55,800

68   Mario has incurred the following costs in relation to unit of inventory:

	$
Raw materials cost	1.50
Import duties	0.40
Direct Labour	0.50
Subcontracted labour costs	0.80
Refundable sales tax	0.20
Storage costs	0.05
Production overheads (per unit)	0.25

There was a problem with the first batch of items produced, so abnormal wastage costs of 0.10 per unit have also been incurred by Mario.

At what value should Mario value this inventory in its Financial Statements?

A $3.50

B $3.45

C $3.80

D $3.70

69 Frankie grows agricultural produce and sells them to the general public.

As well as considering IAS 2 *Inventories*, what other standard will apply to Frankie?

A   IAS 16 *Property, Plant and Equipment*

B   IAS 23 *Borrowing Costs*

C   IAS 41 *Agriculture*

D   IAS 17 *Leases*

70 Magna purchased cattle for $10,500 on 1 January. At 31 December, the cattle has a fair value of $13,000. If Magna sold the cattle, commission of 2% would be payable.

What is the correct accounting treatment for the cattle at 31 December according to IAS 41 *Agriculture*?

A   Hold at cost of $10,500

B   Revalue to $13,000, taking gain of $2,500 to the statement of profit or loss

C   Revalue to $13,000, taking gain of $2,500 to the revaluation surplus

D   Revalue to $12,740, taking gain of $2,240 to the statement of profit or loss

71 AP has the following two legal claims outstanding:

- A legal action claiming compensation of $500,000 filed against AP in March 20X4.

- A legal action taken by AP against a third party, claiming damages of $200,000 was started in January 20X3 and is nearing completion.

In both cases, it is more likely than not that the amount claimed will have to be paid.

How should AP report these legal actions in its financial statements for the year ended 31 March 20X5?

	Legal action against AP	Legal action by AP
A	Disclose by a note	No disclosure
B	Make a provision	No disclosure
C	Make a provision	Disclosure as a note
D	Make a provision	Accrue the income

72 **Which ONE of the following would require a provision for a liability to be created by BW at its reporting date of 31 October 20X5?**

A   The government introduced new laws on data protection which come into force on 1 January 20X6. BW's directors have agreed that this will require a large number of staff to be retrained. At 31 October 20X5, the directors were waiting on a report they had commissioned that would identify the actual training requirements

B   At the date, BW is negotiating with its insurance provider about the amount of an insurance claim that it had filed. On 20 November 20X5, the insurance provider agreed to pay $200,000

C   BW makes refunds to customers for any goods returned within 30 days of sale, and has done so for many years

D   A customer is suing BW for damages alleged to have been caused by BW's product. BW is contesting the claim and, at 31 October 20X5, the directors have been advised by BW's legal advisers it is very unlikely to lose the case

73 **Using the requirements set out in IAS 10 Events after the Reporting Period, which of the following would be classified as an adjusting event after the reporting period in financial statements ended 31 March 20X4 that were approved by the directors on 31 August 20X4?**

A   A reorganisation of the enterprise, proposed by a director on 31 January 20X4 and agreed by the Board on 10 July 20X4.

B   A strike by the workforce which started on 1 May 20X4 and stopped all production for 10 weeks before being settled.

C   The receipt of cash from a claim on an insurance policy for damage caused by a fire in a warehouse on 1 January 20X4. The claim was made in January 20X4 and the amount of the claim had not been recognised at 31 March 20X4 as it was uncertain that any money would be paid. The insurance enterprise settled with a payment of $1.5 million on 1 June 20X4.

D   The enterprise had made large export sales to the USA during the year. The year-end receivables included $2 million for amounts outstanding that were due to be paid in US dollars between 1 April 20X4 and 1 July 20X4. By the time these amounts were received, the exchange rate had moved in favour.

74 Target Ltd is preparing its financial statements for the year ended 30 September 20X7. The company is facing a number of legal claims from its customers with regards to a faulty product sold. The total amount being claimed is $3.5 million. The company's lawyers say that the customers have an 80% chance of being successful.

Per IAS 37 Provisions, Contingent Liabilities and Contingent Assets, what amount, if any, should be recognised in respect of the above in Target plc's statement of financial position as at 30 September 20X7?

A $3.5 million

B $2.8 million

C $0.7 million

D   No amount should be recognised

75   ABC plc has a year end of 31 December 2014. On 15th December 2014 the directors publicly announced their decision to close an operating unit and make a number of employees redundant. Some of the employees currently working in the unit will be transferred to other operating units within ABC. The estimated costs of the closure are as follows:

	$000
Redundancy costs	800
Lease termination costs	200
Relocation of continuing employees to new locations	400
Retraining of continuing employees	300
	1,700

What is the closure provision that should be recognised under IAS 37 – *Provisions, contingent assets and contingent liabilities***?**

A $800,000

B $1,000,000

C $1,400,000

D $1,700,000

76   Tamsin plc's accounting records shown the following:

Income tax payable for the year $60,000

Over provision in relation to the previous year $4,500

Opening provision for deferred tax $2,600

Closing provision for deferred tax $3,200

What is the income tax expense that will be shown in the statement of profit or loss for the year?

A $54,600

B $67,900

C $65,100

D $56,100

77 The following information has been extracted from the accounting records of Clara Ltd:

Estimated income tax for the year ended 30 September 20X0: $75,000

Income tax paid for the year ended 30 September 20X0: $80,000

Estimated income tax for the year ended 30 September 20X1: $83,000

What figures will be shown in the statement of profit or loss for the year ended 30 September 20X1 and the statement of financial position as at that date in respect of income tax?

	Statement of profit or loss	Statement of financial position
A	$83,000	$83,000
B	$88,000	$83,000
C	$83,000	$88,000
D	$88,000	$88,000

78 Hudson has the following balances included on its trial balance at 30 June 2014

Taxation $4,000 Credit

Deferred taxation $12,000 Credit

The balance on Taxation relates to an overprovision from 30 June 2013.

At 30 June 2014, the directors estimate that the provision necessary for taxation on current year profits is $15,000. The carrying value of Hudson's non-current assets exceeds the tax written-down value by $30,000. The rate of tax is 30%.

What is the charge for taxation that will appear in the Statement of Profit or Loss for the year to 30 June 2014?

A $23,000

B $28,000

C $8,000

D $12,000

79 Holmes has the following balances included on its trial balance at 30 June 2014:

Taxation $7,000 Credit

Deferred taxation $16,000 Credit

The balance on Taxation relates to an overprovision from 30 June 2013.

At 30 June 2014, the directors estimate that the provision necessary for taxation on current year profits is $12,000. The balance on the deferred tax account needs to be increased to $23,000, which includes the impact of the increase in property valuation below.

During the year Holmes revalued its property for the first time, resulting in a gain of $10,000. The rate of tax is 30%.

What is the charge for taxation that will appear in the Statement of Profit or Loss for the year to 30 June 2014?

A $9,000

B $12,000

C $23,000

D $1,000

80   Garfish plc had profits after tax of $3.0 million in the year ended 31 December 20X7. On 1 January 20X7, Garfish had 2.4 million ordinary shares in issue. On 1 April 20X7 Garfish made a one for two rights issue at a price of $1.40 when the market price of Garfish's shares was $2.00.

What is the basic earnings per share figure for the year ended 31 December 20X7, according to IAS 33 *Earnings Per Share*?

A   49.5 cents

B   89.1 cents

C   91.2 cents

D   92.6 cents

81   On 1st January 20X4, Sam Ltd had 3 million ordinary shares in issue. On 1st June 20X4, Sam Ltd made a 1 for 3 bonus issue. On 30th September 20X4, Sam Ltd then issued a further 1 million shares at full market price. Sam Ltd had profits attributable to ordinary equity holders of $2million for the year ended 31st December 20X4.

What is the basic earnings per share figure for the year ended 31st December 20X4, according to IAS 33 *Earnings Per Share*?

A   47.1 cents

B   42.9 cents

C   49.3 cents

D   52.2 cents

82   During the year, Mac made a 1 for 3 rights issue at $1.60 when the market price was $2.20. The previous year's financial statements showed an earnings per share figure of 81 cents. There were no other issues of shares during the year.

What will the restated earnings per share figure be for comparative purposes in the current year financial statements?

A   60.8 cents

B   75.5 cents

C   Impossible to calculate

D   81 cents

83 Coral Plc has net profit for the year ended 30 September 20X5 of $10,500,000. Coral has had 6 million shares in issue for many years. In the current year, Coral has issued a convertible bond. It was issued at its nominal value of $2,500,000, and carries an effective interest rate of 8%.

The bond is convertible in five years, with 50 shares issued for every $100 nominal of convertible bond held.

Coral Plc pays tax at a rate of 28%

What is the Diluted Earnings Per Share figure to be disclosed in Coral Plc's financial statements for the year ended 30 September 20X5?

A $1.77

B $1.75

C $1.48

D $1.47

84 Isco's financial statements show a profit for the year of $2million. On 1 January 20X5, Isco had 4 million shares in issue. There were no new issues of shares in the year, but there were 1 million outstanding options to buy shares for $3 each. For the year to 31 December 20X5, the average market value of Isco's shares was $5.00.

What is Isco's diluted earnings per share for the year ended 31 December 20X5?

A 30 cents

B 43.5 cents

C 45.5 cents

D 40 cents

85 Gromit Plc has the following extract from its consolidated profit or loss account:

	$000
Profit for the period	2,800
Other Comprehensive Income	
Revaluation Gain	500
Total Comprehensive Income	3,300
Profit for the period attributable to:	
Parent	2,250
Non-controlling Interest	550
	2,800
Total Comprehensive Income attributable to:	
Parent	2,600
Non-controlling Interest	700
	3,300

What figure should be used as Earnings by Gromit in its Earnings Per Share (EPS) calculation?

A $2,600,000

B $3,300,000

C $2,250,000

D $2,800,000

86   **Which of the following does NOT need to be removed from a company's net profit in a profit or loss account in order to calculate the earnings figure to be used in the Earnings Per Share calculation?**

A   Redeemable preference share dividends

B   Irredeemable preference share dividends

C   Profit attributable to the non-controlling interest

D   An error in expenses discovered before the financial statements have been authorised for issue.

STATEMENT OF CASH FLOWS

87   At 1 October 20X4, BK had the following balance:

Accrued interest payable $12,000 credit

During the year ended 30 September 20X5, BK charged interest payable of $41,000 to its statement of profit or loss. This included the unwinding of a discount relating to a provision stated at its present value of $150,000 at 1 October 20X4. The closing balance on accrued interest payable account at 30 September 20X5 was $15,000 credit, and BK uses a discount rate of 6%.

How much interest paid should BK show on its statement of cash flows for the year ended 30 September 20X5?

A $38,000

B $29,000

C $35,000

D $41,000

88   The following balances were extracted from N's financial statements:

Extracts from the statement of financial position as at 31 December

	20X9	20X8
	$000	$000
Non-current liabilities		
Deferred taxation	38	27
Current liabilities		
Current tax payable	119	106

Extract from statement of profit or loss and other comprehensive income for the year ended 31 December 20X9

	$000
Income tax expense	122

The amount of tax paid that should be included in N's statement of cash flows for the year ended 31 December 20X9 is:

A $98,000

B $109,000

C $122,000

D $241,000

89   Which ONE of the following would be not be shown in a statement of cash flow using the direct method?

A   Cash payments to employees

B   Cash paid to suppliers

C   Cash sales

D   Finance costs

90   IAS 7 Statement of cash flows sets out the three main headings to be used in a statement of cash flows. Items that may appear on a statement of cash flows include:

(i)   Tax paid

(ii)   Purchase of investments

(iii)   Loss on disposal of machinery

(iv)   Purchase of equipment

Which of the above items would be included under the heading "Cash flows from operating activities" according to IAS 7?

A   (i) and (ii)

B   (i) and (iii)

C   (ii) and (iv)

D   (iii) and (iv)

91   During the year to 31st July Smartypants made a profit of $37,500 after accounting for depreciation of $2,500. During the year non-current assets were purchased for $16,000, receivables increased by $2,000, inventories decreased by $3,600 and trade payables increased by $700.

What was the increase in cash and bank balances during the year?

A $21,300

B $32,300

C $24,900

D $26,300

92 Which of the following lists consists of items that would be added to net profit before taxation in the calculation of net cash from operating activities under the indirect method according to IAS 7?

    A   Decrease in trade receivables, increase in trade payables, profit on sale of non-current assets.

    B   Loss on sale of non-current assets, depreciation, increase in trade receivables.

    C   Decrease in inventories, depreciation, profit on sale of non-current assets.

    D   Decrease in trade receivables, increase in trade payables, loss on sale of non-current assets.

93 Butcher plc had the following balances in its statement of financial position as at 30 June 20X0 and 20X1:

	20X0	20X1
Share capital	$150,000	$170,000
Share premium	$95,000	$105,000
10% debentures	$190,000	$170,000

How much will appear in the statement of cash flows for the year ended 30 June 20X1 under the heading 'cash flows from financing activities'?

    A $nil

    B $10,000 inflow

    C $30,000 inflow

    D $40,000 inflow

94 At 1 January 20X0 Casey Ltd had property, plant and equipment with a carrying value of $180,000. In the year ended 31 December 20X0 the company disposed of assets with a carrying value of $60,000 for $50,000. The company revalued a building from $75,000 to $100,000 and charged depreciation for the year of $20,000. At the end of the year, the carrying value of property, plant and equipment was $250,000.

How much will be reported in the statement of cash flows for the year ended 31 December 20X0 under the heading 'cash flows from investing activities'?

    A $75,000 outflow

    B $125,000 outflow

    C $135,000 outflow

    D $50,000 inflow

CONSOLIDATED FINANCIAL STATEMENTS

95 **Which ONE of the following definitions is not included within the definition of control per IFRS 10?**

A   Having power over the investee

B   Having exposure, or rights, to variable returns from its investment with the investee

C   Having the majority of shares in the investee

D   Having the ability to use its power over the investee to affect the amount of the investor's returns

96 Pamela acquired 80% of the share capital of Samantha on 1/1/20X1. Part of the purchase consideration was to pay additional cash on 1/1/20X4 of $200,000. The applicable cost of capital is 10%.

What will the deferred consideration liability be at 31/12/20X2?

A $150,000

B $165,000

C $200,000

D $181,500

97 Philip acquired 85% of the share capital of Stanley on 1/10/20X1 for $500,000. The profit for the year ended 31/12/20X1 for Stanley was $36,000. Profits are deemed to accrue evenly over the year. At 31/12/20X1 the following extracts of the statement of financial position for Stanley has been provided:

Equity share capital $200,000

Retained earnings $180,000

Non-controlling interest is valued using the fair value method. The fair value of non-controlling interest at 1/10/20X1 was $30,000.

What is the goodwill on acquisition?

A $150,000

B $184,650

C $159,000

D $177,000

98 On 30 June 2014 GHI acquired 800,000 of JKL's 1 million shares. The purchase consideration was as follows:

GHI issued 3 shares for every four shares acquired in JKL. On 30 June the market price of a GHI share was $3.80 and the market price of a JKL share was $3.00.

GHI agreed to pay $550,000 in cash to the existing shareholders on 30 June 2015. GHI's borrowing rate was 10% per annum.

GHI paid advisors $100,000 to advise on the acquisition.

What is the cost of investment that will be used in the goodwill calculation in the consolidated accounts of GHI?

A $2,400,000

B $2,780,000

C $2,830,000

D $2,880,000

99 MNO has a 75% owned subsidiary PQR. During the year MNO sold inventory to PQR for an invoiced price of $800,000. PQR have since sold 75% of that inventory on to third parties. The sale was at a mark-up of 25% on cost to MNO. PQR is the only subsidiary of MNO.

What is the adjustment to inventory that would be included in the consolidated statement of financial position of MNO at the year-end resulting from this sale?

A $120,000

B $40,000

C $160,000

D $50,000

100 West Ltd has a 75% subsidiary, Land Ltd, and is preparing its consolidated statement of financial position as at 31 December 20X6. The carrying amount of property, plant and equipment in the two companies at that date is as follows:

West Ltd $300,000

Land Ltd $60,000

On 1 January 20X6 Land Ltd had transferred some property to West Ltd for $40,000. At the date of transfer the property, which had cost $42,000, had a carrying amount of $30,000 and a remaining useful life of five years. The group accounting policy is to depreciate property on a straight-line basis down to a nil residual value. It is also group policy not to revalue non-current assets.

What is the carrying amount of property, plant and equipment in the consolidated statement of financial position of West Ltd as at 31 December 20X6?

A $332,000

B $350,000

C $352,000

D $360,000

101 **Which ONE of the following situations is unlikely to represent control over an investee?**

A Owning 55% and being able to elect 4 of the 7 directors

B Owning 51%, but the constitution requires that decisions need the unanimous consent of shareholders

C Having currently exercisable options which would take the shareholding of the company to 55%

D Owning 40% of the shares, but having the majority of voting rights within the company

102 **Which ONE of the following will not be recognised as part of the cost of an investment in a subsidiary company?**

    A   A cash payment of $50,000 to be made in one year's time

    B   Professional fees of $10,000 in connection with the investment

    C   A share for share exchange of 3 shares in the parent company for every 4 shares held in the subsidiary company

    D   An agreement to pay a further $30,000 if the subsidiary company achieves an operating profit of over $100,000 in the first 3 years after acquisition.

103 Peter plc acquires 80% of the share capital of Paul plc on 1/8/X6 and is preparing its group financial statements for the year ended 31/12/X6.

How will Paul's results be included in the group statement of profit or loss?

    A   80% of Paul's revenue and expenses for the year ended 31/12/X6

    B   100% of Paul's revenue and expenses for the year ended 31/12/X6

    C   80% of Paul's revenue and expenses for the period 1/8/X6-31/12/X6

    D   100% of Paul's revenue and expenses for the period ended 1/8/X6-31/12/X6

104 **Which ONE of the following would result in an unrealised profit within a group scenario?**

    A   A parent sells a building originally costing $800,000 to its subsidiary company for $900,000. The subsidiary still holds this asset at the date of consolidation.

    B   A parent sells a building originally costing $800,000 to its subsidiary company for $900,000. The subsidiary has sold this asset before the date of consolidation.

    C   A parent sells goods which originally cost $14,000 to its subsidiary company for $18,000. The subsidiary company has sold all of these goods at the date of consolidation.

    D   A parent sells goods which originally cost $14,000 to an associate company for $18,000. The associate company has sold all of these goods at the date of consolidation.

105 **An impairment of goodwill in a subsidiary company will be accounted for in which of the following ways?**

    A   It will always be deducted in full from the parent company retained earnings

    B   It will be apportioned between the parent company and the non-controlling interest (NCI) when the NCI is valued at fair value

    C   It will always be apportioned between the parent company and the NCI

    D   It will be apportioned between the parent company and the NCI where the NCI is valued using the proportionate method

106 **Which one of the following is not a condition which must be met if a parent is not producing consolidated accounts?**

A   The activities of the subsidiary are significantly different to the rest of the group and to consolidate them would prejudice the overall group position

B   The ultimate parent company produces consolidated financial statements that comply with IFRS and are publicly available

C   The parent's debt or equity instruments are not traded in a public market

D   The parent itself is a wholly owned subsidiary or a partially owned subsidiary whose owners do not object to the parent not producing consolidated financial statements

107 During the year Fluff sold $168,000 worth of goods to its subsidiary Ball. These goods were sold at a mark-up of 50% on cost. On 31 December Ball still had $36,000 worth of these goods in inventory.

What is the PURP adjustment in the group accounts?

A $56,000

B $12,000

C $84,000

D $18,000

108 STU has an 80% subsidiary, VWX. VWX, which has been a subsidiary of STU for the whole year, reported a profit after tax of $600,000 in its own financial statements. You ascertain the following additional matters:

At the year-end there was unrealised profit of $60,000 on sales by VWX to STU.

During the year the goodwill on acquisition of VWX was impaired by $50,000.

STU measures the non-controlling interest in VWX using the fair value method.

What is the non-controlling interest in VWX that would be reported in the consolidated statement of profit or loss and other comprehensive income of STU for the year?

A $98,000

B $108,000

C $110,000

D $120,000

109 H PLC acquired an 80% holding in S Limited. on 1st April 20X6. From 1st April 20X6 to 31st December 20X6 S sold goods worth $4.3m at cost plus 10% to H. H's inventory at 31st December 20X6 included $2.2m of such inventory. The statements of profit or loss for each company for year to 31st December 20X6 showed the following in respect of cost of sales:

H PLC $14.7m

S LTD $11.6m

Show the cost of sales figure in the consolidated statement of profit or loss for year to 31 December 20X6.

A $18,900,000

B $20,200,000

C $19,100,000

D $19,300,000

110 X PLC acquired a 60% holding in Y Limited on 1 January 20X6. At this date, Y had a building with a fair value $200,000 in excess of its carrying value, which had a remaining life of 10 years. Also, goodwill had been impaired by $55,000 in the year to 31 December 20X6. The balances on operating expenses for the year to 31 December 20X7 are shown below:

X PLC $600,000

Y LTD $350,000

What are consolidated operating expenses for the year to 31 December 20X7?

A $875,000

B $990,000

C $930,000

D $970,000

111 A PLC acquired a 60% holding in B Limited on 1 July 20X6. At this date, A gave B a $500,000 8% loan. The interest on the loan has been accounted for correctly in the individual financial statements. The following totals for finance costs for the year to 31 December 20X6 in the individual financial statements are shown below.

A PLC $200,000

B LTD $70,000

What are consolidated finance costs for the year to 31 December 20X7?

A $215,000

B $225,000

C $230,000

D $250,000

112 Which ONE of the following would have no impact on the profit attributable to the non-controlling interest in the consolidated statement of profit or loss if the non-controlling interest is measured at fair value?

A   The parent transferring an item of inventory to the subsidiary for $10,000 greater than its carrying value, all of which remains in the group at the year end

B   The subsidiary selling an inventory to the parent at a profit of $20,000, which all remains in the group at the year end

C   The subsidiary having an item of plant with a fair value of $500,000 above its carrying value, and a remaining life of 10 years

D   Goodwill impairment

113 AB has owned 80% of CD for many years. In the current year ended 30 June 20X3, AB has reported total revenues of $5.5 million, and CD of $2.1 million. AB has sold goods to CD during the year with a total value of $1 million. Half of these goods sold remain in year end inventories.

What is the consolidated revenue figure for the AB group for the year ended 30 June 20X3?

A $7.6 million

B $4.5 million

C $6.6 million

D $7.1 million

114 Burridge bought 30% of Allen on 1 July 20X4. Allen's statement of profit or loss for the year shows a profit of $400,000. Allen paid a dividend to Burridge of $50,000 on 1 December. At the year end, the investment in Allen was judged to have been impaired by $10,000.

What will be shown under 'Share of profit from associate' in the consolidated statement of profit or loss for the year ended 31 December 20X4?

A   Nil

B $50,000

C $60,000

D $110,000

115 Beasant bought 30% of Arnie on 1 January 20X8, when Arnie had share capital of $100,000 $1 shares and $400,000 retained earnings. Beasant paid by giving the previous owners of Arnie one Beasant share for every 3 shares bought in Arnie. At the date of acquisition, Beasant's shares had a market value of $4.50 and Arnie's had a market value of $2. At 31 December, Arnie's net assets were $460,000.

What is the value shown under 'Investment in Associate in the consolidated statement of financial position as at 31 December 20X8?

A   8,000

B $33,000

C $51,000

D $123,000

116 **Removing unrealised profits on sales between a parent and subsidiary is an example of which concept?**

A   Prudence

B   Going concern

C   Equity accounting

D   Single entity

117 The Nicol group has recently purchased a 20% stake in Hansen plc. The other 80% is owned by Lawro, another listed company, whose directors make up Hansen's board.

What is the most likely treatment for Hansen in the Nicol group accounts?

A   Treat the investment as an associate

B   Treat the investment as a subsidiary

C   Disclose the shareholding only, with no entries in the financial statements

D   Treat the investment as an equity investment per IFRS 9.

118 Badger Plc acquired 30% of Eagle Ltd on 1 July 20X3. Badger has classified Eagle as an associate undertaking. The investment cost $5.5 million. For the year ended 30 September 20X3, Eagle Ltd is reporting a net profit of $625,000.

What is the value of the associate investment in the group Statement of Financial Position of Badger Plc as at 30 September 20X3?

A $5,656,250

B $5,500,000

C $6,125,000

D $5,968,750

119 Green Ltd is an associate undertaking of Purple Plc. Purple Plc owns 30% of the shares in Green Ltd, and has done so for many years. During the year ended 31 December 20X4, Green Ltd made a net profit of $1.5 million. Green sold goods to Purple Plc during the year with a value of $2 million, and half are still in Purple's inventories at year end. All the goods were sold at a margin of 30%.

Purple has recognised previous impairments in relation to its investment in Green Ltd of $225,000. In the current year, Purple wishes to recognise an additional impairment charge of $35,000.

What is the share of profit of associate to be shown in Purple's consolidated statement of Profit or Loss?

A $100,000

B $115,000

C $325,000

D $415,000

120 Which ONE of the following statements regarding consolidated financial statements is correct?

A   For consolidation, it may be acceptable to use financial statements of the subsidiary if the year-end differs from the parent by 2 months.

B   For consolidation, all companies within the group must have the same year end.

C   All companies within a group must have the same accounting policy in their individual financial statements.

D   The profit made on all intra-group sales in the year must be removed from the consolidated financial statements.

INTERPRETATION OF FINANCIAL STATEMENTS

121 Which of the following ratios is likely to be most relevant for a local charity?

A   Operating profit margin

B   Current ratio

C   Earnings per share

D   Return on capital employed

122 Which ONE of the following is not a limitation of applying ratio analysis to published financial statements?

A   Accounting policy choices can limit comparability between different companies

B   Financial statements may contain errors

C   Information within published financial statements is historic and out of date

D   Different ways of calculating certain ratios exist

123 The following information has been taken from Preston's financial statements for the year-ended 31 December 20X7:

Preston has inventory turnover of six times

The year-end receivables collection period is 42 days

Cost of sales for the year was $1,690,000

Credit purchases for the year were $2,150,000

Preston's cash cycle at 31 December 20X7 was 68 days

All calculations should be made to the nearest full day, and the trading year has 365 days.

What is Preston's trade payables collection period as at 31 December 20X7?

A   35 days

B   17 days

C   138 days

D   26 days

124 The following extracts of the financial statements of Wiggo have been obtained:

Revenue	$980,000
Cost of sales	($530,000)
Operating expenses	($210,000)
Equity	$600,000
Loan, repayable 20X8	$300,000
Deferred tax	$44,000
Payables	$46,000

What is the return on capital employed of Wiggo?

A   24.2%

B   25.4%

C   26.7%

D   50%

125 The following extracts of the financial statements of Wiggo have been obtained:

	20X5
Inventories	$130,000
Receivables	$80,000
Cash	$10,000
Loan repayable 20X8	$90,000
Deferred tax	$14,000
Payables	$70,000
Overdraft	$34,000

What is the quick ratio of Wiggo?

A   0.76:1

B   0.87:1

C   1.86:1

D   2.12:1

126 **Which ONE of the following explanations is unlikely to lead to an increase in receivables collection period?**

A   A new contract with a large customer has been won following a competitive tender

B   A large one-off credit sale has been completed just before the year end

C   Difficult economic conditions have led to some customers struggling to pay on time

D   A website has been opened in the year for trade direct to the public

127 Which ONE of the following items is unlikely to be considered a 'one-off' item which would impact the comparability of ratios?

A   A new website selling direct to the public has meant that deliveries are now made to more diverse geographical areas, increasing delivery costs

B   A closure of a department has led to redundancies

C   Sale of surplus property leading to a profit on disposal

D   A storm in the year led to significant damage to the warehouse

128 KRL is a company which manufactures pharmaceuticals, and is investigating a proposed takeover of another entity which is based overseas.

KRL has performed a benchmarking exercise based on the financial statements of the overseas entity, and thinks this entity would fit in with it strategically.

Which ONE of the following would KRL be unlikely to be able to use in order to make the decision?

A   Internal business plans of the takeover target

B   Details of the overseas country in which the target entity operates

C   Press reports of the target entity

D   Recent financial statements of the entity

129 Which ONE of the following is not a valid reason for a decrease in gross profit margin?

A   A major customer renewed their contract during the year following a competitive tender process

B   New plant and equipment used in the manufacturing process has been purchased in the year, which has increased the depreciation expense

C   Delivery costs to customers have risen following an increase in the rates charged by couriers

D   A national recession has led to sales prices being cut in response

130 Marcel Plc has calculated that its current year Price Earnings (P/E) ratio is 12.6.

The sector average P/E ratio is 10.5

Which ONE of the following would be an explanation of the difference between Marcel's P/E ratio and the sector average?

A   Marcel is seen as a less risky investment than the sector average, and there is higher confidence about the future prospects of Marcel.

B   Marcel is seen as a more risky investment than the sector average, however there is higher confidence about the future prospects of Marcel.

C   Marcel is seen as a less risky investment than the sector average, however there is low confidence about the future prospects of Marcel.

D   Marcel is seen as a more risky investment than the sector average, and there is low confidence about the future prospects of Marcel.

131 Why is it important to disclose the Diluted Earnings Per Share (EPS) calculation in a company's financial statements?

    A   It acts as a prediction of the future Earnings Per Share figure

    B   It discloses that Earnings Per Share could have been higher

    C   It forms part of the Price Earnings ratio calculation

    D   It is a warning that the Earnings Per Share calculation could have been lower

132 Apollo Ltd took out a new loan on 1st January 20X6. This loan is carries an effective interest rate of 8%, and the initial proceeds of the loan are $2.5m, which is after paying issue costs of $250k. The coupon rate on the loan is 6%. Apollo must keep to an interest cover ratio of 9 times under the arrangements made with the bank.

What operating profit must be maintained by Apollo in the year ended 31st December 20X6, in order to meet the minimum interest cover ratio specified by the bank?

    A $1,350,000

    B $1,800,000

    C $450,000

    D $1,980,000

The following information is to be used for questions 133 and 134:

Rogers Plc has just completed their financial statements for the year ended 30 June 20X6. They are reporting a net profit of $1,250,000 for the current year, and they have $1 million 50 cent shares in issue. The current market price of Rogers' shares is $3.50.

Rogers Plc has total dividends during the year ended 30 June 20X6 of $1,500,000

---

133 What is the Price Earnings (P/E) ratio of Rogers Plc for the year ended 30 June 20X6?

    A   4.7 times

    B   5.6 times

    C   2.8 times

    D   0.18 times

134 What is the Dividend Yield of Rogers Plc for the year ended 30 June 20X6?

    A   42.9%

    B   46.7%

    C   35.7%

    D   21.4%

135 Alco and Saleco are both food retailers. They are both showing a Return on Capital Employed (ROCE) figure of 10% for the current year. Both companies have the same financial year end.

Alco has reported a net profit (based on profit before interest and tax) of 25% and Saleco has reported a net profit of 2%.

What, if any, is the difference between these two companies, even though they are showing the same ROCE calculation?

A   The companies are identical

B   Alco operates at the high end of the market, and Saleco at the lower end of the market

C   Alco operates at the lower end of the market, and Saleco at the high end of the market

D   There is not enough information in the question to determine the difference between the two companies

136   Which ONE of the following is not a limitation of financial statements?

A   Financial statements often use historic cost, meaning that inflation is not taken into account

B   Companies having different year ends may make comparability difficult, especially in industries with seasonal variations

C   Estimates have to be used within the financial statements for certain items, which may differ from the eventual figure

D   Complex items may not fit into any accounting standards and therefore may be omitted from the financial statements

137 Lepchem is a pharmaceutical company which was launched in September 20X1. Lepchem have been funded through bank loans and equity investment. Lepchem's aim is to develop new pharmaceuticals which could then be sold for a high margin. So far, Lepchem have not managed to successfully develop or sell any pharmaceuticals.

Which ratio is likely to be the most relevant for Lepchem for the year to 31 December 20X1?

A   Current ratio

B   Gross profit margin

C   Operating profit margin

D   Receivables collection period

138   Which ONE of the following is not likely to be a criterion under which a not-for-profit is judged in terms of value for money?

A   The management of resources

B   The success in achieving the organisation's stated aims

C   The return given to investors

D   How well costs are being managed

139 Which ONE of the following measures is likely to be the least relevant to a property management company which rents out properties to businesses?

A   Non-current asset turnover

B   Return on capital employed

C   Average rent earned

D   Inventory turnover period

140 Which of the following accounting standards is least likely to be relevant to a charity which receives local government funding to providing low-cost meals to elderly individuals from an owned premises?

A   IAS 16 Property, Plant and Equipment

B   IAS 20 Government grants

C   IAS 18 Revenue

D   IAS 2 Inventory

Section B

PRACTICE QUESTIONS

CONCEPTUAL FRAMEWORK/FINANCIAL STATEMENTS

141   FINANCIAL STATEMENTS *Walk in the footsteps of a top tutor*

(a)   The IASB's Framework *Conceptual Framework for Financial Reporting* requires financial statements to be prepared on the basis that they comply with certain accounting concepts, underlying assumptions and (qualitative) characteristics. Five of these are:

Matching/accruals

Faithful representation

Prudence

Comparability

Materiality

Required:

Briefly explain the meaning of each of the above concepts/assumptions.   (5 marks)

(b)   For most entities, applying the appropriate concepts/assumptions in accounting for inventories is an important element in preparing their financial statements.

Required:

Illustrate with examples how each of the concepts/assumptions in (a) may be applied to accounting for inventory.   (10 marks)

(Total: 15 marks)

142   FINO *Walk in the footsteps of a top tutor*

(a)   An important requirement of the IASB's *Conceptual Framework for Financial Reporting* is that an entity's financial statements should represent faithfully the transactions and events that it has undertaken.

Required:

Explain what is meant by faithful representation according to the IASB's Conceptual Framework for Financial Reporting.   (5 marks)

(b)   On 1 April 2007, Fino increased the operating capacity of its plant. Due to a lack of liquid funds it was unable to buy the required plant which had a cost of $350,000. On the recommendation of the finance director, Fino entered into an agreement to lease the plant from the manufacturer. The lease required four annual payments in advance of $100,000 each commencing on 1 April 2007. The plant would have a useful life of four years and would be scrapped at the end of this period. The finance director, believing the lease to be an operating lease, commented that the agreement would improve the company's return on capital employed (compared to outright purchase of the plant).

Required:

(i)   **Discuss the validity of the finance director's comment and describe how IAS 17 Leases ensures that leases such as the above are faithfully represented in an entity's financial statements.** **(4 marks)**

(ii)   **Prepare extracts of Fino's statement of profit or loss and statement of financial position for the year ended 30 September 2007 in respect of the rental agreement assuming:**

(1)   **It is an operating lease** **(2 marks)**

(2)   **It is a finance lease (use an implicit interest rate of 10% per annum).** **(4 marks)**

(Total: 15 marks)

143   WARDLE

(a)   An important aspect of the International Accounting Standards Board's *Conceptual Framework for Financial Reporting* is that transactions should be recorded on the basis of faithful representation.

Required:

Explain why it is important that financial statements should show faithful representation, and describe circumstances where the recognition criteria for assets and liabilities may differ from the passing of legal title over items. **(5 marks)**

(b)   Wardle's activities include the production of maturing products which take a long time before they are ready to retail. Details of one such product are that on 1 April 2009 it had a cost of $5 million and a fair value of $7 million. The product would not be ready for retail sale until 31 March 2012.

On 1 April 2009 Wardle entered into an agreement to sell the product to Easyfinance for $6 million. The agreement gave Wardle the right to repurchase the product at any time up to 31 March 2012 at a fixed price of $7,986,000, at which date Wardle expected the product to retail for $10 million. The compound interest Wardle would have to pay on a three-year loan of $6 million would be:

	$
Year 1	600,000
Year 2	660,000
Year 3	726,000

This interest is equivalent to the return required by Easyfinance.

Required:

Assuming the above figures prove to be accurate, prepare extracts from the statement of profit or loss of Wardle for the three years to 31 March 2012 in respect of the above transaction:

(i) Reflecting the legal form of the transaction; (2 marks)

(ii) Reflecting the faithful representation of the transaction. (3 marks)

Note: Statement of financial position extracts are NOT required.

(c) Comment on the effect the two treatments have on the statement of profit or loss and the statements of financial position and how this may affect an assessment of Wardle's performance. (5 marks)

(Total: 15 marks)

144 TUNSHILL

(a) IAS *8 Accounting Policies, Changes in Accounting Estimates and Errors* contains guidance on the use of accounting policies and accounting estimates.

Required:

Explain the basis on which the management of an entity must select its accounting policies and distinguish, with an example, between changes in accounting policies and changes in accounting estimates. (5 marks)

(b) The directors of Tunshill are disappointed by the draft profit for the year ended 30 September 2010. The company's assistant accountant has suggested two areas where she believes the reported profit may be improved:

(i) A major item of plant that cost $20 million to purchase and install on 1 October 2007 is being depreciated on a straight-line basis over a five-year period (assuming no residual value). The plant is wearing well and at the beginning of the current year (1 October 2009) the production manager believed that the plant was likely to last eight years in total (i.e. from the date of its purchase). The assistant accountant has calculated that, based on an eight-year life (and no residual value) the accumulated depreciation of the plant at 30 September 2010 would be $7.5 million ($20 million/8 years × 3). In the financial statements for the year ended 30 September 2009, the accumulated depreciation was $8 million ($20 million/5 years × 2). Therefore, by adopting an eight-year life, Tunshill can avoid a depreciation charge in the current year and instead credit $0.5 million ($8 million − $7.5 million) to the statement of profit or loss in the current year to improve the reported profit. **(5 marks)**

(ii) Most of Tunshill's competitors value their inventory using the average cost (AVCO) basis, whereas Tunshill uses the first in first out (FIFO) basis. The value of Tunshill's inventory at 30 September 2010 (on the FIFO basis) is $20 million, however on the AVCO basis it would be valued at $18 million. By adopting the same method (AVCO) as its competitors, the assistant accountant says the company would improve its profit for the year ended 30 September 2010 by $2 million. Tunshill's inventory at 30 September 2009 was reported as $15 million, however on the AVCO basis it would have been reported as $13.4 million. **(5 marks)**

Required:

Comment on the acceptability of the assistant accountant's suggestions and quantify how they would affect the financial statements if they were implemented under IFRS. Ignore taxation.

(Total: 15 marks)

145   PROMOIL *Walk in the footsteps of a top tutor*

(a)   The definition of a liability forms an important element of the International Accounting Standards Board's *Conceptual Framework for Financial Reporting* which, in turn, forms the basis for IAS 37 *Provisions, Contingent Liabilities and Contingent Assets*.

Required:

Define a liability and describe the circumstances under which provisions should be recognised. Give two examples of how the definition of liabilities enhances the faithful representation of financial statements.   **(5 marks)**

(b)   On 1 October 2007, Promoil acquired a newly constructed oil platform at a cost of $30 million together with the right to extract oil from an offshore oilfield under a government licence. The terms of the licence are that Promoil will have to remove the platform (which will then have no value) and restore the sea bed to an environmentally satisfactory condition in 10 years' time when the oil reserves have been exhausted. The estimated cost of this on 30 September 2017 will be $15 million. The present value of $1 receivable in 10 years at the appropriate discount rate for Promoil of 8% is $0.46.

Required:

(i)   **Explain and quantify how the oil platform should be treated in the financial statements of Promoil for the year ended 30 September 2008;**   **(7 marks)**

(ii)   **Describe how your answer to (b)(i) would change if the government licence did not require an environmental cleanup.**   **(3 marks)**

(Total: 15 marks)

146   WAXWORK

(a)   The objective of IAS 10 *Events after the Reporting Period is* to prescribe the treatment of events that occur after an entity's reporting period has ended.

Required:

Define the period to which IAS 10 relates and distinguish between adjusting and non-adjusting events.   **(5 marks)**

(b)   Waxwork's current year end is 31 March 2009. Its financial statements were authorised for issue by its directors on 6 May 2009 and the AGM (annual general meeting) will be held on 3 June 2009. The following matters have been brought to your attention:

(i)   On 12 April 2009 a fire completely destroyed the company's largest warehouse and the inventory it contained. The carrying amounts of the warehouse and the inventory were $10 million and $6 million respectively. It appears that the company has not updated the value of its insurance cover and only expects to be able to recover a maximum of $9 million from its insurers. Waxwork's trading operations have been severely disrupted since the fire and it expects large trading losses for some time to come. **(4 marks)**

(ii) A single class of inventory held at another warehouse was valued at its cost of $460,000 at 31 March 2009. In April 2009 70% of this inventory was sold for $280,000 on which Waxworks' sales staff earned a commission of 15% of the selling price. **(3 marks)**

(iii) On 18 May 2009 the government announced tax changes which have the effect of increasing Waxwork's deferred tax liability by $650,000 as at 31 March 2009. **(3 marks)**

Required:

Explain the required treatment of the items (i) to (iii) by Waxwork in its financial statements for the year ended 31 March 2009. *Note:* **Assume all items are material and are independent of each other.** **(10 marks as indicated)**

(Total: 15 marks)

147 DARBY

(a) Your assistant has been criticised over a piece of assessed work that he produced for his study course for giving the definition of a non-current asset as 'a physical asset of substantial cost, owned by the company, which will last longer than one year'.

Required:

Explain the weaknesses in the assistant's definition of non-current assets. (4 marks)

(b) The same assistant has encountered the following matters during the preparation of the draft financial statements of Darby for the year ending 30 September 2009. He has given an explanation of his treatment of them.

(i) Darby spent $200,000 sending its staff on training courses during the year. This has already led to an improvement in the company's efficiency and resulted in cost savings. The organiser of the course has stated that the benefits from the training should last for a minimum of four years. The assistant has therefore treated the cost of the training as an intangible asset and charged six months' amortisation based on the average date during the year on which the training courses were completed. **(3 marks)**

(ii) During the year the company started research work with a view to the eventual development of a new processor chip. By 30 September 2009 it had spent $1.6 million on this project. Darby has a past history of being particularly successful in bringing similar projects to a profitable conclusion. As a consequence the assistant has treated the expenditure to date on this project as an asset in the statement of financial position.

Darby was also commissioned by a customer to research and, if feasible, produce a computer system to install in motor vehicles that can automatically stop the vehicle if it is about to be involved in a collision. At 30 September 2009, Darby had spent $2.4 million on this project, but at this date it was uncertain as to whether the project would be successful. As a consequence the assistant has treated the $2.4 million as an expense in the statement of profit or loss. **(4 marks)**

(iii) Darby signed a contract (for an initial three years) in August 2009 with a company called Media Today to install a satellite dish and cabling system to a newly built group of residential apartments. Media Today will provide telephone and television services to the residents of the apartments via the satellite system and pay Darby $50,000 per annum commencing in December 2009. Work on the installation commenced on 1 September 2009 and the expenditure to 30 September 2009 was $58,000. The installation is expected to be completed by 31 October 2009. Previous experience with similar contracts indicates that Darby will make a total profit of $40,000 over the three years on this initial contract. The assistant correctly recorded the costs to 30 September 2009 of $58,000 as a non-current asset, but then wrote this amount down to $40,000 (the expected total profit) because he believed the asset to be impaired.

The contract is not a finance lease. Ignore discounting. **(4 marks)**

Required:

For each of the above items (i) to (iii) comment on the assistant's treatment of them in the financial statements for the year ended 30 September 2009 and advise him how they should be treated under International Financial Reporting Standards.

(Total: 15 marks)

148 REBOUND

(a) Your assistant has been reading the IASB's *Conceptual Framework for Financial Reporting* and as part of the qualitative characteristics of financial statements under the heading of 'relevance' he notes that the predictive value of information is considered important. He is aware that financial statements are prepared historically (i.e. after transactions have occurred) and offers the view that the predictive value of financial statements would be enhanced if forward-looking information (e.g. forecasts) were published rather than backward-looking historical statements.

Required:

By the use of specific examples, provide an explanation to your assistant of how IFRS presentation and disclosure requirements can assist the predictive role of historically prepared financial statements. **(6 marks)**

(b) The following summarised information is available in relation to Rebound, a publicly listed company:

Statement of profit or loss extracts years ended 31 March:

	2011		2010	
	Continuing	Discontinued	Continuing	Discontinued
	$000	$000	$000	$000
Profit after tax				
Existing operations	2,000	(750)	1,750	600
Operations acquired on 1 August 2010	450		nil	

Analysts expect profits from the market sector in which Rebound's existing operations are based to increase by 6% in the year to 31 March 2012 and by 8% in the sector of its newly acquired operations.

On 1 April 2009 Rebound had:

$3 million of 25 cents equity shares in issue.

$5 million 8% convertible loan stock 2016; the terms of conversion are 40 equity shares in exchange for each $100 of loan stock. Assume an income tax rate of 30%.

On 1 October 2010 the directors of Rebound were granted options to buy 2 million shares in the company for $1 each. The average market price of Rebound's shares for the year ending 31 March 2011 was $2·50 each.

Required:

(i)   **Calculate Rebound's estimated profit after tax for the year ending 31 March 2012 assuming the analysts' expectations prove correct;**   **(3 marks)**

(ii)   **Calculate the diluted earnings per share (EPS) on the continuing operations of Rebound for the year ended 31 March 2011 and the comparatives for 2010.**
                                                                                      (6 marks)

                                                                          (Total: 15 marks)

149   BOROUGH

(a)   IAS 37 *Provisions, contingent liabilities and contingent assets* prescribes the accounting and disclosure for those items named in its title.

Required:

Define provisions and contingent liabilities and briefly explain how IAS 37 improves consistency in financial reporting.   **(6 marks)**

(b)   The following items have arisen during the preparation of Borough's draft financial statements for the year ended 30 September 2011:

(i)   On 1 October 2010, Borough commenced the extraction of crude oil from a new well on the seabed. The cost of a 10-year licence to extract the oil was $50 million. At the end of the extraction, although not legally bound to do so, Borough intends to make good the damage the extraction has caused to the seabed environment. This intention has been communicated to parties external to Borough. The cost of this will be in two parts: a fixed amount of $20 million and a variable amount of 2 cents per barrel extracted. Both of these amounts are based on their present values as at 1 October 2010 (discounted at 8%) of the estimated costs in 10 years' time. In the year to 30 September 2011 Borough extracted 150 million barrels of oil.

(ii)   Borough owns the whole of the equity share capital of its subsidiary Hamlet. Hamlet's statement of financial position includes a loan of $25 million that is repayable in five years' time. $15 million of this loan is secured on Hamlet's property and the remaining $10 million is guaranteed by Borough in the event of a default by Hamlet. The economy in which Hamlet operates is currently experiencing a deep recession, the effects of which are that the current value of its property is estimated at $12 million and there are concerns over whether Hamlet can survive the recession and therefore repay the loan.

Required:

Describe, and quantify where possible, how items (i) and (ii) above should be treated in Borough's statement of financial position for the year ended 30 September 2011.

In the case of item (ii) only, distinguish between Borough's entity and consolidated financial statements and refer to any disclosure notes. Your answer should only refer to the treatment of the loan and should not consider any impairment of Hamlet's property or Borough's investment in Hamlet.

Note: the treatment in the income statement is NOT required for any of the items.

The following mark allocation is provided as guidance for this requirement:

(i)   5 marks

(ii)   4 marks   (9 marks)

(Total: 15 marks)

150   TELEPATH

(a)   The objective of IAS 36 *Impairment of* assets is to prescribe the procedures that an entity applies to ensure that its assets are not impaired.

Required:

Explain what is meant by an impairment review. Your answer should include reference to assets that may form a cash generating unit.

Note: you are NOT required to describe the indicators of an impairment or how impairment losses are allocated against assets.   (4 marks)

(b)   (i)   Telepath acquired an item of plant at a cost of $800,000 on 1 April 2010 that is used to produce and package pharmaceutical pills. The plant had an estimated residual value of $50,000 and an estimated life of five years, neither of which has changed. Telepath uses straight-line depreciation. On 31 March 2012, Telepath was informed by a major customer (who buys products produced by the plant) that it would no longer be placing orders with Telepath. Even before this information was known, Telepath had been having difficulty finding work for this plant. It now estimates that net cash inflows earned from the plant for the next three years will be:

		$000
year ended:	31 March 2013	220
	31 March 2014	180
	31 March 2015	170

On 31 March 2015, the plant is still expected to be sold for its estimated realisable value. Telepath has confirmed that there is no market in which to sell the plant at 31 March 2012. Telepath's cost of capital is 10% and the following values should be used:

value of $1 at:	$
end of year 1	0·91
end of year 2	0·83
end of year 3	0·75

(ii) Telepath owned a 100% subsidiary, Tilda that is treated as a cash generating unit. On 31 March 2012, there was an industrial accident (a gas explosion) that caused damage to some of Tilda's plant. The assets of Tilda immediately before the accident were:

	$000
Goodwill	1,800
Patent	1,200
Factory building	4,000
Plant	3,500
Receivables and cash	1,500
	12,000

As a result of the accident, the recoverable amount of Tilda is $6·7 million

The explosion destroyed (to the point of no further use) an item of plant that had a carrying amount of $500,000.

Tilda has an open offer from a competitor of $1 million for its patent. The receivables and cash are already stated at their fair values less costs to sell (net realisable values).

Required:

Calculate the carrying amounts of the assets in (i) and (ii) above at 31 March 2012 after applying any impairment losses.

Calculations should be to the nearest $1,000.

The following mark allocation is provided as guidance for this requirement:

(i) 4 marks

(ii) 7 marks (11 marks)

(Total: 15 marks)

151 LOBDEN

(a) Two of the qualitative characteristics of information contained in the IASB's *Conceptual Framework for Financial Reporting* are understandability and comparability.

Required:

Explain the meaning and purpose of the above characteristics in the context of financial reporting and discuss the role of consistency within the characteristic of comparability in relation to changes in accounting policy. **(6 marks)**

(b) Lobden is a construction contract company involved in building commercial properties. Its current policy for determining the percentage of completion of its contracts is based on the proportion of cost incurred to date compared to the total expected cost of the contract.

One of Lobden's contracts has an agreed price of $250 million and estimated total costs of $200 million. The cumulative progress of this contract is:

Year ended:	30 September 2011	30 September 2012
	$million	$million
Costs incurred	80	145
Work certified and billed	75	160
Billings received	70	150

Based on the above, Lobden prepared and published its financial statements for the year ended 30 September 2011. Relevant extracts are:

Statement of profit or loss

	$million
Revenue (balance)	100
Cost of sales	(80)
Profit (50 × 80/200)	20

Statement of financial position

	$million
Current assets	
Amounts due from customers	
Contract costs to date	80
Profit recognized	20
	100
Progress billings	(75)
	25
Contract receivables (75 – 70)	5

Lobden has received some adverse publicity in the financial press for taking its profit too early in the contract process, leading to disappointing profits in the later stages of contracts. Most of Lobden's competitors take profit based on the percentage of completion as determined by the work certified compared to the contract price.

Required:

(i) Assuming Lobden changes its method of determining the percentage of completion of contracts to that used by its competitors, and that this would represent a change in an accounting estimate, calculate equivalent extracts to the above for the year ended 30 September 2012; **(7 marks)**

(ii) Explain why the above represents a change in accounting estimate rather than a change in accounting policy. **(2 marks)**

(Total: 15 marks)

152 RADAR

(a)   The objective of IFRS 5 *Non-current Assets Held for Sale and Discontinued Operations* specifies, amongst other things, accounting for and presentation and disclosure of discontinued operations.

Required:

Define a discontinued operation and explain why the disclosure of such information is important to users of financial statements. **(5 marks)**

(b)   Radar's sole activity is the operation of hotels all over the world. After a period of declining profitability, Radar's directors made the following decisions during the year ended 31 March 2013:

- •   it disposed of all of its hotels in country A;
- •   it refurbished all of its hotels in country B in order to target the holiday and tourism market. The previous target market in country B had been aimed at business clients.

Required:

Treating the two decisions separately, explain whether they meet the criteria for being classified as discontinued operations in the financial statements for the year ended 31 March 2013. **(4 marks)**

(c)   At a board meeting on 1 July 2012, Pulsar's directors made the decision to close down one of its factories on 31 March 2013. The factory and its related plant would then be sold.

A formal plan was formulated and the factory's 250 employees were given three months' notice of redundancy on 1 January 2013. Customers and suppliers were also informed of the closure at this date.

The directors of Pulsar have provided the following information:

Fifty of the employees would be retrained and deployed to other subsidiaries within the group at a cost of $125,000; the remainder will accept redundancy and be paid an average of $5,000 each.

Factory plant has a carrying amount of $2·2 million, but is only expected to sell for $500,000 incurring $50,000 of selling costs; however, the factory itself is expected to sell for a profit of $1·2 million.

The company rents a number of machines under operating leases which have an average of three years to run after 31 March 2013. The present value of these future lease payments (rentals) at 31 March 2013 was $1 million; however, the lessor has said they will accept $850,000 which would be due for payment on 30 April 2013 for their cancellation as at 31 March 2013.

Penalty payments due to non-completion of supply contracts are estimated at $200,000.

Required:

Explain and quantify how the closure of the factory should be treated in Pulsar's financial statements for the year ended 31 March 2013.

Note: **The closure of the factory does not meet the criteria of a discontinued operation.** **(6 marks)**

(Total: 15 marks)

153 LAIDLAW

(a) The *Conceptual Framework for Financial Reporting* identifies faithful representation as a fundamental qualitative characteristic of useful financial information.

Required:

Distinguish between fundamental and enhancing qualitative characteristics and explain why faithful representation is important. **(5 marks)**

(b) Laidlaw has produced its draft financial statements for the year ended 30 September 2013 and two issues have arisen:

(i) On 1 September 2013, Laidlaw factored (sold) $2 million of trade receivables to Finease. Laidlaw received an immediate payment of $1·8 million and credited this amount to receivables and charged $200,000 to administrative expenses. Laidlaw will receive further amounts from Finease depending on how quickly Finease collects the receivables.

Finease will charge a monthly administration fee of $10,000 and 2% per month on its outstanding balance with Laidlaw. Any receivables not collected after four months would be sold back to Laidlaw; however, Laidlaw expects all customers to settle in full within this period. None of the receivables were due or had been collected by 30 September 2013. **(5 marks)**

(ii) On 1 October 2012, Laidlaw sold a property which had a carrying amount of $3·5 million to a property company for $5 million and recorded a profit of $1·5 million on the disposal. Part of the terms of the sale are that Laidlaw will rent the property for a period of five years at an annual rental of $400,000. At the end of this period, the property company will sell the property through a real estate company/property agent at its fair value which is expected to be approximately $6·5 million. Laidlaw will be given the opportunity to repurchase the property (at its fair value) before it is put on the open market.

All of the above amounts are deemed to be at commercial values. **(5 marks)**

Required:

Explain, and quantify where appropriate, how Laidlaw should account for the above two issues in its financial statements for the year ended 30 September 2013.

Note: **The mark allocation is shown against each of the two issues above.**

(Total: 15 marks)

THE FOLLOWING SIX QUESTIONS (154-158) ARE ALL 10 MARK QUESTIONS, WHICH DO NOT EXIST IN THE NEW EXAM FORMAT. THE FOLLOWING TOPICS ARE LIKELY TO BE INCLUDED AS PART OF A LARGER QUESTION OR A MULTIPLE-CHOICE QUESTION. THESE QUESTIONS ARE DEEMED TO BE GOOD EXAM PRACTICE AND HAVE THEREFORE BEEN LEFT IN THE EXAM KIT.

154 FUNDO

Fundo entered into a 20-year operating lease for a property on 1 October 2000 which has a remaining life of eight years at 1 October 2012. The rental payments are $2·3 million per annum.

Prior to 1 October 2012, Fundo obtained permission from the owner of the property to make some internal alterations to the property so that it can be used for a new manufacturing process which Fundo is undertaking. The cost of these alterations was $7 million and they were completed on 1 October 2012 (the time taken to complete the alterations can be taken as being negligible). A condition of being granted permission was that Fundo would have to restore the property to its original condition before handing back the property at the end of the lease. The estimated restoration cost on 1 October 2012, discounted at 8% per annum to its present value, is $5 million.

Required:

(a) **Explain how the lease, the alterations to the leased property and the restoration costs should be treated in the financial statements of Fundo for the year ended 30 September 2013.** **(4 marks)**

(b) **Prepare extracts from the financial statements of Fundo for the year ended 30 September 2013 reflecting your answer to (a) above.** **(6 marks)**

(Total: 10 marks)

155 SPECULATE

Speculate owns the following properties at 1 April 2012:

Property A: An office building used by Speculate for administrative purposes with a depreciated historical cost of $2 million. At 1 April 2012 it had a remaining life of 20 years. After a reorganisation on 1 October 2012, the property was let to a third party and reclassified as an investment property applying Speculate's policy of the fair value model. An independent valuer assessed the property to have a fair value of $2·3 million at 1 October 2012, which had risen to $2·34 million at 31 March 2013.

Property B: Another office building sub-let to a subsidiary of Speculate. At 1 April 2012, it had a fair value of $1·5 million which had risen to $1·65 million at 31 March 2013.

Required:

(i) **Define investment property under IAS 40 and explain why its accounting treatment is different from that of owner-occupied property;** **(3 marks)**

(ii) **Explain how the treatment of an investment property carried under the fair value model differs from an owner-occupied property carried under the revaluation model.** **(2 marks)**

Prepare extracts from Speculate's entity statement of profit or loss and other comprehensive income and statement of financial position for the year ended 31 March 2013 in respect of the above properties. In the case of property B only, state how it would be classified in Speculate's consolidated statement of financial position.

Note: Ignore deferred tax. **(5 marks)**

(Total: 10 marks)

156 BERTRAND

Bertrand issued $10 million convertible loan notes on 1 October 2010 that carry a nominal interest (coupon) rate of 5% per annum. They are redeemable on 30 September 2013 at par for cash or can be exchanged for equity shares in Bertrand on the basis of 20 shares for each $100 of loan. A similar loan note, without the conversion option, would have required Bertrand to pay an interest rate of 8%.

When preparing the draft financial statements for the year ended 30 September 2011, the directors are proposing to show the loan note within equity in the statement of financial position, as they believe all the loan note holders will choose the equity option when the loan note is due for redemption. They further intend to charge a finance cost of $500,000 ($10 million x 5%) in the income statement for each year up to the date of redemption.

The present value of $1 receivable at the end of each year, based on discount rates of 5% and 8%, can be taken as:

		5%	8%
End of year	1	0·95	0·93
	2	0·91	0·86
	3	0·86	0·79

Required:

(a) Explain why the nominal interest rate on the convertible loan notes is 5%, but for non-convertible loan notes it would be 8%, and briefly comment on the impact of the directors' proposed treatment of the loan notes on the financial statements and the acceptability of this treatment. **(5 marks)**

(b) Prepare extracts to show how the loan notes and the finance charge should be treated by Bertrand in its financial statements for the year ended 30 September 2011. **(5 marks)**

(Total: 10 marks)

157 SHAWLER

(a) Shawler is a small manufacturing company specialising in making alloy castings. Its main item of plant is a furnace which was purchased on 1 October 2009. The furnace has two components: the main body (cost $60,000 including the environmental provision – see below) which has a ten-year life, and a replaceable liner (cost $10,000) with a five-year life.

The manufacturing process produces toxic chemicals which pollute the nearby environment. Legislation requires that a clean-up operation must be undertaken by Shawler on 30 September 2019 at the latest.

Shawler received a government grant of $12,000 relating to the cost of the main body of the furnace only.

The following are extracts from Shawler's statement of financial position as at 30 September 2011 (two years after the acquisition of the furnace):

	Carrying amount	
	$	
Non-current assets		
Furnace: main body	48,000	
replaceable liner	6,000	
Current liabilities		
Government grant	1,200	
Non-current liabilities		
Government grant	8,400	
Environmental provision	18,000	(present value discounted at 8% per annum)

Required:

(i) **Prepare equivalent extracts from Shawler's statement of financial position as at 30 September 2012;** **(3 marks)**

(ii) **Prepare extracts from Shawler's statement of profit or loss for the year ended 30 September 2012 relating to the items in the statement of financial position.**

(3 marks)

(b) On 1 April 2012, the government introduced further environmental legislation which had the effect of requiring Shawler to fit anti-pollution filters to its furnace within two years. An environmental consultant has calculated that fitting the filters will reduce Shawler's required environmental costs (and therefore its provision) by 33%. At 30 September 2012 Shawler had not yet fitted the filters.

Required:

Advise Shawler as to whether they need to provide for the cost of the filters as at 30 September 2012 and whether they should reduce the environmental provision at this date. **(4 marks)**

(Total: 10 marks)

158 FLIGHTLINE

 Timed question with Online tutor debrief

Flightline is an airline which treats its aircraft as complex non-current assets. The cost and other details of one of its aircraft are:

	$000	**Estimated life**
Exterior structure – purchase date 1 April 1995	120,000	20 years
Interior cabin fittings – replaced 1 April 2005	25,000	5 years
Engines (2 at $9 million each) – replaced 1 April 2005		
No residual values are attributed to any of the component parts.	18,000	36,000 flying hours

At 1 April 2008 the aircraft log showed it had flown 10,800 hours since 1 April 2005. In the year ended 31 March 2009, the aircraft flew for 1,200 hours for the six months to 30 September 2008 and a further 1,000 hours in the six months to 31 March 2009.

On 1 October 2008 the aircraft suffered a 'bird strike' accident which damaged one of the engines beyond repair. This was replaced by a new engine with a life of 36,000 hours at cost of $10.8 million. The other engine was also damaged, but was repaired at a cost of $3 million; however, its remaining estimated life was shortened to 15,000 hours. The accident also caused cosmetic damage to the exterior of the aircraft which required repainting at a cost of $2 million. As the aircraft was out of service for some weeks due to the accident, Flightline took the opportunity to upgrade its cabin facilities at a cost of $4.5 million. This did not increase the estimated remaining life of the cabin fittings, but the improved facilities enabled Flightline to substantially increase the air fares on this aircraft

Required:

Calculate the charges to the statement of profit or loss in respect of the aircraft for the year ended 31 March 2009 and its carrying amount in the statement of financial position as at that date. *Note:* **The post accident changes are deemed effective from 1 October 2008.**

(10 marks)

159   APEX   *Walk in the footsteps of a top tutor*

(a)   Apex is a publicly listed supermarket chain. During the current year it started the building of a new store. The directors are aware that in accordance with IAS 23 Borrowing costs certain borrowing costs have to be capitalised.

Required:

Explain the circumstances when, and the amount at which, borrowing costs should be capitalised in accordance with IAS 23.   **(5 marks)**

(b)   Details relating to construction of Apex's new store:

Apex issued a $10 million unsecured loan with a coupon (nominal) interest rate of 6% on 1 April 2009. The loan is redeemable at a premium which means the loan has an effective finance cost of 7.5% per annum. The loan was specifically issued to finance the building of the new store which meets the definition of a qualifying asset in IAS 23. Construction of the store commenced on 1 May 2009 and it was completed and ready for use on 28 February 2010, but did not open for trading until 1 April 2010. During the year trading at Apex's other stores was below expectations so Apex suspended the construction of the new store for a two-month period during July and August 2009. The proceeds of the loan were temporarily invested for the month of April 2009 and earned interest of $40,000.

Required:

Calculate the net borrowing cost that should be capitalised as part of the cost of the new store and the finance cost that should be reported in the statement of profit or loss for the year ended 31 March 2010.   **(5 marks)**

(Total: 10 marks)

160 BARSTEAD   *Walk in the footsteps of a top tutor*

(a) The following figures have been calculated from the financial statements (including comparatives) of Barstead for the year ended 30 September 2009:

Increase in profit after taxation	80%
Increase in (basic) earnings per share	5%
Increase in diluted earnings per share	2%

Required:

Explain why the three measures of earnings (profit) growth for the same company over the same period can give apparently differing impressions. **(4 marks)**

(b) The profit after tax for Barstead for the year ended 30 September 2009 was $15 million. At 1 October 2008 the company had in issue 36 million equity shares and a $10 million 8% convertible loan note. The loan note will mature in 2010 and will be redeemed at par or converted to equity shares on the basis of 25 shares for each $100 of loan note at the loan-note holders' option. On 1 January 2009 Barstead made a fully subscribed rights issue of one new share for every four shares held at a price of $2.80 each. The market price of the equity shares of Barstead immediately before the issue was $3.80. The earnings per share (EPS) reported for the year ended 30 September 2008 was 35 cents.

Barstead's income tax rate is 25%.

Required:

Calculate the (basic) EPS figure for Barstead (including comparatives) and the diluted EPS (comparatives not required) that would be disclosed for the year ended 30 September 2009. **(6 marks)**

(c) The methods by which Accounting Standards are developed differ considerably throughout the world. It is often argued that there are two main systems of regulation that determine the nature of Accounting Standards: a rules-based system and a principles-based system.

Required:

Briefly explain the difference between the two systems and state which system you believe is most descriptive of International Financial Reporting Standards (IFRS).

(5 marks)

(Total: 15 marks)

PREPARATION OF SINGLE COMPANY FINANCIAL STATEMENTS

161 LLAMA

The following trial balance relates to Llama, a listed company, at 30 September 2007:

	$000	$000
Land and buildings – at valuation 1 October 2006 (note (i))	130,000	
Plant – at cost (note (i))	128,000	
Accumulated depreciation of plant at 1 October 2006		32,000
Investments – at fair value through profit and loss (note (i))	26,500	
Investment income		2,200
Cost of sales (note (i))	89,200	
Distribution costs	11,000	
Administrative expenses	12,500	
Loan interest paid	800	
Inventory at 30 September 2007	37,900	
Income tax (note (ii))		400
Trade receivables	35,100	
Revenue		180,400
Equity shares of 50 cents each fully paid		60,000
Retained earnings at 1 October 2006		25,500
2% loan note 2009 (note (iii))		80,000
Trade payables		34,700
Revaluation reserve (arising from land and buildings)		14,000
Deferred tax		11,200
Suspense account (note (iv))		24,000
Bank		6,600
	471,000	471,000

The following notes are relevant:

(i)   Llama has a policy of revaluing its land and buildings at each year end. The valuation in the trial balance includes a land element of $30 million. The estimated remaining life of the buildings at that date (1 October 2006) was 20 years. On 30 September 2007, a professional valuer valued the buildings at $92 million with no change in the value of the land. Depreciation of buildings is charged 60% to cost of sales and 20% each to distribution costs and administrative expenses.

During the year Llama manufactured an item of plant that it is using as part of its own operating capacity. The details of its cost, which is included in cost of sales in the trial balance, are:

	$000
Materials cost	6,000
Direct labour cost	4,000
Machine time cost	8,000
Directly attributable overheads	6,000

The manufacture of the plant was completed on 31 March 2007 and the plant was brought into immediate use, but its cost has not yet been capitalised.

All plant is depreciated at 12.5% per annum (time apportioned where relevant) using the reducing balance method and charged to cost of sales.

The fair value of the investments held at fair value through profit and loss at 30 September 2007 was $27.1 million.

(ii) The balance of income tax in the trial balance represents the under/over provision of the previous year's estimate. The estimated income tax liability for the year ended 30 September 2007 is $18.7 million. At 30 September 2007 there were $40 million of taxable temporary differences. The income tax rate is 25%. *Note:* You may assume that the movement in deferred tax should be taken to the statement of profit or loss.

(iii) The 2% loan note was issued on 1 April 2007 under terms that provide for a large premium on redemption in 2009. The finance department has calculated that the effect of this is that the loan note has an effective interest rate of 6% per annum.

(iv) The suspense account contains the corresponding credit entry for the proceeds of a rights issue of shares made on 1 July 2007. The terms of the issue were one share for every four held at 80 cents per share. Llama's share price immediately before the issue was $1. The issue was fully subscribed.

Required:

(a) **A statement of profit or loss and other comprehensive income for the year ended 30 September 2007.** **(12 marks)**

(b) **A statement of financial position as at 30 September 2007.** **(13 marks)**

(c) **A calculation of the earnings per share for the year ended 30 September 2007.**

 Note: **A statement of changes in equity is not required.** **(5 marks)**

(Total: 30 marks)

162 DEXON

Below is the summarised draft statement of financial position of Dexon at 31 March 2008.

	$000	$000	$000
Assets			
Non-current assets			
Property at valuation (land $20,000; buildings $165,000 (note (ii))			185,000
Plant (note (ii))			180,500
Investments at fair value through profit and loss at 1 April 2007 (note (iii))			12,500
			378,000
Current assets			
Inventory		84,000	
Trade receivables (note (iv))		52,200	
Bank		3,800	140,000
Total assets			518,000

Equity and liabilities			
Equity			
Ordinary shares of $1 each			250,000
Share premium		40,000	
Revaluation reserve		18,000	
Retained earnings – at 1 April 2007	12,300		
– for the year ended 31 March 2008	96,700	109,000	167,000
			417,000
Non-current liabilities			
Deferred tax – at 1 April 2007 (note (v))			19,200
Current liabilities			81,800
Total equity and liabilities			518,000

The following information is relevant:

(i)   Dexon's statement of profit or loss includes $8 million of revenue for credit sales made on a 'sale or return' basis. At 31 March 2008, customers who had not paid for the goods, had the right to return $2.6 million of them. Dexon applied a mark up on cost of 30% on all these sales. In the past, Dexon's customers have sometimes returned goods under this type of agreement.

(ii)   The non-current assets have not been depreciated for the year ended 31 March 2008.

Dexon has a policy of revaluing its land and buildings at the end of each accounting year. The values in the above statement of financial position are as at 1 April 2007 when the buildings had a remaining life of fifteen years. A qualified surveyor has valued the land and buildings at 31 March 2008 at $180 million.

Plant is depreciated at 20% on the reducing balance basis.

(iii)   The investments at fair value through profit and loss are held in a fund whose value changes directly in proportion to a specified market index. At 1 April 2007 the relevant index was 1,200 and at 31 March 2008 it was 1,296.

(iv)   In late March 2008 the directors of Dexon discovered a material fraud perpetrated by the company's credit controller that had been continuing for some time. Investigations revealed that a total of $4 million of the trade receivables as shown in the statement of financial position at 31 March 2008 had in fact been paid and the money had been stolen by the credit controller. An analysis revealed that $1.5 million had been stolen in the year to 31 March 2007 with the rest being stolen in the current year. Dexon is not insured for this loss and it cannot be recovered from the credit controller, nor is it deductible for tax purposes.

(v)   During the year the company's taxable temporary differences increased by $10 million of which $6 million related to the revaluation of the property. The deferred tax relating to the remainder of the increase in the temporary differences should be taken to the statement of profit or loss. The applicable income tax rate is 20%.

(vi)   The above figures do not include the estimated provision for income tax on the profit for the year ended 31 March 2008. After allowing for any adjustments required in items (i) to (iv), the directors have estimated the provision at $11.4 million (this is in addition to the deferred tax effects of item (v)).

(vii)   On 1 September 2007 there was a fully subscribed rights issue of one new share for every four held at a price of $1.20 each. The proceeds of the issue have been received and the issue of the shares has been correctly accounted for in the above statement of financial position.

(viii) In May 2007 a dividend of 4 cents per share was paid. In November 2007 (after the rights issue in item (vii) above) a further dividend of 3 cents per share was paid. Both dividends have been correctly accounted for in the above statement of financial position.

Required:

Taking into account any adjustments required by items (i) to (viii) above:

(a)   **Prepare a statement showing the recalculation of Dexon's profit for the year ended 31 March 2008.**   **(8 marks)**

(b)   **Prepare the statement of changes in equity of Dexon for the year ended 31 March 2008.**   **(8 marks)**

(c)   **Redraft the statement of financial position of Dexon as at 31 March 2008. (9 marks)**

(d)   **Explain the difference between accounting for a prior year error and accounting for an under or overestimate of a provision in the prior year. Your answer should refer to the issue in note (iv).**   **(5 marks)**

   Note: **Notes to the financial statements are NOT required.**

(Total: 30 marks)

163 CAVERN

The following trial balance relates to Cavern as at 30 September 2010:

	$000	$000
Equity shares of 20 cents each (note (i))		50,000
8% loan note (note (ii))		30,600
Retained earnings – 30 September 2009		15,100
Revaluation reserve		7,000
Share premium		11,000
Land and buildings at valuation – 30 September 2009:		
Land ($7 million) and building ($36 million) (note (iii))	43,000	
Plant and equipment at cost (note (iii))	67,400	
Accumulated depreciation plant and equipment – 30 September 2009		13,400
Equity investments (note (iv))	15,800	
Inventory at 30 September 2010	19,800	
Trade receivables	29,000	
Bank		4,600
Deferred tax (note (v))		4,000
Trade payables		21,700
Revenue		182,500
Cost of sales	128,500	
Administrative expenses (note (i))	25,000	
Distribution costs	8,500	
Loan note interest paid	2,400	
Bank interest	300	
Investment income		700
Current tax (note (v))	900	
	340,600	340,600

The following notes are relevant:

(i) Cavern has accounted for a fully subscribed rights issue of equity shares made on 1 April 2010 of one new share for every four in issue at 42 cents each, when the market value of a Cavern share was 82 cents. The company paid ordinary dividends of 3 cents per share on 30 November 2009 and 5 cents per share on 31 May 2010. The dividend payments are included in administrative expenses in the trial balance.

(ii) The 8% loan note was issued on 1 October 2008 at its nominal (face) value of $30 million. The loan note will be redeemed on 30 September 2012 at a premium which gives the loan note an effective finance cost of 10% per annum.

(iii) Non-current assets:

Cavern revalues its land and building at the end of each accounting year. At 30 September 2010 the relevant value to be incorporated into the financial statements is $41.8 million. The building's remaining life at the beginning of the current year (1 October 2009) was 18 years. Cavern does not make an annual transfer from the revaluation reserve to retained earnings in respect of the realisation of the revaluation surplus. Ignore deferred tax on the revaluation surplus.

Plant and equipment includes an item of plant bought for $10 million on 1 October 2009 that will have a 10-year life (using straight-line depreciation with no residual value). Production using this plant involves toxic chemicals which will cause decontamination costs to be incurred at the end of its life. The present value of these costs using a discount rate of 10% at 1 October 2009 was $4 million. Cavern has not provided any amount for this future decontamination cost. All other plant and equipment is depreciated at 12.5% per annum using the reducing balance method.

No depreciation has yet been charged on any non-current asset for the year ended 30 September 2010. All depreciation is charged to cost of sales.

(iv) The equity investments had a fair value of $13.5 million on 30 September 2010. There were no acquisitions or disposals of these investments during the year ended 30 September 2010. The equity investments are recorded as fair value through profit or loss in accordance with IFRS 9 *Financial Instruments*.

(v) A provision for income tax for the year ended 30 September 2010 of $5.6 million is required. The balance on current tax represents the under/over provision of the tax liability for the year ended 30 September 2009. At 30 September 2010 the tax base of Cavern's net assets was $15 million less than their carrying amounts. The movement on deferred tax should be taken to the statement of profit or loss. The income tax rate of Cavern is 25%.

Required:

(a) **Prepare the statement of profit or loss for Cavern for the year ended 30 September 2010.** **(11 marks)**

(b) **Prepare the statement of changes in equity for Cavern for the year ended 30 September 2010.** **(5 marks)**

(c) **Prepare the statement of financial position of Cavern as at 30 September 2010.** **(9 marks)**

(d) **Using the information in note (i), calculate earnings per share for Cavern for the year ended 30 September 2010. Also, calculate the re-stated figure for 2009 if the EPS figure in the original 2009 financial statements was 8c per share.** **(5 marks)**

Notes to the financial statements are not required.

(Total: 30 marks)

164 CANDEL *Walk in the footsteps of a top tutor*

The following trial balance relates to Candel at 30 September 2008:

	$000	$000
Leasehold property – at valuation 1 October 2007 (note (i))	50,000	
Plant and equipment – at cost (note (i))	76,600	
Plant and equipment – accumulated depreciation at 1 October 2007		24,600
Capitalised development expenditure – at 1 October 2007 (note (ii))	20,000	
Development expenditure – accumulated amortisation at 1 October 2007		6,000
Closing inventory at 30 September 2008	20,000	
Trade receivables	43,100	
Bank		1,300
Trade payables and provisions (note (iii))		23,800
Revenue (note (i))		300,000
Cost of sales	204,000	
Distribution costs	14,500	
Administrative expenses (note (iii))	22,200	
Preference dividend paid	800	
Interest on bank borrowings	200	
Equity dividend paid	6,000	
Research and development costs (note (ii))	8,600	
Equity shares of 25 cents each		50,000
8% redeemable preference shares of $1 each (note (iv))		20,000
Retained earnings at 1 October 2007		24,500
Deferred tax (note (v))		5,800
Leasehold property revaluation reserve		10,000
	466,000	466,000

The following notes are relevant:

(i) **Non-current assets – tangible:**

The leasehold property had a remaining life of 20 years at 1 October 2007. The company's policy is to revalue its property at each year end and at 30 September 2008 it was valued at $43 million. Ignore deferred tax on the revaluation.

On 1 October 2007 an item of plant was disposed of for $2.5 million cash. The proceeds have been treated as sales revenue by Candel. The plant is still included in the above trial balance figures at its cost of $8 million and accumulated depreciation of $4 million (to the date of disposal).

All plant is depreciated at 20% per annum using the reducing balance method.

Depreciation and amortisation of all non-current assets is charged to cost of sales.

(ii) **Non-current assets – intangible:**

In addition to the capitalised development expenditure (of $20 million), further research and development costs were incurred on a new project which commenced on 1 October 2007. The research stage of the new project lasted until 31 December 2007 and incurred $1.4 million of costs. From that date the project incurred development costs of $800,000 per month. On 1 April 2008 the directors became confident that the project would be successful and yield a profit well in excess of its costs. The project is still in development at 30 September 2008.

Capitalised development expenditure is amortised at 20% per annum using the straight-line method. All expensed research and development is charged to cost of sales.

(iii)   Candel is being sued by a customer for $2 million for breach of contract over a cancelled order. Candel has obtained legal opinion that there is a 20% chance that Candel will lose the case. Accordingly Candel has provided $400,000 ($2 million × 20%) included in administrative expenses in respect of the claim. The unrecoverable legal costs of defending the action are estimated at $100,000. These have not been provided for as the legal action will not go to court until next year.

(iv)   The preference shares were issued on 1 April 2008 at par. They are redeemable at a large premium which gives them an effective finance cost of 12% per annum.

(v)   The directors have estimated the provision for income tax for the year ended 30 September 2008 at $11.4 million. The required deferred tax provision at 30 September 2008 is $6 million.

Required:

(a)   **Prepare the statement of profit or loss and other comprehensive income for the year ended 30 September 2008.** **(12 marks)**

(b)   **Prepare the statement of changes in equity for the year ended 30 September 2008.**
(3 marks)

(c)   **Prepare the statement of financial position as at 30 September 2008.**   **(10 marks)**

(d)   **In December 2008, the leasehold property was severely damaged following a storm. Explain how this damage should be dealt with in the financial statements for the year ended 30 September 2008. Explain how the treatment may differ depending on whether the building is insured or not.** **(5 marks)**

Note: Notes to the financial statements are not required.   **(Total: 30 marks)**

165 PRICEWELL

 Timed question with Online tutor debrief

The following trial balance relates to Pricewell at 31 March 2009:

	$000	$000
Leasehold property – at valuation 31 March 2008 (note (i))	25,200	
Plant and equipment (owned) – at cost (note (i))	46,800	
Plant and equipment (leased) – at cost (note (i))	20,000	
Accumulated depreciation at 31 March 2008		12,800
Owned plant and equipment		
Leased plant and equipment		5,000
Finance lease payment (paid on 31 March 2009) (note (i))	6,000	
Obligations under finance lease at 1 April 2008 (note (i))		15,600
Construction contract (note (ii))	14,300	
Inventory at 31 March 2009	28,200	
Trade receivables	33,100	
Bank	5,500	
Trade payables		33,400
Revenue (note (iii))		310,000
Cost of sales (note (iii))	234,500	
Distribution costs	19,500	
Administrative expenses	27,500	
Preference dividend paid (note (iv))	2,400	
Equity dividend paid	8,000	
Equity shares of 50 cents each		40,000
6% redeemable preference shares at 31 March 2008 (note (iv))		41,600
Retained earnings at 31 March 2008		4,900
Current tax (note (v))	700	
Deferred tax (note (v))		8,400
	471,700	471,700

The following notes are relevant:

(i) **Non-current assets:**

The 15 year leasehold property was acquired on 1 April 2007 at cost $30 million. The company policy is to revalue the property at market value at each year end. The valuation in the trial balance of $25.2 million as at 31 March 2008 led to an impairment charge of $2.8 million which was reported in the statement of profit or loss and other comprehensive income of the previous year (i.e. year ended 31 March 2008). At 31 March 2009 the property was valued at $24.9 million.

Owned plant is depreciated at 25% per annum using the reducing balance method.

The leased plant was acquired on 1 April 2007. The rentals are $6 million per annum for four years payable in arrears on 31 March each year. The interest rate implicit in the lease is 8% per annum. Leased plant is depreciated at 25% per annum using the straight-line method.

No depreciation has yet been charged on any non-current assets for the year ended 31 March 2009. All depreciation is charged to cost of sales.

(ii) On 1 October 2008 Pricewell entered into a contract to construct a bridge over a river. The agreed price of the bridge is $50 million and construction was expected to be completed on 30 September 2010. The $14.3 million in the trial balance is:

	$000
Materials, labour and overheads	12,000
Specialist plant acquired 1 October 2008	8,000
Payment from customer	(5,700)
	14,300

The sales value of the work done at 31 March 2009 has been agreed at $22 million and the estimated cost to complete (excluding plant depreciation) is $10 million. The specialist plant will have no residual value at the end of the contract and should be depreciated on a monthly basis. Pricewell recognises profits on uncompleted contracts on the percentage of completion basis as determined by the agreed work to date compared to the total contract price.

(iii) Pricewell's revenue includes $8 million for goods it sold acting as an agent for Trilby. Pricewell earned a commission of 20% on these sales and remitted the difference of $6.4 million (included in cost of sales) to Trilby.

(iv) The 6% preference shares were issued on 1 April 2007 at par for $40 million. They have an effective finance cost of 10% per annum due to a premium payable on their redemption.

(v) The directors have estimated the provision for income tax for the year ended 31 March 2009 at $4.5 million. The required deferred tax provision at 31 March 2009 is $5.6 million; all adjustments to deferred tax should be taken to the statement of profit or loss and other comprehensive income. The balance of current tax in the trial balance represents the under/over provision of the income tax liability for the year ended 31 March 2008.

Required:

(a) **Prepare the statement of profit or loss and other comprehensive income for the year ended 31 March 2009.** **(12 marks)**

(b) **Prepare the statement of financial position as at 31 March 2009.** **(13 marks)**

(c) **Explain how revenue should be recognised in relation to goods and services, and explain how the items in notes (ii) and (iii) follow these principles.** **(5 marks)**

Note: **A statement of changes in equity and notes to the financial statements are not required.**

(Total: 30 marks)

 Calculate your allowed time, allocate the time to the separate parts

166 SANDOWN

The following trial balance relates to Sandown at 30 September 2009:

	$000	$000
Revenue (note (i))		380,000
Cost of sales	246,800	
Distribution costs	17,400	
Administrative expenses (note (ii))	50,500	
Loan interest paid (note (iii))	1,000	
Investment income		1,300
Current tax (note (v))	2,100	
Freehold property – at cost 1 October 2000 (note (vi))	63,000	
Plant and equipment – at cost (note (vi))	42,200	
Brand – at cost 1 October 2005 (note (vi))	30,000	
Accumulated depreciation – 1 October 2008 – building		8,000
– plant and equipment		19,700
Accumulated amortisation – 1 October 2008 – brand		9,000
Investment property (note (iv))	26,500	
Inventory at 30 September 2009	38,000	
Trade receivables	44,500	
Bank	8,000	
Trade payables		42,900
Equity shares of 20 cents each		50,000
Equity option		2,000
5% convertible loan note 2012 (note (iii))		18,440
Retained earnings at 1 October 2008		33,260
Deferred tax (note (v))		5,400
	———	———
	570,000	570,000
	———	———

The following notes are relevant:

(i)   Sandown's revenue includes $16 million for goods sold to Pending on 1 October 2008. The terms of the sale are that Sandown will incur ongoing service and support costs of $1.2 million per annum for three years after the sale. Sandown normally makes a gross profit of 40% on such servicing and support work. Ignore the time value of money.

(ii)   Administrative expenses include an equity dividend of 4.8 cents per share paid during the year.

(iii)   The 5% convertible loan note was issued for proceeds of $20 million on 1 October 2007. It has an effective interest rate of 8% due to the value of its conversion option, and can be converted into 50 shares for every $100 owed.

(iv)   The investment property is considered to have a fair value of $29 million at 30 September 2009. Sandown uses the fair value model allowed in IAS 40 to account for investment property.

(v)   The balance on current tax represents the under/over provision of the tax liability for the year ended 30 September 2008. The directors have estimated the provision for income tax for the year ended 30 September 2009 at $16.2 million. At 30 September 2009 the carrying amounts of Sandown's net assets were $13 million in excess of their tax base. The income tax rate of Sandown is 30%.

(vi)   Non-current assets:

The freehold property has a land element of $13 million. The building element is being depreciated on a straight-line basis.

Plant and equipment is depreciated at 40% per annum using the reducing balance method.

Sandown's brand in the trial balance relates to a product line that received bad publicity during the year which led to falling sales revenues. An impairment review was conducted on 1 April 2009 which concluded that, based on estimated future sales, the brand had a value in use of $12 million and a remaining life of only three years. However, on the same date as the impairment review, Sandown received an offer to purchase the brand for $15 million. Prior to the impairment review, it was being depreciated using the straight-line method over a 10-year life.

No depreciation/amortisation has yet been charged on any non-current asset for the year ended 30 September 2009. Depreciation, amortisation and impairment charges are all charged to cost of sales.

Required:

(a)   Prepare the statement of profit or loss for Sandown for the year ended 30 September 2009.   (13 marks)

(b)   Prepare the statement of financial position of Sandown as at 30 September 2009.   (12 marks)

(c)   Explain the purpose of diluted earnings per share, and how it aids the predictive nature of financial statements. Your answer should make reference to note (iii). A calculation of diluted earnings per share is NOT required.   (5 marks)

Notes to the financial statements are not required.

A statement of changes in equity is not required.

(Total: 30 marks)

167 HIGHWOOD

The following trial balance relates to Highwood at 31 March 2011:

	$000	$000
Equity shares of 50 cents each		56,000
Retained earnings (note (i))		1,400
8% convertible loan note (note (ii))		30,000
Freehold property – at cost 1 April 2005 (land element $25m (note (iii)))	75,000	
Plant and equipment – at cost	74,500	
Accumulated depreciation – 1 April 2010 – building		10,000
– plant and equipment		24,500
Current tax (note (iv))		800
Deferred tax (note (iv))		2,600
Inventory – 4 April 2011 (note (v))	36,000	
Trade receivables	47,100	
Bank		11,500
Trade payables		24,500
Revenue		339,650
Cost of sales	207,750	
Distribution costs	27,500	
Administrative expenses (note (vi))	30,700	
Loan interest paid (note (ii))	2,400	
	———	———
	500,950	500,950
	———	———

The following notes are relevant:

(i) An equity dividend of 5 cents per share was paid in November 2010 and charged to retained earnings.

(ii) The 8% $30 million convertible loan note was issued on 1 April 2010 at par. Interest is payable annually in arrears on 31 March each year. The loan note is redeemable at par on 31 March 2013 or convertible into equity shares at the option of the loan note holders on the basis of 30 equity shares for each $100 of loan note. Highwood's finance director has calculated that to issue an equivalent loan note without the conversion rights it would have to pay an interest rate of 10% per annum to attract investors.

The present value of $1 receivable at the end of each year, based on discount rates of 8% and 10% are:

	8%	10%
End of year 1	0·93	0·91
2	0·86	0·83
3	0·79	0·75

(iii)   Non-current assets:

On 1 April 2010 Highwood decided to value its freehold property at its current value. A qualified property valuer reported that the market value of the freehold property on this date was $80 million, of which $30 million related to the land. At this date the remaining estimated life of the property was 20 years. Highwood does not make a transfer to retained earnings in respect of excess depreciation on the revaluation of its assets. Plant is depreciated at 20% per annum on the reducing balance method. All depreciation of non-current assets is charged to cost of sales.

(iv)   Current tax represents the under/over provision of the tax liability for the year ended 31 March 2010. The required provision for income tax for the year ended 31 March 2011 is $19·4 million. The difference between the carrying amounts of the assets of Highwood (including the property revaluation in note (iii) above) and their (lower) tax base at 31 March 2011 is $27 million. Highwood's rate of income tax is 25%.

(v)   The inventory of Highwood was not counted until 4 April 2011 due to operational reasons. At this date its value at cost was $36 million and this figure has been used in the cost of sales calculation above. Between the year end of 31 March 2011 and 4 April 2011, Highwood received a delivery of goods at a cost of $2·7 million and made sales of $7·8 million at a mark-up on cost of 30%. Neither the goods delivered nor the sales made in this period were included in Highwood's purchases (as part of cost of sales) or revenue in the above trial balance.

(vi)   On 31 March 2011 Highwood factored (sold) trade receivables with a book value of $10 million to Easyfinance. Highwood received an immediate payment of $8·7 million and will pay Easyfinance 2% per month on any uncollected balances. Any of the factored receivables outstanding after six months will be refunded to Easyfinance. Highwood has derecognised the receivables and charged $1·3 million to administrative expenses. If Highwood had not factored these receivables it would have made an allowance of $600,000 against them.

Required:

(a)   Prepare the statement of profit or loss and other comprehensive income for Highwood for the year ended 31 March 2011;   **(11 marks)**

(b)   Prepare the statement of changes in equity for Highwood for the year ended 31 March 2011;   **(4 marks)**

(c)   Prepare the statement of financial position of Highwood as at 31 March 2011.
                                                                        (10 marks)

(d)   The methods by which Accounting Standards are developed differ considerably throughout the world. It is often argued that there are two main systems of regulation that determine the nature of Accounting Standards: a rules-based system and a principles-based system.

Required:

Briefly explain the difference between the two systems and state which system you believe is most descriptive of International Financial Reporting Standards (IFRS).
                                                                        (5 marks)

Note: **your answers and workings should be presented to the nearest $1,000**

                                                                        (Total: 30 marks)

168 KEYSTONE

The following trial balance relates to Keystone at 30 September 2011:

	$000	$000
Revenue (note (i))		380,000
Material purchases (note (ii))	64,000	
Production labour (note (ii))	124,000	
Factory overheads (note (ii))	80,000	
Distribution costs	14,200	
Administrative expenses (note (iii))	46,400	
Finance costs	350	
Investment income		800
Leased property – at cost (note (ii))	50,000	
Plant and equipment – at cost (note (ii))	44,500	
Accumulated amortisation/depreciation at 1 October 2010		
– leased property		10,000
– plant and equipment		14,500
Financial asset: equity investments (note (v))	18,000	
Inventory at 1 October 2010	46,700	
Trade receivables	33,550	
Trade payables		27,800
Bank		2,300
Equity shares of 20 cents each		50,000
Retained earnings at 1 October 2010		33,600
Deferred tax (note (vi))		2,700
	———	———
	521,700	521,700
	———	———

The following notes are relevant:

(i)   Revenue includes goods sold and despatched in September 2011 on a 30-day right of return basis. Their selling price was $2·4 million and they were sold at a gross profit margin of 25%. Keystone is uncertain as to whether any of these goods will be returned within the 30-day period.

(ii)   Non-current assets:

During the year Keystone manufactured an item of plant for its own use. The direct materials and labour were $3 million and $4 million respectively. Production overheads are 75% of direct labour cost and Keystone determines the final selling price for goods by adding a mark-up on total cost of 40%. These manufacturing costs are included in the relevant expense items in the trial balance. The plant was completed and put into immediate use on 1 April 2011.

All plant and equipment is depreciated at 20% per annum using the reducing balance method with time apportionment in the year of acquisition.

The directors decided to revalue the leased property in line with recent increases in market values. On 1 October 2010 an independent surveyor valued the leased property at $48 million, which the directors have accepted. The leased property was being amortised over an original life of 20 years which has not changed. Keystone does not make a transfer to retained earnings in respect of excess amortisation. The revaluation gain will create a deferred tax liability (see note (vi)).

All depreciation and amortisation is charged to cost of sales. No depreciation or amortisation has yet been charged on any non-current asset for the year ended 30 September 2011.

(iii)   On 15 August 2011, Keystone's share price stood at $2·40 per share. On this date Keystone paid a dividend (included in administrative expenses) that was calculated to give a dividend yield of 4%.

(iv)   The inventory on Keystone's premises at 30 September 2011 was counted and valued at cost of $54·8 million.

(v)   The equity investments had a fair value of $17·4 million on 30 September 2011. There were no purchases or disposals of any of these investments during the year. Keystone has not made the election in accordance with IFRS 9 Financial Instruments. Keystone adopts this standard when accounting for its financial assets.

(vi)   A provision for income tax for the year ended 30 September 2011 of $24·3 million is required. At 30 September 2011, the tax base of Keystone's net assets was $15 million less than their carrying amounts. This excludes the effects of the revaluation of the leased property. The income tax rate of Keystone is 30%.

Required:

(a)   **Prepare the statement of profit or loss and other comprehensive income for Keystone for the year ended 30 September 2011.**   **(15 marks)**

(b)   **Prepare the statement of financial position for Keystone as at 30 September 2011.**
                                                                                    (10 marks)

   A statement of changes in equity is not required.

(c)   The directors of Baxen, a public listed company, are considering the adoption of International Financial Reporting Standards (IFRS) in the near future. The company has ambitious growth plans which involve extensive trading with many foreign companies and the possibility of acquiring at least one of its trading partners as a subsidiary in the near future.

   Required:

   Identify the advantages that Baxen could gain by adopting IFRS for its financial reporting purposes.   **(5 marks)**

                                                                              (Total: 30 marks)

169 FRESCO

The following trial balance relates to Fresco at 31 March 2012:

	$000	$000
Equity shares of 50 cents each (note (i))		45,000
Share premium (note (i))		5,000
Retained earnings at 1 April 2011		5,100
Leased property (12 years) – at cost (note (ii))	48,000	
Plant and equipment – at cost (note (ii))	47,500	
Accumulated amortisation of leased property at 1 April 2011		16,000
Accumulated depreciation of plant and equipment at 1 April 2011		33,500
Inventory at 31 March 2012	25,200	
Trade receivables (note (iii))	28,500	
Bank		1,400
Deferred tax (note (iv))		3,200
Trade payables		27,300
Revenue		350,000
Cost of sales	298,700	
Lease payments (note (ii))	8,000	
Distribution costs	16,100	
Administrative expenses	26,900	
Bank interest	300	
Current tax (note (iv))	800	
Suspense account (note (i))		13,500
	———	———
	500,000	500,000
	———	———

The following notes are relevant:

(i) The suspense account represents the corresponding credit for cash received for a fully subscribed rights issue of equity shares made on 1 January 2012. The terms of the share issue were one new share for every five held at a price of 75 cents each. The price of the company's equity shares immediately before the issue was $1·20 each.

(ii) Non-current assets:

To reflect a marked increase in property prices, Fresco decided to revalue its leased property on 1 April 2011. The Directors accepted the report of an independent surveyor who valued the leased property at $36 million on that date. Fresco has not yet recorded the revaluation. The remaining life of the leased property is eight years at the date of the revaluation. Fresco makes an annual transfer to retained profits to reflect the realisation of the revaluation reserve. In Fresco's tax jurisdiction the revaluation does not give rise to a deferred tax liability.

On 1 April 2011, Fresco acquired an item of plant under a finance lease agreement that had an implicit finance cost of 10% per annum. The lease payments in the trial balance represent an initial deposit of $2 million paid on 1 April 2011 and the first annual rental of $6 million paid on 31 March 2012. The lease agreement requires further annual payments of $6 million on 31 March each year for the next four years. Had the plant not been leased it would have cost $25 million to purchase for cash.

Plant and equipment (other than the leased plant) is depreciated at 20% per annum using the reducing balance method.

No depreciation/amortisation has yet been charged on any non-current asset for the year ended 31 March 2012. Depreciation/amortisation are charged to cost of sales.

(iii) In March 2012, Fresco's internal audit department discovered a fraud committed by the company's credit controller who did not return from a foreign business trip. The outcome of the fraud is that $4 million of the company's trade receivables have been stolen by the credit controller and are not recoverable. Of this amount, $1 million relates to the year ended 31 March 2011 and the remainder to the current year. Fresco is not insured against this fraud.

(iv) Fresco's income tax calculation for the year ended 31 March 2012 shows a tax refund of $2·4 million. The balance on current tax in the trial balance represents the under/over provision of the tax liability for the year ended 31 March 2011. At 31 March 2012, Fresco had taxable temporary differences of $12 million (requiring a deferred tax liability). The income tax rate of Fresco is 25%.

Required:

(a) **(i)** **Prepare the statement of profit or loss for Fresco for the year ended 31 March 2012.** **(9 marks)**

    (ii) **Prepare the statement of changes in equity for Fresco for the year ended 31 March 2012.** **(5 marks)**

    (iii) **Prepare the statement of financial position of Fresco as at 31 March 2012.**

        (8 marks)

(b) **Calculate the basic earnings per share for Fresco for the year ended 31 March 2012.** **(3 marks)**

(c) The definition of an asset forms an important element of the International Accounting Standards Board's *Framework for the Preparation and Presentation of Financial Statements* which, in turn, forms the basis for a number of financial reporting standards.

Required:

Define an asset and explain the important aspects of the definition. Give two examples of how the definition of assets enhances the reliability of financial statements. **(5 marks)**

(Total: 30 marks)

170 QUINCY

The following trial balance relates to Quincy as at 30 September 2012:

	$000	$000
Revenue (note (i))		213,500
Cost of sales	136,800	
Distribution costs	12,500	
Administrative expenses (note (ii))	19,000	
Loan note interest and dividend paid (notes (ii) and (iii))	20,700	
Investment income		400
Equity shares of 25 cents each		60,000
6% loan note (note (ii))		25,000
Retained earnings at 1 October 2011		18,500
Land and buildings at cost (land element $10 million) (note (iv))	50,000	
Plant and equipment at cost (note (iv))	83,700	
Accumulated depreciation at 1 October 2011: buildings		8,000
plant and equipment		33,700
Equity financial asset investments (note (v))	17,000	
Inventory at 30 September 2012	24,800	
Trade receivables	28,500	
Bank	2,900	
Current tax (note (vi))	1,100	
Deferred tax (note (vi))		1,200
Trade payables		36,700
	———	———
	397,000	397,000
	———	———

The following notes are relevant:

(i)   On 1 October 2011, Quincy sold one of its products for $10 million (included in revenue in the trial balance). As part of the sale agreement, Quincy is committed to the ongoing servicing of this product until 30 September 2014 (i.e. three years from the date of sale). The value of this service has been included in the selling price of $10 million. The estimated cost to Quincy of the servicing is $600,000 per annum and Quincy's normal gross profit margin on this type of servicing is 25%. Ignore discounting.

(ii)   Quincy issued a $25 million 6% loan note on 1 October 2011. Issue costs were $1 million and these have been charged to administrative expenses. The loan will be redeemed on 30 September 2014 at a premium which gives an effective interest rate on the loan of 8%.

(iii) Quincy paid an equity dividend of 8 cents per share during the year ended 30 September 2012.

(iv)   Non-current assets:

Quincy had been carrying land and buildings at depreciated cost, but due to a recent rise in property prices, it decided to revalue its property on 1 October 2011 to market value. An independent valuer confirmed the value of the property at $60 million (land element $12 million) as at that date and the directors accepted this valuation.

The property had a remaining life of 16 years at the date of its revaluation. Quincy will make a transfer from the revaluation reserve to retained earnings in respect of the realisation of the revaluation reserve. Ignore deferred tax on the revaluation.

Plant and equipment is depreciated at 15% per annum using the reducing balance method.

No depreciation has yet been charged on any non-current asset for the year ended 30 September 2012. All depreciation is charged to cost of sales.

(v)   The investments had a fair value of $15.7 million as at 30 September 2012. There were no acquisitions or disposals of these investments during the year ended 30 September 2012.

(vi)   The balance on current tax represents the under/over provision of the tax liability for the year ended 30 September 2011. A provision for income tax for the year ended 30 September 2012 of $7·4 million is required. At 30 September 2012, Quincy had taxable temporary differences of $5 million, requiring a provision for deferred tax. Any deferred tax adjustment should be reported in the statement of profit or loss. The income tax rate of Quincy is 20%.

Required:

(a)   **Prepare the statement of profit or loss and other comprehensive income for Quincy for the year ended 30 September 2012.**   **(11 marks)**

(b)   **Prepare the statement of changes in equity for Quincy for the year ended 30 September 2012.**   **(4 marks)**

(c)   **Prepare the statement of financial position for Quincy as at 30 September 2012.**
                                                                                            (10 marks)

       Notes to the financial statements are not required.

(d)   **Explain the fundamental qualitative characteristics of information contained in the *IASB Conceptual Framework* illustrating your answer with specific references to non-current assets.**   **(5 marks)**

                                                                                        (Total: 30 marks)

171 ATLAS

The following trial balance relates to Atlas at 31 March 2013:

	$000	$000
Equity shares of 50 cents each (note (v))		50,000
Share premium		20,000
Retained earnings at 1 April 2012		11,200
Land and buildings – at cost (land $10 million) (note (ii))	60,000	
Plant and equipment – at cost (note (ii))	94,500	
Accumulated depreciation at 1 April 2012: – buildings		20,000
– plant and equipment		24,500
Inventory at 31 March 2013	43,700	
Trade receivables	42,200	
Bank		6,800
Deferred tax (note (iv)) *opening DT (because there's no date)*		6,200
Trade payables		35,100
Revenue (note (i))		550,000
Cost of sales	411,500	
Distribution costs	21,500	
Administrative expenses	30,900	
Dividends paid	20,000	
Bank interest	700	
Current tax (note (iv))		1,200
	———	———
	725,000	725,000
	———	———

The following notes are relevant:

(i)   Revenue includes the sale of $10 million of maturing inventory made to Xpede on 1 October 2012. The cost of the goods at the date of sale was $7 million and Atlas has an option to repurchase these goods at any time within three years of the sale at a price of $10 million plus accrued interest from the date of sale at 10% per annum. At 31 March 2013 the option had not been exercised, but it is highly likely that it will be before the date it lapses.

(ii)   Non-current assets: On 1 October 2012, Atlas terminated the production of one of its product lines. From this date, the plant used to manufacture the product has been actively marketed at an advertised price of $4.2 million which is considered realistic. It is included in the trial balance at a cost of $9 million with accumulated depreciation (at 1 April 2012) of $5 million.

On 1 April 2012, the directors of Atlas decided that the financial statements would show an improved position if the land and buildings were revalued to market value. At that date, an independent valuer valued the land at $12 million and the buildings at $35 million and these valuations were accepted by the directors. The remaining life of the buildings at that date was 14 years. Atlas does not make a transfer to retained earnings for excess depreciation. Ignore deferred tax on the revaluation surplus.

Plant and equipment is depreciated at 20% per annum using the reducing balance method and time apportioned as appropriate.

All depreciation is charged to cost of sales, but none has yet been charged on any non-current asset for the year ended 31 March 2013.

(iii) At 31 March 2013, a provision is required for directors' bonuses equal to 1% of revenue for the year.

(iv) Atlas estimates that an income tax provision of $27.2 million is required for the year ended 31 March 2013 and at that date the liability to deferred tax is $9.4 million. The movement on deferred tax should be taken to profit or loss. The balance on current tax in the trial balance represents the under/over provision of the tax liability for the year ended 31 March 2012.

(v) On 1 July 2012, Atlas made and recorded a fully subscribed rights issue of 1 for 4 at $1.20 each. Immediately before this issue, the stock market value of Atlas's shares was $2 each.

Required:

(a) (i) **Prepare the statement of profit or loss and other comprehensive income for Atlas for the year ended 31 March 2013;** (9 marks)

   (ii) **Prepare the statement of changes in equity for Atlas for the year ended 31 March 2013;** (4 marks)

   (iii) **Prepare the statement of financial position of Atlas as at 31 March 2013.**

(9 marks)

Note: **Notes to the financial statements are not required.**

(b) **Calculate the basic earnings per share for Atlas for the year ended 31 March 2013.**
(3 marks)

(c) During April 2013, the Atlas land and buildings were hit by a storm and severely damaged. One of the directors has approached you, asking about how this damage should be accounted for:

'I've been reading something online which tells me the building may be impaired. I don't know what that means, so I'll need you to explain it to me.'

Required:

Explain when an impairment review is required and how any impairment is calculated, showing how any impairment adjustment is made in the financial statements. Your answer should make specific reference to the Atlas land and buildings. (5 marks)

(Total: 30 marks)

172 MOBY

The following trial balance relates to Moby as at 30 September 2013:

	$000	$000
Revenue		227,800
Cost of sales	164,500	
Construction contract (note (i))	4,000	
Distribution costs	13,500	
Administrative expenses (note (iii)	16,500	
Bank interest	900	
Lease rental paid on 30 September 2013 (note (ii))	9,200	
Land ($12 million) and building ($48 million) at cost (note (ii))	60,000	
Owned plant and equipment at cost (note (ii))	65,700	
Leased plant at initial carrying amount (note (ii))	35,000	
Accumulated depreciation at 1 October 2012:		
building		10,000
owned plant and equipment		17,700
leased plant		7,000
Inventory at 30 September 2013	26,600	
Trade receivables	38,500	
Bank		7,300
Insurance provision (note (iii))		150
Deferred tax (note (iv))		8,000
Finance lease obligation at 1 October 2012 (note (ii))		29,300
Trade payables		21,300
Current tax (note (iv))		1,050
Equity shares of 20 cents each		45,000
Loan note (note (v))		40,000
Retained earnings at 1 October 2012		19,800
	434,400	434,400

The following notes are relevant:

(i)   The balance on the construction contract is made up of the following items:

Cost incurred to date $14 million

Value of contract billed (work certified) $10 million

The contract commenced on 1 October 2012 and is for a fixed price of $25 million. The costs to complete the contract at 30 September 2013 are estimated at $6 million. Moby's policy is to accrue profits on construction contracts based on a stage of completion given by the work certified as a percentage of the contract price.

(ii)   Non-current assets:

Moby decided to revalue its land and building, for the first time, on 1 October 2012. A qualified valuer determined the relevant revalued amounts to be $16 million for the land and $38.4 million for the building. The building's remaining life at the date of the revaluation was 16 years. This revaluation has not yet been reflected in the trial balance figures. Moby does not make a transfer from the revaluation reserve to retained earnings in respect of the realisation of the revaluation surplus. Deferred tax is applicable to the revaluation surplus at 25%.

The leased plant was acquired on 1 October 2011 under a five-year finance lease which has an implicit interest rate of 10% per annum. The rentals are $9.2 million per annum payable on 30 September each year.

Owned plant and equipment is depreciated at 12.5% per annum using the reducing balance method.

No depreciation has yet been charged on any non-current asset for the year ended 30 September 2013. All depreciation is charged to cost of sales.

(iii)   On 1 October 2012, Moby received a renewal quote of $400,000 from the company's property insurer. The directors were surprised at how much it had increased and believed it would be less expensive for the company to 'self-insure'. Accordingly, they charged $400,000 to administrative expenses and credited the same amount to the insurance provision. During the year, the company incurred $250,000 of expenses relating to previously insured property damage which it has debited to the provision.

(iv)   A provision for income tax for the year ended 30 September 2013 of $3.4 million is required. The balance on current tax represents the under/over provision of the tax liability for the year ended 30 September 2012. At 30 September 2013, the tax base of Moby's net assets was $24 million less than their carrying amounts. This does not include the effect of the revaluation in note (ii) above. The income tax rate of Moby is 25%.

(v)   The $40 million loan note was issued at par on 1 October 2012. No interest will be paid on the loan; however, it will be redeemed on 30 September 2015 for $53,240,000 which gives an effective finance cost of 10% per annum.

Required:

(a)   Prepare the statement of profit or loss and other comprehensive income for Moby for the year ended 30 September 2013.   **(12 marks)**

(b)   Prepare the statement of financial position for Moby as at 30 September 2013.

(13 marks)

Note: **A statement of changes in equity and notes to the financial statements are not required.**

(c)   A review of Moby's financial statements for the year ended 30 September 2012 showed that Moby had an operating profit margin of 6% and a return on capital employed of 20%.

Required:

Calculate the equivalent ratios for the year ended 30 September 2013 and comment on the performance of Moby according to these two measures. For the purposes of capital employed, ALL finance lease liabilities are to be included in debt.   **(5 marks)**

(Total: 30 marks)

173 WELLMAY

The summarised draft financial statements of Wellmay are shown below.

Statement of profit or loss year ended 31 March 2007

	$000
Revenue (note (i))	4,200
Cost of sales	(2,700)
Gross profit	1,500
Operating expenses	(470)
Investment property rental income	20
Finance costs	(55)
Profit before tax	995
Income tax	(360)
Profit for the period	635

Statement of financial position as at 31 March 2007

	$000	$000
Assets		
Non-current assets		
Property, plant and equipment (note (ii))		4,200
Investment property (note (ii))		400
		4,600
Current assets		1,400
Total assets		6,000
Equity and liabilities		
Equity		
Equity shares of 50 cents each		1,200
Reserves:		
Revaluation reserve	350	
Retained earnings – At 1 April 2006	2,215	
Retained earnings – profit for the year	635	3,200
		4,400
Non-current liabilities		
8% Convertible loan note (2010) (note (iii))	600	
Deferred tax (note (iv))	180	780
Current liabilities		820
Total equity and liabilities		6,000

The following information is relevant to the draft financial statements:

(i)   Revenue includes $500,000 for the sale on 1 April 2006 of maturing goods to Westwood. The goods had a cost of $200,000 at the date of sale. Wellmay can repurchase the goods on 31 March 2008 for $605,000 (based on achieving a lender's return of 10% per annum) at which time the goods are estimated to have a value of $750,000.

(ii)   **Non-current assets**

Factory depn of $49,000 was charged to cost of sales

Wellmay owns two properties. One is a factory (with office accommodation) used by Wellmay as a production facility and the other is an investment property that is leased to a third party under an operating lease. Wellmay revalues all its properties to current value at the end of each year and uses the fair value model in IAS 40 Investment property. Relevant details of the fair values of the properties are:

	Factory	Investment property
	$000	$000
Valuation 31 March 2006	1,200	400
Valuation 31 March 2007	1,350	375

The valuations at 31 March 2007 have not yet been incorporated into the financial statements.

(iii)   **8% Convertible loan note (2010)**

On 1 April 2006 an 8% convertible loan note with a nominal value of $600,000 was issued at par. It is redeemable on 31 March 2010 at par or it may be converted into equity shares of Wellmay on the basis of 100 new shares for each $200 of loan note. An equivalent loan note without the conversion option would have carried an interest rate of 10%. Interest of $48,000 has been paid on the loan and charged as a finance cost.

The present value of $1 receivable at the end of each year, based on discount rates of 8% and 10% are:

	8%	10%
End of year 1	0.93	0.91
2	0.86	0.83
3	0.79	0.75
4	0.73	0.68

(iv)   The carrying amounts of Wellmay's net assets at 31 March 2007 are $600,000 higher than their tax base. The rate of taxation is 35%. The income tax charge of $360,000 does not include the adjustment required to the deferred tax provision which should be charged in full to the statement of profit or loss.

Required:

Redraft the financial statements of Wellmay, including a statement of changes in equity, for the year ended 31 March 2007 reflecting the adjustments required by notes (i) to (iv) above.

Note: **Calculations should be made to the nearest $000.**

(15 marks)

174 DUNE

The following trial balance relates to Dune at 31 March 2010:

	$000	$000
Equity shares of $1 each		60,000
5% loan note (note (i))		20,000
Retained earnings at 1 April 2009		38,400
Leasehold (15 years) property – at cost (note (ii))	45,000	
Plant and equipment – at cost (note (ii))	67,500	
Accumulated depreciation – 1 April 2009 – leasehold property		6,000
– plant and equipment		23,500
Investments at fair value through profit or loss (note (iii))	26,500	
Inventory at 31 March 2010	48,000	
Trade receivables	40,700	
Bank	15,500	
Deferred tax (note (v))		6,000
Trade payables		52,000
Revenue (note (iv))		400,000
Cost of sales	294,000	
Distribution costs	26,400	
Administrative expenses (note (i))	34,200	
Dividend paid	10,000	
Loan note interest paid (six months)	500	
Bank interest	200	
Investment income		1,200
Current tax (note (v))		1,400
	———	———
	608,500	608,500
	———	———

The following notes are relevant:

(i) The 5% loan note was issued on 1 April 2009 at its nominal (face) value of $20 million. The direct costs of the issue were $500,000 and these have been charged to administrative expenses. The loan note will be redeemed on 31 March 2012 at a substantial premium. The effective finance cost of the loan note is 10% per annum.

(ii) Non-current assets:

In order to fund a new project, on 1 October 2009 the company decided to sell its leasehold property. From that date it commenced a short-term rental of an equivalent property. The leasehold property is being marketed by a property agent at a price of $40 million, which was considered a reasonably achievable price at that date. The expected costs to sell have been agreed at $500,000. Recent market transactions suggest that actual selling prices achieved for this type of property in the current market conditions are 15% less than the value at which they are marketed. At 31 March 2010 the property had not been sold.

Plant and equipment is depreciated at 15% per annum using the reducing balance method.

No depreciation/amortisation has yet been charged on any non-current asset for the year ended 31 March 2010. Depreciation, amortisation and impairment charges are all charged to cost of sales.

(iii) The investments at fair value through profit or loss had a fair value of $28 million on 31 March 2010. There were no purchases or disposals of any of these investments during the year.

(iv) It has been discovered that goods with a cost of $6 million, which had been correctly included in the count of the inventory at 31 March 2010, had been invoiced in April 2010 to customers at a gross profit of 25% on sales, but included in the revenue (and receivables) of the year ended 31 March 2010.

(v) A provision for income tax for the year ended 31 March 2010 of $12 million is required. The balance on current tax represents the under/over provision of the tax liability for the year ended 31 March 2009. At 31 March 2010 the tax base of Dune's net assets was $14 million less than their carrying amounts. The income tax rate of Dune is 30%.

Required:

Prepare the statement of profit or loss for Dune for the year ended 31 March 2010, and the statement of financial position for Dune as at 31 March 2010. **(15 marks)**

Notes to the financial statements and a statement of changes in equity are not required.

175 TOURMALET

The following extracted balances relate to Tourmalet at 30 September 20X3:

	$000	$000
Ordinary shares of 20 cents each		50,000
Retained earnings at 1 October 20X2		61,800
Revaluation reserve at 1 October 20X2		18,500
6% Redeemable preference shares 20X5 (redeemable 20X8)		30,000
Trade payables		35,300
Tax		2,100
Land and buildings – at valuation (note (iii))	150,000	
Plant and equipment – cost (note (v))	98,600	
Investment property – valuation at 1 October 20X2 (note (iv))	10,000	
Depreciation 1 October 20X2 – land and buildings		9,000
Depreciation 1 October 20X2 – plant and equipment		24,600
Trade receivables	31,200	
Inventory – 1 October 20X2	26,550	
Bank	3,700	
Revenue (note (i))		313,000
Investment income (from properties)		1,200
Purchases	158,450	
Finance lease rental	14,000	
Distribution expenses	26,400	
Administration expenses	23,200	
Interim preference dividend	900	
Ordinary dividend paid	2,500	
	–––––––	–––––––
	545,500	545,500
	–––––––	–––––––

The following notes are relevant:

(i)   Revenue includes $50 million for an item of plant sold at fair value on 1 October 20X2. The plant had a book value of $40 million at the date of its sale, which was charged to cost of sales. On the same date, Tourmalet entered into an agreement to lease back the plant for the next five years (being the estimated remaining life of the plant) at a cost of $14 million per annum payable annually in arrears. An arrangement of this type is deemed to have a financing cost of 12% per annum. No depreciation has been charged on the item of plant in the current year.

(ii)   The inventory at 30 September 20X3 was valued at cost of $28.5 million. This includes $4.5 million of slow moving goods. Tourmalet is trying to sell these to another retailer but has not been successful in obtaining a reasonable offer. The best price it has been offered is $2 million.

(iii)   On 1 October 19W9 Tourmalet had its land and buildings revalued by a firm of surveyors at $150 million, with $30 million of this attributed to the land. At that date the remaining life of the building was estimated to be 40 years.

(iv)   Details of the investment property are:

Value – 1 October 20X2 $10 million

Value – 30 September 20X3 $9.8 million

The company adopts the fair value method in IAS 40 *Investment Property* of valuing its investment property.

(v)   Plant and equipment (other than that referred to in note (i) above) is depreciated at 20% per annum on the reducing balance basis. All depreciation is to be charged to cost of sales.

(vi)   The above balances contain the results of Tourmalet's car retailing operations which ceased on 31 December 20X2 due to mounting losses. The results of the car retailing operation, which is to be treated as a discontinued operation, for the year to 30 September 20X3 are:

	$000
Revenue	15,200
Cost of sales	16,000
Administrative expenses	3,200

Tourmalet is still paying rentals for the lease of its car showrooms. The rentals are included in operating expenses. Tourmalet is hoping to use the premises as an expansion of its administration offices. This is dependent on obtaining planning permission from the local authority for the change of use, however this is very difficult to obtain. Failing this, the best option would be early termination of the lease which will cost $1.5 million in penalties. This amount has not been provided for.

(vii)   The balance on the taxation account in the trial balance is the result of the settlement of the previous year's tax charge. The directors have estimated the provision for income tax for the year to 30 September 20X3 at $9.2 million.

Required:

Prepare the statement of profit or loss for the year ended 30 September 20X3 (15 marks)

Note: **A statement of financial position is NOT required. Disclosure notes are NOT required.**

BUSINESS COMBINATIONS

176 PREMIER *Walk in the footsteps of a top tutor*

On 1 June 2010, Premier acquired 80% of the equity share capital of Sanford. The consideration consisted of two elements: a share exchange of three shares in Premier for every five acquired shares in Sanford and the issue of a $100 6% loan note for every 500 shares acquired in Sanford. The share issue has not yet been recorded by Premier, but the issue of the loan notes has been recorded. At the date of acquisition shares in Premier had a market value of $5 each and the shares of Sanford had a stock market price of $3·50 each. Below are the summarised draft financial statements of both companies.

Statements of profit or loss for the year ended 30 September 2010

	Premier	Sanford
	$000	$000
Revenue	92,500	45,000
Cost of sales	(70,500)	(36,000)
Gross profit	22,000	9,000
Distribution costs	(2,500)	(1,200)
Administrative expenses	(5,500)	(2,400)
Finance costs	(100)	nil
Profit before tax	13,900	5,400
Income tax expense	(3,900)	(1,500)
Profit for the year	10,000	3,900
Other comprehensive income:		
Gain on revaluation of land (note (i))	500	nil
Total comprehensive income	10,500	3,900

Statements of financial position as at 30 September 2010

	Premier	Sanford
Assets		
Non-current assets		
Property, plant and equipment	25,500	13,900
Investments	1,800	nil
	27,300	13,900
Current assets	12,500	2,400
Total assets	39,800	16,300

Equity and liabilities		
Equity		
Equity shares of $1 each	12,000	5,000
Land revaluation reserve – 30 September 2010 (note (i))	2,000	nil
Other equity reserve – 30 September 2009 (note (iv))	500	nil
Retained earnings	12,300	4,500
	26,800	9,500
Non-current liabilities		
6% loan notes	3,000	nil
Current liabilities	10,000	6,800
Total equity and liabilities	39,800	16,300

The following information is relevant:

(i) At the date of acquisition, the fair values of Sanford's assets were equal to their carrying amounts with the exception of its property. This had a fair value of $1.2 million **below** its carrying amount, and had a remaining useful life of 8 years at the date of acquisition. Sanford has not incorporated this in its financial statements.

Premier's group policy is to revalue all properties to current value at each year end. On 30 September 2010, the value of Sanford's property was unchanged from its value at acquisition, but the land element of Premier's property had increased in value by $500,000 as shown in other comprehensive income.

(ii) Sales from Sanford to Premier throughout the year ended 30 September 2010 had consistently been $1 million per month. Sanford made a mark-up on cost of 25% on these sales. Premier had $2 million (at cost to Premier) of inventory that had been supplied in the post-acquisition period by Sanford as at 30 September 2010.

(iii) Premier had a trade payable balance owing to Sanford of $350,000 as at 30 September 2010. This did not agree with the corresponding receivable in Sanford's books due to a $130,000 payment made to Sanford, which Sanford has not yet recorded.

(iv) Premier's investments include an investment in shares which at the date of acquisition were classified as fair value through other comprehensive income (FVTOCI). The investments have increased in value by $300,000 during the year. The other equity reserve relates to these investments and is based on their value as at 30 September 2009. There were no acquisitions or disposals of any of these investments during the year ended 30 September 2010.

(v) Premier's policy is to value the non-controlling interest at fair value at the date of acquisition. For this purpose Sanford's share price at that date can be deemed to be representative of the fair value of the shares held by the non-controlling interest.

(vi) There has been no impairment of consolidated goodwill.

Required:

(a) **Prepare the consolidated statement of profit or loss and other comprehensive income for Premier for the year ended 30 September 2010.** (11 marks)

(b) **Prepare the consolidated statement of financial position for Premier as at 30 September 2010.** (19 marks)

(Total: 30 marks)

177 PARENTIS *Walk in the footsteps of a top tutor*

Parentis, a public listed company, acquired 600 million equity shares in Offspring on 1 April 2006. The purchase consideration was made up of:

- a share exchange of one share in Parentis for two shares in Offspring

- the issue of $100 10% loan note for every 500 shares acquired; and

- a deferred cash payment of 11 cents per share acquired payable on 1 April 2007.

Parentis has only recorded the issue of the loan notes. The value of each Parentis share at the date of acquisition was 75 cents and Parentis has a cost of capital of 10% per annum.

The statement of financial positions of the two companies at 31 March 2007 are shown below:

	Parentis		Offspring	
	$ million	$ million	$ million	$ million
Assets				
Property, plant and equipment (note (i))		640		340
Investments		120		Nil
Intellectual property (note (ii))		Nil		30
		———		———
		760		370
Current assets				
Inventory (note (iii))	76		22	
Trade receivables (note (iii))	84		44	
Bank	Nil	160	4	70
	———	———	———	———
Total assets		920		440
		———		———
Equity and liabilities				
Equity shares of 25 cents each		300		200
Retained earnings				
– 1 April 2006	210		120	
– year ended 31 March 2007	90	300	20	140
	———	———	———	———
		600		340
Non-current liabilities				
10% loan notes		120		20
Current liabilities				
Trade payables (note (iii))	130		57	
Current tax payable	45		23	
Overdraft	25	200	Nil	80
	———	———	———	———
Total equity and liabilities		920		440
		———		———

The following information is relevant:

(i) At the date of acquisition the fair values of Offspring's net assets were approximately equal to their carrying amounts with the exception of its properties. These properties had a fair value of $40 million in excess of their carrying amounts which would create additional depreciation of $2 million in the post acquisition period to 31 March 2007. The fair values have not been reflected in Offspring's statement of financial position.

(ii) The intellectual property is a system of encryption designed for internet use. Offspring has been advised that government legislation (passed since acquisition) has now made this type of encryption illegal. Offspring will receive $10 million in compensation from the government.

(iii) Offspring sold Parentis goods for $15 million in the post acquisition period. $5 million of these goods are included in the inventory of Parentis at 31 March 2007. The profit made by Offspring on these sales was $6 million. Offspring's trade payable account (in the records of Parentis) of $7 million does not agree with Parentis's trade receivable account (in the records of Offspring) due to cash in transit of $4 million paid by Parentis.

(iv) Due to the impact of the above legislation, Parentis has concluded that the consolidated goodwill has been impaired by $40 million.

(v) Parentis's policy is to value the non controlling interests using the fair value of the subsidiary's identifiable net assets. The fair value of the non-controlling interests at the date of acquisition is $125 million.

Required:

(a) Prepare the consolidated statement of financial position of Parentis as at 31 March 2007. (25 marks)

(b) Since the year end, Patronic have been developing a new system of encryption which is legal under the new legislation. Parentis have spent $600k up to 30 June 2009, when the results of testing showed that the encryption would be a success. This has now been moved into full production, and is expected to be completed by 31 December. A competitor has offered Patronic $1.6 million for the encryption, which has been deemed to be its fair value. Therefore it has been included at this amount in the financial statements.

Required:

Explain the accounting treatment for the new system of encryption in the financial statements of Patronic for the year ended 31 March 2010. (5 marks)

(Total: 30 marks)

178 PLATEAU *Walk in the footsteps of a top tutor*

On 1 October 2006 Plateau acquired 3 million equity shares in Savannah by an exchange of one share in Plateau for every two shares in Savannah plus $1.25 per acquired Savannah share in cash. The market price of each Plateau share at the date of acquisition was $6.

Only the cash consideration of the above investments has been recorded by Plateau. In addition $500,000 of professional costs relating to the acquisition of Savannah are also included in the cost of the investment.

The summarised draft statement of financial positions of the companies at 30 September 2007 are:

	Plateau $000	Savannah $000
Assets		
Non-current assets		
Property, plant and equipment	18,400	10,400
Investments in Savannah and Axle	13,250	Nil
Fair value through profit or loss investments	6,500	Nil
	38,150	10,400
Current assets		
Inventory	6,900	6,200
Trade receivables	3,200	1,500
Total assets	48,250	18,100
Equity and liabilities		
Equity shares of $1 each	10,000	4,000
Retained earnings – at 30 September 2006	16,000	6,500
– for year ended 30 September 2007	9,250	2,400
	35,250	12,900
Non-current liabilities		
7% Loan notes	5,000	1,000
Current liabilities	8,000	4,200
Total equity and liabilities	48,250	18,100

The following information is relevant:

(i)   At the date of acquisition the fair values of Savannah's assets were equal to their carrying amounts with the exception of Savannah's land which had a fair value of $500,000 below its carrying amount; it was written down by this amount shortly after acquisition and has not changed in value since then.

(ii)   During the year ended 30 September 2007 Savannah sold goods to Plateau for $2.7 million. Savannah had marked up these goods by 50% on cost. Plateau had a third of the goods still in its inventory at 30 September 2007. There were no intra-group payables/receivables at 30 September 2007.

(iii)   Plateau has a policy of valuing non-controlling interests at fair value at the date of acquisition. The fair value of the shares not owned by Plateau at acquisition was $3.25 million.

(iv)   The fair value through profit or loss investments are included in Plateau's statement of financial position (above) at their fair value on 1 October 2006, but they have a fair value of $9 million at 30 September 2007

(v)   The fair value through profit or loss investments are included in Plateau's statement of financial position (above) at their fair value on 1 October 2006, but they have a fair value of $9 million at 30 September 2007

(vi)   Plateau also acquired 30% of the equity shares of Axle at a cost of $7.50 per share in cash. Since acquisition, Axle have made profits of $5 million.

Required:

Prepare the consolidated statement of financial position for Plateau as at 30 September 2007. **(15 marks)**

179 PATRONIC *Walk in the footsteps of a top tutor*

On 1 August 2007 Patronic purchased 18 million of a total of 24 million equity shares in Sardonic. The acquisition was through a share exchange of two shares in Patronic for every three shares in Sardonic. Both companies have shares with a par value of $1 each. The market price of Patronic's shares at 1 August 2007 was $5.75 per share. Patronic will also pay in cash on 31 July 2009 (two years after acquisition) $2.42 per acquired share of Sardonic. Patronic's cost of capital is 10% per annum. The reserves of Sardonic on 1 April 2007 were $69 million.

Patronic has held an investment of 30% of the equity shares in Acerbic for many years. Acerbic made a profit of $6 million in the year.

The summarised statement of profit or loss for the three companies for the year ended 31 March 2008 are:

	Patronic	Sardonic
	$000	$000
Revenue	150,000	78,000
Cost of sales	(94,000)	(51,000)
Gross profit	56,000	27,000
Distribution costs	(7,400)	(3,000)
Administrative expenses	(12,500)	(6,000)
Finance costs (note (ii))	(2,000)	(900)
Profit before tax	34,100	17,100
Income tax expense	(10,400)	(3,600)
Profit for the period	23,700	13,500

The following information is relevant:

(i) The fair values of the net assets of Sardonic at the date of acquisition were equal to their carrying amounts with the exception of property and plant. Property and plant had fair values of $4.1 million and $2.4 million respectively in excess of their carrying amounts. The increase in the fair value of the property would create additional depreciation of $200,000 in the consolidated financial statements in the post acquisition period to 31 March 2008 and the plant had a remaining life of four years (straight-line depreciation) at the date of acquisition of Sardonic. All depreciation is treated as part of cost of sales.

The fair values have not been reflected in Sardonic's financial statements.

No fair value adjustments were required on the acquisition of Acerbic.

(ii)   The finance costs of Patronic do not include the finance cost on the deferred consideration.

(iii)   Prior to its acquisition, Sardonic had been a good customer of Patronic. In the year to 31 March 2008, Patronic sold goods at a selling price of $1.25 million per month to Sardonic both before and after its acquisition. Patronic made a profit of 20% on the cost of these sales. At 31 March 2008 Sardonic still held inventory of $3 million (at cost to Sardonic) of goods purchased in the post acquisition period from Patronic.

(iv)   Patronic has a policy of valuing non-controlling interests using the fair value at the date of acquisition, which was $30.5 million. An impairment test on the goodwill of Sardonic conducted on 31 March 2008 concluded that it should be written down by $2 million. The value of the investment in Acerbic was not impaired.

(v)   All items in the above statement of profit or loss's are deemed to accrue evenly over the year.

(vi)   Ignore deferred tax.

Required:

(a)   **Calculate the goodwill arising on the acquisition of Sardonic at 1 August 2007.**

(8 marks)

(b)   **Prepare the consolidated statement of profit or loss for the Patronic Group for the year ended 31 March 2008.**

Note: **Assume that the investment in Acerbic has been accounted for using the equity method since its acquisition.**   **(17 marks)**

(c)   At 31 March 2008 the other equity shares (70%) in Acerbic were owned by many separate investors. Shortly after this date Spekulate (a company unrelated to Patronic) accumulated a 60% interest in Acerbic by buying shares from the other shareholders. In May 2008 a meeting of the board of directors of Acerbic was held at which Patronic lost its seat on Acerbic's board.

Required:

Explain, with reasons, the accounting treatment Patronic should adopt for its investment in Acerbic when it prepares its financial statements for the year ending 31 March 2009.   **(5 marks)**

(Total: 30 marks)

180 PEDANTIC *Walk in the footsteps of a top tutor*

On 1 April 2008, Pedantic acquired 60% of the equity share capital of Sophistic in a share exchange of two shares in Pedantic for three shares in Sophistic. The issue of shares has not yet been recorded by Pedantic. At the date of acquisition shares in Pedantic had a market value of $6 each. Below are the summarised draft financial statements of both companies.

Statement of profit or loss for the year ended 30 September 2008

	Pedantic	Sophistic
	$000	$000
Revenue	85,000	42,000
Cost of sales	(63,000)	(32,000)
Gross profit	22,000	10,000
Distribution costs	(2,000)	(2,000)
Administrative expenses	(6,000)	(3,200)
Finance costs	(300)	(400)
Profit before tax	13,700	4,400
Income tax expense	(4,700)	(1,400)
Profit for the year	9,000	3,000

Statements of financial position as at 30 September 2008

	Pedantic	Sophistic
Assets		
Non-current assets		
Property, plant and equipment	40,600	12,600
Current assets	16,000	6,600
Total assets	56,600	19,200
Equity and liabilities		
Equity shares of $1 each	10,000	4,000
Retained earnings	35,400	6,500
		45,400
	10,500	
Non-current liabilities		
10% loan notes	3,000	4,000
Current liabilities	8,200	4,700
Total equity and liabilities	56,600	19,200

The following information is relevant:

(i) At the date of acquisition, the fair values of Sophistic's assets were equal to their carrying amounts with the exception of an item of plant, which had a fair value of $2 million in excess of its carrying amount. It had a remaining life of five years at that date [straight-line depreciation is used]. Sophistic has not adjusted the carrying amount of its plant as a result of the fair value exercise.

(ii) Sales from Sophistic to Pedantic in the post acquisition period were $8 million. Sophistic made a mark up on cost of 40% on these sales. Pedantic had sold $5.2 million (at cost to Pedantic) of these goods by 30 September 2008.

(iii) Other than where indicated, statement of profit or loss items are deemed to accrue evenly on a time basis.

(iv) Sophistic's trade receivables at 30 September 2008 include $600,000 due from Pedantic which did not agree with Pedantic's corresponding trade payable. This was due to cash in transit of $200,000 from Pedantic to Sophistic. Both companies have positive bank balances.

(v) Pedantic has a policy of accounting for any non-controlling interest at fair value. The fair value of the non-controlling interest at the acquisition date was $5.9 million. Consolidated goodwill was not impaired at 30 September 2008.

Required:

(a) Prepare the consolidated statement of profit or loss for Pedantic for the year ended 30 September 2008.   **(9 marks)**

(b) Prepare the consolidated statement of financial position for Pedantic as at 30 September 2008.   **(16 marks)**

(c) Pedantic has been approached by a potential new customer, Trilby, to supply it with a substantial quantity of goods on three months credit terms. Pedantic is concerned at the risk that such a large order represents in the current difficult economic climate, especially as Pedantic's normal credit terms are only one month's credit. To support its application for credit, Trilby has sent Pedantic a copy of Tradhat's most recent audited consolidated financial statements. Trilby is a wholly-owned subsidiary within the Tradhat group. Tradhat's consolidated financial statements show a strong statement of financial position including healthy liquidity ratios.

Required:

Comment on the importance that Pedantic should attach to Tradhat's consolidated financial statements when deciding on whether to grant credit terms to Trilby.

(5 marks)

(Total: 30 marks)

181 PANDAR *Walk in the footsteps of a top tutor*

On 1 April 2009 Pandar purchased 80% of the equity shares in Salva. The acquisition was through a share exchange of three shares in Pandar for every five shares in Salva. The market prices of Pandar's and Salva's shares at 1 April 2009 were $6 per share and $3.20 respectively.

On the same date Pandar acquired 40% of the equity shares in Ambra paying $2 per share.

The summarised statement of profit or loss for the three companies for the year ended 30 September 2009 are:

	Pandar $000	Salva $000	Ambra $000
Revenue	210,000	150,000	50,000
Cost of sales	(126,000)	(100,000)	(40,000)
Gross profit	84,000	50,000	10,000
Distribution costs	(11,200)	(7,000)	(5,000)
Administrative expenses	(18,300)	(9,000)	(11,000)
Investment income (interest and dividends)	9,500		
Finance costs	(1,800)	(3,000)	Nil
Profit (loss) before tax	62,200	31,000	(6,000)
Income tax (expense) relief	(15,000)	(10,000)	1,000
Profit (loss) for the year	47,200	21,000	(5,000)

The following information for the equity of the companies at 30 September 2009 is available:

Equity shares of $1 each	200,000	120,000	40,000
Share premium	300,000	Nil	Nil
Retained earnings 1 October 2008	40,000	152,000	15,000
Profit (loss) for the year ended 30 September 2009	47,200	21,000	(5,000)
Dividends paid (26 September 2009)	Nil	(8,000)	Nil

The following information is relevant:

(i) The fair values of the net assets of Salva at the date of acquisition were equal to their carrying amounts with the exception of an item of plant which had a carrying amount of $12 million and a fair value of $17 million. This plant had a remaining life of five years (straight-line depreciation) at the date of acquisition of Salva. All depreciation is charged to cost of sales.

In addition Salva owns the registration of a popular internet domain name. The registration, which had a negligible cost, has a five year remaining life (at the date of acquisition); however, it is renewable indefinitely at a nominal cost. At the date of acquisition the domain name was valued by a specialist company at $20 million.

The fair values of the plant and the domain name have not been reflected in Salva's financial statements.

No fair value adjustments were required on the acquisition of the investment in Ambra.

(ii)   Immediately after its acquisition of Salva, Pandar invested $50 million in an 8% loan note from Salva. All interest accruing to 30 September 2009 had been accounted for by both companies. Salva also has other loans in issue at 30 September 2009.

(iii)   Pandar has credited the whole of the dividend it received from Salva to investment income.

(iv)   After the acquisition, Pandar sold goods to Salva for $15 million on which Pandar made a gross profit of 20%. Salva had one third of these goods still in its inventory at 30 September 2009. There are no intra-group current account balances at 30 September 2009.

(v)   The non-controlling interest in Salva is to be valued at its (full) fair value at the date of acquisition. For this purpose Salva's share price at that date can be taken to be indicative of the fair value of the shareholding of the non-controlling interest.

(vi)   The goodwill of Salva has not suffered any impairment; however, due to its losses, the value of Pandar's investment in Ambra has been impaired by $3 million at 30 September 2009.

(vii)   All items in the above statement of profit or loss are deemed to accrue evenly over the year unless otherwise indicated.

Required:

(a) (i)   **Calculate the goodwill arising on the acquisition of Salva at 1 April 2009;**
(6 marks)

(ii)   **Calculate the carrying amount of the investment in Ambra to be included within the consolidated statement of financial position as at 30 September 2009.**   **(3 marks)**

(b) **Prepare the consolidated statement of profit or loss for the Pandar Group for the year ended 30 September 2009.**   **(16 marks)**

(c) Some commentators have criticized the use of equity accounting on the basis that it can be used as a form of off statement of financial position financing.

Required:

Explain the reasoning behind the use of equity accounting and discuss the above comment.   **(5 marks)**

(Total: 30 marks)

182 PICANT *Walk in the footsteps of a top tutor*

On 1 April 2009 Picant acquired 75% of Sander's equity shares in a share exchange of three shares in Picant for every two shares in Sander. The market prices of Picant's and Sander's shares at the date of acquisition were $3.20 and $4.50 respectively.

In addition to this Picant agreed to pay a further amount on 1 April 2010 that was contingent upon the post-acquisition performance of Sander. At the date of acquisition Picant assessed the fair value of this contingent consideration at $4.2 million, but by 31 March 2010 it was clear that the actual amount to be paid would be only $2.7 million (ignore discounting). Picant has recorded the share exchange and provided for the initial estimate of $4.2 million for the contingent consideration.

On 1 October 2009 Picant also acquired 40% of the equity shares of Adler paying $4 in cash per acquired share and issuing at par one $100 7% loan note for every 50 shares acquired in Adler. This consideration has also been recorded by Picant.

Picant has no other investments.

The summarised statements of financial position of the three companies at 31 March 2010 are:

	Picant $000	Sander $000	Adler $000
Assets			
Non-current assets			
Property, plant and equipment	37,500	24,500	21,000
Investments	45,000	nil	nil
	82,500	24,500	21,000
Current assets			
Inventory	10,000	9,000	5,000
Trade receivables	6,500	1,500	3,000
Total assets	99,000	35,000	29,000
Equity			
Equity shares of $1 each	25,000	8,000	5,000
Share premium	19,800	nil	nil
Retained earnings – at 1 April 2009	16,200	16,500	15,000
– for the year ended 31 March 2010	11,000	1,000	6,000
	72,000	25,500	26,000
Non-current liabilities			
7% loan notes	14,500	2,000	nil
Current liabilities			
Contingent consideration	4,200	nil	nil
Other current liabilities	8,300	7,500	3,000
Total equity and liabilities	99,000	35,000	29,000

The following information is relevant:

(i)   At the date of acquisition the fair values of Sander's property, plant and equipment was equal to its carrying amount with the exception of Sander's factory which had a fair value of $2 million above its carrying amount. Sander has not adjusted the carrying amount of the factory as a result of the fair value exercise. This requires additional annual depreciation of $100,000 in the consolidated financial statements in the post-acquisition period.

Also at the date of acquisition, Sander had an intangible asset of $500,000 for software in its statement of financial position. Picant's directors believed the software to have no recoverable value at the date of acquisition and Sander wrote it off shortly after its acquisition.

(ii)   At 31 March 2010 Picant's current account with Sander was $3.4 million (debit). This did not agree with the equivalent balance in Sander's books due to some goods-in-transit invoiced at $1.8 million that were sent by Picant on 28 March 2010, but had not been received by Sander until after the year end. Picant sold all these goods at cost plus 50%.

(iii)   Picant's policy is to value the non-controlling interest at fair value at the date of acquisition. For this purpose Sander's share price at that date can be deemed to be representative of the fair value of the shares held by the non-controlling interest.

(iv)   Impairment tests were carried out on 31 March 2010 which concluded that the value of the investment in Adler was not impaired but, due to poor trading performance, consolidated goodwill was impaired by $3.8 million.

(v)   Assume all profits accrue evenly through the year.

Required:

Prepare the consolidated statement of financial position for Picant as at 31 March 2010.

(15 marks)

(Total: 15 marks)

183   PRODIGAL

On 1 October 2010 Prodigal purchased 75% of the equity shares in Sentinel. The acquisition was through a share exchange of two shares in Prodigal for every three shares in Sentinel. The stock market price of Prodigal's shares at 1 October 2010 was $4 per share.

The summarised statements of comprehensive income for the two companies for the year ended 31 March 2011 are:

	Prodigal	Sentinel
	$000	$000
Revenue	450,000	240,000
Cost of sales	(260,000)	(110,000)
Gross profit	190,000	130,000
Distribution costs	(23,600)	(12,000)
Administrative expenses	(27,000)	(23,000)
Finance costs	(1,500)	(1,200)
Profit before tax	137,900	93,800
Income tax expense	(48,000)	(27,800)
Profit for the year	89,900	66,000
Other comprehensive income		
Gain on revaluation of land (note (i))	2,500	1,000
Loss on fair value of equity financial asset investment	(700)	(400)
	1,800	600
Total comprehensive income	91,700	66,600

The following information for the equity of the companies at **1 April 2010** (i.e. before the share exchange took place) is available:

	$000	$000
Equity shares of $1 each	250,000	160,000
Share premium	100,000	nil
Revaluation surplus (land)	8,400	nil
Other equity reserve (re equity financial asset investment)	3,200	2,200
Retained earnings	90,000	125,000

The following information is relevant:

(i) Prodigal's policy is to revalue the group's land to market value at the end of each accounting period. Prior to its acquisition Sentinel's land had been valued at historical cost. During the post acquisition period Sentinel's land had increased in value over its value at the date of acquisition by $1 million. Sentinel has recognised the revaluation within its own financial statements.

(ii) Immediately after the acquisition of Sentinel on 1 October 2010, Prodigal transferred an item of plant with a carrying amount of $4 million to Sentinel at an agreed value of $5 million. At this date the plant had a remaining life of two and half years. Prodigal had included the profit on this transfer as a reduction in its depreciation costs. All depreciation is charged to cost of sales.

(iii) After the acquisition Sentinel sold goods to Prodigal for $40 million. These goods had cost Sentinel $30 million. $12 million of the goods sold remained in Prodigal's closing inventory.

(iv) Prodigal's policy is to value the non-controlling interest of Sentinel at the date of acquisition at its fair value which the directors determined to be $100 million.

(v) The goodwill of Sentinel has not suffered any impairment.

(vi) All items in the above statements of comprehensive income are deemed to accrue evenly over the year unless otherwise indicated.

Required:

(a) (i) Prepare the consolidated statement of profit or loss and other comprehensive income of Prodigal for the year ended 31 March 2011;

(16 marks)

(ii) Prepare the equity section (including the non-controlling interest) of the consolidated statement of financial position of Prodigal as at 31 March 2011.

(9 marks)

Note: you are NOT required to calculate consolidated goodwill or produce the statement of changes in equity.

(b) IFRS 3 *Business combinations* permits a non-controlling interest at the date of acquisition to be valued by one of two methods:

(i) at its proportionate share of the subsidiary's identifiable net assets; or

(ii) at its fair value (usually determined by the directors of the parent company).

Required:

Explain the difference that the accounting treatment of these alternative methods could have on the consolidated financial statements, including where consolidated goodwill may be impaired.

(5 marks)

(Total: 30 marks)

184 PALADIN

On 1 October 2010, Paladin secured a majority equity shareholding in Saracen on the following terms:

an immediate payment of $4 per share on 1 October 2010;

and a further amount deferred until 1 October 2011 of $5·4 million. (CL)

The immediate payment has been recorded in Paladin's financial statements, but the deferred payment has not been recorded. Paladin's cost of capital is 8% per annum.

On 1 February 2011, Paladin also acquired 25% of the equity shares of Augusta paying $10 million in cash. The summarised statements of financial position of the three companies at 30 September 2011 are:

	Paladin	Saracen	Augusta
	$000	$000	$000
Assets			
Non-current assets			
Property, plant and equipment	40,000	31,000	30,000
Intangible assets	7,500		
Investments – Saracen (8 million shares at $4 each)	32,000		
– Augusta	10,000	nil	nil
	89,500	31,000	30,000
Current assets			
Inventory	11,200	8,400	10,000
Trade receivables	7,400	5,300	5,000
Bank	3,400	nil	2,000
Total assets	111,500	44,700	47,000
Equity and liabilities			
Equity			
Equity shares of $1 each	50,000	10,000	10,000
Retained earnings – at 1 October 2010	25,700	12,000	31,800
– for year ended 30 September 2011	9,200	6,000	1,200
	84,900	28,000	43,000
Non-current liabilities			
Deferred tax	15,000	8,000	1,000
Current liabilities			
Bank (DON'T net it off with the Ps assets)	nil	2,500	nil
Trade payables	11,600	6,200	3,000
Total equity and liabilities	111,500	44,700	47,000

The following information is relevant:

(i)   Paladin's policy is to value the non-controlling interest at fair value at the date of acquisition. For this purpose the directors of Paladin considered a share price for Saracen of $3·50 per share to be appropriate.

(ii)   At the date of acquisition, the fair values of Saracen's property, plant and equipment was equal to its carrying amount with the exception of Saracen's plant which had a fair value of $4 million above its carrying amount. At that date the plant had a remaining life of four years. Saracen uses straight-line depreciation for plant assuming a nil residual value.

Also at the date of acquisition, Paladin valued Saracen's customer relationships as a customer base intangible asset at fair value of $3 million. Saracen has not accounted for this asset. Trading relationships with Saracen's customers last on average for six years.

(iii)   At 30 September 2011, Saracen's inventory included goods bought from Paladin (at cost to Saracen) of $2·6 million. Paladin had marked up these goods by 30% on cost. Paladin's agreed current account balance owed by Saracen at 30 September 2011 was $1·3 million.

(iv)   Impairment tests were carried out on 30 September 2011 which concluded that consolidated goodwill was not impaired, but, due to disappointing earnings, the value of the investment in Augusta was impaired by $2·5 million.

(v)   Assume all profits accrue evenly through the year.

Required:

(a)   Prepare the consolidated statement of financial position for Paladin as at 30 September 2011.   (25 marks)

(b)   A financial assistant has observed that the fair value exercise means that a subsidiary's net assets are included at acquisition at their fair (current) values in the consolidated statement of financial position. The assistant believes that it is inconsistent to aggregate the subsidiary's net assets with those of the parent because most of the parent's assets are carried at historical cost.

Required:

Comment on the assistant's observation and explain why the net assets of acquired subsidiaries are consolidated at acquisition at their fair values.   (5 marks)

(Total: 30 marks)

185 PYRAMID

On 1 April 2011, Pyramid acquired 80% of Square's equity shares by means of an immediate share exchange and a cash payment of 88 cents per acquired share, deferred until 1 April 2012. Pyramid has recorded the share exchange, but not the cash consideration. Pyramid's cost of capital is 10% per annum.

The summarised statements of financial position of the two companies as at 31 March 2012 are:

	Pyramid	Square
	$000	$000
Assets		
Non-current assets		
Property, plant and equipment	38,100	28,500
Investments – Square	24,000	
– Cube at cost (note (iv))	6,000	
– Loan notes (note (ii))	2,500	
– Other equity (note (v))	2,000	nil
	———	———
	72,600	28,500
Current assets		
Inventory (note (iii))	13,900	10,400
Trade receivables (note (iii))	11,400	5,500
Bank (note (iii))	900	600
	———	———
Total assets	98,800	45,000
	———	———
Equity and liabilities		
Equity		
Equity shares of $1 each	25,000	10,000
Share premium	17,600	nil
Retained earnings – at 1 April 2011	16,200	18,000
– for year ended 31 March 2012	14,000	8,000
	———	———
	72,800	36,000
Non-current liabilities		
11% loan notes (note (ii))	12,000	4,000
Deferred tax	4,500	nil
Current liabilities (note (iii))	9,500	5,000
	———	———
Total equity and liabilities	98,800	45,000
	———	———

The following information is relevant:

(i)   At the date of acquisition, Pyramid conducted a fair value exercise on Square's net assets which were equal to their carrying amounts with the following exceptions:

•   An item of plant had a fair value of $3 million above its carrying amount. At the date of acquisition it had a remaining life of five years. Ignore deferred tax relating to this fair value.

•   Square had an unrecorded deferred tax liability of $1 million, which was unchanged as at 31 March 2012.

Pyramid's policy is to value the non-controlling interest at fair value at the date of acquisition. For this purpose a share price for Square of $3·50 each is representative of the fair value of the shares held by the non-controlling interest.

(ii)   Immediately after the acquisition, Square issued $4 million of 11% loan notes, $2·5 million of which were bought by Pyramid. All interest due on the loan notes as at 31 March 2012 has been paid and received.

(iii)   Pyramid sells goods to Square at cost plus 50%. Below is a summary of the recorded activities for the year ended 31 March 2012 and balances as at 31 March 2012:

	Pyramid	Square
	$000	$000
Sales to Square	16,000	
Purchases from Pyramid		14,500
Included in Pyramid's receivables	4,400	
Included in Square's payables		1,700

On 26 March 2012, Pyramid sold and despatched goods to Square, which Square did not record until they were received on 2 April 2012. Square's inventory was counted on 31 March 2012 and does not include any goods purchased from Pyramid.

On 27 March 2012, Square remitted to Pyramid a cash payment which was not received by Pyramid until 4 April 2012. This payment accounted for the remaining difference on the current accounts.

(iv)   Pyramid bought 1·5 million shares in Cube on 1 October 2011; this represents a holding of 30% of Cube's equity. At 31 March 2012, Cube's retained profits had increased by $2 million over their value at 1 October 2011. Pyramid uses equity accounting in its consolidated financial statements for its investment in Cube.

(v)   The other equity investments of Pyramid are carried at their fair values on 1 April 2011. At 31 March 2012, these had increased to $2·8 million.

(vi)   There were no impairment losses within the group during the year ended 31 March 2012.

Required:

(a)   **Prepare the consolidated statement of financial position for Pyramid as at 31 March 2012.**   **(25 marks)**

(b)   **Explain the principles of ownership and the single entity concept, making specific relation to Pyramid.**   **(5 marks)**

(Total: 30 marks)

186   VIAGEM

On 1 January 2012, Viagem acquired 90% of the 10 million equity shares of Greca. On 31 December 2012, Viagem will pay the shareholders of Greca $1·76 per share acquired. Viagem's cost of capital is 10% per annum.

Statements of profit or loss for the year ended 30 September 2012

	Viagem	Greca
	$000	$000
Revenue	64,600	38,000
Cost of sales	(51,200)	(26,000)
Gross profit	13,400	12,000
Distribution costs	(1,600)	(1,800)
Administrative expenses	(3,800)	(2,400)
Investment income	500	nil
Finance costs	(420)	nil
Profit before tax	8,080	7,800
Income tax expense	(2,800)	(1,600)
Profit for the year	5,280	6,200

The following information is relevant:

(i) At the date of acquisition, the fair values of Greca's assets were equal to their carrying amounts with the exception of an item of plant which had a fair value of $1·8 million above its carrying amount. The remaining life of the plant at the date of acquisition was three years. Depreciation is charged to cost of sales.

Greca has not incorporated this fair value change into its financial statements.

(ii) Viagem's policy is to value the non-controlling interest at fair value at the date of acquisition.

(iii) Sales from Viagem to Greca throughout the year ended 30 September 2012 had consistently been $800,000 per month. Viagem made a mark-up on cost of 25% on these sales. Greca had $1·5 million of these goods in inventory as at 30 September 2012.

(iv) Viagem's investment income is a dividend received from its investment in a 40% owned associate which it has held for several years. The underlying earnings for the associate for the year ended 30 September 2012 were $2 million.

(v) Although Greca has been profitable since its acquisition by Viagem, the market for Greca's products has been badly hit in recent months and Viagem has calculated that the goodwill has been impaired by $2 million as at 30 September 2012.

Required:

Prepare the consolidated statement of profit or loss for Viagem for the year ended 30 September 2012.   **(15 marks)**

187 PARADIGM

On 1 October 2012, Paradigm acquired 75% of Strata's equity shares by means of a share exchange of two new shares in Paradigm for every five acquired shares in Strata. In addition, Paradigm issued to the shareholders of Strata a $100 10% loan note for every 1,000 shares it acquired in Strata. Paradigm has not recorded any of the purchase consideration, although it does have other 10% loan notes already in issue.

The market value of Paradigm's shares at 1 October 2012 was $2 each.

The summarised statements of financial position of the two companies as at 31 March 2013 are:

	Paradigm	Strata
Assets	$000	$000
Non-current assets		
Property, plant and equipment	47,400	25,500
Financial asset: equity investments (notes (i) and (iii))	7,500	3,200
	54,900	28,700
Current assets		
Inventory (note (ii))	20,400	8,400
Trade receivables	14,800	9,000
Bank	2,100	nil
Total assets	92,200	46,100
Equity and liabilities		
Equity		
Equity shares of $1 each	40,000	20,000
Retained earnings/(losses) – at 1 April 2012	19,200	(4,000)
– for year ended 31 March 2013	7,400	8,000
	66,600	24,000
Non-current liabilities		
10% loan notes	8,000	nil
Current liabilities		
Trade payables	17,600	13,000
Bank overdraft	nil	9,100
Total equity and liabilities	92,200	46,100

The following information is relevant:

(i)   At the date of acquisition, Strata produced a draft statement of profit or loss which showed it had made a net loss after tax of $2 million at that date. Paradigm accepted this figure as the basis for calculating the pre- and post-acquisition split of Strata's profit for the year ended 31 March 2013.

Also at the date of acquisition, Paradigm conducted a fair value exercise on Strata's net assets which were equal to their carrying amounts (including Strata's financial asset equity investments) with the exception of an item of plant which had a fair value of $3 million **below** its carrying amount. The plant had a remaining economic life of three years at 1 October 2012.

Paradigm's policy is to value the non-controlling interest at fair value at the date of acquisition. For this purpose, a share price for Strata of $1·20 each is representative of the fair value of the shares held by the non-controlling interest.

(ii)   Each month since acquisition, Paradigm's sales to Strata were consistently $4·6 million. Paradigm had marked these up by 15% on cost. Strata had one month's supply ($4·6 million) of these goods in inventory at 31 March 2013. Paradigm's normal mark-up (to third party customers) is 40%.

(iii)   The financial asset equity investments of Paradigm and Strata are carried at their fair values as at 1 April 2012. As at 31 March 2013, these had fair values of $7·1 million and $3·9 million respectively.

(iv)   There were no impairment losses within the group during the year ended 31 March 2013.

Required:

Prepare the consolidated statement of financial position for Paradigm as at 31 March 2013.   **(Total: 15 marks)**

188 POLESTAR

On 1 April 2013, Polestar acquired 75% of the equity share capital of Southstar. Southstar had been experiencing difficult trading conditions and making significant losses. In allowing for Southstar's difficulties, Polestar made an immediate cash payment of only $1·50 per share. In addition, Polestar will pay a further amount in cash on 30 September 2014 if Southstar returns to profitability by that date. The value of this contingent consideration at the date of acquisition was estimated to be $1·8 million, but at 30 September 2013 in the light of continuing losses, its value was estimated at only $1·5 million. The contingent consideration has not been recorded by Polestar. Overall, the directors of Polestar expect the acquisition to be a bargain purchase leading to negative goodwill.

At the date of acquisition shares in Southstar had a listed market price of $1·20 each.

Below are the summarised draft financial statements of both companies.

Statements of profit or loss for the year ended 30 September 2013

	Polestar	Southstar
	$000	$000
Revenue	110,000	66,000
Cost of sales	(88,000)	(67,200)
Gross profit (loss)	22,000	(1,200)
Distribution costs	(3,000)	(2,000)
Administrative expenses	(5,250)	(2,400)
Finance costs	(250)	nil
Profit (loss) before tax	13,500	(5,600)
Income tax (expense)/relief	(3,500)	1,000
Profit (loss) for the year	10,000	(4,600)

Statements of financial position as at 30 September 2013

Assets
Non-current assets

	Polestar	Southstar
Property, plant and equipment	41,000	21,000
Financial asset: equity investments (note (iii))	16,000	nil
	57,000	21,000
Current assets	16,500	4,800
Total assets	73,500	25,800

Equity and liabilities

Equity shares of 50 cents each	30,000	6,000
Retained earnings	28,500	12,000
	58,500	18,000
Current liabilities	15,000	7,800
Total equity and liabilities	73,500	25,800

The following information is relevant:

(i)   At the date of acquisition, the fair values of Southstar's assets were equal to their carrying amounts with the exception of a leased property. This had a fair value of $2 million above its carrying amount and a remaining lease term of 10 years at that date. All depreciation is included in cost of sales.

(ii) Polestar transferred raw materials at their cost of $4 million to Southstar in June 2013. Southstar processed all of these materials incurring additional direct costs of $1·4 million and sold them back to Polestar in August 2013 for $9 million. At 30 September 2013 Polestar had $1·5 million of these goods still in inventory. There were no other intra-group sales.

(iii) Polestar has recorded its investment in Southstar at the cost of the immediate cash payment; other equity investments are carried at fair value through profit or loss as at 1 October 2012. The other equity investments have fallen in value by $200,000 during the year ended 30 September 2013.

(iv) Polestar's policy is to value the non-controlling interest at fair value at the date of acquisition. For this purpose, Southstar's share price at that date can be deemed to be representative of the fair value of the shares held by the non-controlling interest.

(v) All items in the above statements of profit or loss are deemed to accrue evenly over the year unless otherwise indicated.

Required:

(a) **Prepare the consolidated statement of profit or loss for Polestar for the year ended 30 September 2013.** **(14 marks)**

(b) **Prepare the consolidated statement of financial position for Polestar as at 30 September 2013.** **(11 marks)**

(c) Polestar has a strategy of buying struggling businesses, reversing their decline and then selling them on at a profit within a short period of time. Polestar is hoping to do this with Southstar.

Required:

As an adviser to a prospective purchaser of Southstar, explain any concerns you would raise about basing an investment decision on the information available in Polestar's consolidated financial statements and Southstar's entity financial statements. **(5 marks)**

(Total: 30 marks)

ANALYSING FINANCIAL STATEMENTS AND PREPARING STATEMENTS OF CASH FLOWS

189 HARDY   *Walk in the footsteps of a top tutor*

Hardy is a public listed manufacturing company. Its summarised financial statements for the year ended 30 September 2010 (and 2009 comparatives are:

Statements of profit or loss for the year ended 30 September:

	2010	2009
	$000	$000
Revenue	29,500	36,000
Cost of sales	(25,500)	(26,000)
Gross profit	4,000	10,000
Distribution costs	(1,050)	(800)
Administrative expenses	(4,900)	(3,900)
Investment income	50	200
Finance costs	(600)	(500)
Profit (loss) before taxation	(2,500)	5,000
Income tax (expense) relief	400	(1,500)
Profit (loss) for the year	(2,100)	3,500

Statements of financial position as at 30 September:

	2010		2009	
	$000	$000	$000	$000
Assets				
Non-current assets				
Property, plant and equipment		17,600		24,500
Investments at fair value through profit or loss		2,400		4,000
		20,000		28,500
Current assets				
Inventory and work-in-progress	2,200		1,900	
Trade receivables	2,200		2,800	
Tax asset	600		nil	
Bank	1,200	6,200	100	4,800
Total assets		26,200		33,300

Equity and liabilities				
Equity				
Equity shares of $1 each		13,000		12,000
Share premium		1,000		nil
Revaluation reserve		nil		4,500
Retained earnings		3,600		6,500
		_____		_____
		17,600		23,000
Non-current liabilities				
Bank loan		4,000		5,000
Deferred tax		1,200		700
Current liabilities				
Trade payables	3,400		2,800	
Current tax payable	nil	3,400	1,800	4,600
	_____	_____	_____	_____
Total equity and liabilities		26,200		33,300
		_____		_____

The following information has been obtained from the Chairman's Statement and the notes to the financial statements:

'Market conditions during the year ended 30 September 2010 proved very challenging due largely to difficulties in the global economy as a result of a sharp recession which has led to steep falls in share prices and property values. Hardy has not been immune from these effects and our properties have suffered impairment losses of $6 million in the year.'

The excess of these losses over previous surpluses has led to a charge to cost of sales of $1·5 million in addition to the normal depreciation charge.

'Our portfolio of investments at fair value through profit or loss has been 'marked to market' (fair valued) resulting in a loss of $1·6 million (included in administrative expenses).'

There were no additions to or disposals of non-current assets during the year.

'In response to the downturn the company has unfortunately had to make a number of employees redundant incurring severance costs of $1·3 million (included in cost of sales) and undertaken cost savings in advertising and other administrative expenses.'

'The difficulty in the credit markets has meant that the finance cost of our variable rate bank loan has increased from 4·5% to 8%. In order to help cash flows, the company made a rights issue during the year and reduced the dividend per share by 50%.'

'Despite the above events and associated costs, the Board believes the company's underlying performance has been quite resilient in these difficult times.'

Required:

Analyse and discuss the financial performance and position of Hardy as portrayed by the above financial statements and the additional information provided.

Your analysis should be supported by any FIVE profitability, liquidity and gearing and other appropriate ratios (up to 5 marks available).

(15 marks)

190 MINSTER *Online question assistance*

Minster is a publicly listed company. Details of its financial statements for the year ended 30 September 20X6, together with a comparative statement of financial position, are:

Statement of financial position at	30 September 20X6		30 September 20X5	
	$000	$000	$000	$000
Non-current assets (note (i))				
Property, plant and equipment		1,280		940
Software		135		Nil
Investments at fair value through profit and loss		150		125
		———		———
		1,565		1,065
Current assets				
Inventories	480		510	
Trade receivables	270		380	
Amounts due from construction contracts	80		55	
Bank	Nil	830	35	980
	———	———	———	———
Total assets		2,395		2,045
Equity and liabilities				
Equity shares of 25 cents each		500		300
Reserves				
Share premium (note (ii))	150		85	
Revaluation reserve	60		25	
Retained earnings	950	1,160	965	1,075
	———	———	———	———
		1,660		1,375
Non-current liabilities				
9% loan note	120		Nil	
Environmental provision	162		Nil	
Deferred tax	18	30	25	25
	———		———	
Current liabilities				
Trade payables	350		555	
Bank overdraft	25		40	
Current tax payable	60	435	50	645
	———	———	———	———
Total equity and liabilities		2,395		2,045
		———		———

Statement of profit or loss for the year ended 30 September 20X6

Revenue	1,397
Cost of sales	(1,110)
Gross profit	287
Operating expenses	(125)
	162
Finance costs (note (i))	(40)
Investment income and gain on investments	20
Profit before tax	142
Income tax expense	(57)
Profit for the year	85

The following supporting information is available:

(i)   Included in property, plant and equipment is a coal mine and related plant that Minster purchased on 1 October 20X5. Legislation requires that in ten years' time (the estimated life of the mine) Minster will have to landscape the area affected by the mining. The future cost of this has been estimated and discounted at a rate of 8% to a present value of $150,000. This cost has been included in the carrying amount of the mine and, together with the unwinding of the discount, has also been treated as a provision. The unwinding of the discount is included within finance costs in the statement of profit or loss.

Other land was revalued (upward) by $35,000 during the year.

Depreciation of property, plant and equipment for the year was $255,000.

There were no disposals of property, plant and equipment during the year.

The software was purchased on 1 April 20X6 for $180,000.

The market value of the investments had increased during the year by $15,000. There have been no sales of these investments during the year.

(ii)   On 1 April 20X6 there was a bonus (scrip) issue of equity shares of one for every four held utilising the share premium reserve. A further cash share issue was made on 1 June 20X6. No shares were redeemed during the year.

(iii) A dividend of 5 cents per share was paid on 1 July 20X6.

Required:

Prepare a statement of cash flows for Minster for the year to 30 September 20X6 in accordance with IAS 7 *Statements of cash flows*. **(15 marks)**

191   TABBA *Walk in the footsteps of a top tutor*

The following draft financial statements relate to Tabba, a private company.

Statements of financial position as at:	30 September 20X5		30 September 20X4	
	$000	$000	$000	$000
Tangible non-current assets (note (ii))		10,600		15,800
Current assets				
Inventories	2,550		1,850	
Trade receivables	3,100		2,600	
Insurance claim (note (iii))	1,500		1,200	
Cash and bank	850	8,000	Nil	5,650
Total assets		18,600		21,450
Equity and liabilities				
Share capital ($1 each)		6,000		6,000
Reserves:				
Revaluation (note (ii))	nil		1,600	
Retained earnings	2,550	2,550	850	2,450
		8,550		8,450
Non-current liabilities				
Finance lease obligations (note (ii))	2,000		1,700	
6% loan notes	800		Nil	
10% loan notes	nil		4,000	
Deferred tax	200		500	
Government grants (note (ii))	1,400	4,400	900	7,100
Current liabilities				
Bank overdraft	nil		550	
Trade payables	4,050		2,950	
Government grants (note (ii))	600		400	
Finance lease obligations (note (ii))	900		800	
Current tax payable	100	5,650	1,200	5,900
Total equity and liabilities		18,600		21,450

The following information is relevant:

(i)   Statement of profit or loss extract for the year ended 30 September 20X5:

	$000
Operating profit before interest and tax	270
Interest expense	(260)
Interest receivable	40
Profit before tax	50
Net tax credit	50
Profit for the period	100

Note: The interest expense includes finance lease interest.

(ii)   The details of the tangible non-current assets are:

	Cost	Accumulated depreciation	Carrying value
	$000	$000	$000
At 30 September 20X4	20,200	4,400	15,800
At 30 September 20X5	16,000	5,400	10,600

During the year Tabba sold its factory for its fair value $12 million and agreed to rent it back, under an operating lease, for a period of five years at $1 million per annum. At the date of sale it had a carrying value of $7.4 million based on a previous revaluation of $8.6 million less depreciation of $1.2 million since the revaluation. The profit on the sale of the factory has been included in operating profit. The surplus on the revaluation reserve related entirely to the factory. No other disposals of non-current assets were made during the year.

Plant acquired under finance leases during the year was $1.5 million. Other purchases of plant during the year qualified for government grants of $950,000 received in the year.

Amortization of government grants has been credited to cost of sales.

(iii) The insurance claim relates to flood damage to the company's inventories which occurred in September 20X4. The original estimate has been revised during the year after negotiations with the insurance company. The claim is expected to be settled in the near future.

Required:

Prepare a statement of cash flows using the indirect method for Tabba in accordance with IAS 7 *Statements of cash flows* for the year ended 30 September 20X5.   **(15 marks)**

192   PINTO

Pinto is a publicly listed company. The statement of cash flows of Pinto is available:

Statement of cash flows of Pinto for the Year to 31 March 2008:

Cash flows from operating activities	$000	$000
Profit before tax		440
Adjustments for:		
Depreciation	280	
Loss on disposal of plant and machinery	90	370
Increase in warranty provision		100
Investment income		(60)
Finance costs		50
Redemption penalty costs included in administrative expenses		20
		920

Working capital adjustments		
Increase in inventories	(400)	
Decrease in trade receivables	60	
Increase in trade payables	360	20
	————	————
Cash generated from operations		940
Interest paid		(50)
Tax refund received		60
		————
Net cash from operating activities		950
Cash flows from investing activities		
Purchase of property, plant and equipment	(1,440)	
Sale of property, plant and equipment	150	
Investment income received (60 – 20 gain on investment property)	40	
	————	
Net cash used in investing activities		(1,250)
Cash flows from financing activities		
Proceeds from issue of shares	1,000	
Repayment of loan notes	(420)	
Dividends paid	(150)	
	————	
Net cash from financing activities		430
		————
Net increase in cash and cash equivalents		130
Cash and cash equivalents at beginning of period		(120)
		————
Cash and cash equivalents at end of period		10
		————

The following supporting information is available:

(i)   An item of plant with a carrying amount of $240,000 was sold at a loss of $90,000 during the year. Depreciation of $280,000 was charged (to cost of sales) for property, plant and equipment in the year ended 31 March 2008.

Pinto uses the fair value model in IAS 40 *Investment Property*. There were no purchases or sales of investment property during the year.

(ii)   The 6% loan notes were redeemed early incurring a penalty payment of $20 thousand which has been charged as an administrative expense in the statement of profit or loss and other comprehensive income.

(iii)   There was an issue of shares for cash on 1 October 2007. There were no bonus issues of shares during the year.

(iv)   Pinto gives a 12 month warranty on some of the products it sells. The amounts shown in current liabilities as warranty provision are an accurate assessment, based on past experience, of the amount of claims likely to be made in respect of warranties outstanding at each year end. Warranty costs are included in cost of sales.

(v)   A dividend of 3 cents per share was paid on 1 January 2008.

Required:

Comment on the cash flow management of Pinto as revealed by the statement of cash flows and the information provided by the above financial statements.

Note: Ratio analysis is not required, and will not be awarded any marks.

(15 marks)

193 HARBIN *Walk in the footsteps of a top tutor*

Shown below are the recently issued (summarised) financial statements of Harbin, a listed company, for the year ended 30 September 2007, together with comparatives for 2006 and extracts from the Chief Executive's report that accompanied their issue.

Statements of profit or loss

	2007	2006
	$000	$000
Revenue	250,000	180,000
Cost of sales	(200,000)	(150,000)
Gross profit	50,000	30,000
Operating expenses	(26,000)	(22,000)
Finance costs	(8,000)	(Nil)
Profit before tax	16,000	8,000
Income tax expense (at 25%)	(4,000)	(2,000)
Profit for the period	12,000	6,000

Statement of financial position

	2007	2006
	$000	$000
Non-current assets		
Property, plant and equipment	210,000	90,000
Goodwill	10,000	Nil
	220,000	90,000
Current assets		
Inventory	25,000	15,000
Trade receivables	13,000	8,000
Bank	nil	14,000
	38,000	37,000
Total assets	258,000	127,000

Equity and liabilities

Equity shares of $1 each	100,000	100,000
Retained earnings	14,000	12,000
	114,000	112,000

Non-current liabilities

8% loan notes	100,000	Nil

Current liabilities

Bank overdraft	17,000	Nil
Trade payables	23,000	13,000
Current tax payable	4,000	2,000
	44,000	15,000
Total equity and liabilities	258,000	127,000

Extracts from the Chief Executive's report:

'Highlights of Harbin's performance for the year ended 30 September 2007:

• an increase in sales revenue of 39%

• gross profit margin up from 16.7% to 20%

• a doubling of the profit for the period.

In response to the improved position the Board paid a dividend of 10 cents per share in September 2007 an increase of 25% on the previous year.'

You have also been provided with the following further information.

On 1 October 2006 Harbin purchased the whole of the net assets of Fatima (previously a privately owned entity) for $100 million. The contribution of the purchase to Harbin's results for the year ended 30 September 2007 was:

	$000
Revenue	70,000
Cost of sales	(40,000)
Gross profit	30,000
Operating expenses	(8,000)
Profit before tax	22,000

There were no disposals of non-current assets during the year.

The following ratios have been calculated for Harbin for the year ended 30 September 2006 and 2007:

	2007	2006
Return on year-end capital employed	11.2%	7.1%
(profit before interest and tax over total assets less current liabilities)		
Net asset (equal to capital employed) turnover	1.2	1.6
Net profit (before tax) margin	6.4%	4.4%
Current ratio	0.9	2.5
Closing inventory holding period (in days)	46	37
Trade receivables' collection period (in days)	19	16
Trade payables' payment period (based on cost of sales) (in days)	42	32
Gearing (debt over debt plus equity)	46.7%	Nil

Required:

Assess the financial performance and position of Harbin for the year ended 30 September 2007 compared to the previous year. Your answer should refer to the information in the Chief Executive's report and the impact of the purchase of the net assets of Fatima. **(15 marks)**

194 GREENWOOD

Greenwood is a public listed company. During the year ended 31 March 2007 the directors decided to cease operations of one of its activities and put the assets of the operation up for sale (the discontinued activity has no associated liabilities). The directors have been advised that the cessation qualifies as a discontinued operation and has been accounted for accordingly.

Extracts from Greenwood's financial statements are set out below.

Note: The statement of profit or loss figures down to the profit for the period from continuing operations are those of the continuing operations only.

Statement of profit or loss for the year ended 31 March

	2007	*2006*
	$000	*$000*
Revenue	27,500	21,200
Cost of sales	(19,500)	(15,000)
Gross profit	8,000	6,200
Operating expenses	(2,900)	(2,450)
	5,100	3,750
Finance costs	(600)	(250)
Profit before taxation	4,500	3,500
Income tax expense	(1,000)	(800)
Profit for the period from continuing operations	3,500	2,700
Profit/(Loss) from discontinued operations	(1,500)	320
Profit for the period	2,000	3,020

Analysis of discontinued operations

Revenue	7,500	9,000
Cost of sales	(8,500)	(8,000)
Gross profit/(loss)	(1,000)	1,000
Operating expenses	(400)	(550)
Profit/(loss) before tax	(1,400)	450
Tax (expense)/relief	300	(130)
	(1,100)	320
Loss on measurement to fair value of disposal group	(500)	–
Tax relief on disposal group	100	–
Profit/(Loss) from discontinued operations	(1,500)	320

Statement of financial positions as at 31 March

	2007		2006	
	$000	$000	$000	$000
Non-current assets		17,500		17,600
Current assets				
Inventory	1,500		1,350	
Trade receivables	2,000		2,300	
Bank	Nil		50	
Assets held for sale (at fair value)	6,000	9,500	Nil	3,700
Total assets		27,000		21,300
Equity and liabilities				
Equity shares of $1 each		10,000		10,000
Retained earnings		4,500		2,500
		14,500		12,500
Non-current liabilities				
5% loan notes		8,000		5,000
Current liabilities				
Bank overdraft	1,150		Nil	
Trade payables	2,400		2,800	
Current tax payable	950	4,500	1,000	3,800
Total equity and liabilities		27,000		21,300

Note: The carrying amount of the assets of the discontinued operation at 31 March 2006 was $6.3 million.

Required:

Analyse the financial performance and position of Greenwood for the two years ended 31 March 2007.

Note: Your analysis should be supported by FIVE appropriate ratios and refer to the effects of the discontinued operation. **(15 marks)**

195   VICTULAR *Walk in the footsteps of a top tutor*

Victular is a public company that would like to acquire (100% of) a suitable private company. It has obtained the following draft financial statements for two companies, Grappa and Merlot. They operate in the same industry and their managements have indicated that they would be receptive to a takeover.

Statements of profit or loss for the year ended 30 September 2008

	$000	Grappa $000	$000	Merlot $000
Revenue		12,000		20,500
Cost of sales		(10,500)		(18,000)
		————		————
Gross profit		1,500		2,500
Operating expenses		(240)		(500)
Finance costs – loan		(210)		(300)
– overdraft		Nil		(10)
– lease		Nil		(290)
		————		————
Profit before tax		1,050		1,400
Income tax expense		(150)		(400)
		————		————
Profit for the year		900		1,000
		————		————
Note: Dividends paid during the year		250		700

Statements of financial position as at 30 September 2008

	$000	$000	$000	$000
Assets				
Non-current assets				
Freehold factory (note (i))		4,400		Nil
Owned plant (note (ii))		5,000		2,200
Leased plant (note (ii))		Nil		5,300
		————		————
		9,400		7,500
Current assets				
Inventory	2,000		3,600	
Trade receivables	2,400		3,700	
Bank	600	5,000	Nil	7,300
	————	————	————	————
Total assets		14,400		14,800
		————		————

Equity and liabilities				
Equity shares of $1 each		2,000		2,000
Property revaluation reserve	900		Nil	
Retained earnings	2,600	3,500	800	800
		5,500		2,800
Non-current liabilities				
Finance lease obligations (note (iii))	Nil		3,200	
7% loan notes	3,000		Nil	
10% loan notes	Nil		3,000	
Deferred tax	600		100	
Government grants	1,200	4,800	Nil	6,300
Current liabilities				
Bank overdraft	Nil		1,200	
Trade payables	3,100		3,800	
Government grants	400		Nil	
Finance lease obligations (note (iii))	Nil		500	
Taxation	600	4,100	200	5,700
Total equity and liabilities		14,400		14,800

Notes

(i) Both companies operate from similar premises.

(ii) Additional details of the two companies' plant are:

	Grappa $000	Merlot $000
Owned plant – cost	8,000	10,000
Leased plant – original fair value	Nil	7,500

There were no disposals of plant during the year by either company.

(iii) The interest rate implicit within Merlot's finance leases is 7.5% per annum. For the purpose of calculating ROCE and gearing, **all** finance lease obligations are treated as long-term interest bearing borrowings.

(iv) The following ratios have been calculated for Grappa and can be taken to be correct:

Return on year end capital employed (ROCE)	14.8%
(capital employed taken as shareholders' funds plus long-term interest bearing borrowings – see note (iii) above)	
Pre-tax return on equity (ROE)	19.1%
Net asset (total assets less current liabilities) turnover	1.2 times
Gross profit margin	12.5%
Operating profit margin	10.5%
Current ratio	1.2:1
Closing inventory holding period	70 days

Trade receivables' collection period	73 days
Trade payables' payment period (using cost of sales)	108 days
Gearing (see note (iii) above)	35.3%
Interest cover	6 times
Dividend cover	3.6 times

Required:

(a)   Calculate for Merlot the ratios equivalent to all those given for Grappa above.

(4 marks)

(b)   Assess the relative performance and financial position of Grappa and Merlot for the year ended 30 September 2008 to inform the directors of Victular in their acquisition decision.

(11 marks)

(Total: 15 marks)

196   COALTOWN   *Walk in the footsteps of a top tutor*

 Timed question with Online tutor debrief

Coaltown is a wholesaler and retailer of office furniture. Extracts from the company's financial statements are set out below:

Statement of profit or loss and other comprehensive income for the year ended:

		31 March 2009		31 March 2008	
		$000	$000	$000	$000
Revenue	– cash	12,800		26,500	
	– credit	53,000	65,800	28,500	55,000
Cost of sales			(43,800)		(33,000)
Gross profit			22,000		22,000
Operating expenses			(11,200)		(6,920)
Finance costs – loan notes		(380)		(180)	
– overdraft		(220)	(600)	nil	(180)
Profit before tax			10,200		14,900
Income tax expense			(3,200)		(4,400)
Profit for period			7,000		10,500
Other comprehensive income					
Gain on property revaluation			5,000		1,200
Total comprehensive income for the year			12,000		11,700

Statement of changes in equity for the year ended 31 March 2009:

	$000 Equity shares	$000 Share premium	$000 Revaluation reserve	$000 Retained earnings	$000 Total
Balances b/f	8,000	500	2,500	15,800	26,800
Share issue	8,600	4,300			12,900
Comprehensive income			5,000	7,000	12,000
Dividends paid				(4,000)	(4,000)
Balances c/f	16,600	4,800	7,500	18,800	47,700

Statements of financial position as at 31 March:

	2009 $000	2009 $000	2008 $000	2008 $000
Assets				
Non-current assets (see note)				
Cost		93,500		80,000
Accumulated depreciation		(43,000)		(48,000)
		50,500		32,000
Current assets				
Inventory	5,200		4,400	
Trade receivables	7,800		2,800	
Bank	nil	13,000	700	7,900
Total assets		63,500		39,900
Equity and liabilities				
Equity shares of $1 each		16,600		8,000
Share premium		4,800		500
Revaluation reserve		7,500		2,500
Retained earnings		18,800		15,800
		47,700		26,800
Non-current liabilities		4,000		3,000
10% loan notes				
Current liabilities	3,600		nil	
Bank overdraft				
Trade payables	4,200		4,500	
Taxation	3,000		5,300	
Warranty provision	1,000	11,800	300	10,100
Total equity and liabilities		63,500		39,900

During the year the company redesigned its display areas in all of its outlets. The previous displays had cost $10 million and had been written down by $9 million. There was an unexpected cost of $500,000 for the removal and disposal of the old display areas. Also during the year the company revalued the carrying amount of its property upwards by $5 million, the accumulated depreciation on these properties of $2 million was reset to zero. All depreciation is charged to operating expenses.

Required:

Prepare a statement of cash flows for Coaltown for the year ended 31 March 2009 in accordance with IAS 7 *Statement of Cash Flows* by the indirect method. **(15 marks)**

197 QUARTILE

Quartile sells jewellery through stores in retail shopping centres throughout the country. Over the last two years it has experienced declining profitability and is wondering if this is related to the sector as whole. It has recently subscribed to an agency that produces average ratios across many businesses. Below are the ratios that have been provided by the agency for Quartile's business sector based on a year end of 30 June 2012, as well as some ratios for Quartile that have already been completed.

	Sector	Quartile
Return on year-end capital employed (ROCE)	16·8%	
Net asset (total assets less current liabilities) turnover	1·4 times	1.6 times
Gross profit margin	35%	
Operating profit margin	12%	7.5%
Current ratio	1·25:1	
Average inventory turnover	3 times	4.5 times
Trade payables' payment period	64 days	
Debt to equity	38%	

The financial statements of Quartile for the year ended 30 September 2012 are:

Statement of profit or loss

	$000	$000
Revenue		56,000
Opening inventory	8,300	
Purchases	43,900	
	52,200	
Closing inventory	(10,200)	(42,000)
Gross profit		14,000
Operating costs		(9,800)
Finance costs		(800)
Profit before tax		3,400
Income tax expense		(1,000)
Profit for the year		2,400

Statement of financial position

	$000	$000
Assets		
Non-current assets		
Property and shop fittings		25,600
Deferred development expenditure		5,000
		30,600
Current assets		
Inventory	10,200	
Bank	1,000	11,200
Total assets		41,800
Equity and liabilities		
Equity		
Equity shares of $1 each		15,000
Property revaluation reserve		3,000
Retained earnings		8,600
		26,600
Non-current liabilities		
10% loan notes		8,000
Current liabilities		
Trade payables	5,400	
Current tax payable	1,800	7,200
Total equity and liabilities		41,800

Note: The deferred development expenditure relates to an investment in a process to manufacture artificial precious gems for future sale by Quartile in the retail jewellery market.

Required:

(a)   **Prepare the missing ratios for Quartile**   (4 marks)

(b)   **Assess the financial and operating performance of Quartile in comparison to its sector averages.**   (11 marks)

(Total: 15 marks)

198 MONTY

Monty is a publicly listed company. Its financial statements for the year ended 31 March 2013 including comparatives are shown below:

Statements of profit or loss and other comprehensive income for the year ended:

	31 March 2013	31 March 2012
	$000	$000
Revenue	31,000	25,000
Cost of sales	(21,800)	(18,600)
	———	———
Gross profit	9,200	6,400
Distribution costs	(3,600)	(2,400)
Administrative expenses	(2,200)	(1,600)
Finance costs – loan interest	(150)	(250)
– lease interest	(250)	(100)
	———	———
Profit before tax	3,000	2,050
Income tax expense	(1,000)	(750)
	———	———
Profit for the year	2,000	1,300
Other comprehensive income (note (i))	1,350	nil
	———	———
	3,350	1,300
	———	———

Statements of financial position as at:

	31 March 2013		31 March 2012	
	$000	$000	$000	$000
Assets				
Non-current assets				
Property, plant and equipment		14,000		10,700
Deferred development expenditure		1,000		nil
		———		———
		15,000		10,700
Current assets				
Inventory	3,300		3,800	
Trade receivables	2,950		2,200	
Bank	50	6,300	1,300	7,300
	———		———	
Total assets		21,300		18,000
		———		———

Equity and liabilities

Equity

Equity shares of $1 each		8,000		8,000
Revaluation reserve		1,350		nil
Retained earnings		3,200		1,750
		12,550		9,750
Non-current liabilities				
8% loan notes	1,400		3,125	
Deferred tax	1,500		800	
Finance lease obligation	1,200	4,100	900	4,825
Current liabilities				
Finance lease obligation	750		600	
Trade payables	2,650		2,100	
Current tax payable	1,250	4,650	725	3,425
Total equity and liabilities		21,300		18,000

Notes:

(i) On 1 July 2012, Monty acquired additional plant under a finance lease that had a fair value of $1·5 million. On this date it also revalued its property upwards by $2 million and transferred $650,000 of the resulting revaluation reserve this created to deferred tax. There were no disposals of non-current assets during the period.

(ii) Depreciation of property, plant and equipment was $900,000 and amortisation of the deferred development expenditure was $200,000 for the year ended 31 March 2013.

Required:

Prepare a statement of cash flows for Monty for the year ended 31 March 2013, in accordance with IAS 7 *Statement of Cash Flows*, using the indirect method.

(15 marks)

199 KINGDOM

Kingdom is a public listed manufacturing company. Its draft summarised financial statements for the year ended 30 September 2013 (and 2012 comparatives) are:

Statements of profit or loss and other comprehensive income for the year ended 30 September:

	2013	2012
	$000	$000
Revenue	44,900	44,000
Cost of sales	(31,300)	(29,000)
Gross profit	13,600	15,000
Distribution costs	(2,400)	(2,100)
Administrative expenses	(7,850)	(5,900)
Investment properties – rentals received	350	400
– fair value changes	(700)	500
Finance costs	(600)	(600)
Profit before taxation	2,400	7,300
Income tax	(600)	(1,700)
Profit for the year	1,800	5,600
Other comprehensive income	(1,300)	1,000
Total comprehensive income	500	6,600

Statements of financial position as at 30 September:

	2013		2012	
	$000	$000	$000	$000
Assets				
Non-current assets				
Property, plant and equipment		26,700		25,200
Investment properties		4,100		5,000
		30,800		30,200
Current assets				
Inventory	2,300		3,100	
Trade receivables	3,000		3,400	
Bank	nil	5,300	300	6,800
Total assets		36,100		37,000

Equity and liabilities

Equity

Equity shares of $1 each	17,200	15,000
Revaluation reserve	1,200	2,500
Retained earnings	7,700	8,700
	26,100	26,200

Non-current liabilities

12% loan notes	5,000	5,000

Current liabilities

Trade payables	4,200		3,900		
Accrued finance costs	100		50		
Bank	200		nil		
Current tax payable	500	5,000	1,850	5,800	

Total equity and liabilities	36,100	37,000

The following information is relevant: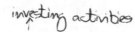

On 1 July 2013, Kingdom acquired a new investment property at a cost of $1·4 million. On this date, it also transferred one of its other investment properties to property, plant and equipment at its fair value of $1·6 million as it became owner-occupied on that date. Kingdom adopts the fair value model for its investment properties.

Kingdom also has a policy of revaluing its other properties (included as property, plant and equipment) to market value at the end of each year. Other comprehensive income and the revaluation reserve both relate to these properties.

Depreciation of property, plant and equipment during the year was $1·5 million. An item of plant with a carrying amount of $2·3 million was sold for $1·8 million during September 2013.

Required:

Prepare the statement of cash flows for Kingdom for the year ended 30 September 2013 in accordance with IAS *7 Statement* of Cash *Flows* using the indirect method.

(15 marks)

200 BENGAL

Bengal is a public company. Its most recent financial statements are shown below:

Statements of profit or loss for the year ended 31 March

	2011	2010
	$000	$000
Revenue	25,500	17,250
Cost of sales	(14,800)	(10,350)
Gross profit	10,700	6,900
Distribution costs	(4,800)	(3,300)
Finance costs	(650)	(100)
Profit before taxation	5,250	3,500
Income tax expense	(2,250)	(1,000)
Profit for the year	3,000	2,500

Statement of cash flows for the year ended 31 March 2011:

	$000	$000
Cash flows from operating activities:		
Profit from operations		5,900
Adjustments for:		
depreciation of non-current assets		640
increase in inventories		(1,800)
increase in receivables		(1,000)
increase in payables		650
Cash generated from operations		4,390
Finance costs paid		(650)
Income tax paid		(1,250)
Net cash from operating activities		2,490
Cash flows from investing activities:		
Purchase of property, plant and equipment	(6,740)	
Purchase of intangibles	(6,200)	
Net cash used in investing activities		(12,940)
Cash flows from financing activities:		
Issue of 8% loan note	7,000	
Equity dividends paid	(750)	
Net cash from financing activities		6,250
Net decrease in cash and cash equivalents		(4,200)
Cash and cash equivalents at beginning of period		4,000
Cash and cash equivalents at end of period		(200)

Notes

(i)   There were no disposals of non-current assets during the period; however Bengal does have some non-current assets classified as 'held for sale' at 31 March 2011.

(ii)   Depreciation of property, plant and equipment for the year ended 31 March 2011 was $640,000.

A disappointed shareholder has observed that although revenue during the year has increased by 48% (8,250/17,250 × 100), profit for the year has only increased by 20% (500/2,500 × 100).

Required:

Using the information in the question and your answer to (a) above, comment on the performance (including addressing the shareholder's observation) and financial position of Bengal for the year ended 31 March 2011.

Note: up to 3 marks are available for the calculation of appropriate ratios.

(15 marks)

Section A

ANSWERS TO OBJECTIVE TEST QUESTIONS

CONCEPTUAL FRAMEWORK/INTERNATIONAL FINANCIAL REPORTING STANDARDS

1 **D**

The allocation of EW's administration costs would not be included as these costs are not directly incurred as a result of carrying out the construction. All of the others are costs which would not have been incurred without the related asset being built.

2 **B**

The cost of the decommissioning is assumed to be an obligation for the company. If so, an amount should be included in the cost of the asset when it is first recognised (on 1 July 20X4).

The amount to include in the cost of the asset for decommissioning costs is the present value of the expected future decommissioning costs. The present value is calculated by multiplying the expected future cost by a discount factor, which in this case is the discount factor for Year 5 (20X9) at 12%. $4,000,000 × 0.567 = $2.268 million.

Therefore:

Debit:	Cost of asset	$2.268 million
Credit:	Provision for decommissioning costs	$2.268 million

The asset is depreciated in the normal way, which in this example is on a straight-line basis over five years.

In addition, the decommissioning cost should be increased to $4 million by the end of Year 5. This is done by making a finance charge each year. This is charged at the cost of capital (12%) and applied to the balance on the provision account. The finance charge for the year to 30 June 20X5 is 12% × $2.268 million = $272,160.

Debit:	Finance charge (expense)	$272,160
Credit:	Provision for decommissioning costs	$272,160

	$
Depreciation charge ($2.268 million/5 years)	453,600
Finance charge	272,160
	———
Total charge	725,760
	———

If you selected A, you have included the depreciation without the finance cost. If you selected C, you have just spread the present value of the dismantling over 5 years. If you selected D, you have expensed the whole asset value.

3   A

	Land	Buildings	Total
	$ million	$ million	$ million
At 30 June 20X5			
Carrying amount	1.00	4.80	5.80
Building depreciation = $5 million/50 years = $100,000 per year			
Revalued amount	1.24	5.76	7.00
Transfer to revaluation reserve			1.20
At 30 June 20X7			
Carrying amount	1.24	5.52	6.76
Building depreciation = $5.76 million/48 years = $120,000 per year			
Disposal value			6.80
Gain on disposal			0.04

The gain on disposal is $40,000. The $1.2 million balance on the revaluation reserve is transferred from the revaluation reserve to another reserve account (probably retained earnings) but is not reported through the statement of profit or loss for the year.

If you selected answer B, you have forgotten to record depreciation between 30 June 20X5 and 30 June 20X7. If you selected answer C, you have based the profit on the original depreciation. If you selected D, you have incorrectly transferred the remaining revaluation reserve into the statement of profit or loss.

4   A

The grant should be released over the useful life, not based on the possibility of the item being repaid. Therefore the $1m should be released over 5 years, being a release of $200,000 a year. At 30 June 20X1, 6 months should be released, meaning $100,000 has been released. This leaves $900,000 in deferred income.

If you selected B you have released a full year of the grant. If you selected C or D, you have released the grant over the potential repayment period rather than the useful life.

5   B

This is a revenue grant, and would therefore be released to the statement of profit or loss over the 4 year life. By the end of year one, $250,000 would have been credited to the statement of profit or loss, leaving $750,000 held in deferred income. At this point the amount is repaid, meaning that the deferred income is removed, as well as the $250,000 income previously recorded.

If you selected A, you have not removed the income that was released in the prior year. If you selected C, you have missed that $250,000 would have been released in the previous year. If you have chosen D, you have made errors over the deferring of the grant and that the repayment would be treated as an expense.

6   B

Asset A would be classed as a non-current asset held for sale under IFRS 5. Assets C and D would both be classified as Property, Plant and Equipment per IAS 16.

7   B

The weighted average cost of borrowing is 7.33% (($1m × 6%) + ($2m × 8%))/$3m.

Therefore the amount to be capitalised = 7.33% × $600,000 × 8/12 = $29,333.

If you selected A, you forgot to time apportion the borrowing costs for the construction period. If you selected D you have used 6% rather than the weighted average. If you selected C you have just used 7% as the average rather than calculating the weighted average.

8   A

IAS 16 states that when the revaluation model is used, revaluations should be made with sufficient regularity to ensure that the carrying value of the assets remain close to fair value. IAS 16 also states that, if one item in a class of assets is revalued, all the assets in that class must be revalued.

9   A

The finance was not made available until after the year end. Therefore the criteria of recognising the item as an asset were not met, as the resources were not available to complete the project.

Even though the brand (B) is internally generated in the subsidiary's accounts, it can be recognised as part of the fair value exercise for the group. Item C can be recognised as a purchased intangible and item D meets the criteria for being capitalised has development costs.

10   D

Item A cannot be capitalised because it does not meet all the criteria, i.e. it is not viable.

Item B is research and cannot be capitalised.

Item C cannot be capitalised because it does not meet all the criteria, i.e. making a loss.

11   D

Key staff cannot be capitalised as firstly they are not controlled by an entity.

Secondly, the value that one member of key staff contributes to an entity cannot be measured reliably.

Members of key staff are separable, and would be expected to contribute future economic benefits to an entity, but they do not meet the definition of an asset, and therefore cannot be capitalised.

12   A

The costs of $750,000 relate to ten months of the year. Therefore per month the costs were $75,000.

As the project was confirmed as feasible on 1 January 20X5, the costs can be capitalised from this date. Therefore four months of these costs can be capitalised = $75,000 × 4 = $300,000

This asset should be amortised from when the products go on sale, and therefore one month's amortisation should be charged to 30 June 20X5. Amortisation is ($300,000/5) × 1/12 = $5,000

Therefore, the carrying value of the asset as at 30 June 20X5 is $300,000-$5,000 = $295,000

If you chose B you have forgotten to amortise the development costs. If you chose A or D you have either capitalised the full amount or capitalised none of the costs.

13   B

The brand of Basil can be measured reliably, so this should be accounted for as a separate intangible on consolidation by Sybil.

The customer list cannot be valued reliably, and so will form part of the overall goodwill calculation of Basil. It will be subsumed within the goodwill value.

14   A

In a cash generating unit, no asset should be impaired below its recoverable amount. The valuation of $2.5 million is an indication that the property is not impaired and should therefore be left at $2.3 million.

$2.5 million cannot be chosen as the company uses the cost model. If you chose item C or D then you have impaired the asset.

15   C

The cash generating unit is impaired by $1,180,000, being the difference between the recoverable amount of $4 million and the total carrying values of the assets of $5,180,000. In a cash generating unit, no asset should be impaired below its recoverable amount, meaning that the property and other net assets are not impaired. The impairment is allocated to goodwill first, resulting in the entire $700,000 being written off. This leaves a remaining impairment of $480,000 to be allocated across plant and intangibles.

This should be allocated on a pro-rata basis according to their carrying value. The plant and intangible have a total carrying value of $1,750,000 ($950,000 plant and $800,000 intangible). Therefore the impairment should be allocated to plant as follows:

$950,000/$1,750,000 × $480,000 = $261,000.

The carrying value of plant is therefore $950,000 - $261,000 = $689,000

If you selected D you have chosen the impairment rather than the carrying amount. If you selected A or B you have pro-rated the impairment over the property or other net assets as well as the plant and intangibles.

16   A

The recoverable amount of an asset is the higher of its present value and fair value less costs to sell. Therefore the recoverable amount is $6,500.

If you selected D, you selected the lower of present value and fair value less costs to sell. If you selected B you have taken the carrying amount at the date of the accident. If you selected C you have chosen the impairment loss rather than the carrying value.

17   A

Assets held for sale should be held at the lower of carrying value and fair value less costs to sell. Therefore the asset should be held at $750.

Item B is just the fair value. Item C is the fair value plus the costs to sell, which is incorrect. Item D is the carrying value.

18   C

A sale has to be expected within 12 months, not one month. The others are all criteria which must be met to classify an asset as held for sale.

19   B

One line should be shown regarding profit from discontinued operations. This line is the profit after tax from the discontinued operation, with a full breakdown of the amount in the notes to the accounts.

20   B

Although Sector X is the only operation of Total Co in Country A, it is not a separate major line of geographical operations, as it only contributes 0.5% of Total Co revenue. Therefore Total Co would not report this as a discontinued operation.

Sector Y is a separate major line of business operations, as it contributes a significant amount of Total Co revenue, and produces a different item from the other parts of Total Co. Therefore, Total Co would report Sector Y as a discontinued operation.

21   B

Although disclosing discontinued operations separately may help with business valuation, and understanding the business, the primary reason discontinued operations are separately presented is to enhance the predictive nature of the financial statements. Financial statements are historic, and this is a major limitation of them. Including information about discontinued operations means that the users of the financial statements can use the continuing operations only when predicting the future performance of an entity.

22   D

The objectives of financial statements are set out in the IASB *Framework*. Note that providing information about 'changes in the financial position', as well as information about financial position and financial performance, is included in these objectives.

23   B

You should learn the IASB definitions of both assets and liabilities. The definition in the question is in two parts: (1) a liability is a present obligation that has arisen out of a past event, and (2) it is certain or probable that settlement of this obligation will result in an outflow of economic benefits, such as a payment of money. It is also necessary for the amount of the liability to be measured reliably.

24   D

While prudence is an important concept in producing unbiased information, it is not outlined as one of the characteristics of financial information.

25   D

It is important to learn that the two fundamental characteristics are relevance and faithful representation.

26   D

The IFRS foundation is the overall supervisory body. The IFRS Interpretations Committee deals with conflicting interpretations of accounting standards worldwide, the International Accounting Standards Board issues International Financial Reporting Standards and the IFRS Advisory Council gives advice to the board.

27   B

The IFRS foundation is the overall supervisory body. The IFRS Interpretations Committee deals with conflicting interpretations of accounting standards worldwide, the International Accounting Standards Board issues International Financial Reporting Standards and the IFRS Advisory Council gives advice to the board.

28   D

Faithful representation means presenting transactions according to their economic substance rather than their legal form. Items A to C all represent incorrect accounting treatments, and item D reflects that a sale and repurchase agreement with a bank may represent a secured loan rather than a sale.

29   B

All other definitions include some part of the correct answer, but are incomplete.

30   A

There only has to be probable flow of economic benefits, rather than a certain flow. Also, the cost or value must be capable of reliable measurement, or no amount can be put into the financial statements.

31   D

Information is relevant if it influences the economic decisions of the users. The other definitions describe good treatment but are not explaining the concept of relevance.

32   B

IFRS is based on a principles-based framework, as it is based on the IASB's *The Conceptual Framework for Financial Reporting.* Accounting standards do contain elements of rules, but are also based on the same framework. It does not represent a legal obligation, and it is not an ethical code.

33   D

Harmonisation would not provide greater compatibility with legal systems, as legal systems differ worldwide. Greater compatibility would arise when a country develops its own accounting standards within the context of their specific legal framework.

34   D

All of the listed examples are advantages except (iv) as a principles-based framework recognises that is not possible to draw up a set of rules to cover every eventuality and therefore does not attempt to do so.

35   C

The prior period error is corrected by restating the comparative amounts for the previous period at their correct value. A note to the accounts should disclose the nature of the error, together with other details.

36   B

Level 3 inputs do include the best information available, but this is not regarded as the most reliable evidence of fair value, as level 1 inputs are likely to be the most reliable evidence.

37   B

A change in the method of inventory valuation would be classified as a change in accounting policy under IAS 8. The allowance for receivables, useful life and depreciation method are all accounting estimates.

38   C

A change in accounting policy may be made firstly if this is required by an IFRS (mandatory change). If there is no requirement, an entity can choose to change their accounting policy if they believe a new accounting policy would result in a more reliable and relevant presentation of events and transactions.

Entities cannot change their accounting policies simply to make financial reporting easier, or to try and show a more favourable picture of results.

39   D

All of the given methods can be used.

40   A

In times of rising prices, asset values will be understated, as historical cost will not be a true representation of the asset values. Additionally, the real purchase cost of replacement items will not be incorporated, meaning that profits are overstated.

B and D relate to asset values being overstated, which is incorrect. Unrecognised gains is irrelevant.

41   D

The capital maintenance concept aims to ensure that excess dividends are not paid in times of rising prices, by considering the effects of both inflation and specific price rises.

A, B and C are all key concepts regarding financial statements, but do not cover rising prices.

42   B

	B/f	Interest 7%	Payment	c/f
	$	$	$	$
31/10/X3	45,000	3,150	(10,975)	37,175
31/10/X4	37,175	2,602	(10,975)	28,802

The figure to the right of the payment in the next year is the non-current liability. Once a payment has been made, $28,802 will still be owed, making this the non-current liability.

The current liability will be the difference between the total liability of $37,175 and the non-current liability of $28,802, which is $8,373.

If you selected C, you chose the year end liability rather than the non-current liability. If you selected A, you recorded the payment in advance rather than arrears. If you selected D you recorded the payment in advance and chose the year end liability rather than the non-current liability.

43 B

The expense in relation to an operating lease should be expensed into the statement of profit or loss on a straight-line basis over the lease term. The total amount to be paid is $30,000 (paying $1,000 a month for 3 years, less the first six month rent-free period).

This would be spread across the 3 year lease period, giving an expense of $10,000 a year. As the lease was only entered into six months into the year, six months expense should be recorded. This gives an expense of $5,000. As nothing has been paid by the year end, an accrual of $5,000 would also be shown in the statement of financial position.

If you chose A you have recorded a full year's payment. If you chose D you have accounted for it on a cash basis. If you chose C you have not spread the costs evenly across the lease.

44 A

Initial value of lease liability: $100,000 FV - $13760 deposit = $86,240

	Balance b/f	Payment	Subtotal	Interest	Balance c/f
20X3	86,240	(20,000)	66,240	5,299	71,539
20X4	71,539	(20,000)	51,539	4,123	55,662
20X5	55,662	(20,000)	35,662		

The non-current liability is the figure to the right of the payment in the following year, therefore $35,662. The current liability is the total liability of $55,662 less the non-current liability of $35,662, which is $20,000.

The finance cost is the figure in the interest column for 20X4.

If you chose B you have done the entries for year one. If you chose C or D, you have recorded the payments in arrears, not in advance.

45 C

SPL expense = $20,000 total payments/3 years = $6,667

SFP accrual = $6,667 (Expensed $6,667, paid nothing)

If you chose A you have taken the annual payment. If you chose D you have taken the cash paid. If you chose B you have deducted the expense from the annual payment.

46 A

Reverse operating lease treatment - Dr Liability 210,000, Cr RE b/f 210,000

Include depreciation of asset of $127,000 ($635,000/5) - Dr RE b/f 127,000, Cr NCA 127,000

Include finance cost for lease of $77,470 ($635,000 × 12.2%) – Dr RE b/f 77,470, Cr Liability 77,470

This gives a net adjustment of $5,530 to be credited to opening retained earnings.

If you selected B, you have missed the depreciation. If you selected C or D, you have either reversed the whole entry or nothing.

47   D

The asset would initially be capitalised at $87,000. This is then depreciated over six years, being the shorter of the useful life and the lease term. The lease term is taken to be seven years due to the nominal rent in the final two years of the lease.

This would give a depreciation expense of $14,500 a year. After two years, accumulated depreciation would be $29,000 and therefore the carrying value would be $58,000.

If you chose A, you have used a useful life of 7 years. If you chose B you have used a useful life of 5 years. If you chose C you have used $89,000 rather than $87,000 initially.

48   C

The payment of cash is irrelevant in relation to revenue recognition

49   D

DT should not record any revenue as it has not yet transferred the risks and rewards of ownership of the goods to XX. However, as it has received a deposit, it should create a deferred income liability for $90,000.

50   C

The asset should be depreciated for six months prior to the disposal, leading to a depreciation expense of $40,000 ($1.6 million/20 years × 6/12).

This gives the asset a carrying value of $1,560,000 and means that the profit on disposal is $440,000.

Finally, the rent expense should be expensed into the statement of profit or loss on a straight line basis. As 6 months have elapsed, the expense should be $75,000.

If you chose A or B, you have not depreciated the asset for the first six months. If you chose D, you have applied a full year's depreciation.

51   D

The sale should be treated as a loan secured against the inventory. The inventory would remain in the books of Mango, and a $500,000 loan would be recorded. This loan would include interest at 10% a year. In year one, $50,000 would therefore be recorded as a finance cost.

Answers A and B treat this as a sale, which is incorrect. Deferred income is not taken to the statement of profit or loss, so item C is incorrect.

52   B

The amount payable each year is based on the coupon rate of 7%, giving an amount of $210,000 payable each year ($3 million × 7%). This should be discounted at the market rate of interest of 9% to find the value of the liability.

Year 1 ($210,000 × 0.914)	191,940
Year 2 ($210,000 × 0.837)	175,770
Year 3 ($3,210,000 × 0.766)	2,458,860
	————
Total present value of debt	**2,829,570**
	————
Equity element	**170,430**
	————

If you chose A, you used the incorrect discount rate. If you chose C you forgot to calculate the repayment of $3 million. If you chose D you have no used split accounting.

53   B

The loan notes should initially be recorded at their net proceeds, being the $100,000 raised less the $3,000 issue costs, giving $97,000. This should then be held at amortised cost, taking the effective rate of interest to the statement of profit or loss. The annual payment will be the coupon rate, which will be 5% × $100,000 = $5,000 a year.

Applying this to an amortised cost table gives $7,981, as shown below.

	B/f	Interest 8%	Payment	c/f
	$	$	$	$
20X4	97,000	7,760	(5,000)	99,760
20X5	99,760	**7,981**		

If you chose C, you have done the calculation you 20X4. If you chose D, you have used 8% of the full $100,000 and done the calculation for 20X4. If you chose A, you have used 8% of the full $100,000

54   A

The business model test must also be passed, which means that the objective is to hold the instrument to collect the cash flows rather than to sell the asset. The others are irrelevant.

55   A

The default position for equity investments is fair value through profit or loss, meaning the investment is revalued each year end, with the gain or loss being taken to the statement of profit or loss. Fair value through other comprehensive income is the alternative position. Amortised cost is the treatment for debt instruments, and net proceeds relates to financial liabilities.

56   C

The investment should be classified as Fair Value through other comprehensive income.

As such, they will initially be valued inclusive of transaction costs.

Therefore, the initial value is 10,000 × $3.50 = $35,000+$500 = $35,500.

At year-end, these will be revalued to fair value of $4.50 each, therefore 10,000*$4.50 = $45,000.

The gain is therefore $45,000-$35,500 = $9,500.

If you chose A, you have not capitalised the initial transaction costs. If you chose B, you have selected the fair value. If you chose D, you have selected the cost.

57   B

Financial Assets held for trading will be valued at Fair Value through Profit or Loss. These are therefore valued excluding any transaction costs (which will be expensed to profit or loss).

The initial value of the investment is therefore 15,000 × $6.50 = $97,500

The shares will be revalued to fair value as at year end, and the gain will be taken to profit or loss.

The year-end value of the shares is 15,000 × $7.75 = $116,250, giving a gain of $18,750. This is recognised within profit or loss.

If you chose A you have recognised the gain in the incorrect place. If you chose C or D you have incorrectly capitalised the transaction costs.

58   B

Transaction costs are included when measuring all financial assets and liabilities at amortised costs, and when valuing financial assets valued at fair value through other comprehensive income.

Financial assets valued at fair value through profit or loss are expensed through the profit or loss account on initial valuation and not included in the initial value of the asset.

59   B

	$m
Price	90
Total cost – incurred to date	(77)
– estimated future	(33)
	———
Overall loss	(20)
	———

Stage of completion = work certified 63/total price 90 = 70%

	$m
Revenue (70% of 90)	63
Cost of sales (Balancing figure)	(83)
	———
FULL loss to be recognised immediately	(20)
	———

Answer A has based cost of sales on stage of completion, as has item C. Item D has the full costs in cost of sales but has recognised revenue on the costs incurred basis of stage of completion.

60   D

	$m
Price	40
Total cost – incurred to date	(16)
– estimated future	(18)
	———
Overall profit	6
	———

Stage of completion = 45%

	$m
Revenue (45% of 40)	18
Cost of sales (45% of total costs of 34)	(15.3)
Overall profit	2.7

Items A and B incorrectly include the full revenue. Item C includes the actual costs to date incorrectly.

61 D

Contract price	200,000
Total contract cost (130,000 + 20,000)	(150,000)
Estimated total profit	50,000

Stage of completion 180,000/200,000 = 90%

Profit earned = 50,000 × 90% =	45,000
Recognised in previous year	(15,000)
Current year profit	30,000

Item B is the full profit. Item C is the profit earned to date without deducting the previous year, and item A is the previous year's profit.

62 A

Cost to date	90,000
Profit to date	30,000
Invoiced to customer	(80,000)
Gross amount due	40,000

The difference between the amount invoiced of $80,000 and the amount received of $65,000 would be shown within trade receivables.

Item B has not deducted the amount invoiced. Item C is the profit added to the amount invoiced. Item D is the gross amount plus the difference between the amount invoiced and received.

63 D

The amounts due from/to customers shown in the Statement of Financial Position are made up of total costs incurred plus recognised profits/less recognised losses, less amounts invoiced to customers.

If customers have not paid all the amounts they have been invoiced, the outstanding balance will be shown under trade receivables.

64   A

Using the work certified basis, the percentage completion of this contract is 1,050/1,500= 70%

Therefore 70% of the total contract costs should be recognised, giving 800 × 70% = $560,000

As $240,000 of costs were recognised in the prior year, costs of $560,000-$240,000 = $320,000 should be recognised in the current year profit or loss statement.

65   D

The contract price was $4.5m, but the reimbursement of $650,000 can also be included in revenue, giving total contract revenue of $5,150,000.

Original contract costs were $3.75m, this should be increased by the additional costs incurred of $820,000 and the penalty to be incurred of $150,000. Therefore total costs are $4,720,000.

The overall profit on the contract is therefore $5,150,000 - $4,720,000 = $430,000

If you chose C, you have not included the reimbursement. If you chose B, you have missed out the penalty. If you chose A you have included the full $820,000 in revenue.

66   C

IAS 2 states that:

(a)   selling costs cannot be included in inventory cost, therefore item (i) cannot be included

(b)   general overheads cannot be included (item (iii))

(c)   overhead costs should be added to inventory cost on the basis of normal capacity of the production facilities, therefore item (vi) cannot be included in cost

(d)   the cost of **factory** management and administration can be included, so that item (iv) can be included in inventory values.

67   D

	Cost	Recoverable amount (Net Realisable Value)	Lower of cost and recoverable amount
Item 1	$24,000	See note 1	$24,000
Item 2	$33,600	$31,800 (note 2)	$31,800
			$55,800

Notes:

(1)   The recoverable amount is not known, but it must be above cost because the contract is expected to produce a high profit margin. The subsequent fall in the cost price to $20,000 is irrelevant for the inventory valuation.

(2)   The recoverable amount is $36,000 minus 50% of $8,400.

68   B

The costs of inventory should include all costs of bringing inventory to its present location and condition, so Mario should include the raw materials cost, import duties, direct labour, subcontracted labour and production overheads in its inventory.

Sales tax would not be included as it is refundable.

Storage costs are specifically excluded from the value of inventory, as they are incurred once the inventory is ready to be sold.

Abnormal wastage costs are excluded from the valuation of inventory per IAS2.

69   C

The crops grown will be treated as agricultural produce and therefore IAS 41 will apply.

70   D

Biological assets should be revalued to fair value less point of sale costs at the year end, with the gain or loss being taken to the statement of profit or loss.

If you chose A, you have used the cost model. If you chose B or C, you have not deducted the point of sale costs.

71   C

The legal action against AP is a contingent liability. As it is probable, AP should make a provision. The legal action taken by AP is a contingent asset. As it is probable, it should be disclosed in a note.

72   C

A provision is only required when (i) there is a present obligation arising as a result of a past event, (ii) it is probable that an outflow of resources embodying economic benefits will be required to settle the obligation, and (iii) a reliable estimate can be made of the amount. Only answer C meets all these criteria. Answer A is incorrect because the obligation does not exist at the reporting date and also cannot be reliably measured at present. Answer B is an example of an adjusting event after the reporting date as it provides evidence of conditions existing at the reporting. Answer D is a contingent liability. However, as it is remote, no provision is necessary.

73   C

The warehouse fire is an adjusting event as it occurred before the reporting date. Settlement of the insurance claim should therefore be included in the financial statements.

The other events are non-adjusting as they occurred after the reporting date and do not provide evidence of conditions existing at the reporting date. Issue B is a brand new event, and therefore should not be adjusted. As it is clearly material, the event should be disclosed in the notes to the accounts.

74   A

Per IAS 37, the amount payable relates to a past event (the sale of faulty products) and the likelihood of payout is probable (i.e. more likely than not). Hence, the full amount of the payout should be provided for. If you chose B or C, you have weighted the amount based on the probability rather than using the best estimate.

75   B

The costs associated with ongoing activities (being the relocation and retraining of employees) should not be provided for.

76   D

The tax expense in the statement of profit or loss is made up of the current year estimate, the prior year overprovision and the movement in deferred tax. The prior year overprovision must be deducted from the current year expense, and the movement in deferred tax must be added to the current year expense, as the deferred tax liability has increased.

Tax expense = $60,000 - $4,500 + $600 = $56,100

If you chose A, you have deducted the movement in deferred tax, even though the liability has increased. If you chose C you have added the overprovision. If you chose B you have added the overprovision and the closing deferred tax liability.

77   B

The tax expense in the statement of profit or loss is made up of the current year estimate and the prior year underprovision. The year end liability in the statement of financial position is made up of the current year estimate only.

Tax expense = $83,000 + $5,000 underprovision from previous year = $88,000

Tax liability = $83,000 year end estimate only.

If you chose A, C or D, you have got the liability and expense confused.

78   C

Deferred tax provision required	9,000 (30,000 × 30%)
Opening balance per TB	12,000
Reduction in provision	(3,000)

Tax expense:

Current year estimate	15,000
Prior year overprovision	(4,000)
Deferred tax, as above	(3,000)
	————
Charge for year	8,000
	————

If you chose A, you have added in the full deferred tax liability. If you chose B you have added the full liability and the overprovision. If you chose D, you have not dealt with the overprovision.

79   A

Deferred taxation increase (23,000-16,000) = 7,000	
Less tax on revaluation gain	(3,000) recognised as OCI (10,000 × 30%)
	————
Charge to SPL	4,000
	————

Tax expense:

Current year estimate	12,000
Prior year overprovision	(7,000)
Deferred tax, as above	4,000
	———
Charge for year	9,000
	———

If you chose B, you have used the full deferred tax increase. If you chose C you have added the overprovision. If you chose D you have deducted the deferred tax movement.

80   B

Earnings per share

EPS = $3,000,000/3,366,667 **(W1)** = 89.1c

(W1) Weighted average number of shares

Step 1 – Theoretical ex-rights price (TERP)

2 shares @ $2 =	$4
1 share @ $1.40 =	$1.40
	——
3 shares	$5.40

TERP = $5.40/3 = $1.80

Step 2 – Rights fraction

$$\frac{2.00}{1.80}$$

Step 3 – Weighted average number of shares (WANS)

Date	Number	Fraction of year	Rights fraction	Weighted Average
1 January	2,400,000	3/12	2/1.8	666,667
1 April	3,600,000	9/12		2,700,000
				————
				3,366,667
				————

If you chose C or D, you have failed to apply the rights fraction correctly. If you chose A you have applied the fraction but not time apportioned the number of shares.

81   A

Earnings per share

EPS = $2,000,000/4,250,000 *(W1)* = 47.1c

(W1) Weighted average number of shares

Date	Number	Fraction of year	Bonus fraction	Weighted Average
1 January	3,000,000	5/12	4/3	1,666,667
1 June	4,000,000	4/12		1,333,333
30 September	5,000,000	3/12		1,250,000
				4,250,000

If you chose C or D, you have failed to apply the bonus fraction correctly. If you chose B you have applied the bonus fraction for more than the first 5 months.

82   B

The prior year earnings per share figure must be restated by the inverse of the rights fraction that relates to the current year earnings per share calculation.

The current year rights fraction is calculated below.

Step 1 – Theoretical ex-rights price (TERP)

3 shares @ $2.20 =	$6.60
1 share @ $1.40 =	$1.60
4 shares	$8.20

TERP = $8.20/4 = $2.05

Step 2 – Rights fraction

$$\frac{2.20}{2.05}$$

Therefore the restated earnings per share figure is 81c × 2.05/2.20 = 75.5c.

If you chose A, you have restated the prior year by ¾. If you chose D you have not restated the prior year.

83   D

Diluted EPS is calculated as 10,644,000/7,250,000 = $1.47

The Earnings adjustment is:	$	
Earnings for Basic EPS	10,500,000	
Plus interest saved (2.5m*8%)	200,000	
Less tax (200,000*28%)	(56,000)	
Earnings for Diluted EPS	10,644,000	
Shares for Basic EPS	6,000,000	
Shares issued on conversion	1,250,000	(2,500,000/100)*50
Shares for Diluted EPS	7,250,000	

84   C

To calculate diluted earnings per share with an option, you need to work out the number of 'free' shares that will be issued if the options are exercised, and add that to the weighted average number of shares.

If the options are exercised, $3million will be received ($3 × 1 million options).

At the market value of $5, $3million would buy 600,000 shares ($3m/$5).

Therefore the cash received is the equivalent of 600,000 shares. As there are 1 million options, this means that 400,000 shares are being issued for free.

Diluted EPS = $2m/(4 million + 600,000) = **45.5 cents**

85   C

The Earnings figure for the EPS calculation is the profit attributable to the parent company shareholders.

86   A

Redeemable preference dividends will already have been removed from net profit when arriving at this figure in a profit or loss account. Therefore this adjustment is not necessary. All the other items will need to be removed from the overall net profit figure in the profit or loss account.

STATEMENT OF CASH FLOWS

87   B

	$
Accrued interest b/f	12,000
Interest per statement of profit or loss	41,000
Less unwinding (this is unpaid, $150k, × 6%)	(9,000)
Accrued interest c/f	(15,000)
	———
Paid	29,000
	———

If you chose A, you have ignored the unwinding of the discount. If you chose C you have made an error between the opening and closing liability. If you chose D you have simply taken the expense for the year.

88   A

		Tax liabilities	
		B/f (27 + 106)	133
Paid	98	Statement of profit or loss	122
C/f (38 + 119)	157		
	———		———
	255		255
	———		———

89 D

Finance costs are added back in the indirect method but are not included in the direct method.

90 B

Purchase of investments and purchase of equipment would both be shown within cash flows from investing activities.

91 D

	$
Profit	37,500
Depreciation	2,500
Increase in receivables	(2,000)
Decrease in inventory	3,600
Increase in payables	700
Cash generated from operations	42,300
Purchase of non-current assets	(16,000)
Net increase in cash and cash equivalents	26,300

If you chose A, you have deducted depreciation. If you chose C you have deducted the payables movement. If you chose B, you have added the movement in receivables.

92 D

Profit on disposal of non-current assets will be deducted from profit, as it relates to non-cash income. Increases in receivables would be deducted as they have a negative impact on cash flow.

93 B

There will be an inflow of $30,000 relating to a share issue (being the total movement in share capital and share premium), and a $20,000 outflow on repayment of the debentures. Therefore the overall movement will be a net $10,000 inflow.

94 A

PPE			
B/f	180	Disposal (CV)	60
Revaluation	25	Depreciation	20
Paid (Balance)	**125**	C/f	250
	330		330

The amounts to be shown in investing activities will be:

Purchase of PPE: ($125,000) (See working above)

Sale of PPE: $50,000 (Given in question)

This gives a **net outflow of $75,000**

If you chose B or D, you have only accounted for one of the cash flows. If you chose C, you have missed the disposal from your PPE working.

CONSOLIDATED FINANCIAL STATEMENTS

95   C

While having the majority of shares may be a situation which leads to control, it does not feature in the definition of control per IFRS 10.

96   D

The deferred consideration needs to initially be discounted to present value on 1 January 20X1.

$200,000/1.1^2 = $150,000 on 1 January 20X1.

At 31 December 20X2, the discount will have been unwound for 2 years.

$150,000 × 10% = $15,000 to 31 December 20X1, making the liability $165,000 at 31 Dec 20X1.

$165,000 × 10% = $16,500 to 31 December 20X2, making the liability **$181,500** at 31 Dec 20X2.

If you chose C, you have not discounted the consideration. If you chose A, you have not unwound the discount. If you chose B, you have only done the first year calculation.

97   C

Cost of investment	$500,000
Fair value of NCI	$30,000
	$530,000
Less: Net assets at acquisition	($371,000) (see below)
Goodwill at acquisition	$159,000

To work out the net assets at acquisition, the retained earnings at acquisition must be calculated. The retained earnings at the end of the year are given as $180,000, and there has been a profit of $36,000 for the year. As Philip has owned Stanley for 3 months, then 3 months of this profit is regarded as post acquisition. Therefore $9,000 has been made since acquisition.

Once this has been worked out, the retained earnings at acquisition can be calculated by deducting the post-acquisition retained earnings of $9,000 from the closing retained earnings of $180,000 to give $171,000.

This means that net assets at acquisition = $200,000 share capital + $171,000 retained earnings = $371,000.

If you chose A, you have not time apportioned the retained earnings. If you chose B or D, you have ignored the non-controlling interest.

98   B

The cost of investment is worked out as follows:

Shares: 800,000 × ¾ × $3.80 = $2,280,000

Deferred cash = $550,000 × 1/1.1 = $500,000

The professional fees cannot be capitalised as part of the cost of investment. Therefore the total cost of investment is $2,280,000 + $500,000 = **$2,780,000**

If you chose A, you have used the wrong share price. If you chose C, you have not discounted the deferred cash. If you chose D, you have capitalised the professional fees.

99   B

The profit on the $800,000 sale is $160,000 ($800,000 × 25/125).

As 75% of the goods have been sold on to third parties, 25% remain in inventory at the year end. Unrealised profits only arise on goods remaining in inventory at the year end, so the unrealised profit is $40,000.

100   C

The unrealised profit on the non-current asset transfer needs to be removed.

The carrying value at the year end after the transfer is $32,000 ($40,000 less 1 year's depreciation).

The carrying value of the asset if it had never been transferred would have been $24,000 ($30,000 less 1 year's depreciation).

Therefore the unrealised profit on the non-current asset is $8,000.

The total PPE is therefore $300,000 + $60,000 - $8,000 = **$352,000.**

101   B

The fact that unanimous consent is required would suggest that there is no control over the investee.

102   B

Any incidental costs associated with the acquisition should be expensed as incurred. Deferred consideration, share for share exchanges and contingent consideration can all be included as part of the cost of an investment in a subsidiary company.

103   D

All of Paul's revenue and expenses will be time-apportioned from the date of acquisition to the date of consolidation to reflect the period for which these were controlled by Peter.

104   A

The asset has not been sold outside of the group and therefore there is an unrealised profit to adjust for on consolidation.

105   B

Where the NCI is valued at fair value, the goodwill impairment will be split between the parent and the NCI in accordance with their shareholdings.

106 A

The activities of the subsidiary are irrelevant when making the decision as to whether to produce consolidated financial statements or not.

107 B

	$	
Sales value	168	150%
Cost value	112	100%
Profit	56	50%

Workings:

Mark up means profit is based on cost, therefore cost represents 100%. If profit is 50%, the sales value must be worth 150%. $36,000 of goods are still in inventory. This represents 150%.

The profit element = $36,000/150 × 50 = $12,000

If you chose A or C, you have calculated the profit based on the total sales in the year. If you chose D, you used margin rather than mark-up.

108 A

NCI % × S's PAT = 20% × $600k =	$120k
NCI% × PURP (S selling to P) = 20% × 60k =	($12k)
NCI% × Impairment (NCI at FV) = 20% × $100k =	($10k)

Total NCI = $120k - $12k - $10k = **$98k**

If you chose B, C or D, you have missed the PURP, impairment or both.

109 D

Cost of sales = $14.7m + $8.7m (9/12 × $11.6m) - $4.3m (I/C sale) + $200k (PURP) = **$19.3m**

The PURP is $2.2m × 10/110 = $200k.

If you chose B, you have not time-apportioned the results. If you chose A you have deducted the PURP rather than adding it. If you chose C, you have missed the PURP.

110 D

Operating expenses = $600,000 + $350,000 + $20,000 (FV depreciation) = $970,000

The only adjustments to the statement of profit or loss should be the current year income or expenses. Therefore the prior year fair value depreciation and goodwill impairment are ignored.

111 B

The finance costs for the subsidiary must be time apportioned for six months, as A has only owned them for that period of time. Also, the intra-group interest must be split out. The intra-group interest would not have existed in the first half of the year, as the loan was only given to B in July.

The intra-group interest for the second 6 months would have been $20,000 ($500,000 × 8% × 6/12). Without this, B's finance costs would have been $50,000 for the year. Splitting this evenly across the year would mean that $25,000 was incurred in each six month period.

Therefore the total finance costs would be $200,000 + $25,000 = **$225,000.**

112 A

The parent transferring inventory at a profit would mean that the parent's profits are overstated. This would have no impact on the non-controlling interest.

113 C

Consolidated revenue: AB $5.5m+ CD $2.1m- $1m intercompany = $6.6 million

All intercompany sales and cost of sales are removed from the group accounts.

114 B

The dividend would not have been in Allen's statement of profit or loss, so no adjustment to this would be made. The adjustment to remove the dividend would be made in investment income, where Burridge will have recorded the income in its individual financial statements.

The profit needs to be time-apportioned for the six months of ownership, with the $10,000 impairment then deducted.

Share of profit of associate = 30% × $200,000 ($400,000 × 6/12) – $10,000 = **$50,000**

If you chose D, you have not time-apportioned the associate. If you chose C, you have not deducted the impairment.

115 B

Beasant own 30% of Arnie's shares, which is 30,000 shares (30% of Arnie's 100,000 shares).

As Beasant gave 1 share away for every 3 purchased, Beasant gave 10,000 shares away. These had a market value of $4.50 and were therefore worth $45,000.

After that, Beasant must include 30% of Arnie's post acquisition movement in net assets. Arnie has made a post-acquisition loss of $40,000 (net assets at acquisition were $500,000 and net assets at 31 December were $460,000). Therefore Beasant's share of this is a $12,000 loss (30%).

Cost of investment	$45,000
Share of post-acquisition loss	($12,000)
	———
Investment in associate	$33,000

If you chose D, you based the consideration on 30,000 shares rather than 10,000. If you chose C, you have ignored share capital from the net assets movement. If you chose A, you have used the wrong share price for consideration.

116 D

Removing unrealised profits is an example of the single entity concept, as you are treating the two companies as if they were a single economic entity.

117 D

Normally 20% would suggest that Nicol have significant influence, making Hansen an associate. However, Lawro having 80% and controlling the entire board would mean that it is unlikely that Nicol have any kind of influence and therefore treat the investment as a trade investment.

118 A

	$
Cost of Investment	5,500,000
Badger % of post-acquisition profits	156,250
30% × (625,000 × 3/12)	
Total	**5,656,250**

119 C

The share of profit is calculated as follows:

	$
Share of Net Profit: 30% * 1,500,000	450,000
Share of PURP: 30%*[(2m*50%)*30%]	(90,000)
Current Year impairment	(35,000)
Total	**325,000**

120 A

IFRS 10 states that where the reporting date for a parent is different from that of a subsidiary, the

subsidiary should prepare additional financial information as of the same date as the financial statements of the parent unless it is impracticable to do so.

If it is impracticable to do so, IFRS 10 allows use of subsidiary financial statements made up to a date of not more than three months earlier or later than the parent's reporting date, with due adjustment for significant transactions or other events between the dates.

The companies do not have to have the same policies in their individual financial statements, but adjustments will be made to prepare the consolidated financial statements using the group policies.

Only the profit relating to goods remaining in the group at year end needs to be adjusted.

INTERPRETATION OF FINANCIAL STATEMENTS

121 B

A, C and D are all ratios associated with profit. A charity is more likely to be concerned with liquidity rather than the profits made by the entity.

122 B

Published financial statements should not contain errors, as they have been through an audit. Even if errors were contained, this is not a limitation of ratio analysis, it is a problem with the preparation of financial statements.

123 A

Inventory turnover is six times, so inventory days must be 365/6 = 61 days.

The cash collection period is inventory days, plus receivables days, less payables days.

Therefore the trade payables period is 61+42-68 = 35 days

124 C

Return on capital employed is calculated as profit from operations/capital employed. Capital employed consists of debt and equity. In this calculation, the deferred tax and payables are not included. Therefore the return on capital employed = $240,000/$900,000 = **26.7%**

125 B

The quick ratio is made up of the current assets excluding inventory divided by the current liabilities. In the case of Wiggo, this will be receivables and cash divided by payables and the overdraft, = ($80,000 + $10,000)/($70,000+$34,000) = **0.87:1**

126 D

A new website selling direct to the public is unlikely to be on credit terms, as payment will be taken on the order. This should therefore reduce the receivables collection period.

127 A

While the website is new in the year, the additional delivery costs are likely to be incurred every year in the future, meaning it is not a 'one-off' item.

128 A

Internal business plans would be internal information for an entity, therefore KRL would not be able to obtain this information publically.

Details of an overseas market would be useful to help KRL plan its post-acquisition strategy, press reports would be available and useful when considering an acquisition target. The recent financial statements are also likely to be publicly available and useful in determining the validity of a purchase.

129 C

Delivery costs to customers come after gross profit in the statement of profit or loss, so the increased prices will have no impact on the gross profit margin.

130 A

P/E ratio is seen as a marker of risk, and a high P/E ratio is indicative of a lower perceived risk than a company with a lower P/E ratio. Therefore Marcel is seen as less risky than the sector average.

P/E ratio is also indicative of market confidence, and a high P/E ratio means that high future growth is expected. Therefore, there is more confidence about the future prospects of Marcel than the sector average.

131 D

Diluted EPS is not a prediction of the future EPS figure as firstly there is no forecast made of the earnings figure. Secondly, if there were a range of conversion terms for a convertible, the terms giving the maximum number of issued shares would always be used in the Diluted EPS calculation, rather than the most likely conversion terms.

You cannot show your Diluted EPS figure if it is lower than the Basic EPS, you are only permitted to disclose it if it is lower than Basic EPS.

The Price Earnings ratio calculation is the current share price over the Basic EPS calculation.

Diluted EPS is a warning to shareholders that the EPS calculation could have been lower if the commitments to issue ordinary shares had been issued as shares in the current period.

132 B

The finance cost in the profit or loss account will be based on the effective interest rate, so the charge will be $2.5m × 8% = $200,000.

If the interest cover to be maintained is 9, then the minimum operating profit to be maintained must be $200 × 9 = $1.8m

Option A used the coupon rate of 6% to calculate the finance cost, giving $150k.

Option C used the difference between the effective and coupon rate which is $50k.

Option D includes the transaction costs in the initial value of the loan, when calculating effective interest, giving $220k.

133 B

Price Earnings (P/E) Ratio is Current Market Price per share/ Earnings Per Share.

The Earnings Per Share (EPS) for Rogers is net profit/ number of ordinary shares in issue.

Therefore, EPS is 1,250/2000 = $0.625, or 62.5c

P/E ratio is therefore 3.50/0.625 = 5.6 times

If you chose A, you used the dividend rather than the profit to calculate EPS

If you chose C, you used the $1m value of the shares in issue to calculate EPS

If you chose D, you inverted the fraction to calculate the P/E ratio

134 D

The dividend yield is calculated as the Dividend per share/ Current share price × 100%.

Dividend per share is Total dividends/ Total number of shares

Dividend per share is therefore $1.5m/2m = $0.75, or 75c

The current share price is $3.50

Therefore the dividend yield is 0.75/3.5 × 100% = 21.4%

If you chose A, you used the $1m value of the shares rather than the 2m number

If you chose B, you inverted the fraction for P/E ratio

If you chose C, you used profit rather than dividend per share to calculate the dividend yield.

135 B

ROCE can be sub-divided into net profit × asset turnover.

Alco has a higher net profit, and therefore must be a high end retailer. Its asset turnover is 0.4 times, so it does not use assets intensively to generate a profit. This would be expected at a high end retailer, as they are not volume driven.

Saleco has a low net profit, and therefore must be a lower end retailer. Its asset turnover is 5 times, so it uses assets intensively to generate a profit. This would be expected at a lower end retailer, as they are volume driven.

136 D

While complex items may exist which don't fit easily into an accounting standard, these cannot simply be omitted from the financial statements. IFRS is a principles-based framework, so these would be accounted for using the principles contained within the IASB's *Conceptual Framework for Financial Reporting*.

137 A

Lepchem have not yet made any sales, so any ratio involving profit or revenue is irrelevant. The current ratio will be relevant, as Lepchem may have cash flow problems as they spend cash to develop new pharmaceuticals without any cash receipt until they are successful. This could threaten Lepchem's ability to continue as a going concern.

138 C

Not-for-profit entities do not exist to make profits, therefore the return given to investors is irrelevant.

139 D

With a property management company, the value in the business is linked to the properties and the income which they can generate. Therefore the revenue and profits generated will be relevant. However, there will be no real inventory so inventory turnover is unlikely to be a key measure that is used.

140 C

The entity is likely to need to be able to account for both PPE and inventory, and will have to account for any grants received from the local government. The charity is unlikely to have significant revenue, as their income is grant-based.

Section B

ANSWERS TO PRACTICE QUESTIONS

CONCEPTUAL FRAMEWORK/FINANCIAL STATEMENTS

141 FINANCIAL STATEMENTS *Walk in the footsteps of a top tutor*

Key answer tips

Part (a) was extremely straightforward requiring the definitions of assumed knowledge accounting concepts. To score full marks here a candidate would need to support their definitions with an example. Part (b) required candidates to relate the accounting concepts specifically to inventory, again an example would be required to add depth to your answer – simply restating what has already been written in part (a) would not score any marks. The highlighted words are key phrases that markers are looking for.

(a)   The accruals basis requires transactions (or events) to be recognised when they occur (rather than on a cash flow basis). Revenue is recognised when it is earned (rather than when it is received) and expenses are recognised when they are incurred (i.e. when the entity has received the benefit from them), rather than when they are paid.

Financial information should faithfully represent the transactions of the period. This means that the information should be complete, neutral and free from bias.

Prudence is used where there are elements of uncertainty surrounding transactions or events. Prudence requires the exercise of a degree of caution when making judgements or estimates under conditions of uncertainty. Thus when estimating the expected life of a newly acquired asset, if we have past experience of the use of similar assets and they had had lives of (say) between five and eight years, it would be prudent to use an estimated life of five years for the new asset.

Comparability is essential when assessing the performance of an entity by using its financial statements and is an enhancing characteristic from the IASB's framework. Assessing the performance of an entity over time (trend analysis) requires that the financial statements used have been prepared on a comparable (consistent) basis. Generally this can be interpreted as using consistent accounting policies (unless a change is required to show a fairer presentation). A similar principle is relevant to comparing one entity with another; however it is more difficult to achieve consistent accounting policies across entities.

Information is material if its omission or misstatement could influence (economic) decisions of users based on the reported financial statements. Clearly an important aspect of materiality is the (monetary) size of a transaction, but in addition the nature of the item can also determine that it is material. For example the monetary results of a new activity may be small, but reporting them could be material to any assessment of what it may achieve in the future. Materiality is considered to be a threshold quality, meaning that information should only be reported if it is considered material. Too much detailed (and implicitly immaterial) reporting of (small) items may confuse or distract users.

(b)   Accounting for inventory, by adjusting purchases for opening and closing inventories is a classic example of the application of the accruals principle whereby revenues earned are matched with costs incurred. Closing inventory is by definition an example of goods that have been purchased, but not yet consumed. In other words the entity has not yet had the 'benefit' (i.e. the sales revenue they will generate) from the closing inventory; therefore the cost of the closing inventory should not be charged to the current year's statement of profit or loss.

Consignment inventory is where goods are supplied (usually by a manufacturer) to a retailer under terms which mean the legal title to the goods remains with the supplier until a specified event (say sale to the public), despite being kept at the retailers' premises. Until the goods have been sold to the public, the risks and rewards relating to those goods lie with the manufacturer, meaning it should be included within their inventory, otherwise the inventory value is not complete.

At the year end, the value of an entity's closing inventory is, by its nature, uncertain. In the next accounting period it may be sold at a profit or a loss. Accounting standards require inventory to be valued at the lower of cost and net realisable value. This is the application of prudence. If the inventory is expected to sell at a profit, the profit is deferred (by valuing inventory at cost) until it is actually sold. However, if the goods are expected to sell for a (net) loss, then that loss must be recognised immediately by valuing the inventory at its net realisable value.

There are many acceptable ways of valuing inventory (e.g. average cost or FIFO). In order to meet the requirement of comparability, an entity should decide on the most appropriate valuation method for its inventory and then be consistent in the use of that method. Any change in the method of valuing (or accounting for) inventory would break the principle of comparability.

For most businesses inventories are a material item. An error (omission or misstatement) in the value or treatment of inventory has the potential to affect decisions users may make in relation to financial statements. Therefore (correctly) accounting for inventory is a material event. Conversely there are occasions where on the grounds of immateriality certain 'inventories' are not (strictly) accounted for correctly. For example, at the year end a company may have an unused supply of stationery. Technically this is inventory, but in most cases companies would charge this 'inventory' of stationery to the statement of profit or loss for the year in which it was purchased rather than show it as an asset.

Note: Other suitable examples would be acceptable.

Examiner's comments

Part (a) asked candidates to explain the meaning of five common accounting concepts/assumptions followed by a section requiring candidates to illustrate how these could be applied to a specific item, namely inventory. The first part of this question really bordered on the level of the lower paper F3 Financial Accounting. Not surprisingly many candidates did very well on this section, but there were a significant number of candidates that showed a very poor and deeply worrying lack of knowledge of basic concepts. There was also evidence of further poor examination; the question asked candidates to explain the concepts whereas many answer gave unsupported examples of the concepts. For example an answer that says providing for bad debts is an example of prudence is quite true, but it is not an explanation of prudence. Other weak answers said things like income and expenditure should be matched or accountants use substance over form; again these are not explanations of the concepts. A few candidates got carried away with this section not realising that there was only 1 mark for each explanation.

Part (b), requiring the application of the concepts to inventory, was very mixed. Well-prepared candidates often gained full marks and weaker candidates scored very little. Many markers reported that candidates were repeating their answers to part (a) and made no attempt to relate the concepts to inventory. Some candidates related the concepts to other accounting items, for example leasing was often cited as an example of substance over form; it is, but this is nothing to with inventory.

Other candidates wrote all they knew about the rules for inventory without relating it to which concepts the rules were applying. Neither of the above examples would gain any marks because they are not answering the question asked.

A few candidates seemed to think it was an auditing paper and described the audit work they would do in relation to inventory.

ACCA marking scheme		
		Marks
(a)	explanations 1 mark each	5
(b)	examples 2 marks each	10
		———
Total		15
		———

Key answer tips

Part (a) simply requires the discussion of faithful representation – to add depth to your answer make sure you include examples. Part (b) required you to criticise the finance director's current accounting treatment/demonstrate how IAS 17 enables a faithful representation and to show how the lease would be accounted for both as an operating and a finance lease. The highlighted words are key phrases that markers are looking for.

(a)   **Faithful representation**

The Framework states that in order to be useful, information must faithfully representation the information that it intends to purport. The Framework describes faithful representation as where the financial statements (or other information) have the characteristic that they faithfully represent the transactions and other events that have occurred. If information is to represent faithfully the transactions and other events that it purports to represent, this means that the information should be complete, neutral and free from bias. Thus a statement of financial position should faithfully represent transactions that result in assets, liabilities and equity of an entity. Some would refer to this as showing a true and fair view. An essential element of faithful representation is the application of the concept of the recognition criteria of assets and liabilities, largely surrounding the control of assets and the passing of risks and rewards over items. There are many examples where recording the legal form of a transaction does not convey its real substance or commercial reality. For example an entity may sell some inventory to a finance house and later buy it back at a price based on the original selling price plus a finance cost. Such a transaction is really a secured loan attracting interest costs. To portray it as a sale and subsequent repurchase of inventory would not be a faithful representation of the transaction. The 'sale' would probably create a 'profit', there would be no finance cost in the statement of comprehensive income and the statement of financial position would not show the asset of inventory or the liability to the finance house. A further example is that an entity may issue loan notes that are (optionally) convertible to equity. In the past, sometimes management has argued that as they expect the loan note holders to take the equity option, the loan notes should be treated as equity (which of course would flatter the entity's gearing). Ratios such as return on capital employed (ROCE), asset turnover, interest cover and gearing are often used to assess the performance of an entity. If these ratios were calculated from financial statements that have been manipulated, they would be distorted (usually favourably) from the underlying substance. Clearly users cannot rely on such financial statements or any ratios calculated from them.

(b)   (i)   The finance director's comment that the ROCE would improve, based on the agreement being classified as an operating lease is correct (but see below). Over the life of the lease the reported profit is not affected by the lease being designated as an operating or finance lease, but the statement of financial position is. This is because the depreciation and finance costs charged on a finance lease would equal (over the full life of the lease) what would be charged as lease rentals if it were classed as an operating lease instead. However, classed as an operating lease, there would not be a leased asset or lease obligation recorded in the statement of financial position; whereas there would be if it were a finance lease or an outright purchase. Thus capital employed under an operating lease would be lower leading to a higher (more favourable) ROCE. IAS 17 *Leases* defines a finance lease as one which transfers to the lessee substantially all the risks and rewards incidental to ownership (an application of the principle of substance over form). In this case, as the asset will be used by Fino for four years (its entire useful life) and then be scrapped, it is almost certain to require classification as a finance lease. Thus the finance director's comments are unlikely to be valid.

Fino

(ii)   (1)   **Operating lease**

	$
Statement of profit or loss – cost of sales	
(machine rental) (100,000 × 6/12)	50,000
Statement of financial position	
Current assets	
Prepayment (100,000 × 6/12)	50,000

        (2)   **Finance lease**

Statement of profit or loss	
– cost of sales (depreciation) (350,000/4 × 6/12)	43,750
– finance costs (see working)	12,500
Statement of financial position	
Non-current assets	
Leased plant (Cost 350,000 less depreciation 43,750)	306,250
Non-current liabilities	
Lease obligation (250,000 – 75,000)	175,000
Current liabilities	
Accrued interest (see working)	12,500
Lease obligation (100,000 – 25,000 see below)	75,000
	———
	87,500

Working:	
Cost	350,000
Deposit	(100,000)
	———
	250,000
Interest to 30 September 2007 (6 months at 10%)	12,500
	———
Total obligation at 30 September 2007	262,500
	———

The payment of $100,000 on 1 April 2008 will contain $25,000 of interest ($250,000 × 10%) and a capital repayment of $75,000.

Examiner's comments

Part (a) Answers to this question were very mixed and covered the whole range of marks. Good answers to part (a) recognised the important issues; however weaker candidates could not adequately identify that faithful representation necessitated reflecting the commercial substance of transactions rather than their legal form. Many answers dealt with all the qualitative characteristics of financial information. These seemed more a regurgitation of what had been taught/learned rather than answering the question asked.

Part (b)(i) required candidates to assess the differential effect of treating a lease as an operating lease compared to a finance lease and relating this to the director's comments in relation to ROCE.

There were a number of good answers to this section, most recognising that the lease was in fact a finance lease along with the effect that this would have on the financial statements and the ROCE. Weaker answers spent too much time defining a finance lease (this was not required) and not addressing the issue of the effect on ROCE. In a few very poor answers the point was missed altogether with candidates discussing leasing as a means of purchasing assets when cash was unavailable.

---

143 WARDLE

(a)   For financial statements to achieve a faithful representation, information should be complete, neutral and free from bias. A key component for recognising an asset is control, whether an asset is a resource controlled by an entity. For an asset to control a resource, it is often considered that they are exposed to the majority of the risks and rewards associated with that asset.

Examples where the risks and rewards may differ from the passing of legal title:

- Finance lease agreements. Under a finance lease, legal title may not pass to the lessee, but the risks and rewards associated with the asset pass to them. Therefore the asset is controlled by the lessee and should be recorded in their books, along with the associated liability.

- Sale and repurchase agreements. These often mean that an entity 'sells' an asset to a third party, but continued to enjoy the future benefits embodied in that asset. Under faithful representation this transaction would not be represented faithfully by recording it as a sale (in all probability this would be a financing transaction).

- Consignment inventory. This is where goods are supplied (usually by a manufacturer) to a retailer under terms which mean the legal title to the goods remains with the supplier until a specified event (say payment in three months). If the retailer bears the risk of the item not selling, then it is likely that the goods should be treated as their inventory and should therefore be derecognised in the books of the manufacturer.

- Sale and finance leaseback. Under a finance leaseback, the risks and rewards associated with the asset would remain with the selling company. Therefore the asset would be brought back under a finance lease, with the corresponding liability.

(b)　**Extracts from the statement of profit or loss**

(i)　**reflecting the legal form:**

Year ended:	31 March 2010	31 March 2011	31 March 2012	Total
	$000	$000	$000	$000
Revenue	6,000	nil	10,000	16,000
Cost of sales	(5,000)	nil	(7,986)	(12,986)
Gross profit	1,000	nil	2,014	3,014
Finance costs	nil	nil	nil	nil
Net profit	1,000	nil	2,014	3,014

(ii)　**reflecting faithful representation:**

Year ended:	31 March 2010	31 March 2011	31 March 2012	Total
	$000	$000	$000	$000
Revenue	nil	nil	10,000	10,000
Cost of sales	(nil)	nil	(5,000)	(5,000)
Gross profit	nil	nil	5,000	5,000
Finance costs	(600)	(660)	(726)	(1,986)
Net profit	(600)	(660)	4,274	3,014

(c)　It can be seen from the above that the two treatments have no effect on the total net profit reported in the statement of comprehensive incomes, however, the profit is reported in different periods and the classification of costs is different. In effect the legal form creates some element of profit smoothing and completely hides the financing cost. Although not shown, the effect on the statements of financial position is that recording the legal form of the transaction does not show the inventory, nor does it show the in-substance loan. Thus recording the legal form would be an example of off balance sheet (statement of financial position) financing. The effect on an assessment of Wardle using ratio analysis may be that recording the legal form rather than the substance of the transaction would be that interest cover and inventory turnover would be higher and gearing lower. All of which may be considered as reporting a more favourable performance.

ACCA marking scheme		Marks
(a)	1 mark per valid point	5
(b)	(i) and (ii) – 1 mark per reported profit figure	5
(c)	1 mark per valid point	5
Total		15

144 TUNSHILL

Key answer tips

This question covers IAS 8 *Accounting Policies, Changes in Accounting Estimates and Errors* which is considered to be an underpinning standard from your F3 studies. Part (a) requires you to demonstrate your knowledge of the standard and part (b) requires the application of that knowledge. This question illustrates the importance of assumed knowledge standards so ensure that you do not neglect these from your studies.

(a)   Management's choices of which accounting policies they may adopt are not as wide as generally thought. Where an International Accounting Standard, IAS or IFRS (or an Interpretation) specifically applies to a transaction or event the accounting policy used must be as prescribed in that Standard (taking in to account any Implementation Guidance within the Standard). In the absence of a Standard, or where a Standard contains a choice of policies, management must use its judgement in applying accounting policies that result in information that is relevant and reliable given the circumstances of the transactions and events. In making such judgements, management should refer to guidance in the Standards related to similar issues and the definitions, recognition criteria and measurement concepts for assets, liabilities, income and expenses in the IASB's Conceptual Framework for Financial Reporting. Management may also consider pronouncements of other standard-setting bodies that use a similar conceptual framework to the IASB.

A change in an accounting policy usually relates to a change of principle, basis or rule being applied by an entity. Accounting estimates are used to measure the carrying amounts of assets and liabilities, or related expenses and income. A change in an accounting estimate is a reassessment of the expected future benefits and obligations associated with an asset or a liability. Thus, for example, a change from non-depreciation of a building to depreciating it over its estimated useful life would be a change of accounting policy. To change the estimate of its useful life would be a change in an accounting estimate.

(b)   (i)   The main issue here is the estimate of the useful life of a non-current asset. Such estimates form an important part of the accounting estimate of the depreciation charge. Like most estimates, an annual review of their appropriateness is required and it is not unusual, as in this case, to revise the estimate of the remaining useful life of plant. It appears, from the information in the question, that the increase in the estimated remaining useful life of the plant is based on a genuine reassessment by the production manager. This appears to be an acceptable reason for a revision of the plant's life, whereas it would be unacceptable to increase the estimate simply to improve the company's reported profit. That said, the assistant accountant's calculation of the financial effect of the revised life is incorrect. Where there is an increase (or decrease) in the estimated remaining life of a non-current asset, its carrying amount (at the time of the revision) is allocated over the new remaining life (after allowing for any estimated residual value). The carrying amount at 1 October 2009 is $12 million ($20 million – $8 million accumulated depreciation) and this should be written off over the estimated remaining life of six years (eight years in total less two already elapsed). Thus a charge for depreciation of $2 million would be required in the year ended 30 September 2010 leaving a carrying amount of $10 million ($12 million – $2 million) in the statement of financial position at that date. A depreciation charge for the current year cannot be avoided and there will be no credit to the statement of profit or loss as suggested by the assistant accountant. It should be noted that the incremental effect of the revision to the estimated life of the plant would be to improve the reported profit by $2 million being the difference between the depreciation based on the old life ($4 million) and the new life ($2 million).

(ii) The appropriateness of the proposed change to the method of valuing inventory is more dubious than the previous example. Whilst both methods (FIFO and AVCO) are acceptable methods of valuing inventory under IAS 2 Inventories, changing an accounting policy to be consistent with that of competitors is not a convincing reason. Generally changes in accounting policies should be avoided unless a change is required by a new or revised accounting standard or the new policy provides more reliable and relevant information regarding the entity's position. In any event the assistant accountant's calculations are again incorrect and would not meet the intention of improving reported profit. The most obvious error is that changing from FIFO to AVCO will cause a reduction in the value of the closing inventory at 30 September 2010 effectively reducing, rather than increasing, both the valuation of inventory and reported profit. A change in accounting policy must be accounted for as if the new policy had always been in place (retrospective application). In this case, for the year ended 30 September 2010, both the opening and closing inventories would need to be measured at AVCO which would reduce reported profit by $400,000 (($20 million – $18 million) – ($15 million – $13.4 million) – i.e. the movement in the values of the opening and closing inventories). The other effect of the change will be on the retained earnings brought forward at 1 October 2009. These will be restated (reduced) by the effect of the reduced inventory value at 30 September 2009 i.e. $1.6 million ($15 million – $13.4 million). This adjustment would be shown in the statement of changes in equity.

ACCA marking scheme			Marks
(a)		1 mark per valid point	5
(b)	(i)	recognise as a change in accounting estimate	1
		appears an acceptable basis for change	1
		correct method is to allocate carrying amount over new remaining life	1
		depreciation for current year should be $2 million	1
		carrying amount at 30 September 2010 is $10 million	1
			5
	(ii)	proposed change is probably not for a valid reason	1
		change would cause a decrease (not an increase) in profit	1
		changes in policy should be applied retrospectively	1
		decrease in year to 30 September 2010 is $400,000	1
		retained earnings restated by $1.6 million	1
			5
Total			15

145 PROMOIL *Walk in the footsteps of a top tutor*

Key answer tips

This question covers IAS 37 provisions, contingent assets and contingent liabilities. Part (a) requires the definition of liabilities and provisions and how the definitions enhance the faithful representation of financial statements. Part (b) requires both the discussion and accounting for a long-term environmental provision – don't miss the discussion element as you will be restricted on the marks that can be achieved.

(a) A liability is a present obligation of an entity arising from past events, the settlement of which is expected to result in an outflow of economic benefits (normally cash). Provisions are defined as liabilities of uncertain timing or amount, i.e. they are normally estimates. In essence provisions should be recognised if they meet the definition of a liability. Equally they should not be recognised if they do not meet the definition. A statement of financial position would not give a 'fair representation' if it did not include all of an entity's liabilities (or if it did include, as liabilities, items that were not liabilities). These definitions ensure financial statements are presented fairly by preventing profits from being 'smoothed' by making a provision to reduce profit in years when they are high and releasing those provisions to increase profit in years when they are low. It also means that the statement of financial position cannot avoid the immediate recognition of long-term liabilities (such as environmental provisions) on the basis that those liabilities have not matured.

(b) (i) Future costs associated with the acquisition/construction and use of non-current assets, such as the environmental costs in this case, should be treated as a liability as soon as they become unavoidable. For Promoil this would be at the same time as the platform is acquired and brought into use. The provision is for the present value of the expected costs and this same amount is treated as part of the cost of the asset. The provision is 'unwound' by charging a finance cost to the statement of comprehensive income each year and increasing the provision by the finance cost. Annual depreciation of the asset effectively allocates the (discounted) environmental costs over the life of the asset.

Statement of profit or loss for the year ended 30 September 2008	$000
Depreciation (see below)	3,690
Finance costs ($6.9 million × 8%)	552

Statement of financial position as at 30 September 2008
Non-current assets

Cost ($30 million + $6.9 million ($15 million × 0.46))	36,900
Depreciation (over 10 years)	(3,690)
	33,210

Non-current liabilities

Environmental provision ($6.9 million × 1.08)	7,452

(ii)   If there was no legal requirement to incur the environmental costs, then Promoil should not provide for them as they do not meet the definition of a liability. Thus the oil platform would be recorded at $30 million with $3 million depreciation and there would be no finance costs.

However, if Promoil has a published policy that it will voluntarily incur environmental cleanup costs of this type (or if this may be implied by its past practice), then this would be evidence of a 'constructive' obligation under IAS 37 and the required treatment of the costs would be the same as in part (i) above.

Examiner's comments

Part (a) asked candidates to define liabilities and provisions and describe when and when they should not be recognised, along with giving two examples of how the definitions have enhanced the faithful representation of financial statements. In general this was well answered with most candidates scoring well on the definitions, but many of the examples given were rather trivial such as accrued audit fees or trade creditors. These types of liability have never been at issue in terms of the reliability of financial statements, whereas when and if environmental provisions should be recognised and the use of 'big bath' and 'profit smoothing' provisions do need robust definitions in order to ensure their correct treatment.

Part (b)(i) asked candidates how the construction of an oil platform and the related environmental 'clean up 'costs should be treated. It required candidates to discount the future clean up costs and provide for them immediately with the same amount being added to the cost of the oil platform.

On the whole most candidates that attempted this question had the right idea, if not a perfect understanding. Common errors were not to include the cleanup costs in non-current assets (some even deducted them), failure to discount the cleanup costs and it was very common not to 'unwind' the liability to arrive at a finance cost.

Weaker candidates thought this was a construction contract question.

In **part (ii)** of this section, the question asked how the answer would differ if there was no requirement to undertake the environmental costs. Most candidates did say that the company would not have to provide for the costs, but stopped at that. An important aspect of this subject area is whether, in the absence of a legal requirement, there may be a constructive obligation. Only a few candidates discussed this aspect.

---

146 WAXWORK

(a)   Events after the reporting period are defined by IAS 10 Events after the Reporting Period as those events, both favourable and unfavourable, that occur between the end of the reporting period and the date that the financial statements are authorised for issue (normally by the Board of directors).

An adjusting event is one that provides further evidence of conditions that existed at the end of the reporting period, including an event that indicates that the going concern assumption in relation to the whole or part of the entity is not appropriate. Normally trading results occurring after the end of the reporting period are a matter for the next reporting period, however, if there is an event which would normally be treated as non-adjusting that causes a dramatic downturn in trading (and profitability) such that it is likely that the entity will no longer be a going concern, this should be treated as an adjusting event.

A non-adjusting event is an event after the end of the reporting period that is indicative of a condition that arose after the end of the reporting period and, subject to the exception noted above, the financial statements would not be adjusted to reflect such events.

The outcome (and values) of many items in the financial statements have a degree of uncertainty at the end of the reporting period. IAS 10 effectively says that where events occurring after the end of the reporting period help to determine what those values were at the end of the reporting period, they should be taken in account (i.e. adjusted for) in preparing the financial statements.

If non-adjusting events, whilst not affecting the financial statements of the current year, are of such importance (i.e. material) that without disclosure of their nature and estimated financial effect, users' ability to make proper evaluations and decisions about the future of the entity would be affected, then they should be disclosed in the notes to the financial statements.

(b)   (i)   This is normally classified as a non-adjusting event as there was no reason to doubt that the value of warehouse and the inventory it contained was worth less than its carrying amount at 31 March 2009 (the last day of the reporting period). The total loss suffered as a result of the fire is $16 million. The company expects that $9 million of this loss will be recovered from an insurance policy. Recoveries from third parties should be assessed separately from the related loss. As this event has caused serious disruption to trading, IAS 10 would require the details of this non-adjusting event to be disclosed as a note to the financial statements for the year ended 31 March 2009 as a total loss of $16 million and the effect of the insurance recovery to be disclosed separately.

The severe disruption in Waxwork's trading operations since the fire, together with the expectation of large trading losses for some time to come, may call in to question the going concern status of the company. If it is judged that Waxwork is no longer a going concern, then the fire and its consequences become an adjusting event requiring the financial statements for the year ended 31 March 2009 to be redrafted on the basis that the company is no longer a going concern (i.e. they would be prepared on a liquidation basis).

(ii)   70% of the inventory amounts to $322,000 (460,000 × 70%) and this was sold for a net amount of $238,000 (280,000 × 85%). Thus a large proportion of a class of inventory was sold at a loss after the reporting period. This would appear to give evidence of conditions that existed at 31 March 2009 i.e. that the net realisable value of that class of inventory was below its cost. Inventory is required to be valued at the lower of cost and net realisable value, thus this is an adjusting event. If it is assumed that the remaining inventory will be sold at similar prices and terms as that already sold, the net realisable value of the whole of the class of inventory would be calculated as:

$280,000/70% = $400,000, less commission of 15% = $340,000.

Thus the carrying amount of the inventory of $460,000 should be written down by $120,000 to its net realisable value of $340,000.

In the unlikely event that the fall in the value of the inventory could be attributed to a specific event that occurred after the date of the statement of financial position then this would be a non-adjusting event.

(iii)   The date of the government announcement of the tax change is beyond the period of consideration in IAS 10. Thus this would be neither an adjusting nor a non-adjusting event. The increase in the deferred tax liability will be provided for in the year to 31 March 2010. Had the announcement been before 6 May 2009, it would have been treated as a non-adjusting event requiring disclosure of the nature of the event and an estimate of its financial effect in the notes to the financial statements.

ACCA marking scheme				Marks
(a)	Definition			1
	discussion of adjusting events			2
	reference to going concern			1
	discussion of non-adjusting events			1
	Maximum			5
(b)	(i) to (iii) 1 mark per valid point as indicated		Maximum	10
Total				15

Examiner's comments

I was particularly disappointed with candidates' performance on this question. Part (a) was straightforward for anyone who had read IAS 10 Events after the Reporting Period (or variant equivalents) and the three illustrative examples are well documented in the Standard and text books. In part (a) many candidates attempted to distinguish between adjusting and non-adjusting events through the use of examples rather than by description. Examples were not asked for in Part (a) and therefore did not earn marks.

In **part (a)** there was a lot of confusion over the period covered by the Standard, many candidates thought there is a set time (e.g. 3 or 6 months) or that the period extends to the AGM. To state that an adjusting event requires adjustment – and a non-adjusting event doesn't – did not earn any marks as it says nothing and certainly does not relate to the issues raised by IAS 10. Many candidates also thought that the determining factor regarding whether to adjust or not lies with whether the item is material or not. Several candidates suggested that examples (ii) and (iii) were not material, despite the note to the question providing clear guidance on this point. Weaker candidates confused the topic with prior period adjustments and the use of provisions and contingent items.

Unsurprisingly, if candidates were not able to correctly answer part (a), they did not gain many marks in the examples in part (b), however many candidates who did know the definitions in (a) still could not apply the circumstances to the part (b) scenarios. There were a lot of comments in (b) that contradicted definitions given in part (a).

(b)(i) This example dealt with the consequences a fire after the reporting period. The common errors were to say this was an adjusting event (it was non-adjusting), most candidates netted off potential insurance proceeds from the losses and did not appreciate that the losses and the related insurance claim required different considerations. Hardly anyone realised that the subsequent disruption of trading may have brought into question the going concern of the company (which would then make it an adjusting event). Even those candidates who correctly stated this was a non-adjusting event proceeded, often at great length, to itemise the journal entries needed as if it was an adjusting event (without any mention of the going concern aspects). **(ii)** This was an example of sale of inventory at a loss after the reporting period. Most candidates focused on the sale itself and said it should be dealt with in the following year therefore no adjustment was required. Some correctly appreciated that the relevant issue was that the inventory's value should be adjusted because its net realisable value was below cost. However two further errors were common; either they did not extend the lower of NRV or cost principle to the whole of the inventory (instead just the 70% that had been sold) or they wanted to put the sale through the current year's accounts rather than just write the inventory down. Weaker candidates stated the transaction was a non-adjusting event, as it took place after the reporting date, but, in contradiction, then proceeded to explain at great length the adjustments that the sale and commission would create. **(iii)** This concerned a change in taxation legislation after the financial statements had been authorised. The main point of this example was the timing of the event, specifically after the financial statements had been authorised by the board and was thus neither an adjusting nor non-adjusting event (it was outside the scope of the Standard). Most candidates did not appreciate the timing of the event and even those that did still wanted to adjust for it and proceeded to explain the nature and purpose of deferred tax.

I would also point out that there were many candidates that were on the right lines with this question, but simply did not discuss all the elements of the scenarios which inevitably limited the marks gained.

147 DARBY

(a)   There are four elements to the assistant's definition of a non-current asset and he is substantially incorrect in respect of all of them.

The term non-current assets will normally include intangible assets and certain investments; the use of the term 'physical asset' would be specific to tangible assets only.

Whilst it is usually the case that non-current assets are of relatively high value this is not a defining aspect. A waste paper bin may exhibit the characteristics of a non-current asset, but on the grounds of materiality it is unlikely to be treated as such. Furthermore the past cost of an asset may be irrelevant; no matter how much an asset has cost, it is the expectation of future economic benefits flowing from a resource (normally in the form of future cash inflows) that defines an asset according to the IASB's *Conceptual Framework for Financial Reporting*.

The concept of ownership is no longer a critical aspect of the definition of an asset. It is probably the case that most noncurrent assets in an entity's statement of financial position are owned by the entity; however, it is the ability to 'control' assets (including preventing others from having access to them) that is now a defining feature. For example: this is an important characteristic in treating a finance lease as an asset of the lessee rather than the lessor.

It is also true that most non-current assets will be used by an entity for more than one year and a part of the definition of property, plant and equipment in IAS 16 *Property, plant and equipment* refers to an expectation of use in more than one period, but this is not necessarily always the case. It may be that a non-current asset is acquired which proves unsuitable for the entity's intended use or is damaged in an accident. In these circumstances assets may not have been used for longer than a year, but nevertheless they were reported as non-currents during the time they were in use. A non-current asset may be within a year of the end of its useful life but (unless a sale agreement has been reached under IFRS 5 *Non-current assets held for sale and discontinued operations*) would still be reported as a non-current asset if it was still giving economic benefits. Another defining aspect of non-current assets is their intended use i.e. held for continuing use in the production, supply of goods or services, for rental to others or for administrative purposes.

(b) (i) The expenditure on the training courses may exhibit the characteristics of an asset in that they have and will continue to bring future economic benefits by way of increased efficiency and cost savings to Darby. However, the expenditure cannot be recognised as an asset on the statement of financial position and must be charged as an expense as the cost is incurred. The main reason for this lies with the issue of 'control'; it is Darby's employees that have the 'skills' provided by the courses, but the employees can leave the company and take their skills with them or, through accident or injury, may be deprived of those skills. Also the capitalisation of staff training costs is specifically prohibited under International Financial Reporting Standards (specifically IAS 38 *Intangible assets*).

(ii) The question specifically states that the costs incurred to date on the development of the new processor chip are research costs. IAS 38 states that research costs must be expensed. This is mainly because research is the relatively early stage of a new project and any future benefits are so far in the future that they cannot be considered to meet the definition of an asset (probable future economic benefits), despite the good record of success in the past with similar projects.

Although the work on the automatic vehicle braking system is still at the research stage, this is different in nature from the previous example as the work has been commissioned by a customer, As such, from the perspective of Darby, it is work in progress (a current asset) and should not be written off as an expense. A note of caution should be added here in that the question says that the success of the project is uncertain which presumably means it may not be completed. This does not mean that Darby will not receive payment for the work it has carried out, but it should be checked to the contract to ensure that the amount it has spent to date ($2.4 million) will be recoverable. In the event that say, for example, the contract stated that only $2 million would be allowed for research costs, this would place a limit on how much Darby could treat as work in progress. If this were the case then, for this example, Darby would have to expense $400,000 and treat only $2 million as work in progress.

(iii) The question suggests the correct treatment for this kind of contract is to treat the costs of the installation as a non-current asset and (presumably) depreciate it over its expected life of (at least) three years from when it becomes available for use. In this case the asset will not come into use until the next financial year/reporting period and no depreciation needs to be provided at 30 September 2009.

The capitalised costs to date of $58,000 should only be written down if there is evidence that the asset has become impaired. Impairment occurs where the recoverable amount of an asset is less than its carrying amount. The assistant appears to believe that the recoverable amount is the future profit, whereas (in this case) it is the future (net) cash inflows. Thus any impairment test at 30 September 2009 should compare the carrying amount of $58,000 with the expected net cash flow from the system of $98,000 ($50,000 per annum for three years less future cash outflows to completion the installation of $52,000 (see note below)). As the future net cash flows are in excess of the carrying amount, the asset is not impaired and it should not be written down but shown as a non-current asset (under construction) at cost of $58,000.

Note: As the contract is expected to make a profit of $40,000 on income of $150,000, the total costs must be $110,000, with costs to date at $58,000 this leaves completion costs of $52,000.

ACCA marking scheme		
		Marks
(a)	1 mark per valid point	4
	Maximum	4.0
(b)	(i) to (iii)– 1 mark per valid point as indicated	11.0
	Maximum	11.0
Total		15

Examiner's comments

Part (a) asked candidates to criticise the definition included in the question of non-current assets that had been given by an assistant. Many candidates did not directly criticise the points in the assistant's definition, instead they gave the definition of non-current assets as per the IASB Framework without comparing it to the given definition. This is a classic example of not answering the question that was asked. Good answers did focus on issues of control (rather than ownership) and reference to intangible assets as well, as 'physical' assets. Some answers 'rambled on' giving examples of every type of non-current assets the candidate could think of (again nothing to do with the question asked).

Part (b) gave three examples of how the assistant had treated items in the financial statements and asked candidates to comment (and advise) on their treatment. **Item (i)** was expenditure on staff training costs that the assistant wanted to treat as an intangible assets. Most candidates realised that such costs could not be treated as an asset and should be expensed, but very few said why.

Item (ii) gave two examples of research expenditure. Again most candidates correctly said that (in most cases) research cannot be treated as an asset. Despite saying this some candidates thought that as the company had a successful history of bringing projects similar to the first example to profitable conclusions, it was acceptable to treat these research costs as an asset. The second example was research commissioned by a customer and as such was in fact work-in-progress and therefore should not have been written off (as suggested by the assistant). Even where candidates did advocate the correct treatment, they rarely explained why.

The last **item (iii)** caused most difficulty. It was about whether expenditure on a partially completed non-current asset (a satellite dish system) was impaired. The assistant thought it was because the expected profit from the asset was less than the amount already spent on it. What most candidates failed to realise was that the asset would only be impaired where the recoverable amount, being the value in use (based on future cash flows, not profit), was less than the carrying amount (ignoring the possibility of selling the asset).

Many candidates thought this was a (long-term) construction contract, presumably because the asset would be used to earn revenue for at least three years. In fact the period of construction of the asset was only two months and the contract was for the rental (not the construction) of the asset (the question specifically said that it was not a finance lease). This showed a fundamental lack of understanding of what construction contracts are.

148 REBOUND

(a) Two important and interrelated aspects of relevance are its confirmatory and predictive roles. The Framework specifically states that to have predictive value, information need not be in the form of an explicit forecast. The serious drawback of forecast information is that it does not have (strong) confirmatory value; essentially it will be an educated guess.

IFRS examples of enhancing the predictive value of historical financial statements are:

(i) The disclosure of continuing and discontinued operations. This allows users to focus on those areas of an entity's operations that will generate its future results. Alternatively it could be thought of as identifying those operations which will not yield profits or, perhaps more importantly, losses in the future.

(ii) The separate disclosure of non-current assets held for sale. This informs users that these assets do not form part of an entity's long-term operating assets.

(iii) The separate disclosure of material items of income or expense (e.g. a gain on the disposal of a property). These are often 'one off' items that may not be repeated in future periods. They are sometimes called 'exceptional' items or described in the Framework as 'unusual, abnormal and infrequent' items.

(iv) The presentation of comparative information (and the requirement for the consistency of its presentation such as retrospective application of changes in accounting policies) allows for a degree of trend analysis. Recent trends may help predict future performance.

(v) The requirement to disclose diluted EPS is often described as a 'warning' to shareholders of what EPS would have been if any potential (future) equity shares such as convertibles and options had already been exercised.

(vi) The Framework's definitions of assets (resources from which *future* economic benefits should flow) and liabilities (obligations which will result in *a future* outflow of economic benefits) are based on an entity's future prospects rather than its past costs.

Note: other examples may be acceptable.

(b)   (i)   The estimated profit after tax for Rebound for the year ending 31 March 2012 would be:

	$000
Existing operations (continuing only) ($2 million × 1·06)	2,120
Newly acquired operations ($450,000 × 12/8 months × 1·08)	729
	2,849

Note: the profit from newly acquired operations in 2011 was for only eight months; in 2012 it will be for a full year.

(ii)   Diluted EPS on continuing operations

	2011	*comparative 2010*
$\dfrac{\$2{,}730{,}000 \text{ (see workings)}}{14{,}600{,}000 \text{ (see workings)}} \times 100$	18.7 cents	
$\dfrac{\$2{,}030{,}000 \text{ (see workings)}}{14{,}000{,}000 \text{ (see workings)}} \times 100$		14.5 cents

Workings (figures in brackets are in '000 or $000)

The earnings are calculated as follows:

	2011	*comparative 2010*
	$000	$000
Continuing operations:		
Existing operations	2,000	1,750
Newly acquired operations	450	nil
Re convertible loan stock (see below)	280	280
	2,730	2,030

The weighted average number of shares (in '000) is calculated as follows:

At 1 April 2009 (3,000 × 4 (i.e. shares of 25 cents each))	12,000	12,000
Re convertible loan stock (see below)	2,000	2,000
Re share options (see below)	600 (weighted for six months)	nil
	14,600	14,000

Convertible loan stock:

On an assumed conversion there would be an increase in income of $280,000 ($5,000 × 8% × 0·7 after tax).

There would be an increase in the number of shares of 2 million ($5,000/$100 × 40). These adjustments would apply fully to both years.

Share options:

Exercising the options would create proceeds of $2 million (2,000 × $1). At the market price of $2˙50 each this would buy 800,000 shares ($2,000/$2˙50) thus the diluting number of shares is 1˙2 million (2,000 – 800).

. This would be weighted for 6/12 in 2011 as the grant was half way through the year.

ACCA marking scheme				
				Marks
(a)	1 mark per valid point/example			6
(b)	(i)	profit from continuing operations		1
		profit from newly acquired operations		2
				—
			Maximum	3
				—
	(ii)	EPS for 2010 and 2011 at 3 marks each		6
				—
Total				**15**
				—

149 BOROUGH

(a) IAS 37 *Provisions, contingent liabilities and contingent assets* defines provisions as liabilities of uncertain timing or amount that should be recognised where there is a present obligation (as a result of past events), it is probable (more than a 50% chance) that there will be an outflow of economic benefits and the amounts can be estimated reliably. The obligation may be legal or constructive.

A contingent liability has more uncertainty in that it is a **possible** obligation (less than a 50% chance) whose existence will be confirmed only by one or more future uncertain events not wholly within the control of the entity. An existing obligation where the amount cannot be reliably measured is also a contingent liability.

The Standard seeks to improve consistency in the reporting of provisions. In the past some entities created 'general' (rather than specific) provisions for liabilities that did not really exist (known as 'big bath' provisions); equally many entities did not recognise provisions where there was a present obligation. The latter often related to deferred liabilities such as future environmental costs. The effect of such inconsistencies was that comparability was weakened and profit was frequently manipulated.

(b) (i) Although the information in the question says the environmental provision is not a legal obligation, it implies that it is a constructive obligation (Borough has created an expectation that it will pay the environmental costs) and therefore these costs should be provided for. The obligation for the fixed element of the cost arose as soon as the extraction commenced, whereas the variable element accrues in line with the extraction of oil. The present value of the environmental cost is shown as a non-current liability (credit) with the debit added to the cost of the licence and (effectively) charged to income as part of the annual amortisation charge.

The relevant extracts from Borough's statement of financial position as at 30 September 2011 are:

	$000
Non-current asset	
Licence for oil extraction (50,000 + 20,000)	70,000
Amortisation (10 years)	(7,000)
	———
Carrying amount	63,000
	———
Non-current liability	
Environmental provision ((20,000 + (150,000 × 0·02 cents)) × 1·08 finance cost)	24,840
	———

(ii) From Borough's perspective, as a separate entity, the guarantee for Hamlet's loan is a contingent liability of $10 million. As Hamlet is a separate entity, Borough has no liability for the secured amount of $15 million, not even for the potential shortfall for the security of $3 million. The $10 million contingent liability would be disclosed in the notes to Borough's financial statements.

In Borough's consolidated financial statements, the full liability of $25 million would be included in the statement of financial position as part of the group's non-current liabilities – there would be no contingent liability disclosed.

The concerns over the potential survival of Hamlet due to the effects of the recession may change the disclosure in Borough's entity financial statements. If Borough deems it probable that Hamlet is not a going concern the $10 million loan, which was previously a contingent liability, would become an actual liability and should be provided for on Borough's entity statement of financial position and disclosed as a current (not a non-current) liability.

ACCA marking scheme			Marks
(a)		definition of provisions	2
		definition of contingent liabilities	2
		how the Standard improves comparability	2
		Maximum	6
(b)	(i)	it is a constructive obligation	1
		explanation of treatment	1
		non-current asset (including amortisation)	1½
		environmental provision (including unwinding of discount)	1½
	(ii)	entity financial statements contingent liability of $10 million	1
		no obligation for secured $15 million	1
		consolidated statements show full $25 million as a liability	1
		if not a going concern, guarantee would be shown as an actual (current) liability in entity financial statements	1
			9
Total			15

150 TELEPATH

(a) An impairment review is the procedure to determine if and by how much an asset may have been impaired. An asset is impaired if its carrying amount is greater than its recoverable amount. The recoverable amount of an asset is defined as the higher of its fair value less costs to sell or its value in use, which is the present values of the future net cash flows the asset will generate.

The problem in applying this definition is that assets rarely generate cash flows in isolation; most assets generate cash flows in combination with other assets. IAS 36 introduces the concept of a cash generating unit (CGU) which is the smallest identifiable group of assets that generate cash inflows that are independent of other assets. Where an asset forms part of a CGU any impairment review must be made on the group of assets as a whole. If impairment losses are then identified, they must be allocated and/or apportioned to the assets of the CGU as prescribed by IAS 36.

(b) (i) The carrying amount of the plant at 31 March 2012, before the impairment review, is $500,000 (800,000 – (150,000 × 2)) where $150,000 is the annual depreciation charge ((800,000 cost – 50,000 residual value)/5 years).

This needs to be compared with the recoverable amount of the plant which must be its value in use as it has no market value at this date.

Value in use:

		Cash flow $000	Discount factor at 10%	Present value $000
year ended:	31 March 2013	220	0·91	200
	31 March 2014	180	0·83	149
	31 March 2015	170 + 50	0·75	165
				514

At 31 March 2012, the plant's value in use of $514,000 is greater than its carrying amount of $500,000. This means the plant is not impaired and it should continue to be carried at $500,000.

(ii)

	Per question $000	Plant write off $000		Impairment losses $000
Goodwill	1,800	1,800	write off in full	nil
Patent	1,200	1,200	at realisable value	1,000
Factory	4,000	4,000	pro rata loss of 40%	2,400
Plant	3,500	3,000	pro rata of 40%	1,800
Receivables and cash	1,500	1,500	realisable value	1,500
	12,000	11,500	Value in use	6,700

The plant with a carrying amount of $500,000 that has been damaged to the point of no further use should be written off (it no longer meets the definition of an asset). The carrying amounts in the second column above are after writing off this plant.

After this, firstly, goodwill is written off in full.

Secondly, any remaining impairment loss should write off the remaining assets pro rata to their carrying amounts, except that no asset should be written down to less than its fair value less costs to sell (net realisable value).

After writing off the damaged plant the remaining impairment loss is $4·8 million (11·5m – 6·7m) of which $1·8 million is applied to the goodwill, $200,000 to the patent (taking it to its realisable value) and the remaining $2·8 million is apportioned pro rata at 40% (2·8m/(4m + 3m)) to the factory and the remaining plant.

The carrying amounts of the assets of Tilda, at 31 March 2012 after the accident, are as shown in the third column above.

ACCA marking scheme				
				Marks
(a)		1 mark per valid point		—
			Maximum	4
(b)	(i)	carrying amount before impairment test		1
		value in use		2
		conclude not impaired and carry at $500,000		1
			Maximum	4
	(ii)	damaged plant written off		1
		goodwill written off		1
		patent at $1 million		1
		cash and receivables already at realisable value – no impairment		1
		calculation of remaining loss/pro rata percentage		1
		apply to building and plant only		2
			Maximum	7
Total				15

151 LOBDEN

(a) The main objective of financial statements is to provide information that is useful to a wide range of users for the purpose of making economic decisions. Therefore, it is important that the activities and events of the entity, as expressed within the financial statements, are understood by users, meaning that their usefulness and relevance is maximised. This can present management with a problem because clearly not all users have the same (financial) abilities and knowledge. For the purpose of understandability, management are allowed to assume users do have a reasonable knowledge of accounting and business and are prepared to study the financial statements diligently. Importantly, this characteristic cannot be used by management to avoid disclosing complex information that may be relevant in user decision-making. However, management must recognise that too much or overly complex disclosure can obscure the more important aspects of an entity's performance, i.e. important information should not be 'buried' in the detail of unfathomable information.

Comparability is the main tool by which users can assess the performance of an entity. This can be done through trend analysis of the same entity's financial statements over time (say five years), or by comparing one entity with other (suitable) entities (or business sector averages) for the same time period. This means that the measurement and disclosure (classification) of like transactions should be consistent over time for the same entity, and (ideally) between different entities. Consistency and comparability are facilitated by the existence and disclosure of accounting policies. The above illustrates the close correlation between comparability and consistency. However, it is not always possible for an entity to apply the same accounting policies every year; sometimes they have to change (e.g. because of a new accounting standard or a change in legislation). Similarly, it is not practical for accounting standards to require all entities to adopt the same accounting policies.

Thus, if an entity does change an accounting policy, this breaks the principle of consistency. In such circumstances, IFRSs normally require that any reported comparatives (previous year's financial statements) are restated as if the new policy had been in force when those statements were originally reported. In this way, although there has been a change of policy, comparability has been maintained.

It is more difficult to address the issue of consistency across entities; as already stated, accounting standards cannot prescribe the use of the same policy for all entities (this would be uniformity). However, accounting standards do prohibit certain accounting treatments (considered inappropriate or inferior) and they do require entities to disclose their accounting policies, such that users become aware of differences between entities and this may allow them to make value adjustments when comparing entities using different policies.

(b) (i) **Lobden's statement of profit or loss (extracts) for the year ended:**

		30 September 2012
		$million
Revenue (based on work certified)	(160 – 100)	60
Cost of sales (balance)		(48)
Profit	((50 × 160/250) – 20)	12

Statement of financial position (extracts) as at:

		30 September 2012
		$million
Current assets:		
Amounts due from customers		
Contract costs to date		145
Profit recognised (cumulative 20 + 12)		32
		177
Progress billings (cumulative)		(160)
Amounts due from customers		17
Contract receivables	(160 – 150)	10

(ii) The relevant issue here is what constitutes the accounting policy for construction contracts. Where there is uncertainty in the outcome of a contract, the appropriate accounting policy would be the completed contract basis (i.e. no profit is taken until the contract is completed). Similarly, any expected losses should be recognised immediately. Where the outcome of a contract is reasonably foreseeable, the appropriate accounting policy is to accrue profits by the percentage of completion method. If this is accepted, it becomes clear that the different methods of determining the percentage of completion of construction contracts are different accounting estimates. Thus the change made by Lobden in the year to 30 September 2012 represents a change of accounting estimate. This approach complies with the guidance in IAS 11 *Construction Contracts* paras 30 and 38.

ACCA marking scheme			Marks
(a)	1 mark per valid point: understandability		2
	comparability		4
		Maximum	6
(b)	(i) revenue		2
	cost of sales		½
	recognised profit		2
	amounts due from customers		2
	contract receivables		½
		Maximum	7
	(ii) discussion		1
	conclusion		1
		Maximum	2
Total			15

152 RADAR

(a) A discontinued operation is a component (see below) of an entity that has either already been disposed of or is classified as held for sale that represents a separate major line of business or geographical area of business operations (or is part of a co-ordinated plan to dispose of such). It also applies to a subsidiary that is acquired specifically with a view to resale.

A component of an entity has operations and cash flows that are clearly distinguished for reporting purposes from those of the rest of an entity. It would normally be a cash generating unit (or a group of cash generating units) or a subsidiary.

This information is important to users of financial statements when they are forming an assessment of the likely future performance of an entity. For example, if a group made a large profit from one of its subsidiaries that it has recently sold (or will soon sell), this will have a material effect on any forecast of the group's future profit. This is because the profits from the subsidiary disposed of will no longer contribute to future group profit (though the re-investment of any sale proceeds from the disposal could). Also, the converse would be true where the disposal or closure of a loss-making subsidiary could improve future profitability.

(b) IFRS 5 *Non-current Assets Held for Sale and Discontinued Operations* has been criticised for the use of the term '*a separate major line of business or geographical area of business operations*' to identify a discontinued operation as it may mean different things to different people and lead to inconsistency (and thus a lack of comparability). Despite this, the disposal of hotels in country A would seem to represent a separate geographical location and should be treated as a discontinued operation, even though the group will continue to operate hotels in other countries. The example of country B is less conclusive. Some might argue that a change in the target market (to holiday and tourism) does represent a different 'line of business operations' that has a different pricing structure, operating costs (such as providing 'all-inclusive' holidays) and profit margins than that of business clients. Also, the refurbishment of the hotels would seem to indicate catering to a different market. Others may argue that this is simply adapting a product (as all companies have to do) and does not represent a change to a separate line of business.

(c) On its own, a board decision to close the factory is not sufficient to justify the creation of a provision under IAS *37 Provisions, Contingent Liabilities and Contingent Assets.* However, by formulating a plan and informing interested parties (employees, customers and suppliers), this is likely to constitute a constructive obligation for a restructuring provision by raising a valid expectation of the closure.

The amounts that should be provided for at 31 March 2013 are:

(workings in brackets are in $000)

	$000
– redundancy (200 employees × 5)	1,000
– impairment loss on plant (2,200 – (500 – 50))	1,750 (may be shown as a separate provision)
– onerous contract (lower amount)	850
– penalty payments	200
	3,800

The $3·8 million should be charged to the statement of profit or loss for the year ended 31 March 2013 and the same amount reported in the statement of financial position as at 31 March 2013 as a current liability/plant impairment (assuming all parts of the factory closure will be completed within the next 12 months).

The factory and the plant would be disclosed in the statement of financial position as non-current assets held for sale at the lower of their carrying amount (the factory) or fair value less cost to sell (the plant).

The $125,000 retraining costs cannot be provided for as they are part of future activities and the anticipated $1·2 million profit on the disposal of the factory cannot be recognised until it is realised.

ACCA marking scheme		Marks
(a)	1 mark per valid point	5
(b)	operations in country A is a discontinued operation	2
	discussion of issue for country B	2
	Maximum	4

(c)	information points to a constructive obligation	1
	provide for redundancy	1
	but not for retraining	1
	impairment of plant 1,750 (cannot recognise/offset gain on property)	1
	onerous contract – lower amount provided for	1
	provide for penalty	1
	Maximum	6
Total		**15**

153 LAIDLAW

(a) The *Conceptual Framework for Financial Reporting* implies that the two fundamental qualitative characteristics (relevance and faithful representation) are vital as, without them, financial statements would not be useful, in fact they may be misleading. As the name suggests, the four enhancing qualitative characteristics (comparability, verifiability, timeliness and understandability) improve the usefulness of the financial information. Thus financial information which is not relevant or does not give a faithful representation is not useful (and worse, it may possibly be misleading); however, financial information which does not possess the enhancing characteristics can still be useful, but not as useful as if it did possess them.

In order for financial statements to be useful to users (such as investors or loan providers), they must present financial information faithfully, i.e. financial information must faithfully represent the economic phenomena which it purports to represent (e.g. in some cases it may be necessary to treat a sale and repurchase agreement as an in-substance (secured) loan rather than as a sale and subsequent repurchase). Faithfully represented information should be complete, neutral and free from error. Substance is not identified as a separate characteristic because the IASB says it is implied in faithful representation such that faithful representation is only possible if transactions and economic phenomena are accounted for according to their substance and economic reality.

(b) (i) When dealing with the factoring of receivables, probably the most important aspect of the transaction is which party bears the risk of any non-payment by the customer (irrecoverable receivables). In this case, that party is Laidlaw as it will have to 'buy back' any receivables not settled within four months of their 'sale'. Thus Finease is acting as an administrator (for a fee of $10,000 per month) and as a provider of finance (charging 2% interest per month).

Laidlaw should not 'derecognise' the receivables as suggested in the question, but instead treat the $1·8 million cash received from Finease as a current liability (a loan or financing arrangement secured on the receivables). Laidlaw should charge $10,000 as an administration fee and $36,000 ($1·8 million x 2%) as interest (for the month of September 2013), to profit or loss as administrative expenses and finance costs respectively. Both these amounts should also be added to the current liability (the amount owed to Finease) which at 30 September 2013 would amount to $1,846,000.

(ii) The critical aspect of these transactions (the sale, the rental and the potential repurchase) is that they are (or will be) all carried out at commercial values. Thus Laidlaw has adopted the correct treatment by recording the disposal of the property as a 'true' sale and, presumably, charged $400,000 to profit or loss under operating lease arrangements for the rental of the property for the year ended 30 September 2013. The fact that Laidlaw will be given the opportunity to repurchase the property in five years' time before it is put on the open market is not an asset and should not be recognised as such, nor does it affect the substance of the sale. This is because the price of the potential repurchase is at what is expected to be its fair value and is therefore not favourable to Laidlaw.

		ACCA marking scheme	
			Marks
(a)		1 mark per valid point	5
(b)	(i)	'buy back' means Laidlaw bears the risk of non-payment	1
		Finease earns administration and financing fees	1
		receivables are not derecognised (remain on statement of financial position)	1
		$1·8 million is a loan secured on receivables	1
		$10,000 and $36,000 charged to profit or loss as administrative expenses and finance costs respectively	1
		Maximum	5
	(ii)	all transactions at commercial values	2
		thus accounting for as a disposal is correct	1
		rental correctly charged at $400,000	1
		option is not an asset as a repurchase would apply at market values	1
		Maximum	5
Total			15

154 FUNDO

(a) The alterations to the leased property do not affect the lease itself and this should continue to be treated as an operating lease and charging profit or loss with the annual rental of $2·3 million.

The initial cost of the alterations should be capitalised and depreciated over the remaining life of the lease. In addition to this, IAS 37 *Provisions, Contingent Assets and Contingent Liabilities* requires that the cost of restoring the property to its original condition should be provided for on 1 October 2012 as this is when the obligation to incur the restoration cost arises (as the time taken to do the alterations is negligible). The present value of the restoration costs, given as $5 million, should be added to the initial cost of the alterations and depreciated over the remaining life of the lease. A corresponding provision should be created and a finance cost of 8% per annum should be charged to profit or loss and accrued on this provision.

(b) **Extracts from the financial statements of Fundo**

	$000
Statement of profit or loss for the year ended 30 September 2013	
Operating lease rental	2,300
Depreciation of alterations to leased property (12,000/8 years)	1,500
Finance cost (5,000 × 8%)	400

Statement of financial position as at 30 September 2013

Non-current assets

Alterations to leased property (7,000 + 5,000)	12,000
Accumulated depreciation (above)	(1,500)
	———
Carrying amount	10,500
	———
Non-current liabilities	
Provision for property restoration costs (5,000 + 400 above)	5,400
	———

ACCA marking scheme		
		Marks
(a)	1 mark per valid point	4
(b)	statement of profit or loss	
	operating lease rental	1
	depreciation charge	1
	finance cost	1
	statement of financial position	
	alterations to leased property, at cost	1
	accumulated depreciation	1
	non-current liability (provision)	1
		———
	Maximum	6
		———
Total		**10**
		———

155 SPECULATE

(a) (i) An investment property is land or buildings (or a part thereof) held by the owner to generate rental income or for capital appreciation (or both) rather than for production or administrative use. Generally, non-investment properties generate cash flows in combination with other assets, whereas a property that meets the definition of an investment property means that it will generate cash flows that are largely independent of the other assets held by an entity and such properties do not form part of the entity's normal operations.

(ii) Superficially, the revaluation model and fair value sound very similar; both require properties to be valued at their fair value which is usually a market-based assessment (often by an independent valuer). However, any gain (or loss) over a previous valuation is taken to profit or loss if it relates to an investment property, whereas for an owner-occupied property, any gain is taken to a revaluation reserve (via other comprehensive income and the statement of changes in equity). A loss on the revaluation of an owner-occupied property is charged to profit or loss unless it has a previous surplus in the revaluation reserve which can be used to offset the loss until it is exhausted. A further difference is that owner-occupied property continues to be depreciated after revaluation, whereas investment properties are not depreciated.

(b)   **Extracts from Speculate's financial statements for the year ended 31 March 2013**

(workings in brackets in $000)

Statement of profit or loss and other comprehensive income

	$000
Depreciation of office building (A) (2,000/20 years × 6/12)	(50)
Gain on investment properties: A (2,340 – 2,300)	40
B (1,650 – 1,500)	150
Other comprehensive income (A see below)	350

Statement of financial position

Non-current assets

Investment properties (A and B) (2,340 + 1,650)	3,990

Equity

Revaluation reserve (A) (2,300 – (2,000 – 50))	350

In Speculate's consolidated financial statements property B would be accounted for under IAS 16 *Property, Plant and Equipment* and be classified as owner-occupied. Further information is required to determine the depreciation charge.

ACCA marking scheme		
		Marks
(a)	(i) 1 mark per valid point	3
	(ii) 1 mark per valid point	2
	Maximum	5
(b)	depreciation of property A for 6 months	1
	gain on investment properties A and B	1
	carrying amounts at 31 March 2013	1
	OCI/revaluation reserve at 31 March 2013	1
	property B classified as owner-occupied in consolidated financial statements	1
	Maximum	5
Total		**10**

156   BERTRAND

(a)   (i)   The interest rate (5%) for the convertible loan notes is lower because of the potential value of the conversion option. The cost of equivalent loan notes without the option is 8%, the difference is mainly due to the market expectation of the higher worth of Bertrand's equity shares (compared to the cash alternative) when the loan notes are due for redemption. From the entity's viewpoint, the conversion option means lower payments of interest (to help cash flow), but it will eventually cause a dilution of earnings.

(ii)   If the directors' treatment were acceptable, the use of the conversion option (compared to issuing non-convertible loans) would improve profit and earnings per share because of lower interest rates (and hence interest charges) and the company's gearing would be lower as the loan notes would not be shown as debt. However, this proposed treatment is not acceptable. A convertible loan note is a complex (hybrid) financial instrument and IFRS requires that the proceeds of the issue should be allocated between equity (the value of the option) and debt and the finance charge should be based on that of an equivalent non-convertible loan (8% in this case).

(b)   **Extracts from the financial statements of Bertrand**

Income statement for the year ended 30 September 2011

Finance costs (9,190 × 8%)	735
	rounded

Statement of financial position as at 30 September 2011

Equity	
Equity option	810
Non-current liabilities	
8% convertible loan notes ((9,190 × 1·08) − 500)	9,425
	rounded

Working

Year ended 30 September	Cash flow	Discount rate at	Discounted cash flows
	$000	8%	$000
2011	500	0·93	465
2012	500	0·86	430
2013	10,500	0·79	8,295
			———
value of debt component			9,190
value of equity option component (= balance)			810
			———
total proceeds			10,000
			———

ACCA marking scheme			
			Marks
(a)	(i)	1 mark per valid point	2
	(ii)	1 mark per valid point	3
(b)		finance cost	2
		value of equity option	1
		value of debt at 30 September 2011	2
			—
		Maximum	5
			—
Total			**10**
			—

157 SHAWLER

(a)   (i)   **Shawler statement of financial position (extract) as at 30 September 2012**

Carrying amount

Non-current assets: $

Furnace: main body   42,000   (48,000 – (60,000/10 years))

replaceable liner   4,000   (6,000 – (10,000/5 years))

Current liabilities

Government grant   1,200   (prior year amount transferred to the income statement)

Non-current liabilities

Government grant   7,200   (8,400 – 1,200 (12,000/10 years) transferred to current liabilities)

Environmental provision   19,440   (18,000 × 1·08)

(ii)   **Statement of profit or loss (extract) year ended 30 September 2012**

$

Depreciation (6,000 + 2,000)   8,000

Government grant (credited)   (1,200)

Finance costs (18,000 × 8%)   1,440

(b)   Although the legislation requiring the fitting of the filters has been passed, it does not come into force for two years. Even if Shawler has the intention of fitting the filters within this period, this still is not an obligating event; therefore no provision should be made for this future cost. Surprisingly, even if Shawler had not fitted the filters before the date required by the legislation, it would still not require a provision. However, there could be a separate provision required for a liability to a fine.

As it would be the fitting of the filters that directly causes the reduction in the environmental clean-up costs, it follows that until the filters are actually fitted, Shawler could not reduce its environmental provision.

ACCA marking scheme				
				Marks
(a)	(i)	furnace		1
		government grant (½ for split)		1
		environmental provision		1
				—
			Maximum	3
				—
	(ii)	depreciation		1
		government grant (credit)		1
		finance costs		1
				—
			Maximum	3
				—
(b)		not an obligating event as legislation not yet in force		1
		need not provide for cost of filters even when it is in force		1
		may need separate provision for a fine		1
		cannot reduce the environmental provision		1
				—
			Maximum	4
				—
Total				10
				—

158 FLIGHTLINE

Flightline – Statement of profit or loss for the year ended 31 March 2009

	$000
Depreciation (w (i))	13,800
Loss on write off of engine (w (iii))	6,000
Repairs – engine	3,000
– Exterior painting	2,000

Statement of financial position as at 31 March 2009

Non-current asset – Aircraft

	Cost	Accumulated depreciation	Carrying amount
	$000	$000	$000
Exterior (w (i))	120,000	84,000	36,000
Cabin fittings (w (ii))	29,500	21,500	8,000
Engines (w (iii))	19,800	3,700	16,100
	169,300	109,200	60,100

Workings (figures in brackets in $000)

(i) The exterior of the aircraft is depreciated at $6 million per annum (120,000/ 20 years). The cabin is depreciated at $5 million per annum (25,000/5 years). The engines would be depreciated by $500 ($18 million/36,000 hours) i.e. $250 each, per flying hour.

The carrying amount of the aircraft at 1 April 2008 is:

	Cost	Accumulated depreciation	Carrying amount
	$000	$000	$000
Exterior (13 years old)	120,000	78,000	42,000
Cabin (3 years old)	25,000	15,000	10,000
Engines (used 10,800 hours)	18,000	5,400	12600
	163,000	98,400	64,600

Depreciation for year to 31 March 2009:	$000
Exterior (no change)	6,000
Cabin fittings – six months to 30 September 2008 (5,000 × 6/12)	2,500
– six months to 31 March 2009 (w (ii))	4,000
Engines – six months to 30 September 2008 (500 × 1,200 hours)	600
– six months to 31 March 2009 ((400 + 300) w (iii))	700
	13,800

(ii) Cabin fittings – at 1 October 2008 the carrying amount of the cabin fittings is $7.5 million (10,000 – 2,500). The cost of improving the cabin facilities of $4.5 million should be capitalised as it led to enhanced future economic benefits in the form of substantially higher fares. The cabin fittings would then have a carrying amount of $12 million (7,500 + 4,500) and an unchanged remaining life of 18 months. Thus depreciation for the six months to 31 March 2009 is $4 million (12,000 × 6/18).

(iii) Engines – before the accident the engines (in combination) were being depreciated at a rate of $500 per flying hour. At the date of the accident each engine had a carrying amount of $6 million ((12,600 – 600)/2). This represents the loss on disposal of the written off engine. The repaired engine's remaining life was reduced to 15,000 hours. Thus future depreciation on the repaired engine will be $400 per flying hour, resulting in a depreciation charge of $400,000 for the six months to 31 March 2009. The new engine with a cost of $10.8 million and a life of 36,000 hours will be depreciated by $300 per flying hour, resulting in a depreciation charge of $300,000 for the six months to 31 March 2009. Summarising both engines:

	Cost	Accumulated depreciation	Carrying amount
	$000	$000	$000
Old engine	9,000	3,400	5,600
New engine	10,800	300	10,500
	19,800	3,700	16,100

Note: Marks are awarded for clear calculations rather than for detailed explanations. Full explanations are given for tutorial purposes

ACCA marking scheme	Marks
Statement of comprehensive income	
depreciation – exterior	1
– cabin fittings	2
– engines	2
loss on write off of engine repairs	1
Repairs	1
Statement of financial position	
carrying amount at 31 March 2009	3
Total	10

Examiner's comments

A significant number of candidates did not start this question and many more that did appeared to run out of time. There were no general issues here with candidates not understanding what they were meant to do or not reading the requirements properly, however many answers lacked a methodical approach meaning they got hopelessly lost in the detail. Generally the exterior structure of the aircraft was dealt with correctly although many capitalised the repainting costs (which is revenue expenditure). For the cabin fittings, the upgrade was often correctly capitalised but then the depreciation was calculated on (total) cost, not the new carrying amount and also over the wrong period. The engines caused the most problems. Candidates often tried to perform the calculations of them together, instead of separating them, and then became confused in what they were doing.

Conclusion

As reported in the introduction, the overall performance of candidates was rather disappointing with too many candidates pinning their hopes on passing by just learning the main topics or relying on numerical skills alone. There was evidence of poor examination technique, including poor planning, time management and question spotting. Markers reported that the scripts of poorly prepared candidates did not seem to have mastered the understanding and techniques examinable at F3. Basic depreciation, accruals and an inability to correctly classify items in the financial statements (e.g. receivables included in the statement of comprehensive income) were notable weaknesses of some of these candidates.

In fairness, many of the above comments on the individual questions have concentrated candidates' weak areas. This has been done for reasons of directing future study and highlighting poor techniques such that candidates can improve future performance. This does give a pessimistic view of performance, but I would like draw attention to a good number of excellent papers where it was apparent that candidates had done a great deal of studying and were rewarded appropriately.

159 APEX *Walk in the footsteps of a top tutor*

Key answer tips

This question focuses on IAS 23 Borrowing costs, being a specific element of accounting for tangible assets and should be a relatively straightforward question to answer and score well on if borrowing costs have been revised. The highlighted words are key phrases that markers are looking for.

(a)   Where borrowing costs are directly incurred on a 'qualifying asset', they must be capitalised as part of the cost of that asset. A qualifying asset may be a tangible or an intangible asset that takes a substantial period of time to get ready for its intended use or eventual sale. Property construction would be a typical example, but it can also be applied to intangible assets during their development period. Borrowing costs include interest based on its effective rate (which incorporates the amortisation of discounts, premiums and certain expenses) on overdrafts, loans and (some) other financial instruments and finance charges on finance leased assets. They may be based on specifically borrowed funds or on the weighted average cost of a pool of funds. Any income earned from the temporary investment of specifically borrowed funds would normally be deducted from the amount to be capitalised.

Capitalisation should commence when expenditure is being incurred on the asset, which is not necessarily from the date funds are borrowed. Capitalisation should cease when the asset is ready for its intended use, even though the funds may still be incurring borrowing costs. Also capitalisation should be suspended if there is a suspension of active development of the asset.

Any borrowing costs that are not eligible for capitalisation must be expensed. Borrowing costs cannot be capitalised for assets measured at fair value.

(b)   The finance cost of the loan must be calculated using the effective rate of 7.5%, so the total finance cost for the year ended 31 March 2010 is $750,000 ($10 million × 7.5%). As the loan relates to a qualifying asset, the finance cost (or part of it in this case) can be capitalised under IAS 23.

The Standard says that capitalisation commences from when expenditure is being incurred (1 May 2009) and must cease when the asset is ready for its intended use (28 February 2010); in this case a 10-month period. However, interest cannot be capitalised during a period where development activity is suspended; in this case the two months of July and August 2009. Thus only eight months of the year's finance cost can be capitalised = $500,000 ($750,000 × 8/12). The remaining four-months finance costs of $250,000 must be expensed. IAS 23 also says that interest earned from the temporary investment of specific loans should be deducted from the amount of finance costs that can be capitalised. However, in this case, the interest was earned during a period in which the finance costs were NOT being capitalised, thus the interest received of $40,000 would be credited to the statement of comprehensive income and not to the capitalised finance costs.

In summary:

	$
Statement of profit or loss for the year ended 31 March 2010:	
Finance cost (debit)	(250,000)
Investment income (credit)	40,000
Statement of financial position as at 31 March 2010:	
Property, plant and equipment (finance cost element only)	500,000

ACCA marking scheme		
		Marks
(a)	1 mark per valid point	5
(b)	use of effective rate of 7.5%	1
	capitalise for eight months	2
	charge to statement of comprehensive income	1
	interest received to statement of comprehensive income	1
		―
	Maximum	5
		―
Total		10
		―

Examiner's comments

This question was based on the relatively infrequently examined topic of borrowing costs and as such caught out many candidates who had not covered this in their revision. A considerable number of candidates did not attempt this question. Those that had studied the topic scored well thus answers tended to be very polarised, either very good or very poor.

Part (a) asked for the circumstances when borrowing costs should be capitalised. This should have proved straightforward. An answer such as 'Borrowing costs relating to assets that take a substantial time to complete are capitalised at the effective rate interest from the date construction starts and should end when the asset is ready for use.' would alone have attracted at least three of the five marks available for this part.

Further discussion of the suspension of capitalisation where construction activity is suspended and the deduction of any (temporary) investment income from capitalised cost would have been all that was necessary to gain the full marks.

Instead many answers just guessed at the rules or interpreted the requirement to be about what other costs could be capitalised during the construction of non-current assets (the topic of a recent past question).

Part (b) was a numerical example designed to put the above rules into practice. The main errors made by candidates were using the nominal/coupon rate of 6% instead of the effective rate of 7.5% to calculate the interest to be either capitalised or expensed and not correctly calculating the period of capitalisation. A number of candidates spent time calculating what the liability for the loan would be in the statement of financial position – this was not asked for and gained no marks.

160 BARSTEAD *Walk in the footsteps of a top tutor*

Key answer tips

This question not only required the calculation of EPS but also how the three different measures of profit can give the users of the financial statements differing impressions. To score well in this question you need to have a firm grasp of accounting for basic and diluted EPS. The highlighted words are key phrases that markers are looking for.

(a)   Whilst profit after tax (and its growth) is a useful measure, it may not give a fair representation of the true underlying earnings performance. In this example, users could interpret the large annual increase in profit after tax of 80% as being indicative of an underlying improvement in profitability (rather than what it really is: an increase in absolute profit). It is possible, even probable, that (some of) the profit growth has been achieved through the acquisition of other companies (acquisitive growth). Where companies are acquired from the proceeds of a new issue of shares, or where they have been acquired through share exchanges, this will result in a greater number of equity shares of the acquiring company being in issue. This is what appears to have happened in the case of Barstead as the improvement indicated by its earnings per share (EPS) is only 5% per annum. This explains why the EPS (and the trend of EPS) is considered a more reliable indicator of performance because the additional profits which could be expected from the greater resources (proceeds from the shares issued) is matched with the increase in the number of shares. Simply looking at the growth in a company's profit after tax does not take into account any increases in the resources used to earn them. Any increase in growth financed by borrowings (debt) would not have the same impact on profit (as being financed by equity shares) because the finance costs of the debt would act to reduce profit.

The calculation of a diluted EPS takes into account any potential equity shares in issue. Potential ordinary shares arise from financial instruments (e.g. convertible loan notes and options) that may entitle their holders to equity shares in the future. The diluted EPS is useful as it alerts existing shareholders to the fact that future EPS may be reduced as a result of share capital changes; in a sense it is a warning sign. In this case the lower increase in the diluted EPS is evidence that the (higher) increase in the basic EPS has, in part, been achieved through the increased use of diluting financial instruments. The finance cost of these instruments is less than the earnings their proceeds have generated leading to an increase in current profits (and basic EPS);

however, in the future they will cause more shares to be issued. This causes a dilution where the finance cost per potential new share is less than the basic EPS.

(b) (Basic) EPS for the year ended 30 September 2009

($15 million/43.25 million × 100)	34.7	cents
Comparative (basic) EPS (35 × 3.60/3.80)	33.2	cents

Effect of rights issue (at below market price)

100 shares at $3.80	380
25 shares at $2.80	70
	____
125 shares at $3.60 (calculated theoretical ex-rights value)	450

Weighted average number of shares

36 million × 3/12 × $3.80/$3.60	9.50	million
45 million × 9/12	33.75	million
	43.25	million

Diluted EPS for the year ended 30 September 2009

($15.6 million/45.75 million × 100)	34.1	cents
Adjusted earnings		
15 million + (10 million × 8% × 75%)	$15.6	million
Adjusted number of shares		
43.25 million + (10 million × 25/100)	45.75	million

(c) A rules-based accounting system is likely to be very descriptive and is generally considered to be a system which relies on a series of detailed rules or accounting requirements that prescribe how financial statements should be prepared. Such a system is considered less flexible, but often more comparable and consistent, than a principles-based system. Some would argue that rules-based systems can lead to looking for 'loopholes'. By contrast, a principles-based system relies on generally accepted accounting principles that are conceptually based and are normally underpinned by a set of key objectives. They are more flexible than a rules-based system, but they do require judgment and interpretation which could lead to inconsistencies between reporting entities and can sometimes lead to the manipulation of financial statements.

Because IFRSs are based on *The Conceptual Framework for Financial Reporting,* they are often regarded as being a principles-based system. Of course IFRSs do contain many rules and requirements (often lengthy and complex), but their critical feature is that IFRS 'rules' are based on underlying concepts. In reality most accounting systems have an element of both rules and principles and their designation as rules-based or principles-based depends on the relative importance and robustness of the principles compared to the volume and manner in which the rules are derived.

ACCA marking scheme			
			Marks
(a)	1 mark per valid point		4
		Maximum	4.0
(b)	Basic EPS for 2009		3.0
	Restated EPS for 2008		1.0
	Diluted EPS for 2009		2.0
		Maximum	6.0
(c)	One mark per sensible comment		5.0
Total			15

PREPARATION OF SINGLE COMPANY FINANCIAL STATEMENTS

161 LLAMA

Key answer tips

This published accounts question has a heavy IAS 16 focus so there are many easy marks available. For parts (a) and (b) you need to ensure that you set your answer up in advance outlining the proformas. Once these have been set up, keep moving through the question building up the answer as you go. Part (c) required the calculation of EPS following a rights issue of shares. Ensure that you use the profit figure calculated in part (a) to do this.

(a) **Llama – Statement of profit or loss – Year ended 30 September 2007**

	$000	$000
Revenue		180,400
Cost of sales (w (i))		(81,700)
Gross profit		98,700
Distribution costs (11,000 + 1,000 depreciation)	(12,000)	
Administrative expenses (12,500 + 1,000 depreciation)	(13,500)	(25,500)
Investment income	2,200	
Gain on fair value of investments (27,100 – 26,500)	600	2,800
Finance costs (w (ii))		(2,400)
Profit before tax		73,600
Income tax expense		
(18,700 – 400 – (11,200 – 10,000) deferred tax)		(17,100)
Profit for the period		56,500

Other comprehensive income	
Loss on revaluation	(3,000)
Total comprehensive income	53,500

(b) **Llama – Statement of financial position as at 30 September 2007**

	$000	$000
Assets		
Non-current assets		
Property, plant and equipment (w (iv))		228,500
Investments at fair value through profit and loss		27,100
		255,600
Current assets		
Inventory	37,900	
Trade receivables	35,100	73,000
Total assets		328,600
Equity and liabilities		
Equity		
Equity shares of 50 cents each ((60,000 + 15,000) w (iii))		75,000
Share premium (w (iii))	9,000	
Revaluation reserve (14,000 – 3,000 (w (iv)))	11,000	
Retained earnings (56,500 + 25,500)	82,000	102,000
		177,000
Non-current liabilities		
2% loan note (80,000 + 1,600 (w (ii)))	81,600	
Deferred tax (40,000 × 25%)	10,000	91,600
Current liabilities		
Trade payables	34,700	
Bank overdraft	6,600	
Current tax payable	18,700	60,000
Total equity and liabilities		328,600

Workings (monetary figures in brackets are in 000)

(i) Cost of sales:

	$000
Per question	89,200
Plant capitalised (w (iv))	(24,000)
Depreciation (w (iv)) – buildings	3,000
– plant	13,500
	81,700

(ii) The loan has been in issue for six months. The total finance charge should be based on the effective interest rate of 6%. This gives a charge of $2.4 million (80,000 × 6% × 6/12). As the actual interest paid is $800,000 an accrual (added to the carrying amount of the loan) of $1.6 million is required.

(iii) The rights issue was 30 million shares (60 million/50 cents is 120 million shares at 1 for 4) at a price of 80 cents this would increase share capital by $15 million (30 million × 50 cents) and share premium by $9 million (30 million × 30 cents).

(iv) Non-current assets/depreciation:

Land and buildings:

On 1 October 2006 the value of the buildings was $100 million (130,000 − 30,000 land). The remaining life at this date was 20 years, thus the annual depreciation charge will be $ million (3,000 to cost of sales and 1,000 each to distribution and administration). Prior to the revaluation at 30 September 2007 the carrying amount of the building was $95 million (100,000 − 5,000). With a revalued amount of $92 million, this gives a revaluation deficit of $3 million which should be debited to the revaluation reserve. The carrying amount of land and buildings at 30 September 2007 will be $122 million (92,000 buildings + 30,000 land (unchanged)).

Plant

The existing plant will be depreciated by $12 million ((128,000 − 32,000) × 12½%) and have a carrying amount of $84 million at 30 September 2007.

The plant manufactured for internal use should be capitalised at $24 million (6,000 + 4,000 + 8,000 + 6,000). Depreciation on this will be $1.5 million (24,000 × 12½% × 6/12). This will give a carrying amount of $22.5 million at 30 September 2007. Thus total depreciation for plant is $13.5 million with a carrying amount of $106.5 million (84,000 + 22,500)

	$000
Summarising the carrying amounts:	
Land and buildings	122,000
Plant	106,500
	———
Property, plant and equipment	228,500
	———

(c) **Earnings per share (eps) for the year ended 30 September 2007**

Theoretical ex rights price			$
Holding	4	at $1	4
Issue (1 for 4)	1	at 80 cents	0.8
	—		—
New holding	5	**TERP = 96 cents (bal.fig)**	4.8
	—		—

Weighted average number of shares

120,000,000	× 9/12 × **1/0.96**	93,750,000
150,000,000 (120 × 5/4)	× 3/12	37,500,000
		131,250,000

Earnings per share ($56,500,000/131,250,000) **43 cents**

Examiner's comments

Most candidates did well on this question scoring good marks. The main adjustments contained in the question were generally well understood and correctly accounted for. Again, in order to assist future studies, the common errors were:

– Confusion over the timing of the revaluation of the land and buildings. The question clearly stated that the revaluation was at the end of the year. This meant that the annual deprecation charge for the buildings should be based on the value at the beginning of the year (i.e. the value included in the trial balance) and the revaluation (giving a impairment/deficit in this example) should be based on the carrying amount of the asset after the year's depreciation had been deducted.

   Most candidates did correctly identify the capitalisation of the internally manufactured plant, although many did not realise that this occurred half way through the year necessitating time-apportioned depreciation.

– Another common error was to reduce cost of sales by the closing inventory; by definition cost of sales has already been adjusted for closing inventory.

– A number of candidates did not appreciate that the loan interest paid was for only six months and that the year's finance costs should be based on the effective interest rate of 6% rather than the nominal rate of 2%. Those that did correctly account for the accrued finance costs in the statement of comprehensive income often forgot to add it to the carrying amount of the loan in the statement of financial position.

– The tax calculation was often confused. The opening credit balance of $400,000 was often treated as charge (debit) and the adjustment for deferred tax was often taken as $40 million rather than 25% of $40 million.

– A very common and basic error was to include the bank overdraft in current assets.

– Answers to the calculation of the eps were very mixed. A significant number of candidates did not attempt it and those that did often struggled with effect of the rights issue on the ex-rights price and the weighting exercise.

ACCA marking scheme		
		Marks
(a)	Statement of profit or loss	
	Revenue	½
	Cost of sales	3½
	Distribution costs and administrative expenses	3
	Investment income and gain on investment	1½
	Finance costs	1½
	Tax	2
		───
		12
		───
(b)	Statement of financial position	
	Property, plant and equipment	3
	Investments	1
	Current assets	1
	Equity shares	1
	Share premium	1
	Revaluation reserve	1
	Retained earnings	1
	2% loan notes	1½
	Deferred tax	1
	Trade payables and overdraft	1
	Income tax provision	½
		───
		13
		───
(c)	Earnings per share	
	Calculation of theoretical ex rights price	1
	Rights fraction	1
	Weighted average number of shares (1 for time apportionment, 1 for applying fraction to start of year)	2
	Earnings and calculation of eps	1
		───
		5
		───
Total		25
		───

162 DEXON

Key answer tips

Part (a) required a recalculation of profit – you were expected to consider how the further information would therefore affect profit. Remember a credit entry to the statement of comprehensive income will increase profit whereas a debit entry will reduce profit. Part (b) required you to prepare a SOCIE, many easy marks could be gained here – you need to recognise that the share issue had already been recorded so you are required to work backwards to find the opening balances. Part (c) required you to restate the statement of financial position. An added complication in this question exists with deferred tax. You are required to calculate the deferred tax relating to the revaluation reserve as well the statement of comprehensive income movement.

(a)

	$000	$000
Retained profit for period per question		96,700
Dividends paid (w (i))		15,500
Draft profit for year ended 31 March 2008		112,200
Discovery of fraud (w (ii))		(2,500)
Goods on sale or return (w (iii))		(600)
Depreciation (w (iv)) – buildings (165,000/15 years)	11,000	
– plant (180,500 × 20%)	36,100	(47,100)
Increase in investments ((12,500 × 1,296/1,200) – 12,500)		1,000
Provision for income tax		(11,400)
Increase in deferred tax (w (v))		(800)
Recalculated profit for year ended 31 March 2008		50,800

(b) **Dexon – Statement of Changes in Equity – Year ended 31 March 2008**

	Ordinary shares $000	Share premium $000	Revaluation reserve $000	Retained earnings $000	Total $000
At 1 April 2007	200,000	30,000	18,000	12,300	260,300
Prior period adjustment (w (ii))				(1,500)	(1,500)
Restated earnings at 1 April 2007				10,800	
Rights issue (see below)	50,000	10,000			60,000
Total comprehensive income					
(from (a) and (w (iv))			4,800	50,800	55,600
Dividends paid (w (i))				(15,500)	(15,500)
At 31 March 2008	250,000	40,000	22,800	46,100	358,900

Rights issue: 250 million shares in issue after a rights issue of one for four would mean that 50 million shares were issued (250,000 × 1/5). As the issue price was $1.20, this would create $50 million of share capital and $10 million of share premium.

(c) **Dexon – Statement of financial position as at 31 March 2008:**

Non-current assets	$000	$000
Property (w (iv))		180,000
Plant (180,500 – 36,100 depreciation see (a))		144,400
Investments at fair value through profit and loss (12,500 + 1,000 see (a))		13,500
		337,900
Current assets		
Inventory (84,000 + 2,000 (w (iii)))	86,000	
Trade receivables (52,200 – 4,000 – 2,600 (w (ii) and (iii)))	45,600	
Bank	3,800	135,400
Total assets		473,300

Equity and liabilities		
Equity (from (b))		
Ordinary shares of $1 each		250,000
Share premium	40,000	
Revaluation reserve	22,800	
Retained earnings	46,100	108,900
		358,900
Non-current liabilities		
Deferred tax (19,200 + 2,000 (w (v)))		21,200
Current liabilities (81,800 + 11,400 income tax)		93,200
Total equity and liabilities		473,300

Workings (figures in brackets in $000)

(i) **Dividends paid**

The dividend in May 2007 would be $8 million (200 million shares at 4 cents) and in November 2007 would be $7.5 million (250 million shares × 3 cents). Total dividends would therefore have been $15.5 million.

(ii) The discovery of the fraud means that $4 million should be written off trade receivables. $1.5 million debited to retained earnings as a prior period adjustment (in the statement of changes in equity) and $2.5 written off in the statement of comprehensive income for the year ended 31 March 2008.

(iii) **Goods on sale or return**

The sales over which customers still have the right of return should not be included in Dexon's recognised revenue. The reversing effect is to reduce the relevant trade receivables by $2.6 million, increase inventory by $2 million (the cost of the goods (2,600 × 100/130)) and reduce the profit for the year by $600,000.

(iv) **Property**

The carrying amount of the property (after the year's depreciation) is $174 million (185,000 – 11,000). A valuation of $180 million would create a revaluation surplus of $6 million of which $1.2 million (6,000 × 20%) would be transferred to deferred tax.

(v) **Deferred tax**

An increase in the taxable temporary differences of $10 million would create a transfer (credit) to deferred tax of $2 million (10,000 × 20%). Of this $1.2 million relates to the revaluation of the property and is debited to the revaluation reserve. The balance, $800,000, is charged to the statement of comprehensive income.

(d)   Prior year errors relate to either failing to use, or deliberate misuse of, information that was available when the financial statement of those periods were authorised for issue. This information could reasonably have been expected to have been taken into account for the preparation of those financial statements.

Prior year errors are applied retrospectively, as if the error had never occurred. This involves restating the prior year comparative financial statements, and potentially making an adjustment in the opening retained earnings.

In this case, the credit controller had committed a fraud in the prior year, therefore knowing that the financial statements were misleading. As the prior year financial statements have not been given, the only adjustment made has been to adjust the opening retained earnings in the statement of changes in equity.

A provision is an accounting estimate. Provisions are liabilities of uncertain timing or amount, and the final amount often depends on the future outcome of certain events, such as a court case.

As long as management apply their best estimate when creating a provision, any changes between the estimated and final amounts are applied prospectively. This change is applied in the year that the new information becomes available, and no prior year adjustment is required.

Examiner's comments

This question asked candidates to recalculate the annual profit, prepare a statement of changes in equity (SOCIE) and redraft a given statement of financial position after accounting for a series of adjustments. The adjustments required were for: reversing a sale or return transaction, depreciation (after a revaluation), an increase in the value of investments, correcting for a discovered fraud, tax and deferred tax and dealing with the effects of a share issue and dividend payments.

For those that knew how to tackle this type of question, the recalculation/restatement of the annual profit was done quite well with many candidates gaining 5 or 6 out of the 8 marks available. The most common errors were:

-    failing to add back the dividends to the retained earnings for the year to give a starting point for the profit for the year

-    adjusting for the sales revenue rather than the profit made on goods subject to an outstanding sale and return agreement (some adjusted for both the sales revenue and the cost of sales which was marked as correct)

-    taking the revaluation of the land and buildings as if it were at the beginning of the year (the question clearly stated it was at the end of the year)

-    deducting the whole of the cost of a fraud from the current year's profit (part of it related to the previous year and should have been treated as a prior period adjustment in the SOCIE)

-    taking the whole of the increase in deferred tax to the statement of comprehensive income (part of it related to the property revaluation and should also have been included in the SOCIE). Many of the errors made in the recalculation of the profit for the year were carried on to the SOCIE or/and the statement of financial position. Additionally in the SOCIE many candidates did not realise that the share issue had already been accounted for (the question made this quite clear) thus they treated the figures in the statement of financial position as if they were at the beginning of the year rather than at the end of the year and consequently calculated the wrong share capital and share premium movements. Very few included the deferred tax effect of the revaluation and an incorrect calculation of the dividends was also common (or omitted completely).

The statement of financial position was generally well done and most of the errors that were made generally related to the following through of earlier (previously mentioned) errors. For example it was common not to eliminate the sale and return receivable and not to include the related inventory in current assets. Strangely a few candidates spent time trying to calculate an ex-rights price for the share issue. This was not asked for.

ACCA marking scheme			
			Marks
(a)	Adjustments:		
	add back dividends		1
	balance of fraud loss		1
	goods on sale or return		1
	depreciation charges		2
	investment gain		1
	taxation provision		1
	deferred tax		1
	Maximum		8
(b)	Statement of changes in equity		
	balances b/f		1
	restated earnings b/f		1
	rights issue		2
	total comprehensive income		3
	dividends paid		1
	Maximum		8
(c)	Statement of financial position		
	Property		1
	Plant		1
	Investment		1
	Inventory		1
	trade receivables		2
	equity from (b)		1
	deferred tax		1
	current liabilities		1
	Maximum		9
(d)	Explanation of prior year error		1
	Retrospective application		1
	Change to Dexon's retained earnings in the scenario		1
	Change in provision represents accounting estimate		1
	Accounting estimates applied prospectively		1
	Other sensible comments		1 each
			Max 5
	Total		30

163 CAVERN

Key answer tips

This is a typical style question requiring the preparation of financial statements from a trial balance. This is a time consuming question so ensure you get the straightforward marks for tax and non-current assets. Be wary of the share issue that has already been recorded – you will need to work backwards to determine the value of the share issued and the opening balance.

(a) **Cavern – Statement of profit or loss and other comprehensive income for the year ended 30 September 2010**

	$000
Revenue	182,500
Cost of sales (w (i))	(137,400)
Gross profit	45,100
Distribution costs	(8,500)
Administrative expenses (25,000 – 18,500 dividends (w (iii)))	(6,500)
Loss on investments (700 – (15,800 – 13,500))	(1,600)
Finance costs (300 + 400 (w (ii)) + 3,060 (w (iv)))	(3,760)
Profit before tax	24,740
Income tax expense (5,600 + 900 – 250 (w (v)))	(6,250)
Profit for the year	18,490
Other comprehensive income	
Gain on revaluation of land and buildings (w (ii))	800
Total comprehensive income	19,290

(b) **Cavern – Statement of changes in equity for the year ended 30 September 2010**

	Share capital $000	Share premium $000	Revaluation reserve $000	Retained earnings $000	Total equity $000
Balance at 1 October 2009	40,000	nil	7,000	15,100	62,100
Rights issue (w (iii))	10,000	11,000			21,000
Dividends (w (iii))				(18,500)	(18,500)
Comprehensive income			800	18,490	19,290
Balance at 30 September 2010	50,000	11,000	7,800	15,090	83,890

(c)   **Cavern – Statement of financial position as at 30 September 2010**

Assets	$000	$000
Non-current assets		
Property, plant and equipment (41,800 + 51,100 (w (ii)))		92,900
Financial asset investments		13,500
		106,400
Current assets		
Inventory	19,800	
Trade receivables	29,000	
		48,800
Total assets		155,200
Equity and liabilities		
Equity (see (b) above)		
Equity shares of 20 cents each		50,000
Share premium	11,000	
Revaluation reserve	7,800	
Retained earnings	15,090	
		33,890
		83,890
Non-current liabilities		
Provision for decontamination costs (4,000 + 400 (w (ii)))	4,400	
8% loan note (w (iv))	31,260	
Deferred tax (w (v))	3,750	
		39,410
Current liabilities		
Trade payables	21,700	
Bank overdraft	4,600	
Current tax payable	5,600	
		31,900
Total equity and liabilities		155,200

Workings (monetary figures in brackets in $'000)

(i)   **Cost of sales**

Per trial balance	128,500
Depreciation of building (36,000/18 years)	2,000
Depreciation of new plant (14,000/10 years)	1,400
Depreciation of existing plant and equipment	5,500
((67,400 – 10,000 – 13,400) × 12.5%)	
	137,400

(ii) **Property, plant and equipment**

The new plant of $10 million should be grossed up by the provision for the present value of the estimated future decontamination costs of $4 million to give a gross cost of $14 million. The 'unwinding' of the provision will give rise to a finance cost in the current year of $400,000 (4,000 × 10%) to give a closing provision of $4.4 million.

The gain on revaluation and carrying amount of the land and building will be:

Valuation – 30 September 2009	43,000
Building depreciation (w (i))	(2,000)
Carrying amount before revaluation	41,000
Revaluation – 30 September 2010	41,800
Gain on revaluation	800

The carrying amount of the plant and equipment will be:

New plant (14,000 – 1,400)	12,600
Existing plant and equipment (67,400 – 10,000 – 13,400 – 5,500)	38,500
	51,100

(iii) **Rights issue/dividends paid**

Based on 250 million (50 million × 5 – as shares are 20 cents each) shares in issue at 30 September 2010, a rights issue of 1 for 4 on 1 April 2010 would have resulted in the issue of 50 million new shares (250 million – (250 million × 4/5)). This would be recorded as share capital of $10 million (50,000 × 20 cents) and share premium of $11 million (50,000 × (42 cents – 20 cents)).

The dividend of 3 cents per share paid on 30 November 2009 would have been based on 200 million shares and been $6 million. The dividend of 5 cents per share paid on 31 May 2010 would have been based on 250 million shares and been $12.5 million. Therefore the total dividends paid, incorrectly included in administrative expenses, were $18.5 million.

(iv) **Loan note**

The finance cost of the loan note, at the effective rate of 10% applied to the carrying amount of the loan note of $30.6 million, is $3.06 million. The interest actually paid is $2.4 million. The difference between these amounts of $660,000 (3,060 – 2,400) is added to the carrying amount of the loan note to give $31.26 million (30,600 + 660) for inclusion as a non-current liability in the statement of financial position.

(v) **Deferred tax**

Provision required at 30 September 2010 (15,000 × 25%)	3,750
Provision at 1 October 2009	(4,000)
Credit (reduction in provision) to income statement	250

(d) **Earnings per share:**

EPS = $18,490,000/235,810,811 **(W1)** = 7.8c

(W1) Weighted average number of shares

Step 1 – Theoretical ex-rights price (TERP)

4 shares @ $0.82 =	$3.28
1 share @ $0.42 =	$0.42
5 shares	$3.70

TERP = $3.70/5 = $0.74

Step 2 – Bonus fraction

$$\frac{0.82}{0.74}$$

Step 3 – Weighted average number of shares (WANS)

Date	Number	Fraction of year	Rights fraction	Weighted Average
1 October	200,000,000	6/12	0.82/0.74	110,810,811
1 April	250,000,000	9/12		125,000,000
				235,810,811

Re-stated 2009 EPS = 8c × (0.74/0.82) = 7.2c

ACCA marking scheme		
		Marks
(a)	statement of profit or loss	
	Revenue	1½
	cost of sales	3
	distribution costs	½
	administrative expenses	1
	investment income loss	1
	finance costs	2½
	income tax expense	2
	gain on revaluation of land and buildings	½
	Maximum	11
(b)	Statement of changes in equity	
	balances b/f	½
	rights issue	1
	dividends	1
	revaluation gain	½
	profit for year	1
	Maximum	4

(c)	statement of financial position		
	property, plant and equipment		2½
	financial asset investments		½
	inventory		½
	trade receivables		½
	contamination provision		1
	8% loan note		1
	deferred tax		1
	trade payables		½
	bank overdraft		½
	current tax payable		1
		Maximum	9
(d)	Theoretical ex-rights price		1
	Rights fraction		1
	Weighted average number of shares		2
	Use of own PAT from part (a)		½
	Restated 2009 EPS		½
			5
	Total		30

164 CANDEL *Walk in the footsteps of a top tutor*

Key answer tips

Make sure you remember to complete all parts of the question – a statement of changes in equity is required as well as a statement of comprehensive income and statement of financial position. Be wary of the revaluation. The revaluation takes place at the end of the year, therefore a full year depreciation should be applied before you undertake the revaluation.

(a) **Candel – Statement of profit or loss and other comprehensive income for the year ended 30 September 2008**

	$000
Revenue (300,000 – 2,500)	297,500
Cost of sales (w (i))	(225,400)
Gross profit	72,100
Distribution costs	(14,500)
Administrative expenses (22,200 – 400 + 100 see note below)	(21,900)
Finance costs (200 + 1,200 (w (ii)))	(1,400)
Profit before tax	34,300

(Income tax expense (11,400 + (6,000 − 5,800 deferred tax))	(11,600)
Profit for the year	22,700
Other comprehensive income	
Loss on leasehold property revaluation (w (iii))	(4,500)
Total comprehensive income for the year	18,200

Note: As it is considered that the outcome of the legal action against Candel is unlikely to succeed (only a 20% chance) it is inappropriate to provide for any damages. The potential damages are an example of a contingent liability which should be disclosed (at $2 million) as a note to the financial statements. The unrecoverable legal costs are a liability (the start of the legal action is a past event) and should be provided for in full.

(b)   **Candel – Statement of changes in equity for the year ended 30 September 2008**

	Equity shares	Revaluation reserve	Retained earnings	Total equity
	$000	$000	$000	$000
Balances at 1 October 2007	50,000	10,000	24,500	84,500
Dividend			(6,000)	(6,000)
Comprehensive income		(4,500)	22,700	18,200
Balances at 30 September 2008	50,000	5,500	41,200	96,700

(c)   **Candel – Statement of financial position as at 30 September 2008**

	$000	$000
Assets		
Non-current assets (w (iii))		
Property, plant and equipment (43,000 + 38,400)		81,400
Development costs		14,800
		96,200
Current assets		
Inventory	20,000	
Trade receivables	43,100	63,100
Total assets		159,300
Equity and liabilities:		
Equity (from (b))		
Equity shares of 25 cents each		50,000
Revaluation reserve	5,500	
Retained earnings	41,200	46,700
		96,700
Non-current liabilities		
Deferred tax	6,000	
8% redeemable preference shares (20,000 + 400 (w (ii)))	20,400	26,400

Current liabilities

Trade payables (23,800 – 400 + 100 – re legal action)	23,500	
Bank overdraft	1,300	
Current tax payable	11,400	36,200

Total equity and liabilities	159,300

Workings (figures in brackets in $000)

(i) **Cost of sales:**

	$000
Per trial balance	204,000
Depreciation (w (iii)) – leasehold property	2,500
– plant and equipment	9,600
Loss on disposal of plant (4,000 – 2,500)	1,500
Amortisation of development costs (w (iii))	4,000
Research and development expenses (1,400 + 2,400 (w (iii)))	3,800
	225,400

(ii)

Tutorial note

This requires knowledge of accounting for financial instruments under IAS 32 &IFRS 9.

The finance cost of $1.2 million for the preference shares is based on the effective rate of 12% applied to $20 million issue proceeds of the shares for the six months they have been in issue (20m × 12% × 6/12). The dividend paid of $800,000 is based on the nominal rate of 8%. The additional $400,000 (accrual) is added to the carrying amount of the preference shares in the statement of financial position. As these shares are redeemable they are treated as debt and their dividend is treated as a finance cost.

(iii) **Non-current assets:**

Leasehold property

Valuation at 1 October 2007	50,000
Depreciation for year (20 year life)	(2,500)
Carrying amount at date of revaluation	47,500
Valuation at 30 September 2008	(43,000)
Revaluation deficit	4,500

Tutorial note

Remember to write off the disposed asset, both cost and b/fwd accumulated depreciation before calculating the current year depreciation charge.

	$000
Plant and equipment per trial balance (76,600 – 24,600)	52,000
Disposal (8,000 – 4,000)	(4,000)
	48,000
Depreciation for year (20%)	(9,600)
Carrying amount at 30 September 2008	38,400

Tutorial note

Remember research costs are to be expensed and development costs are to be capitalised only when the recognition criteria in IAS38 are met. In this question- the directors do not become confident that the project will be successful until 1 April – therefore development costs on the new project in January – March must be expensed.

Capitalised/deferred development costs	
Carrying amount at 1 October 2007 (20,000 – 6,000)	14,000
Amortised for year (20,000 × 20%)	(4,000)
Capitalised during year (800 × 6 months)	4,800
Carrying amount at 30 September 2008	14,800

Note: Development costs can only be treated as an asset from the point where they meet the recognition criteria in IAS 38 *Intangible assets*. Thus development costs from 1 April to 30 September 2008 of $4.8 million (800 × 6 months) can be capitalised. These will not be amortised as the project is still in development. The research costs of $1.4 million plus three months' development costs of $2.4 million (800 × 3 months) (i.e. those incurred before the criteria were met) must be expensed.

(d)   The damage would be a non-adjusting event, as the conditions (the storm damage) did not exist at the year end.

As it is a non-adjusting event, no double entries would need to be made, but a disclosure note should be included. This disclosure note would include a description of the event as well as any estimated financial effect and other consequences such as delays in production.

If the building was insured, the disclosure note would include the potential amount and timing of any insurance reimbursements.

If the building was uninsured, then the event may mean that Candel are unable to continue as a going concern. If this is the case, then the financial statements will need to be produced on the break-up basis. This would mean that all assets would be held at their sale values, with all assets and liabilities being classed as 'current'.

Examiner's comments

This was a fairly standard question requiring candidates to prepare an statement of profit or loss, a statement of financial position and a statement of changes in equity (SOCIE) after accounting for a series of adjustments.

The adjustments required were for depreciation (after a revaluation), correcting a sale of plant included as a revenue sale, capitalisation of development costs, dealing with a contingent liability, using the effective interest rate on preference shares and current and deferred tax.

The ability to produce financial statements from a trial balance seems well understood, but some of the adjustments created difficulties:

— careless mistake was to add back the sale proceeds of the plant to revenues (it should have been deducted)

— timing of the revaluation of a leasehold property was at the end of the period, but many candidates answered as if it was at the beginning of the period

— research and development caused many problems. Development costs can only be capitalised from the point at which management become confident of the success of the project. Up to this point they must be written off along with research expenditure. Very few candidates could put this into practice.

— reversal of a provision for a contingent liability (they should not be provide for); however the associated unrecoverable legal costs should have been provided for. Candidates often only got one of these two adjustments correct. A similar error occurred with the related current liability.

— deferred tax caused problems; ether the movement was credited to income (it should have been debited) or the whole of the provision was charged to income (rather than the movement).

The statement of financial position was generally well answered when allowing for 'knock on' errors from the statement of comprehensive income calculations.

The SOCIE was more mixed; it was often completely ignored and errors such as including in the SOCIE the issue of the redeemable preference shares and their dividend (they are debt) and not including the equity dividend.

---

165 PRICEWELL

(a) **Pricewell – Statement of profit or loss for the year ended 31 March 2009:**

	$000
Revenue (310,000 + 22,000 (w (i)) – 6,400 (w (ii)))	325,600
Cost of sales (w (iii))	(255,100)
Gross profit	70,500
Distribution costs	(19,500)
Administrative expenses	(27,500)
Finance costs (4,160 (w (v)) + 1,248 (w (vi)))	(5,408)
Profit before tax	18,092
Income tax expense (4,500 +700 – (8,400 – 5,600 deferred tax)	(2,400)
Profit for the year	15,692

(b) **Pricewell – Statement of financial position as at 31 March 2009:**

Assets	$000	$000
Non-current assets		
Property, plant and equipment (24,900 + 41,500 w (iv))		66,400
Current assets		
Inventory	28,200	
Amount due from customer (w (i))	17,100	
Trade receivables	33,100	
Bank	5,500	83,900
Total assets		150,300
Equity and liabilities:		
Equity shares of 50 cents each		40,000
Retained earnings (w (vii))		12,592
		52,592
Non-current liabilities		
Deferred tax	5,600	
Finance lease obligation (w (vi))	5,716	
6% Redeemable preference shares (41,600 + 1,760 (w (v)))	43,360	54,676
Current liabilities		
Trade payables	33,400	
Finance lease obligation (10,848 – 5,716) (w (vi)))	5,132	
Current tax payable	4,500	43,032
Total equity and liabilities		150,300

Workings (figures in brackets in $000)

		$000
(i)	**Construction contract:**	
	Selling price	50,000
	Estimated cost	
	To date	(12,000)
	To complete	(10,000)
	Plant	(8,000)
	Estimated profit	20,000

Work done is agreed at $22 million so the contract is 44% complete (22,000/50,000).

	$000
Revenue	22,000
Cost of sales (= balance)	(13,200)
Profit to date (44% × 20,000)	8,800

	$000
Cost incurred to date materials and labour	12,000
Plant depreciation (8,000 × 6/24 months)	2,000
Profit to date	8,800
	22,800
Cash received	(5,700)
Amount due from customer	17,100

(ii) Pricewell is acting as an agent (not the principal) for the sales on behalf of Trilby. Therefore the statement of comprehensive income should only include $1.6 million (20% of the sales of $8 million). Therefore $6.4 million (8,000 − 1,600) should be deducted from revenue and cost of sales. It would also be acceptable to show agency sales (of $1.6 million) separately as other income.

Cost of sales

	$000
Per question	234,500
Contract (w (i))	13,200
Agency cost of sales (w (ii))	(6,400)
Depreciation (w (iv)) – leasehold property	1,800
– owned plant ((46,800 − 12,800) × 25%)	8,500
– leased plant (20,000 × 25%)	5,000
Surplus on revaluation of leasehold property (w (iv))	(1,500)
	255,100

	$000

(iv) Non-current assets

Leasehold property	
valuation at 31 March 2008	25,200
depreciation for year (14 year life remaining)	(1,800)
carrying amount at date of revaluation valuation at 31 March 2009	23,400
valuation at 31 March 2008	(24,900)
revaluation surplus (to statement of comprehensive income – see below)	1,500

The $1.5 million revaluation surplus is credited to the statement of comprehensive income as this is the partial reversal of the $2.8 million impairment loss recognised in the statement of comprehensive income in the previous period (i.e. year ended 31 March 2008).

Plant and equipment

– owned (46,800 – 12,800 – 8,500)	25,500
– leased (20,000 – 5,000 – 5,000)	10,000
– contract (8,000 – 2,000 (w (i)))	6,000
Carrying amount at 31 March 2009	41,500

(v) The finance cost of $4,160,000 for the preference shares is based on the effective rate of 10% applied to $41.6 million balance at 1 April 2008. The accrual of $1,760,000 (4,160 – 2,400 dividend paid) is added to the carrying amount of the preference shares in the statement of financial position. As these shares are redeemable they are treated as debt and their dividend is treated as a finance cost.

(vi) Finance lease liability

balance at 31 March 2008	15,600
interest for year at 8%	1,248
lease rental paid 31 March 2009	(6,000)
total liability at 31 March 2009	10,848
interest next year at 8%	868
lease rental due 31 March 2010	(6,000)
total liability at 31 March 2010	5,716

(vii) Retained earnings

balance at 1 April 2008	4,900
profit for year	15,692
equity dividend paid	(8,000)
balance at 31 March 2009	12,592

(c) In revenue relating to both goods and services, the amount of revenue must be measured reliably. There must also be probably economic benefits and the costs incurred or to be incurred must be capable of reliable measurement.

Revenue relating to the sale of goods also must mean that the risks and rewards associated with the goods have been transferred to the buyer.

Revenue relating to the rendering of services can be recognised if the stage of completion can be measured reliably.

In relation to the construction contract, a service is being provided, in the form of building an asset for the customer. The revenue is therefore recognised on a stage of completion basis. If the costs to complete could not be measured, then the revenue could only be recognised to the level of recoverable costs.

In relation to the agency transaction, the revenue can be recognised as Pricewell have no more risks and rewards in relation to the transaction. However, as an agent, Pricewell's revenue only consists of their commission.

ACCA marking scheme		
		Marks
(a)	Statement of comprehensive income	
	Revenue	2
	Cost of sales	5
	Distribution costs	½
	Administrative expenses	½
	Finance costs	2
	Income tax expense	2
		___
	Maximum	12
(b)	Statement of financial position	
	Property, plant and equipment	2½
	Inventory	½
	Due on construction contract	2
	Trade receivables	½
	Bank	½
	Equity shares	½
	Retained earnings (1 for dividend)	1½
	Deferred tax	1
	Finance lease – non-current liability	½
	Preference shares	1
	Trade payables	½
	Finance lease – current liability	1
	Current tax payable	1
		___
	Maximum	13
		___
(c)	Criteria for revenue recognition	2
	Criteria for goods/services	2
	Application to scenario	2
		___
		5 max
		___
Total		30
		___

166 SANDOWN

Key answer tips

This question required the preparation of a statement of profit or loss and a statement of financial position and had the usual published accounts adjustments such as tax and non-current asset accounting. Be wary when dealing with the convertible loan this has already been accounted for in 2008 and you are now required to account for the second year of the convertible loan.

(a) **Sandown – Statement of profit or loss for the year ended 30 September 2009**

	$000
Revenue (380,000 – 4,000 (w (i)))	376,000
Cost of sales (w (ii))	(265,300)
Gross profit	110,700
Distribution costs	(17,400)
Administrative expenses (50,500 – 12,000 (w (iii)))	(38,500)
Investment income (1,300 + 2,500 (w (iv))	3,800
Finance costs (w (v))	(1,475)
Profit before tax	57,125
Income tax expense (16,200 + 2,100 – 1,500 (w (vi)))	(16,800)
Profit for the year	40,325

(b) **Sandown – Statement of financial position as at 30 September 2009**

	$000	$000
Assets		
Non-current assets		
Property, plant and equipment (w (vii))		67,500
Intangible – brand (15,000 – 2,500 (w (ii)))		12,500
Investment property (w (iv))		29,000
		109,000
Current assets		
Inventory	38,000	
Trade receivables	44,500	
Bank	8,000	90,500
Total assets		199,500

Equity and liabilities

Equity

Equity shares of 20 cents each		50,000
Equity option		2,000
Retained earnings (33,260 + 40,325 – 12,000 dividend (w (iii)))		61,585
		113,585

Non-current liabilities

Deferred tax (w (vi))	3,900	
Deferred income (w (i))	2,000	
5% convertible loan note (w (v))	18,915	24,815

Current liabilities

Trade payables	42,900	
Deferred income (w (i))	2,000	
Current tax payable	16,200	61,100

Total equity and liabilities		199,500

Workings (figures in brackets in $000)

(i) IAS 18 Revenue requires that where sales revenue includes an amount for after sales servicing and support costs then a proportion of the revenue should be deferred. The amount deferred should cover the cost and a reasonable profit (in this case a gross profit of 40%) on the services. As the servicing and support is for three years and the date of the sale was 1 October 2008, revenue relating to two years' servicing and support provision must be deferred: ($1.2 million × 2/0.6) = $4 million. This is shown as $2 million in both current and non-current liabilities.

(ii) **Cost of sales**

Per question		246,800
Depreciation	– building (50,000/50 years – see below)	1,000
	– plant and equipment (42,200 – 19,700) × 40%))	9,000
Amortisation	– brand (1,500 + 2,500 – see below)	4,000
Impairment of brand (see below)		4,500
		265,300

The cost of the building of $50 million (63,000 – 13,000 land) has accumulated depreciation of $8 million at 30 September 2008 which is eight years after its acquisition. Thus the life of the building must be 50 years. The brand is being amortised at $3 million per annum (30,000/10 years). The impairment occurred half way through the year, thus amortisation of $1.5 million should be charged prior to calculation of the impairment loss. At the date of the impairment review the brand had a carrying amount of $19.5 million (30,000 – (9,000 + 1,500)). The recoverable amount of the brand is its fair value of $15 million (as this is higher than its value in use of $12 million) giving an impairment loss of $4.5 million (19,500 – 15,000). Amortisation of $2.5 million (15,000/3 years × 6/12) is required for the second-half of the year giving total amortisation of $4 million for the full year.

(iii) A dividend of 4.8 cents per share would amount to $12 million (50 million × 5 (i.e. shares are 20 cents each) × 4.8 cents). This is not an administrative expense but a distribution of profits that should be accounted for through equity.

(iv) The gain on the investment property is shown below

Fair value at 1 October 2008	26,500
Fair value at 30 September 2009	29,000
	———
Gain on investment property	2,500
	———

The investment property is to be reported in the statement of financial position at fair value of $29 million at 30 September 2009 which gives a fair value increase (credited to the statement of comprehensive income) of $2.5 million.

(v) The finance cost of the convertible loan note is based on its effective rate of 8% applied to $18,440,000 carrying amount at 1 October 2008 = $1,475,000 (rounded). The accrual of $475,000 (1,475 – 1,000 interest paid) is added to the carrying amount of the loan note giving a figure of $18,915,000 (18,440 + 475) in the statement of financial position at 30 September 2009.

(vi) **Deferred tax**

Credit balance required at 30 September 2009 (13,000 × 30%)	3,900
Balance at 1 October 2008	(5,400)
	———
Credit (reduction in balance) to statement of comprehensive income	1,500
	———

(vii) **Non-current assets**

Freehold property (63,000 – (8,000 + 1,000)) (w (ii))	54,000
Plant and equipment (42,200 – (19,700 + 9,000)) (w (ii))	13,500
	———
Property, plant and equipment	67,500
	———

(c) Diluted earnings per share (DEPS) acts as a warning to the shareholders, and should be shown alongside basic earnings per share (EPS). Diluted earnings per share shows how the current EPS figure could fall in the future based on items that are currently in existence, such as convertible loans or options.

This can aid the predictive nature of financial statements as shareholders are given information that could potentially occur in the future. This increases the relevance of the financial statements and provides information which could affect the decisions taken by the users.

In the scenario, Sandown has convertible loans in issue, and the DEPS figure will be calculated by looking at two items. Firstly, Sandown's profit will increase if the loans are converted as there will no longer be the finance cost in the statement of profit or loss. As interest is tax deductible, the increase in earnings will consist of the interest saved less and additional tax payable on the profits.

The second item is that the number of shares will increase. From the scenario, it can be calculated that an additional 10 million shares will be issued ($20m × 50/100).

The additional earnings are added to the current profit, with the additional shares added to the current number of shares for the calculation of diluted EPS.

Examiner's comments

A 'familiar' question requiring candidates to prepare a statement of comprehensive income and a statement of financial position. A series of adjustments were required: for deferred revenue, a dividend paid, an effective interest rate calculation, basic depreciation, taxation and the impairment and amortisation of a brand.

As with question 1 this was a popular question and many candidates scored well. The ability to produce financial statements from a trial balance seems well understood, but some of the adjustments created difficulties:

- few candidates correctly calculated the amount of revenue to be deferred in relation to a sale (of $16 million) with ongoing service support. Most candidates deferred the whole of the revenue rather than the amount of the support costs (plus appropriate profit) relating to the remaining two years of service support. Some candidates increased revenue rather than defer it and some thought it was an in-substance loan

- many candidates applied the effective rate of interest (8%) to the nominal amount ($20 million) of a convertible loan rather than its carrying amount of $18.44 million. A few candidates made complicated calculations of the split between debt and equity for the loan not realising that it was the second year after its issue and the split had been made a year before

- most candidates got the taxation aspects correct, but there were still some basic errors such as charging the whole of the deferred tax provision to income (rather than the movement) and treating the underpayment of tax in the previous period as a credit.

- it was worrying that a number of candidates made basic errors on straight forward depreciation calculations. Some used the straight line method for the plant (not reading the question properly which stated the use of the reducing balance method) and some charged the accumulated depreciation to cost of sales rather than the charge for the period. Amortisation and impairment of the brand caused many problems; not calculating two 6 month charges (before and after the impairment) and not using the (higher) realisable value of the brand as the basis for the impairment charge.

The statement of financial position was generally well answered; most problems were follow-on errors from mistakes made in the statement of comprehensive income. A number of candidates are still incorrectly treating dividends as part of the statement of comprehensive income. Overall, a well-answered question.

---

167 HIGHWOOD

(a) **Highwood – Statement of profit or loss and other comprehensive income for the year ended 31 March 2011**

	$000
Revenue	339,650
Cost of sales (w (i))	(216,950)
Gross profit	122,700
Distribution costs	(27,500)
Administrative expenses (30,700 – 1,300 + 600 allowance (w (ii)))	(30,000)
Finance costs (w (iii))	(2,848)
Profit before tax	62,352
Income tax expense (19,400 – 800 + 400 (w (iv)))	(19,000)
Profit for the year	43,352
Other comprehensive income:	
Gain on revaluation of property (w (i))	15,000
Deferred tax on revaluation (w (i))	(3,750)
Total comprehensive income	54,602

(b) **Highwood – Statement of changes in equity for the year ended 31 March 2011**

	Share capital $000	Equity option $000	Revaluation reserve $000	Retained earnings $000	Total equity $000
Balance at 1 April 2010 (see below)	56,000	nil	nil	7,000	63,000
8% loan note issue (w (iii))		1,524			1,524
Dividend paid (w (v))				(5,600)	(5,600)
Comprehensive income			11,250	43,352	54,602
Balance at 31 March 2011	56,000	1,524	11,250	44,752	113,526

Note: the retained earnings of $1·4 million in the trial balance is after deducting the dividend paid of $5·6 million (w (v)), therefore the retained earnings at 1 April 2010 were $7 million.

(c) **Highwood – Statement of financial position as at 31 March 2011**

Assets	$000	$000
Non-current assets		
Property, plant and equipment (77,500 + 40,000) (w (i))		117,500
Current assets		
Inventory (36,000 – 2,700 + 6,000) (w (i))	39,300	
Trade receivables (47,100 + 10,000 – 600 allowance) (w (ii))	56,500	95,800
		———
Total assets		213,300
		———
Equity and liabilities		
Equity (see answer (ii))		
Equity shares of 50 cents each		56,000
Other component of equity – equity option		1,524
Revaluation reserve		11,250
Retained earnings		44,752
		———
		113,526
Non-current liabilities		
Deferred tax (w (iv))	6,750	
8% convertible loan note (28,476 + 448) (w (iii))	28,924	35,674
	———	
Current liabilities		
Trade payables	24,500	
Liability to Easyfinance (w (ii))	8,700	
Bank overdraft	11,500	
Current tax payable	19,400	64,100
	———	———
Total equity and liabilities		213,300
		———

Workings (figures in brackets in $'000)

(i) Cost of sales and non-current assets	$000
Cost of sales per question	207,750
Depreciation – building (see below)	2,500
– plant and equipment (see below)	10,000
Adjustment/increase to closing inventory (see below)	(3,300)
	———
	216,950
	———

Freehold property

The revaluation of the property will create an initial revaluation reserve of $15 million (80,000 – (75,000 – 10,000)). $3·75 million of this (25%) will be transferred to deferred tax leaving a net revaluation reserve of $11·25 million. The building valued at $50 million will require a depreciation charge of $2·5 million (50,000/20 years remaining) for the current year. This will leave a carrying amount in the statement of financial position of $77·5 million (80,000 − 2,500).

Plant and equipment:

	Cost	Accumulated depreciation
	$000	$000
1 April 2010	74,500	24,500
Charge for year ((74,500 − 24,500) × 20%)		10,000
31 March 2011	74,500	34,500

The carrying amount in the statement of financial position is $40 million.

Inventory adjustment

Goods delivered (deduct from closing inventory)

	(2,700)
Cost of goods sold (7,800 × 100/130) (add to closing inventory)	6,000
Net increase in closing inventory	3,300

(ii) Factored receivables

As Highwood still bears the risk of the non-payment of the receivables, the substance of this transaction is a loan. Thus the receivables must remain on Highwood's statement of financial position and the proceeds of the 'sale' treated as a current liability. The difference between the factored receivables (10,000) and the loan received (8,700) of $1·3 million, which has been charged to administrative expenses, should be reversed except for $600,000 which should be treated as an allowance for uncollectible receivables.

(iii) 8% convertible loan note

This is a compound financial instrument having a debt (liability) and an equity component. These must be quantified and accounted for separately:

year ended 31 March	outflow	10%	present value
	$000		$000
2011	2,400	0·91	2,184
2012	2,400	0·83	1,992
2013	32,400	0·75	24,300
Liability component			28,476
Equity component (balance)			1,524
Proceeds of issue			30,000

The finance cost for the year will be $2,848,000 (28,476 × 10% rounded). Thus $448,000 (2,848 − 2,400 interest paid) will be added to the carrying amount of the loan note in the statement of financial position.

(iv) Deferred tax

credit balance required at 31 March 2011 (27,000 × 25%)	6,750
revaluation of property (w (i))	(3,750)
balance at 1 April 2010	(2,600)
charge to income statement	400

(v) The dividend paid in November 2010 was $5·6 million. This is based on 112 million shares in issue (56,000 × 2 the shares are 50 cents each) times 5 cents.

(d) A rules-based accounting system is likely to be very descriptive and is generally considered to be a system which relies on a series of detailed rules or accounting requirements that prescribe how financial statements should be prepared. Such a system is considered less flexible, but often more comparable and consistent, than a principles-based system. Some would argue that rules-based systems can lead to looking for 'loopholes'. By contrast, a principles-based system relies on generally accepted accounting principles that are conceptually based and are normally underpinned by a set of key objectives. They are more flexible than a rules-based system, but they do require judgement and interpretation which could lead to inconsistencies between reporting entities and can sometimes lead to the manipulation of financial statements.

Because IFRSs are based on *The Conceptual Framework for Financial Reporting,* they are often regarded as being a principles-based system. Of course IFRSs do contain many rules and requirements (often lengthy and complex), but their critical feature is that IFRS 'rules' are based on underlying concepts. In reality most accounting systems have an element of both rules and principles and their designation as rules-based or principles-based depends on the relative importance and robustness of the principles compared to the volume and manner in which the rules are derived.

ACCA marking scheme			
			Marks
(a)	Statement of profit or loss		
	revenue		½
	cost of sales		4
	distribution costs		½
	administrative expenses		1½
	finance costs		1½
	income tax expense		1½
	other comprehensive income		1½
		Maximum	11
(b)	Statement of changes in equity		
	opening balance on retained earnings		1
	other component of equity (equity option)		1
	dividend paid		1
	comprehensive income		1
		Maximum	4

(c)	Statement of financial position		
	property, plant and equipment		2½
	inventory		1
	trade receivables		1
	deferred tax		1
	issue of 8% loan note		1½
	liability to Easyfinance		1
	bank overdraft		½
	trade payables		½
	current tax payable		1
		Maximum	10
(d)	One mark per sensible comment		5
Total			**30**

168 KEYSTONE

(a) **Keystone – Statement of profit or loss and other comprehensive income for the year ended 30 September 2011**

	$000	$000
Revenue (380,000 – 2,400 (w (i)))		377,600
Cost of sales (w (ii))		(258,100)
Gross profit		119,500
Distribution costs		(14,200)
Administrative expenses (46,400 – 24,000 dividend (50,000 × 5 × 2·40 × 4%))		(22,400)
Investment income		800
Loss on fair value of investments (18,000 – 17,400)		(600)
Finance costs		(350)
Profit before tax		82,750
Income tax expense (24,300 + 1,800 (w (v)))		(26,100)
Profit for the year		56,650
Other comprehensive income		
Revaluation of leased property	8,000	
Transfer to deferred tax (w (v))	(2,400)	5,600
Total comprehensive income for the year		62,250

(b)   **Keystone – Statement of financial position as at 30 September 2011**

	$000	$000
Assets		
Non-current assets		
Property, plant and equipment (w (iv))		78,000
Financial asset: equity investments		17,400
		95,400
Current assets		
Inventory (w (iii))	56,600	
Trade receivables (33,550 – 2,400 (w (i)))	31,150	87,750
Total assets		183,150
Equity and liabilities		
Equity		
Equity shares of 20 cents each		50,000
Revaluation reserve (w (iv))	5,600	
Retained earnings (33,600 + 56,650 – 24,000 dividend paid)	66,250	71,850
		121,850
Non-current liabilities		
Deferred tax (w (v))		6,900
Current liabilities		
Trade payables	27,800	
Bank overdraft	2,300	
Current tax payable	24,300	54,400
Total equity and liabilities		183,150

Workings (figures in brackets in $000)

(i)   Where there is uncertainty over goods sold on a sale or return basis they should not be recognised as revenue until they have been formally accepted by the buyer. Thus $2·4 million should be removed from revenue and receivables. The goods should be added to the inventory at 30 September 2011 at their cost of $1·8 million (2·4 million × 75%).

(ii)   Cost of sales

	$000
opening inventory	46,700
materials (64,000 – 3,000)	61,000
production labour (124,000 – 4,000)	120,000
factory overheads (80,000 – (4,000 × 75%))	77,000
Amortisation of leased property (w (iv))	3,000
Depreciation of plant (1,000 + 6,000 (w (iv)))	7,000
Closing inventory (w (iii))	56,600
	258,100

The cost of the self-constructed plant is $10 million (3,000 + 4,000 + 3,000 for materials, labour and overheads respectively that have also been deducted from the above items in cost of sales). It is not permissible to add a profit margin to self-constructed assets.

(iii)   Inventory at 30 September 2011:

	$000
per count	54,800
goods on sale or return (w (i))	1,800
	56,600

(iv)   Non-current assets:

The leased property has been amortised at $2·5 million per annum (50,000/20 years). The accumulated amortisation of $10 million therefore represents four years, thus its remaining life at the date of revaluation is 16 years.

	$000
carrying amount at date of revaluation (50,000 – 10,000)	40,000
revalued amount	48,000
gross gain on revaluation	8,000
transfer to deferred tax (at 30%)	(2,400)
net gain to revaluation reserve	5,600

The revalued amount of $48 million will be amortised over its remaining life of 16 years at $3 million per annum.

The self-constructed plant will be depreciated for six months by $1 million (10,000 × 20% × 6/12) and have a carrying amount at 30 September 2011 of $9 million. The plant in the trial balance will be depreciated by $6 million ((44,500 – 14,500) × 20%) for the year and have a carrying amount at 30 September 2011 of $24 million.

In summary:

	$000
Leased property (48,000 – 3,000)	45,000
Plant (9,000 + 24,000)	33,000
Property, plant and equipment	78,000

(v) Deferred tax

Provision required at 30 September 2011 ((15,000 + 8,000) × 30%)	6,900
Provision at 1 October 2010	(2,700)
Increase required	4,200
Transferred from revaluation reserve (w (iv))	(2,400)
Balance: charge to statement of profit or loss	1,800

(c) There are several aspects of Baxen's business strategy where adopting IFRS would be advantageous.

It is unclear how sophisticated or developed the 'local' standards which it currently uses are, however, it is widely accepted that IFRS are a set of high quality and transparent global standards that are intended to achieve consistency and comparability across the world. They have been produced in co-operation with other internationally renowned standard setters, with the aspiration of achieving consensus and global convergence. Thus if Baxen does adopt IFRS it is likely that its status and reputation (for example, an improved credit rating) in the eyes of other entities would be enhanced.

Other more specific advantages might be:

Its own financial statements would be comparable with other companies that use IFRS. This would help the company to better assess and rank prospective investments in its foreign trading partners.

Should Baxen acquire (as a subsidiary) any foreign companies, it would make the task of consolidation much simpler as there would be no need to reconcile its foreign subsidiary's financial statements to the local generally accepted accounting principles (GAAP) that Baxen currently uses. The use of IFRSs may make the audit fee less expensive.

If Baxen needs to raise finance in the future (highly likely because of its ambitions), it will find it easier to get a listing on any security exchange that is a member of the International Organisation of Securities Commissions (IOSCO) as they recognise IFRS for listing purposes. This flexibility to raise funding also means that Baxen's financing costs should be lower.

ACCA marking scheme		
		Marks
(a)	Statement of profit or loss	
	revenue	1
	cost of sales	7
	distribution costs	½
	administrative expenses	1½
	investment income	1
	loss on fair value of investment	1
	finance costs	½
	income tax expense	1½
	other comprehensive income	1
	Maximum	15
(b)	Statement of financial position	
	property, plant and equipment	1
	equity investments	½
	inventory	½
	trade receivables	1
	equity shares	½
	revaluation reserve	1½
	retained earnings	1½
	deferred tax	1
	trade payables	½
	bank overdraft	½
	current tax payable	½
	Maximum	10
(c)	One mark per sensible comment	5
Total		**30**

169 FRESCO

(a) (i) **Fresco – Statement of profit or loss and other comprehensive income for the year ended 31 March 2012**

	$000
Revenue	350,000
Cost of sales (w (i))	(311,000)
Gross profit	39,000
Distribution costs	(16,100)
Administrative expenses (26,900 + 3,000 re fraud)	(29,900)
Finance costs (300 + 2,300 (w (ii)))	(2,600)
Loss before tax	(9,600)
Income tax relief (2,400 + 200 (w (iii)) – 800)	1,800
Loss for the year	(7,800)
Other comprehensive income	
Revaluation of leased property (w (ii))	4,000
Total comprehensive losses	(3,800)

(ii) **Fresco – Statement of changes in equity for the year ended 31 March 2012**

	Share capital $000	Share premium $000	Revaluation reserve $000	Retained earnings $000	Total equity $000
Balances at 1 April 2011	45,000	5,000	nil	5,100	55,100
Prior period adjustment (re fraud)				(1,000)	(1,000)
Restated balance				4,100	
Rights share issue (see below)	9,000	4,500			13,500
Total comprehensive losses (see (i) above)			4,000	(7,800)	(3,800)
Transfer to retained earnings			(500)	500	
Balances at 31 March 2012	54,000	9,500	3,500	(3,200)	63,800

The rights issue was 18 million shares (45,000/50 cents each × 1/5) at 75 cents = $13·5 million. This equates to the balance on the suspense account. This should be recorded as $9 million equity shares (18,000 × 50 cents) and $4·5 million share premium (18,000 × (75 cents – 50 cents)).

The discovery of the fraud represents an error part of which is a prior period adjustment ($1 million) in accordance with IAS 8 *Accounting policies, changes in accounting estimates and errors*.

(iii) **Fresco – Statement of financial position as at 31 March 2012**

Assets	$000	$000
Non-current assets		
Property, plant and equipment (w (ii))		62,700
Current assets		
Inventory	25,200	
Trade receivables (28,500 – 4,000 re fraud)	24,500	
Current tax refund	2,400	52,100
Total assets		114,800
Equity and liabilities		
Equity (see (ii) above)		
Equity shares of 50 cents each		54,000
Reserves		
Share premium	9,500	
Revaluation	3,500	
Retained earnings	(3,200)	9,800
		63,800
Non-current liabilities		
Finance lease obligation (w (ii))	15,230	
Deferred tax (w (iii))	3,000	18,230
Current liabilities		
Trade payables	27,300	
Finance lease obligation (19,300 – 15,230 (w (ii)))	4,070	
Bank overdraft	1,400	32,770
Total equity and liabilities		114,800

(b) **Fresco – Basic earnings per share for the year ended 31 March 2012**

Loss per statement of comprehensive income	$7·8 million
Weighted average number of shares (w (iv))	99 million
Loss per share	7·9 cents

Workings (figures in brackets are in $000)

	$000
(i) Cost of sales	
Per question	298,700
Amortisation of – leased property (w (ii))	4,500
Amortisation of – leased plant (w (ii))	5,000
Depreciation of other plant and equipment ((47,500 – 33,500) × 20%)	2,800
	311,000

(ii) Non-current assets

Carrying amount 1 April 2011 (48,000 – 16,000)	32,000
Revaluation reserve	4,000
	———
Revalued amount 1 April 2011	36,000
Amortisation year to 31 March 2012 (over 8 years)	(4,500)
	———
Carrying amount 31 March 2012	31,500
	———

$500,000 (4,000/8 years) of the revaluation surplus will be transferred to retained earnings (reported in the statement of changes in equity).

Leased plant:

Fair value 1 April 2011	25,000
Deposit	2,000
	———
	23,000
Interest at 10%	2,300
Payment 31 March 2012	(6,000)
	———
Lease obligation 31 March 2012	19,300
Interest at 10%	1,930
Payment 31 March 2013	(6,000)
	———
Lease obligation 31 March 2013	15,230
	———

Amortisation for the leased plant for the year ended 31 March 2012 is $5 million (25,000/5 years).

Summarising the carrying amount of property, plant and equipment as at 31 March 2012:

Leased property	31,500
Owned plant (47,500 – 33,500 – 2,800)	11,200
Leased plant (25,000 – 5,000)	20,000
	———
	62,700
	———

(iii) Deferred tax

Provision required at 31 March 2012 (12,000 × 25%)	3,000
Provision at 1 April 2011	(3,200)
	———
Credit (reduction in provision) to income statement	200
	———

(iv)   Theoretical ex-rights value:

	Shares	$	$
Holding (say)	100	1·20	120
Rights taken up	20	0·75	15
	120		135

Theoretical ex-rights value   1·125 ($135/120 shares)

Weighted average number of shares:
1 April 2011 to 31 December 2011
1 January 2012 to 31 March 2012   90 million × 1·20/1·125 × 9/12 = 72 million
                                                          108 million × 3/12 = 27 million

Weighted average for the year   99 million

(c)   An asset is a resource controlled by the entity as a result of past events and from which future economic benefits are expected to flow to the entity.

Control is an important aspect of the definition as it reflects the concept of substance over form. This suggests that an asset does not have to be legally owned by an entity for it to be recognised in the statement of financial position. Another important aspect of the definition is the future economic benefits that must be expected to flow to the entity. In practice, when considering whether assets should be recognised, entities should consider whether they have accepted the risks and rewards of ownership of the asset.

In essence, an asset that satisfies the definition should be recognised and this helps to ensure reliability of financial statements as it prevents entities from removing assets (and their associated liabilities) from the statement of financial position in order to show improved return on assets and reduced gearing (this practice is commonly referred to as "off-balance sheet financing").

An example of this is in IAS 17 *Leases* as the definition of a finance lease is based on whether the entity has accepted the risks and rewards of ownership of the asset leased. If so, the entity must recognise the asset together with a liability for the finance lease obligation.

Reliability is further enhanced by not allowing entities to reflect assets if their future benefits is not reasonably certain. Entities may try to argue that assets can be recognised in an attempt to inflate profits, as the alternative to asset recognition would be to charge the cost as an expense in the income statement. A specific example of this is in IAS 38 *Intangible Assets* which requires a strict number of criteria to be satisfied before development costs can be capitalised. Most of these criteria are based on whether the project will be completed and result in future profits, i.e. that there will be future economic benefits.

170 QUINCY

(a) **Quincy – Statement of profit or loss and other comprehensive income for the year ended 30 September 2012**

	$000
Revenue (213,500 – 1,600 (w (i)))	211,900
Cost of sales (w (ii))	(147,300)
Gross profit	64,600
Distribution costs	(12,500)
Administrative expenses (19,000 – 1,000 loan issue costs (w (iv)))	(18,000)
Loss on fair value of equity investments (17,000 – 15,700)	(1,300)
Investment income	400
Finance costs (w (iv))	(1,920)
Profit before tax	31,280
Income tax expense (7,400 + 1,100 – 200 (w (v)))	(8,300)
Profit for the year	22,980
Other comprehensive income	
Gain on revaluation of land and buildings (w (iii))	18,000
Total comprehensive income	40,980

(b) **Quincy – Statement of changes in equity for the year ended 30 September 2012**

	Share capital	Revaluation reserve	Retained earnings	Total equity
	$000	$000	$000	$000
Balance at 1 October 2011	60,000	nil	18,500	78,500
Total comprehensive income		18,000	22,980	40,980
Transfer to retained earnings (w (iii))		(1,000)	1,000	nil
Dividend paid (60,000 × 4 × 8 cents)	(19,200)	(19,200)		
Balance at 30 September 2012	60,000	17,000	23,280	100,280

(c) **Quincy – Statement of financial position as at 30 September 2012**

Assets	$000	$000
Non-current assets		
Property, plant and equipment (57,000 + 42,500 (w (iii)))		99,500
Equity financial asset investments		15,700
		115,200

Current assets		
Inventory	24,800	
Trade receivables	28,500	
Bank	2,900	56,200
Total assets		171,400
Equity and liabilities		
Equity		
Equity shares of 25 cents each		60,000
Revaluation reserve	17,000	
Retained earnings	23,280	40,280
		100,280
Non-current liabilities		
Deferred tax (w (v))	1,000	
Deferred revenue (w (i))	800	
6% loan note (2014) (w (iv))	24,420	26,220
Current liabilities		
Trade payables	36,700	
Deferred revenue (w (i))	800	
Current tax payable	7,400	44,900
Total equity and liabilities		171,400

Workings (figures in brackets in $000)

(i)   Sales made which include revenue for ongoing servicing work must have part of the revenue deferred. The deferred revenue must include the normal profit margin (25%) for the deferred work. At 30 September 2012, there are two more years of servicing work, thus $1·6 million ((600 × 2) × 100/75) must be treated as deferred revenue, split equally between current and non-current liabilities.

(ii)   Cost of sales

	$000
Per trial balance	136,800
Depreciation of building (w (iii))	3,000
Depreciation of plant (w (iii))	7,500
	147,300

(iii) Non-current assets

Land and buildings:

The gain on revaluation and carrying amount of the land and buildings is:

	Land $000		Building $000
Carrying amount as at 1 October 2011	10,000	(40,000 –8,000)	32,000
Revalued amount as at this date	(12,000)	(60,000 – 12,000)	(48,000)
Gain on revaluation	2,000		16,000

Building depreciation year to 30 September 2012 (48,000/16 years)   3,000

The transfer from the revaluation reserve to retained earnings in respect of 'excess' depreciation (as the revaluation is realised) is $1 million (48,000 – 32,000)/16 years.

The carrying amount at 30 September 2012 is $57 million (60,000 – 3,000).

Plant and equipment:

	$000
Carrying amount as at 1 October 2011 (83,700 – 33,700)	50,000
Depreciation at 15% per annum	(7,500)
Carrying amount as at 30 September 2012	42,500

(iv) Loan note

The finance cost of the loan note is charged at the effective rate of 8% applied to the carrying amount of the loan. The issue costs of the loan ($1 million) should be deducted from the proceeds of the loan ($25 million) and not treated as an administrative expense. This gives an initial carrying amount of $24 million and a finance cost of $1,920,000 (24,000 × 8%). The interest actually paid is $1·5 million (25,000 × 6%) and the difference between these amounts, of $420,000 (1,920 – 1,500), is accrued and added to the carrying amount of the loan note. This gives $24·42 million (24,000 + 420) for inclusion as a non-current liability in the statement of financial position.

Note: The loan interest paid of $1·5 million plus the dividend paid of $19·2 million (see (b)) equals the $20·7 million shown in the trial balance for these items.

(v) Deferred tax

	$000
Provision required as at 30 September 2012 (5,000 × 20%)	1,000
Less provision b/f	(1,200)
Credit to income statement	200

(d)   The two fundamental qualitative characteristics of information are relevance and faithful representation.

Information is relevant if it has the ability to influence the economic decisions of the users, and it provided in time to influence those decisions. Information that is relevant has predictive or confirmatory value.

In relation to property, plant and equipment, it could be argued that the revaluation model is more relevant, as it provides a closer approximation to the current value of the assets at the year end.

A counter-argument to this could be that this value is more difficult to verify, as it is an estimate rather than historical cost, which is based on the factual price paid for the asset.

Events should be faithfully represented in the financial statements, meaning that transactions should be recorded according to their economic substance rather than their legal form.

In respect of non-current assets, the key element of an asset definition is control. This means that the party with control over the asset must include it in their financial statements. Based on this, assets held under finance leases must be included within the lessee's financial statements despite legally not being owned.

ACCA marking scheme		
		Marks
(a)	statement of profit or loss	
	revenue	1½
	cost of sales	2
	distribution costs	½
	administrative expenses	1
	loss on investments	1
	investment income	½
	finance costs	1½
	income tax expense	2
	gain on revaluation of land and buildings	1
	Maximum	11
(b)	statement of changes in equity	
	balances b/f	1
	total comprehensive income	1
	dividend paid	1
	transfer of revaluation surplus to retained earnings	1
	Maximum	4
(c)	statement of financial position	
	property, plant and equipment	2½
	equity investments	1
	inventory	½
	trade receivables	½
	bank	½
	deferred tax	1
	deferred revenue	1
	6% loan note	1½
	trade payables	½
	current tax payable	1
	Maximum	10

(d)	Explanation of relevance	1
	Explanation of faithful representation	1
	Discussion of non-current assets	3
		—
		5
		—
Total		30
		—

171 ATLAS

(a) (i) **Atlas – Statement of profit or loss and other comprehensive income for the year ended 31 March 2013**

Monetary figures in brackets are in $000

	$000
Revenue (550,000 – 10,000 in substance loan)	540,000
Cost of sales (w (i))	(420,600)
	———
Gross profit	119,400
Distribution costs	(21,500)
Administrative expenses (30,900 + 5,400 re directors' bonus of 1% of sales made)	(36,300)
Finance costs (700 + 500 (10,000 × 10% × 6/12 re in substance loan))	(1,200)
	———
Profit before tax	60,400
Income tax expense (27,200 – 1,200 + (9,400 – 6,200) deferred tax)	(29,200)
	———
Profit for the year	31,200
Other comprehensive income	
Revaluation gain on land and buildings (w (ii))	7,000
	———
Total comprehensive income for the year	38,200
	———

(ii) **Atlas – Statement of changes in equity for the year ended 31 March 2013**

	Share capital $000	Share premium $000	Revaluation reserve $000	Retained earnings $000	Total equity $000
Balances at 1 April 2012	40,000	6,000	nil	11,200	57,200
Share issue (see below)	10,000	14,000			24,000
Total comprehensive income (see (i) above)			7,000	31,200	38,200
Dividend paid				(20,000)	(20,000)
	———	———	———	———	———
Balances at 31 March 2013	50,000	20,000	7,000	22,400	99,400
	———	———	———	———	———

The rights issue of 20 million shares (50,000/50 cents each × 1/5) at $1·20 has been recorded as $10 million equity shares (20 million × $0·50) and $14 million share premium (20 million × ($1·20 – $0·50)).

(iii)   **Atlas – Statement of financial position as at 31 March 2013**

Assets	$000	$000
Non-current assets		
Property, plant and equipment (44,500 + 52,800 (w (ii)))		97,300
Current assets		
Inventory (43,700 + 7,000 re in substance loan)	50,700	
Trade receivables	42,200	92,900
Plant held for sale (w (ii))		3,600
Total assets		193,800
Equity and liabilities		
Equity (see (ii) above)		
Equity shares of 50 cents each		50,000
Share premium	20,000	
Revaluation reserve	7,000	
Retained earnings	22,400	49,400
		99,400
Non-current liabilities		
In substance loan from Xpede (10,000 + 500 accrued interest)	10,500	
Deferred tax	9,400	19,900
Current liabilities		
Trade payables	35,100	
Income tax	27,200	
Accrued directors' bonus	5,400	
Bank overdraft	6,800	74,500
Total equity and liabilities		193,800

(b)   **Atlas – Basic earnings per share for the year ended 31 March 2013**

Earnings per statement of comprehensive income	$31·2 million
Weighted average number of shares (w (iii))	96·7 million
Earnings per share	32·3 cents

Workings (figures in brackets are in $000)

		$000
(i)	Cost of sales	
	Per question	411,500
	Closing inventory re in substance loan	(7,000)
	Depreciation of buildings (w (ii))	2,500
	Depreciation of plant and equipment (w (ii))	13,600
		420,600

(ii)   Non-current assets

Land and buildings

The gain on revaluation and carrying amount of the land and buildings will be:

	$000
Carrying amount at 1 April 2012 (60,000 – 20,000)	40,000
Revaluation at that date (12,000 + 35,000)	47,000
Gain on revaluation	7,000
Buildings depreciation (35,000/14 years)	(2,500)
Carrying amount of land and buildings at 31 March 2013 (47,000 – 2,500)	44,500

Plant

The plant held for sale should be shown separately and not be depreciated after 1 October 2012.

Other plant	
Carrying amount at 1 April 2012 (94,500 – 24,500)	70,000
Plant held for sale (9,000 – 5,000)	(4,000)
	66,000
Depreciation for year ended 31 March 2013 (20% reducing balance)	(13,200)
Carrying amount at 31 March 2013	52,800

Plant held for sale:	
At 1 April 2012 (from above)	4,000
Depreciation to date of reclassification (4,000 × 20% × 6/12)	(400)
Carrying amount at 1 October 2012	3,600

Total depreciation of plant for year ended 31 March 2013 (13,200 + 400)   13,600

As the fair value of the plant held for sale at 1 October 2012 is $4·2 million, it should continue to be carried at its (lower) carrying amount (and no longer depreciated).

(iii) Earnings per share

Theoretical ex-rights value:

	Shares	$	$
Holding (say)	100	2·00	200
Rights taken up (1 for 4)	25	1·20	30
	125		230

Theoretical ex-rights value   1·84 ($230/125 shares)

Weighted average number of shares:

1 April 2012 to 30 June 2012	80 million × $2·00/$1·84 × 3/12 =	21·7 million
1 July 2012 to 31 March 2013	100 million × 9/12 =	75·0 million
Weighted average for the year		96·7 million

(c) An impairment review is required when indications of impairment exist. Indications can be from a number of external and internal factors. In Atlas' case, the storm damage is the indication that the asset may be impaired.

The asset will be impaired if the carrying value of the asset is greater than its recoverable amount. The recoverable amount of an asset is defined as the greater of the asset's value in use and fair value less costs to sell.

The impairment will be taken to the statement of profit or loss as an expense unless a revaluation surplus exists for that asset, in which case the impairment would be deducted from this. In the case of Atlas, there is a revaluation surplus. Therefore any impairment loss would be deducted from this first, with any excess loss of more than $7m taken to the statement of profit or loss as an expense.

ACCA marking scheme				Marks
(a)	(i)	Statement of profit or loss and other comprehensive income		
		revenue		1
		cost of sales		3
		distribution costs		½
		administrative expenses		1
		finance costs		1
		income tax		1½
		other comprehensive income		1
			Maximum	9
	(ii)	Statement of changes in equity		
		balances b/f		1
		rights issue		1
		total comprehensive income		1
		dividend paid		1
			Maximum	4

	(iii)	Statement of financial position	
		property, plant and equipment	2 ½
		inventory	1
		trade receivables	½
		plant held for sale (at 3,600)	1
		in substance loan	1
		deferred tax	1
		trade payables	½
		current tax	½
		directors' bonus	½
		bank overdraft	½
		Maximum	9
(b)		Basic earnings per share	
		earnings per statement of comprehensive income	½
		theoretical ex-rights value	1
		calculation of weighted average number of shares	1½
		Maximum	3
(c)		Needed when indications of impairment exist	1
		Storm damage is Atlas' indication	1
		Impaired if CV greater than recoverable amount	1
		Definition of recoverable amount	1
		Recognition of impairment loss	1
		Recognition through revaluation surplus of Atlas	1
Total			**30**

172 MOBY

(a) **Moby – Statement of profit or loss and other comprehensive income for the year ended 30 September 2013**

	$000
Revenue (227,800 + 10,000 construction contract (w (i)))	237,800
Cost of sales (w (ii))	(187,900)
Gross profit	49,900
Distribution costs	(13,500)
Administrative expenses (16,500 – 150 disallowed provision – see below)	(16,350)
Profit from operations	20,050
Finance costs (900 + 4,000 loan + 2,930 lease (w (iv)))	(7,830)
Profit before tax	12,220
Income tax expense (3,400 – 1,050 – 2,000 (w (v)))	(350)
Profit for the year	11,870

Other comprehensive income

Items which will not be reclassified to profit or loss:

Gain on revaluation of land and buildings (w (iii))	4,400
Deferred tax on gain (4,400 × 25%)	(1,100)
	———
Total other comprehensive income for the year	3,300
	———
Total comprehensive income for the year	15,170
	———

(b)   **Moby – Statement of financial position as at 30 September 2013**

Assets	$000	$000
Non-current assets		
Property, plant and equipment (w (iii))		115,000
Current assets		
Inventory	26,600	
Amount due from contract customer (w (i))	6,000	
Trade receivables	38,500	71,100
	———	———
Total assets		186,100
		———
Equity and liabilities		
Equity		
Equity shares of 20 cents each		45,000
Revaluation reserve	3,300	
Retained earnings (19,800 + 11,870)	31,670	34,970
	———	———
		79,970
Non-current liabilities		
Lease obligation (w (iv))	16,133	
Deferred tax (w (v))	7,100	
Loan note (40,000 × 1·1)	44,000	67,233
	———	
Current liabilities		
Lease obligation (23,030 – 16,133 (w (iv)))	6,897	
Trade payables	21,300	
Bank overdraft	7,300	
Current tax payable	3,400	38,897
	———	———
Total equity and liabilities		186,100
		———

Workings (monetary figures in brackets in $000)

(i)   Construction contract:

	$000	$000
Total contract revenue		25,000
Costs incurred to date	14,000	
Estimated costs to complete	6,000	(20,000)
Total contract profit		5,000

Percentage of completion is 40% (10,000/25,000)

Amounts to include in financial statements for the year ended 30 September 2013:

Revenue	10,000
Cost of sales (= balancing figure)	(8,000)
Profit for year (40% × 5,000)	2,000

Amount due from customer:

Contract costs to date	14,000
Profit for year	2,000
	16,000
Progress billings (work certified)	(10,000)
Amount due from customer	6,000

(ii)   Cost of sales:

	$000
Per question	164,500
Construction contract costs	8,000
Depreciation of building (w (iii))	2,400
Depreciation of owned plant (w (iii))	6,000
Depreciation of leased plant (w (iii))	7,000
	187,900

(iii)   Non-current assets:

	$000	$000
Land and building		
Carrying amount 1 October 2012 (60,000 – 10,000)		50,000
Revalued land	16,000	
Revalued building	38,400	54,400
Revaluation gain		4,400
Depreciation for year (38,400/16 years)		(2,400)
Carrying amount at 30 September 2013 (54,400 – 2,400)		52,000
Owned plant		
Carrying amount 1 October 2012 (65,700 – 17,700)		48,000
Depreciation for year (48,000 x 12·5%)		(6,000)
Carrying amount at 30 September 2013		42,000
Leased plant		
Carrying amount 1 October 2012 (35,000 – 7,000)		28,000
Depreciation for year (35,000/5 years)		(7,000)
Carrying amount at 30 September 2013		21,000
Carrying amount of property, plant and equipment at 30 September 2013: (52,000 + 42,000 + 21,000)		115,000

(iv)   Lease obligation:

	$000
Liability at 1 October 2012	29,300
Interest at 10% for year ended 30 September 2013	2,930
Rental payment 30 September 2013	(9,200)
Liability at 30 September 2013	23,030
Interest at 10% for year ended 30 September 2014	2,303
Rental payment 30 September 2014	(9,200)
Liability at 30 September 2014	16,133

(v) Deferred tax:

		$000	$000
	Provision b/f at 1 October 2012		(8,000)
	Provision c/f required at 30 September 2013		
	Taxable differences: per question	24,000	
	on revaluation of land and buildings	4,400	
		28,400	
		× 25%	7,100
	Net reduction in provision		(900)
	Charged to other comprehensive income on revaluation gain (4,400 × 25%)		(1,100)
	Credit to profit or loss		2,000

(c) Operating profit margin: 8.4%

(20,050/237,800)

Return on capital employed: 13.6%

(20/050/(67,030+79,970)

The operating profit margin has increased during the year, suggesting that Moby has either managed to raise prices while keeping costs fixed, or cut cost while raising prices.

This is more impressive when the revaluation is taken into account, as this will have led to higher depreciation than last year.

Upon further investigation, it is likely that the new construction contract in the year has had a positive impact on this, as it has generated a profit margin of 20%.

The return on capital employed gives a more negative view on the performance, as it has decreased significantly in the year. Some of this decrease could be attributed to the revaluation in the year, as this has created a revaluation surplus in equity. As this will have no impact on improving profit in the year, this gives a misleading comparison from the prior year.

If the $3.3m revaluation surplus is removed, the return on capital employed would only become 13.9%, still significantly lower than in 2012.

While the operating margin has improved, the reason for the decline in return on capital employed is likely to be due to the loan notes issued in the year. It is not clear what these loan notes have been used for, but it seems like this has not been used to sufficiently increase profits to make the return comparable with the prior year.

It may be that the funds from the loan were used to grow the business which has not yet had a full year to take effect, in which case next year's results may be a fairer comparison.

			Marks
ACCA marking scheme			
(a)	Statement of profit or loss and other comprehensive income		
	revenue		1½
	cost of sales		3
	distribution costs		½
	administrative expenses		1
	finance costs		2
	income tax expense		2
	gain on revaluation of land and buildings		1
	deferred tax on gain		1
		Maximum	12
(b)	Statement of financial position		
	property, plant and equipment		2½
	inventory		½
	amount due on contract		1½
	trade receivables		½
	equity shares		½
	revaluation reserve		1
	retained earnings		1
	non-current lease obligation		1
	deferred tax		1
	loan note		1
	current lease obligation		½
	bank overdraft		½
	trade payables		½
	current tax payable		1
		Maximum	13
(c)	Calculation of ratios using own figures:		
	Operating profit margin		½
	Return on capital employed		1½
	One mark per sensible comment (Maximum of 3)		3
Total			30

173 WELLMAY

Statement of profit or loss and other comprehensive income year ended 31 March 2007

	$000	$000
Revenue (4,200 – 500 (w (i)))		3,700
Cost of sales (w (ii))		(2,500)
Gross profit		1,200
Operating expenses		(470)
Investment property – rental income	20	
– fair value loss (400 –375)	(25)	(5)
Finance costs (w (iii))		(113)
Profit before tax		687
Income tax (360 + 30 (w (v)))		(390)
Profit for the period		297

Statement of changes in equity – year ended 31 March 2007

	Equity shares	Equity option	Revaluation reserve	Retained earnings	Total
	$000	$000	$000	$000	$000
Balances at 1 April 2006	1,200		350	2,215	4,165
Equity conversion option (w (iv))		40			40
Revaluation of factory (w (vi))			190		190
Profit for the period				297	297
Balances at 31 March 2007	1,200	40	540	2,512	4,292

Statement of financial position as at 31 March 2007

	$000	$000
Non-current assets		
Property, plant and equipment (w (vi))		4,390
Investment property (w (vi))		375
		4,765
Current assets (1,400 + 200 inventory (w (i)))		1,600
Total assets		6,365
Equity and liabilities (see statement of changes in equity above)		
Equity shares of 50 cents each		1,200
Equity option (w (iv))		40
		1,240

Reserves:		
Revaluation reserve	540	
Retained earnings	2,512	3,052
		4,292
Non-current liabilities		
Deferred tax (w (v))	210	
8% Convertible loan note ((560 + 8) (w (iv)))	568	778
Current liabilities	820	
Loan from Westwood (500 + 50 accrued interest (w (i)))	550	1,295
Total equity and liabilities		6,365

Workings (All figures in $000)

(i) The 'sale' to Westwood is, in substance, a secured loan. The repurchase price is the cost of sale plus compound interest at 10% for two years. The correct accounting treatment is to reverse the sale with the goods going back into inventory and the 'proceeds' treated as a loan with accrued interest of 10% ($50,000) for the current year.

(ii) **Cost of sales**

From draft financial statements	2,700
Sale of goods added back to inventory (see above)	(200)
	2,500

(iii) **Finance costs**

From draft financial statements	55
Additional accrued interest on convertible loan (w (iv))	8
Finance cost on in-substance loan (500 × 10%)	50
	113

(iv)   **Convertible loan**

This is a compound financial instrument that contains an element of debt and an element of equity (the option to convert). IAS 32 *Financial instruments: disclosure and presentation* requires that the substance of such instruments should be applied to the reporting of them. The value of the debt element is calculated by discounting the future cash flows (at 10%). The residue of the issue proceeds is recorded as the value of the equity option.

	Cash flows	Factor at 10%	Present value $000
Year 1 interest	48	0.91	43.6
Year 2 interest	48	0.83	39.8
Year 3 interest	48	0.75	36.0
Year 4 interest, redemption premium and capital	648	0.68	440.6
Total value of debt component			560.0
Proceeds of the issue			600.0
Equity component (residual amount)			40.0

For the year ended 31 March 2007, the interest cost for the convertible loan in the statement of comprehensive income should be increased from $48,000 to $56,000 (10% × 560) by accruing $8,000, which should be added to the carrying value of the debt.

(v)   **Taxation**

The required deferred tax balance is $210,000 (600 × 35%), the current balance is $180,000, and thus a further transfer of $30,000 (via the statement of comprehensive income) is required.

(vi)   **Properties**

The fair value model in IAS 40 Investment property requires the loss of $25,000 on the fair value of investment properties to be reported in the statement of comprehensive income. This differs from revaluations of other properties. IAS 16 Property, plant and equipment requires surpluses and deficits to be recorded as movements in equity (a revaluation reserve). After depreciation of $40,000 for the year ended 31 March 2007, the factory (used by Wellmay) would have a carrying amount of $1,160,000 (1,200 – 40). The valuation of $1,350,000 at 31 March 2007 would give a further revaluation surplus of $190,000 (1,350 – 1,160) and a carrying amount of property, plant and equipment of $4,390,000 (4,200 + 190) at that date.

174 DUNE

Key answer tips

This question contained many of the usual adjustments that you would expect with a published accounts question such as depreciation and tax adjustments. You were also expected to demonstrate your knowledge of accounting for held for sale assets and financial assets and liabilities in this time-consuming question.

(a) **Dune – Statement of profit or loss for the year ended 31 March 2010**

	$000
Revenue (400,000	400,000
Cost of sales (w (i))	(306,100)
Gross profit	93,900
Distribution costs	(26,400)
Administrative expenses (34,200 – 500 loan note issue costs)	(33,700)
Investment income	1,200
Profit (gain) on investments at fair value through profit or loss (28,000 – 26,500)	1,500
Finance costs (200 + 1,950 (w (iii)))	(2,150)
Profit before tax	34,350
Income tax expense (12,000 – 1,400 – 1,800 (w (iv)))	(8,800)
Profit for the year	25,550

(b) **Dune – Statement of financial position as at 31 March 2010**

	$000	$000
Assets		
Non-current assets		
Property, plant and equipment (w (v))		37,400
Investments at fair value through profit or loss		28,000
		65,400
Current assets		
Inventory	48,000	
Trade receivables	40,700	
Bank	15,500	104,200
Non-current assets held for sale (w (ii))		33,500
Total assets		203,100

Equity and liabilities

Equity

Equity shares of $1 each	60,000
Retained earnings (38,400 + 25,550 – 10,000 dividend paid)	53,950

113,950

Non-current liabilities

Deferred tax (w (v))	4,200	
5% loan notes (2012) (w (iii))	20,450	24,650

Current liabilities

Trade payables	52,000	
Accrued loan note interest (w (iii))	500	
Current tax payable	12,000	64,500

Total equity and liabilities	203,100

Workings (figures in brackets in $000)

(i) **Cost of sales**

	$000
Per question	294,000
Depreciation of leasehold property (see below)	1,500
Impairment of leasehold property (see below)	4,000
Depreciation of plant and equipment ((67,500 – 23,500) × 15%)	6,600
	306,100

(ii) The leasehold property must be classed as a non-current asset held for sale from 1 October 2009 at its fair value less costs to sell. It must be depreciated for six months up to this date (after which depreciation ceases). This is calculated at $1.5 million (45,000/15 years × 6/12). Its carrying amount at 1 October 2009 is therefore $37.5 million (45,000 – (6,000 + 1,500)).

Its fair value less cost to sell at this date is $33.5 million ((40,000 × 85%) – 500). It is therefore impaired by $4 million (37,500 – 33,500).

(iii) The finance cost of the loan note, at the effective rate of 10% applied to the correct carrying amount of the loan note of $19.5 million is, $1.95 million (the issue costs must be deducted from the proceeds of the loan note; they are not an administrative expense). The interest actually paid is $500,000 (20,000 × 5% × 6/12); however, a further $500,000 needs to be accrued as a current liability (as it will be paid soon). The difference between the total finance cost of $1.95 million and the $1 million interest payable is added to the carrying amount of the loan note to give $20.45 million (19,500 + 950) for inclusion as a non-current liability in the statement of financial position.

(iv) **Deferred tax**

Provision required at 31 March 2010 (14,000 × 30%)	4,200
Provision at 1 April 2009	(6,000)
Credit (reduction in provision) to statement of profit or loss	1,800

(v) **Property, plant and equipment**

Property, plant and equipment (67,500 − 23,500 − 6,600)	37,400

ACCA marking scheme		
		Marks
(a)	**Statement of profit or loss**	
	revenue	½
	cost of sales	2
	distribution costs	½
	administrative expenses	1
	investment income	½
	gain on investments	½
	finance costs	1½
	income tax expense	2
		───
	Maximum	7½
(b)	**Statement of financial position**	
	property, plant and equipment	½
	investments	½
	inventory	½
	trade receivables	½
	bank	½
	non-current asset held for sale	1
	equity shares	½
	retained earnings (1 for dividend)	1
	deferred tax	1
	5% loan note	1
	trade payables	½
	accrued loan note interest	½
	current tax payable	½
		───
	Maximum	7½
		───
Total		15
		───

Examiner's comments

This was a question of preparing financial statements from a trial balance with various adjustments required. These involved the dealing with the use of the effective interest rate for a loan, a fair value investment, an impairment of a leasehold property (including presenting it as 'held for sale'), and accounting for taxation. The most common errors were:

- loan: the issue costs were often ignored and calculating the finance charge at the nominal rate of 5% instead of the effective rate of 10%. Omission of accrued interest from current liabilities or including it at the incorrect amount

- despite the investment being described as 'fair value through profit and loss', many candidates credited the gain directly to equity

- leasehold property: a failure to depreciate it up to the date it became 'held for sale'; not calculating the subsequent impairment loss and most candidates continuing to show it as a non-current (rather than a current) asset

- there were many errors in the treatment of the taxation, including: debiting (should be credited) the over provision of the previous year's tax; treating the closing provision (rather than the movement) of deferred tax as the charge in the statement of profit or loss; and confusion over which amounts of tax should appear as non-current and current liabilities.

175 TOURMALET

Tourmalet – Statement of profit or loss for the year ending 30 September 20X3

	$000
Continuing operations	
Revenue (313,000 – 50,000 – 15,200 (discontinued)	247,800
Cost of sales (W1 – 16,000 discontinued**)**	(128,800)
Gross profit	119,000
Distribution expenses	(26,400)
Administrative expenses (W2)	(20,000)
Finance costs (W3)	(7,800)
Loss on investment properties (10,000 – 9,800)	(200)
Investment income	1,200
Profit before tax	65,800
Income tax expense (9,200 – 2,100)	(7,100)
Profit for the period from continuing operations	58,700
Discontinued operations	
Loss for the period from discontinued operations (15,200 – 16,000 – 3,200 – 1,500) (W4)	(5,500)
Profit for the period	53,200

Workings

(W1) Cost of sales:

	$000
Opening inventory	26,550
Purchases	158,450
Sale and leaseback	(40,000)
Profit on disposal (W5)	(2,000)
Depreciation (W2)	27,800
Closing inventory (28,500 – (4,500 – 2,000) see below)	(26,000)
	144,800

The slow moving inventory should be written down to its estimated realisable value. Despite the optimism of the Directors, it would seem prudent to base the realisable value on the best offer so far received (i.e. $2 million).

(W2) **Non-current assets depreciation**

	$000
Buildings $120/40 years	3,000
Plant – per trial balance ((98,600 – 24,600) × 20%)	14,800
Finance lease plant (W5)	10,000
	———
	27,800
	———

For information only:

In the statement of financial position	Cost/valuation	Accumulated depreciation	Net book value
	$000	$000	$000
Land and buildings	150,000	12,000	138,000
Plant – per trial balance	98,600	39,400	59,200
Finance leased plant (W5)	50,000	10,000	40,000
			———
			237,200
			———

(W3) **Finance costs**

	$000
Finance lease interest (W5)	6,000
Preference dividends (30,000 × 6% – half accrued)	1,800
	———
	7,800
	———

(W4) The penalty on the early termination of the lease has been accrued for as it would appear to be unlikely that the permission for change of use will be granted. The $1.5m has therefore been included in the loss from discontinuing operations.

(W5) **Step 1:** Correct incorrect treatment of disposal proceeds

Note: Asset already removed from trial balance figures so need to remove the incorrect entries from revenue/cost of sales and calculate the profit on disposal (to be spread over the five year lease term).

	$000	$000
Dr Revenue	50,000	
Cr Cost of sales		40,000
Cr Profit on disposal (1 year)		2,000
Cr Deferred income (4 years)		8,000

Step 2: Recognise asset/lease liability under rules from IAS 17

	$000	$000
Dr Non-current asset	50,000	
Cr Finance lease		50,000
Dr Depreciation expense	10,000	
Cr Accumulated depreciation		10,000
(50,000 / 5 years)		

Amortised cost:

Year	B/f	Int – 12%	o/s	Rental	C/f
	$000	$000	$000	$000	$000
1	50,000	6,000	56,000	(14,000)	42,000
2	42,000	5,040	47,040	(14,000)	33,040

Note: This statement of financial position is provided for information only. It does not form part of the answer or marking scheme.

Tourmalet – Statement of financial position as at 30 September 20X3

	$000	$000
Non-current assets		
Property, plant and equipment (W2)		237,200
Investment properties		9,800
		247,000
Current assets		
Inventory (W1)	26,000	
Trade receivables	31,200	
Bank	3,700	60,900
Total assets		307,900
Equity and liabilities		
Equity:		
Ordinary shares of 20c each		50,000
Retained earnings (61,800 + 53,200 – 2,500)	112,500	
Revaluation reserve	18,500	131,000
		181,000
Non-current liabilities		
6% Redeemable preference shares	30,000	
Finance lease (W5)	33,040	
Deferred income (W5)	6,000	

Current liabilities		69,040
Trade payables	35,300	
Accrued penalty cost (W4)	1,500	
Finance lease (W5)	8,960	
Deferred income (W5)	2,000	
Preference dividend accrual	900	
((30,000 × 6% payable) – 900 paid)		
Taxation	9,200	
		57,860
Total equity and liabilities		307,900

BUSINESS COMBINATIONS

176 PREMIER *Walk in the footsteps of a top tutor*

Key answer tips

This question requires the preparation of both a consolidated statement of profit or loss and other comprehensive income and a statement of financial position which makes it particularly time consuming. Ensure you get the easy, basic consolidation marks by combining the parent and subsidiary results first. Remember the statement of profit or loss is for a period, so the results of the subsidiary must be time apportioned to reflect the post acquisition period but the statement of financial position is at a point in time and the subsidiary results must not be time apportioned.

(a) **Consolidated statement of profit or loss and other comprehensive income for the year ended 30 September 2010**

	$000
Revenue (92,500 + (45,000 × 4/12) – 4,000 intra-group sales)	103,500
Cost of sales (W6)	(78,850)
Gross profit	24,650
Distribution costs (2,500 + (1,200 × 4/12))	(2,900)
Administrative expenses (5,500 + (2,400 × 4/12))	(6,300)
Finance costs	(100)
Profit before tax	15,350
Income tax expense (3,900 + (1,500 × 4/12))	(4,400)
Profit for the year	10,950

Other comprehensive income:	
Gain on FVTOCI investments	300
Gain on revaluation of property	500
Total other comprehensive income for the year	800
Total comprehensive income	11,750
Profit for year attributable to:	
Equity holders of the parent	10,760
Non-controlling interest (W7)	190
	10,950
Total comprehensive income attributable to:	
Equity holders of the parent (10,760 + 300 + 500)	11,560
Non-controlling interest (from above)	190
	11,750

Sanford's profits for the year ended 30 September 2010 of $3.9 million are $2.6 million (3,900 × 8/12) pre-acquisition and $1.3 million (3,900 × 4/12) post-acquisition.

(b) **Consolidated statement of financial position as at 30 September 2010.**

	$000
Non-current assets	
Property, plant and equipment	38,250
(25,500 + 13,900 – 1,200 (FV adj) + 50 (FV adj))	
Goodwill (W3)	9,300
Investments (1,800 – 800 (consideration) + 300 (gain on FVTOCI))	1,300
	48,850
Current assets (12,500 + 2,400 +130 – 130 (cash in transit) – 350 (intra-group) – 400 (W2)(a))	14,150
	63,000

Equity	
Equity shares of $1 each ((12,000 + 2,400 (W3))	14,400
Share premium (W3)	9,600
Land revaluation reserve	2,000
Other equity reserve (500 + 300 (gain on FVTOCI))	800
Retained earnings (W5)	13,060
	39,860
Non-controlling interest (W4)	3,690
	43,550
Non-current liabilities	
6% loan notes	3,000
Current liabilities (10,000 + 6,800 – 350 intra group balance)	16,450
	63,000

Tutorial note

Per IFRS 9 Financial Instruments, investments classified at fair value through other comprehensive income (FVTOCI) should be taken to the statement of financial position at their fair value at the year end and the gain or loss reported in other equity. The gain or loss, must also be disclosed as other comprehensive income at the foot of the profit or loss account.

Workings in $000

(W1) **Group structure**

Premier
              1 June 2010 (4/12)   80%
Sanford

(W2) **Net assets**

Tutorial note

A net asset working really helps.

	At acquisition	At reporting date	Post acq
Share capital	5,000	5,000	–
Retained earnings (4,500 – (3900 × 4/12))	3,200	4,500	1,300
Property fair value	(1,200)	(1,200)	–
Depreciation reduction		50	50
PURP (below)		(400)	(400)
	7,000	7,950	950
	W3		W4/W5

The unrealised profit (PURP) in inventory is calculated as $2 million × 25/125 = $400,000.

The depreciation reduction is calculated as $1,200/8 years × 4/12 = $50,000.

Tutorial note

The fair value adjustment for property is a downwards fair value adjustment and therefore should be deducted from W2 and non-current assets. The reduction in depreciation should be added back in W2 and added back to non-current assets.

(W3) **Goodwill**

Parent holding (investment) at fair value:	
Shares ((5,000 × 80%) × 3/5 × $5)	12,000
Loan note issue ((5,000 × 80%) / 500 × 100)	800
	12,800
NCI value at acquisition ((5,000 × 20%) × $3.50)	3,500
	16,300
Less:	
Fair value of net assets at acquisition (W2)	(7,000)
Goodwill on acquisition	9,300

Tutorial note

The 2.4 million shares (5,000 × 80% × 3/5) issued by Premier at $5 each would be recorded as share capital of $2.4 million and share premium of $9.6 million.

(W4)	**Non-controlling interest (SOFP)**	
	NCI value at acquisition	3,500
	NCI share of post acquisition reserves	190
	(7,950 – 7,000 (W2)) × 20%	
		3,690

(W5)	**Consolidated retained earnings**	
	Premier	12,300
	Post acquisition in Sanford post acquisition reserves	
	(7,950 – 7,000 (W2)) × 80%	760
		13,060

(W6)	**Cost of sales**	
	Premier	70,500
	Sanford (36,000 × 4/12)	12,000
	Intra-group purchases	(4,000)
	PURP in inventory	400
	Reduction of depreciation charge	(50)
		78,850

(W7)	**NCI (in SPorL):**	
		$000
	NCI share of subsidiary profit (20% × (3,900 × 4/12)	260
	Less: 20% PURP (20% × 400)	(80)
	Add: 20% × reduction in depreciation (20% × 50)	10
		190

		ACCA marking scheme		
				Marks
(a)		statement of comprehensive income:		
		Revenue		1½
		cost of sales		3
		distribution costs		½
		administrative expenses		½
		finance costs		½
		income tax		½
		other comprehensive income – gain on investments		½
		other comprehensive income – gain on property		½
		non-controlling interest – profit for year		1
		split of total comprehensive income		½
				———
			Maximum	9
(b)		statement of financial position:		
		property, plant and equipment		2
		Goodwill		3½
		Investments		1
		current assets		1½
		equity shares		1
		share premium		1
		revaluation reserve		½
		other equity reserve		1
		retained earnings		1½
		non-controlling interest		1½
		6% loan notes		½
		current liabilities		1
				———
			Maximum	16
				———
	Total			25
				———

177   PARENTIS *Walk in the footsteps of a top tutor*

Key answer tip

This question requires the preparation of a statement of financial position for a parent and subsidiary. The cost of investment includes the more technical aspects of fair value adjustments. A complication in this question involves the intellectual property write off and the government compensation. This adjustment is not essential to securing a pass in the question.

(a) **Consolidated statement of financial position of Parentis as at 31 March 2007**

	$ million	$ million
Non-current assets		
Property, plant and equipment (640 + 340 + 40 FV adj − 2 FV depn)		1,018
Intellectual property (30 − 30)		
Goodwill (W3)		130
		1,148
Current assets		
Inventory (76 + 22 − 2 PURP)	96	
Trade receivables (84 + 44 − 4 CIT − 7 intra-group)	117	
Receivable re intellectual property	10	
Bank (4 + 4 Cash-in-transit)	8	231
Total assets		1,379
Equity and liabilities		
Equity shares 25c each (W3)		375
Reserves:		
Share Premium (W3)	150	
Retained earnings (W5)	261	411
		786
Non-controlling interest (W4)		114
Total equity		
		900
Non-current liabilities		
10% loan notes (120 + 20)		140
Current liabilities		
Trade payables (130 + 57 − 7 intra-group)	180	
Cash consideration due 1 April 2007 (60 + 6 interest)	66	
Overdraft	25	
Taxation (45 + 23)	68	339
Total equity and liabilities		1,379

Workings (Note: All figures in $ million)

(W1) Group structure

Parentis

1 April 20X6   75%

Offspring

(W2) **Net assets**

	At acquisition	At reporting date	Post acq
	$000	$000	$000
Share capital	200	200	–
Retained earnings	120	140	20
Fair value adjustment	40	40	–
Fair value depreciation		(2)	(2)
Intellectual property w/off		(30)	(30)
Compensation receivable		10	10
PURP		(2)	(2)
	360	356	(4)
	W3		W4/W5

(W3) **Goodwill**

Tutorial note

The acquisition of 600 million shares represents 75% of Offspring's 800 million shares ($200m/25c). The share exchange of 300 million (i.e. 1 for 2) at $0.75 each will result in an increase in equity share capital of $75 million (the nominal value) and create a share premium balance of $150 million (i.e. $0.50 premium on 300 million shares).

Parent holding (investment) at fair value:	
Share exchange ((600 × 1 / 2) × $0.75)	225
10% loan notes (see below)	120
Cash (600 × $0.11/1.1 i.e. discounted at 10%)	60
	405
NCI value at acquisition (given)	125
	530
Less:	
Fair value of net assets at acquisition (W2)	(360)
Goodwill on acquisition	170
Impairment	(40)
	130

Tutorial note

The issue of the 10% loan notes is calculated as 600 million/500 × $100 = $120 million.

(W4) Non-controlling interest

NCI value at acquisition	125
NCI share of post-acquisition reserves (25% × ($356 − 360) (W2))	(1)
NCI share of impairment (25% × $40)	(10)
	———
	114
	———

(W5) Retained earnings

Parentis	300
Unwinding of the discount (60 × 10%)	(6)
Goodwill impairment (40 × 75%)	(30)
75% Offspring post-acquisition reserves (75% × ($356 − 360) (W2))	(3)
	———
	261
	———

Tutorial note

The unrealised profit in inventory (PURP) is $5m/$15m of the profit of $6 million made by Offspring. Offspring's retained earnings should be updated to reflect the unreal profit at (W2).

(b) The development of the encryption will be classed as research and development costs per IAS 38 Intangible Assets. Initially, the costs will be treated as research, as there is no probable economic benefit until the results of the testing have proved to be positive. As the costs are to be treated as research, these will be expensed in the statement of profit or loss. From 30 June 2009, the costs appear to qualify as development costs and therefore the costs between this date and the completion of the project can be capitalised as an intangible asset. The asset should then be held at cost until the project begins, and then be amortised over the expected life of the project. The bid from a competitor may represent a market value for the asset, but the asset cannot be revalued. Intangibles can only be revalued if an active market exists. This will not be the case for the development costs, as one of the key criteria for an active market is that items are homogenous. This will not exist in relation to the development project, so the asset will remain under the cost model.

178 PLATEAU *Walk in the footsteps of a top tutor*

Key answer tip

Part (a) required the preparation of a statement of financial position that is relatively straightforward. Ensure that you do not include the associate on a line-by-line basis and equity account instead. One of the complications in this question is a negative fair value adjustment. The highlighted words are key phrases that markers are looking for.

(a)   **Consolidated statement of financial position of Plateau as at 30 September 2007**

	$000	$000
Assets		
Non-current assets:		
Property, plant and equipment (18,400 + 10,400)		28,800
Goodwill (W3)		6,000
Investments – associate (W6)		10,500
– other (fair value through profit or loss)		9,000
		———
		54,300
Current assets		
Inventory (6,900 + 6,200 – 300 PURP) (W7)	12,800	
Trade receivables (3,200 + 1,500)	4,700	17,500
	———	
Total assets		71,800
		———
Equity		
Equity shares of $1 each (10,000 + 1,500) (W3)		11,500
Reserves:		
Share premium (W3)	7,500	
Retained earnings (W5)	30,700	38,200
	———	———
		49,700
Non-controlling interest (W4)		3,900
		———
Total equity		53,600
Non-current liabilities		
7% Loan notes (5,000 + 1,000)		6,000
Current liabilities (8,000 + 4,200)		12,200
		———
Total equity and liabilities		71,800
		———

Workings

(W1) Group structure

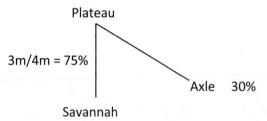

Plateau

3m/4m = 75%

Axle   30%

Savannah

Savannah was acquired on 1 October 2006 and so have been held for 1 year.

(W2) Net assets of Savannah

Tutorial note

A net asset working really helps.

	At acquisition	At reporting date	Post acq
	$000	$000	$000
Share capital	4,000	4,000	
Retained earnings	6,500	8,900	2,400
Fair value adjustment	(500)	–	500
PURP on inventory (W7)		(300)	(300)
	10,000	12,600	2,600
	W3		W4/W5

Tutorial note

The fair value adjustment does not need recording at the reporting date since Savannah had written the asset down in their books after acquisition. It should have been written down at acquisition and hence the adjustment is required at this date.

(W3) **Goodwill**

	$000
Parent holding (investment) at fair value:	
Share exchange((3,000 × ½) × $6)	9,000
Cash (3,000 × $1.25)	3,750
	12,750
NCI value at acquisition	3,250
	16,000
Less:	
Fair value of net assets at acquisition (W2)	(10,000)
	6,000

Tutorial note

The share consideration given on the acquisition of Savannah has not been recorded. Therefore share capital should be increased by (3,000 × ½ × $1) $1,500 and share premium should be increased by (3,000 × ½ × $5) $7,500.

(W4) **Non-controlling interest**

NCI value at acquisition	3,250
NCI share of post acquisition reserves ((12,600 – 10,000) × 25% (W2))	650
	3,900

(W5) **Consolidated reserves**

	$000
Plateau (16,000 + 9,250)	25,250
Acquisition costs to be expensed	(500)
Fair value through profit or loss investments (9,000 – 6,500)	2,500
Savannah (75% × (12,600 – 10,000))	1,950
Axle (W6)	1,500
	30,700

(W6) Investment in Associate

Cost of investment (30% × 4,000 × $7.50)	9,000
Post acquisition profits (30% × 5,000)	1,500
	———
	10,500
	———

(W7) Provision for unrealised profit on inventory

Profit on sale = 50/150 × 2,700 = 900

Profit in inventory = 1/3 × 900 = 300

Examiner's comments

The main areas where candidates went wrong were:

In **part (a)**

– most candidates incorrectly deducted a $500,000 reduction in the fair value of the land from the property, plant and equipment. This effectively double counted the fall in value as the question clearly stated that the land had already been written down in the post acquisition period. The point of the information is that the fall in the value of the land should have been treated as an adjustment between pre and post acquisition profits (affecting goodwill). Also many candidates failed to adjust for the $100,000 additional deprecation on the plant.

– some confusion existed over the value of the associate with many simply showing it in the statement of financial position at cost rather than using equity accounting. A very small minority proportionally consolidated the associate (some even proportionately consolidated the subsidiary).

– many candidates did correctly calculate the unrealised profit on inventory but did not always eliminate it from retained earnings.

– surprisingly, many candidates failed to adjust share capital and premium for the share issue relating to the acquisition.

– generally candidates scored well in the calculation of retained earnings, but the most common errors were not adjusting the subsidiary's post acquisition profit for the revaluation of land (mentioned earlier) and not including the gain on investments (often incorrectly shown as a revaluation reserve).

179 PATRONIC *Walk in the footsteps of a top tutor*

Key answer tip

Part (a) requires the calculation of goodwill considering fair value adjustment s to both the purchase consideration and the subsidiaries net assets. Part (b) requires the preparation of a consolidated statement of comprehensive income – be careful to ensure that you pro-rate the subsidiaries results to take into account that they have only been a subsidiary for eight months. Part (c) requires you to discuss the criteria of an associate company and to identify that Acerbic is no longer an associate. The highlighted words are key phrases that markers are looking for.

(a)   **Cost of control in Sardonic:**

	$000	$000
Parent holding (investment) at fair value:		
Share exchange (18,000 × 2/3 × $5.75)		69,000
Deferred payment ((18,000 × 2.42) × $1/1.1^2$)		36,000
		————
		105,000
NCI value at acquisition		30,500
		————
		135,500
Less:		
Equity shares	24,000	
Pre-acquisition reserves:		
At 1 April 2007	69,000	
To date of acquisition (13,500 × 4/12)	4,500	
Fair value adjustments (4,100 + 2,400)	6,500	
	————	
		(104,000)
		————
		31,500
		————

Tutorial note

The acquisition of 18 million out of a total of 24 million equity shares is a 75% interest.

(b)   **Patronic Group**

Consolidated statement of profit or loss for the year ended 31 March 2008

	$000
Revenue (150,000 + (78,000 × 8/12) − (1,250 × 8 months intra group))	192,000
Cost of sales (W1)	(119,100)
Gross profit	72,900
Distribution costs (7,400 + (3,000 × 8/12))	(9,400)
Administrative expenses (12,500 + (6,000 × 8/12))	(16,500)
Finance costs (W2)	(5,000)
Impairment of goodwill	(2,000)
Share of profit from associate (6,000 × 30%)	1,800
Profit before tax	41,800
Income tax expense (10,400 + (3,600 × 8/12))	(12,800)
Profit for the year	29,000
Attributable to:	
Equity holders of the parent	27,400
Non-controlling interest (W3)	1,600
	29,000

(c)   An associate is defined by IAS 28 *Investments in Associates and Joint Ventures* as an investment over which an investor has significant influence. There are several indicators of significant influence, but the most important are usually considered to be a holding of 20% or more of the voting shares and board representation. Therefore it was reasonable to assume that the investment in Acerbic (at 31 March 2008) represented an associate and was correctly accounted for under the equity accounting method.

The current position (from May 2008) is that although Patronic still owns 30% of Acerbic's shares, Acerbic has become a subsidiary of Spekulate as it has acquired 60% of Acerbic's shares. Acerbic is now under the control of Spekulate (part of the definition of being a subsidiary), therefore it is difficult to see how Patronic can now exert significant influence over Acerbic. The fact that Patronic has lost its seat on Acerbic's board seems to reinforce this point. In these circumstances the investment in Acerbic falls to be treated under IFRS 9 *Financial Instruments*. It will cease to be equity accounted from the date of loss of significant influence. Its carrying amount at that date will be its initial recognition value under IFRS 9 (stated and fair value) and thereafter it will be accounted for in accordance with IFRS 9.

Workings

(W1) **Cost of sales**

	$000	$000
Patronic		94,000
Sardonic (51,000 × 8/12)		34,000
Intra group purchases (1,250 × 8 months)		(10,000)
Additional depreciation: plant (2,400/ 4 years × 8/12)	400	
Property (per question)	200	600
Unrealised profit in inventories (3,000 × 20/120)		500
		119,100

Tutorial note:

For both sales revenues and cost of sales, only the post acquisition intra group trading should be eliminated.

(W2) **Finance costs**

	$000
Patronic per question	2,000
Unwinding interest – deferred consideration (36,000 × 10% × 8/12)	2,400
Sardonic (900 × 8/12)	600
	5,000

(W3) **Non-controlling interest**

NCI share of S's post acquisition profit (13,500 × 8/12 × 25%)	2,250
Less NCI share of FV depreciation (600 (W1) × 25%)	(150)
Less NCI share of impairment (2,000 × 25%)	(500)
	1,600

Examiner's comments

Required the calculation of goodwill and the preparation of a consolidated statement of comprehensive income for a parent, subsidiary and an associate (equity accounted) followed by a short 4 mark section requiring an explanation of how an investment in an associate should be treated after it became a subsidiary of another company. The consolidation was generally well answered, but answers to the written section were more 'patchy'.

The main areas where candidates went wrong were:

In **part (a)** – goodwill calculation

– most candidates correctly calculated the share exchange consideration, but failed to discount (for two years) the deferred cash consideration correctly. The calculation of the pre-acquisition equity was also done quite well, but the most common mistakes were not including an apportionment (4 months) of the current year's profit as part of the pre-acquisition figure and incorrectly including post acquisition adjustments for additional depreciation and unrealised profits as pre-acquisition items. It was also common for candidates to forget to include the subsidiary's share capital in the calculation of equity.

Part (b) – consolidated statement of comprehensive income

– a surprisingly common error was not time apportioning (for 8 months) the subsidiary's results, instead a full year's results were often included. This is a fundamental error showing a lack of understanding of the principle that a subsidiary's results are only included the consolidated accounts from date it becomes a member of the group. A small minority of candidates proportionally consolidated, rather than equity accounted, the associate (some even proportionately consolidated the subsidiary), however this error is now becoming much less common.

– many candidates did not correctly eliminate the intra-group trading; either no adjustment at all or eliminating pre-acquisition trading as well.

– the unrealised profit in inventory was often calculated as a gross profit percentage, whereas the question stated it was a mark up was on cost. It was also common for this adjustment to be deducted from cost of sales rather than added.

– impairment/amortisation of goodwill was often omitted.

– the finance cost relating to the unwinding of the deferred consideration was omitted by most candidates.

– the calculation of the non-controlling interest (now called non-controlling interest) was sometimes ignored or did not take account the post acquisition additional depreciation adjustment or time apportionment.

In **part (c)** the answers were very disappointing; many not attempting it all. The question was based on how an associate, that had previously been equity accounted, would be treated in the following year when it had lost its 'significant influence' due to the associate becoming a subsidiary of another entity. Of those that did attempt this section many wasted time by reproducing (as an answer) the scenario given in the question rather than actually answering the question. Others did not think the investment should be treated any differently in the following year saying that the percentage of share ownership is all that matters (despite the loss of a seat on the board). Some candidates thought the question asked for an explanation of how the investment should be treated in the current year. The correct answer is that it should be treated as an 'ordinary investment' (no longer an associate) under IFRS 9.

ACCA marking scheme		
		Marks
(a) Goodwill of Sardonic:		
consideration		2
net assets acquired calculated as:		
equity shares		1
pre acquisition reserves		2
fair value adjustments		1
Maximum		6
(b) Statement of comprehensive income:		
revenue		2
cost of sales		5
distribution costs and administrative expenses		1
finance costs		2
impairment of goodwill		1
share of associate's profit		1
income tax		1
Non-controlling interest		2
Maximum		15
(c) 1 mark per relevant point to		4
Total		25

180 PEDANTIC *Walk in the footsteps of a top tutor*

Key answer tips

This question requires the preparation of a fairly straightforward consolidated statement of comprehensive income and a consolidated statement of financial position. The biggest problem for candidates is to complete the tasks in the exam time available. Ensure you pro-rate the subsidiary's results in part (a) to gain the easy marks available.

(a) **Consolidated statement of profit or loss for the year ended 30 September 2008**

	$000
Revenue (85,000 + (42,000 × 6/12) − 8,000 intra-group sales)	98,000
Cost of sales (W8)	(72,000)
	————
Gross profit	26,000
Distribution costs (2,000 + (2,000 × 6/12))	(3,000)
Administrative expenses (6,000 + (3,200 × 6/12))	(7,600)
Finance costs (300 + (400 × 6/12))	(500)
	————
Profit before tax	14,900
Income tax expense (4,700 + (1,400 × 6/12))	(5,400)
	————
Profit for the year	9,500
	————

Attributable to:

Equity holders of the parent	9,300
Non-controlling interest (W9)	200
	9,500

(b) **Consolidated statement of financial position as at 30 September 2008**

Assets

Non-current assets

Property, plant and equipment

(40,600 + 12,600 + 2,000 − 200 depreciation adjustment (W2))	55,000
Goodwill (W3)	4,500
	59,500
Current assets (W7)	21,400
Total assets	80,900

Equity and liabilities

Equity attributable to owners of the parent

Equity shares of $1 each (10, 000 + 1,600 (W3))	11,600
Share premium (W3)	8,000
Retained earnings (W5)	35,700
	55,300
Non-controlling interest (W4)	6,100
Total equity	61,400
Non-current liabilities	
10% loan notes (4,000 + 3,000)	7,000
Current liabilities (8,200 + 4,700 − 400 intra-group balance)	12,500
Total equity and liabilities	80,900

Workings (figures in brackets in $000)

(W1) **Group structure**

Pedantic

60%

Sophistic

Investments occurred on 1 April 2008 so has been held for 6 months.

(W2) **Net assets of Sophistic**

	At acquisition	At reporting date	Post acq
	$000	$000	$000
Share capital	4,000	4,000	–
Retained earnings	5,000	6,500	1,500
Fair value adjustment:			
Plant	2,000	2,000	–
Depreciation (2,000 / 5 years) × 6 months		(200)	(200)
PURP on inventory (W6)		(800)	(800)
	11,000	11,500	500
	W3		W4/W5

(W3) **Goodwill**

	$000
Parent holding (investment) at fair value:	
Share exchange ((4,000 × 60%) × 2/3 × $6)	9,600
NCI value at acquisition (given)	5,900
	15,500
Less:	
Fair value of net assets at acquisition (W2)	(11,000)
	4,500

Tutorial note

The share consideration given on the acquisition of Sophistic has not been recorded. Therefore share capital should be increased by ((4,000 ×60%) × 2/3 × $1) $1,600 and share premium should be increased by ((4,000 × 60%) × 2/3 × $5) $8,000.

(W4) **Non-controlling interest (SOFP)**

	$000
NCI value at acquisition	5,900
NCI share of post acquisition reserves	200
((11,500 – 11,000) × 40%)	
	6,100

(W5) **Consolidated reserves**

	$000
Pedantic	35,400
Sophistic (60% × (11,500 – 11,000))	300
	35,700

(W6) **Provision for unrealised profit on inventory**

The unrealised profit (PURP) in inventory is calculated as ($8 million – $5.2 million) × 40/140 = $800,000.

(W7) **Current assets**

	$000
Pedantic	16,000
Sophistic	6,600
PURP in inventory	(800)
Cash in transit	200
Intra-group balance	(600)
	21,400

(W8) **Cost of sales**

	$000
Pedantic	63,000
Sophistic (32,000 × 6/12)	16,000
Intra-group sales	(8,000)
PURP in inventory	800
Additional depreciation (2,000/5 years × 6/12)	200
	72,000

(W9) **Non-controlling interest (SPorL)**

NCI share of S's post acquisition profit (3,000 × 6/12 × 40%)	600
Less NCI share of FV depreciation (200 (W8) × 40%)	(80)
Less NCI share of PURP (800 × 40%)	(320)
	200

(c) Although the concept behind the preparation of consolidated financial statements is to treat all the members of the group as if they were a single economic entity, it must be understood that the legal position is that each member is a separate legal entity and therefore the group itself does not exist as a separate legal entity. This focuses on a criticism of group financial statements in that they aggregate the assets and liabilities of all the members of the group. This can give the impression that all of the group's assets would be available to discharge all of the group's liabilities. This is not the case.

Applying this to the situation in the question, it would mean that any liability of Trilby to Pedantic would not be a liability of any other member of the Pedantic group. Thus the fact that the consolidated statement of financial position of Tradhat shows a strong position with healthy liquidity is not necessarily of any reassurance to Pedantic. Any decision on granting credit to Trilby must be based on Trilby's own (entity) financial statements (which Pedantic should obtain), not the group financial statements. The other possibility, which would take advantage of the strength of the group's statement of financial position, is that Pedantic could ask Tradhat if it would act as a guarantor to Trilby's (potential) liability to Pedantic. In this case Tradhat would be liable for the debt to Pedantic in the event of a default by Trilby.

181 PANDAR *Walk in the footsteps of a top tutor*

(a) (i) **Goodwill in Salva at 1 April 2009:**

	$000	$000
Parent holding (investment) at fair value:		
Share exchange		
((120 million × 80%) × 3/5 × $6)		345,600
NCI value at acquisition		
(120 million × 20% × $3.20)		76,800
		———
		422,400
Equity shares	120,000	
Reserves at 1 October 2008	152,000	
Profit to date of acquisition (see below)	11,500	
Fair value adjustments (5,000 + 20,000)	25,000	308,500
	———	———
Goodwill arising on acquisition		113,900
		———

Tutorial note

The interest on the loan note is $2 million ($50 million × 8% × 6/12). This is in Salva's profit in the post-acquisition period. Thus Salva's profit of $21 million has a split of $11.5 million pre-acquisition ((21 million + 2 million interest) × 6/12) and $9.5 million post-acquisition.

(ii) **Carrying amount of investment in Ambra at 30 September 2009**

	$000
Cost (40 million × 40% × $2)	32,000
Share of post-acquisition losses (5,000 × 40% × 6/12)	(1,000)
Impairment charge	(3,000)
	———
	28,000
	———

(b)   **Pandar Group**

Consolidated statement of profit or loss for the year ended 30 September 2009

	$000	$000
Revenue (210,000 + (150,000 × 6/12) – 15,000 intra-group sales)		270,000
Cost of sales (w (W1))		(162,500)
Gross profit		107,500
Distribution costs (11,200 + (7,000 × 6/12))		(14,700)
Administrative expenses (18,300 + (9,000 × 6/12))		(22,800)
Investment income (W2)		1,100
Finance costs (W3)		(2,300)
Share of loss from associate (5,000 × 40% × 6/12)	(1,000)	
Impairment of investment in associate	(3,000)	(4,000)
Profit before tax		64,800
Income tax expense (15,000 + (10,000 × 6/12))		(20,000)
Profit for the year		44,800
Attributable to:		
Owners of the parent		43,000
Non-controlling interest (W4)		1,800
		44,800

Workings (figures in brackets in $000)

(W1) **Cost of sales**

	$000
Pandar	126,000
Salva (100,000 × 6/12)	50,000
Intra-group purchases	(15,000)
Additional depreciation: plant (5,000/5 years × 6/12)	500
Unrealised profit in inventories (15,000/3 × 20%)	1,000
	162,500

Tutorial note

As the registration of the domain name is renewable indefinitely (at only a nominal cost) it will not be amortised.

(W2) Investment income

	$000
Per statement of comprehensive income	9,500
Intra-group interest (50,000 × 8% × 6/12)	(2,000)
Intra-group dividend (8,000 × 80%)	(6,400)
	1,100

(W3) Finance costs

	$000
Pandar	1,800
Salva post-acquisition ((3,000 – 2,000) × 6/12 + 2,000)	2,500
Intra-group interest (W2)	(2,000)
	2,300

(W4) Non-controlling interest

NCI % × Salva's post-acquisition profit (20% × 9,500 see part (i) above)	1,900
Less: NCI % × FV depreciation (20% × 500 (W1))	(100)
	1,800

(b) In recent years many companies have increasingly conducted large parts of their business by acquiring substantial non-controlling interests in other companies. There are broadly three levels of investment. Below 20% of the equity shares of an investee would normally be classed as an ordinary financial asset investment, measured according to the IFRS 9 *Financial Instruments* rules for the particular category of asset.

A holding of above 50% normally gives control and would create subsidiary company status and consolidation is required. Between these two, in the range of over 20% up to 50%, the investment would normally be deemed to be an associate. (**Note:** The level of shareholding is not the only determining criterion.) The relevance of this level of shareholding is that it is presumed to give significant influence over the operating and financial policies of the investee (but this presumption can be rebutted). If such an investment were treated as an ordinary investment, the investing company would have the opportunity to manipulate its profit. The most obvious example of this would be by exercising influence over the size of the dividend the associated company paid. This would directly affect the reported profit of the investing company. Also, as companies tend not to distribute all of their profits as dividends, over time the cost of the investment in the statement of financial position may give very little indication of its underlying value.

Equity accounting for associated companies is an attempt to remedy these problems. In the statement of profit or loss any dividends received from an associate are replaced by the investor's share of the associate's results. In the statement of financial position the investment is initially recorded at cost and subsequently increased by the investor's share of the retained earnings of the associate (any other gains such as the revaluation of the associate's assets would also be included in this process). This treatment means that the investor would show the same profit irrespective of the size of the dividend paid by the associate and the statement of financial position more closely reflects the worth of the investment.

The problem of off statement of financial position finance relates to the fact that it is the net assets that are shown in the investor's statement of financial position. Any share of the associate's liabilities is effectively hidden because they have been offset against the associate's assets. As a simple example, say a holding company owned 100% of another company that had assets of $100 million and debt of $80 million; both the assets and the debt would appear on the consolidated statement of financial position. Whereas if this single investment was replaced by owning 50% each of two companies that had the same statements of financial position (i.e. $100 million assets and $80 million debt), then under equity accounting only $20 million $((100 - 80) \times 50\% \times 2)$ of net assets would appear on the statement of financial position thus hiding the $80 million of debt. Because of this problem, it has been suggested that proportionate consolidation is a better method of accounting for associated companies, as both assets and debts would be included in the investor's statement of financial position.

IAS 28 *Investments in Associates and Joint Ventures* does not permit the use of proportionate consolidation of associates.

ACCA marking scheme				Marks
(a)	(i)	Goodwill of Salva:		
		Consideration		2.0
		net assets acquired calculated as:		
		equity shares		1.0
		pre acquisition reserves		2.0
		fair value adjustments		1.0
			Maximum	6.0
	(ii)	Carrying value of Ambra		
		Cost		1.0
		share of post-acquisition losses		1.0
		impairment charge		1.0
			Maximum	3.0
(b)		Statement of comprehensive income:		
		Revenue		2.0
		cost of sales		4.0
		distribution costs and administrative expenses		1.0
		investment income		2.5
		finance costs		1.5
		share of associate's losses and impairment charge		1.0
		income tax		1.0
		non-controlling interests		2.0
		domain name not amortised		1.0
			Maximum	16.0
(c)		One mark per sensible comment		5
Total				30

Examiner's comments

Question 1 required calculation of consolidated goodwill (a)(i), the carrying amount of an associate (a)(ii) and the preparation of a consolidated statement of comprehensive income (b) of a parent and a single subsidiary and an associate that had been acquired half way through the accounting period. The question involved a share exchange, fair value adjustments and the elimination of intra-group trading and unrealised profits on inventory. This was generally well answered; most candidates have grasped the main principles of consolidation with only the more complex aspects posing problems. There were a very small minority of candidates that used proportional consolidation (for the associate and some even for the subsidiary) and a similar number failed to time apportion the consolidation. This gave the impression that such candidates have never practised any past questions.

The main areas where candidates made errors were:

In **part (a)** calculation of goodwill and associate:

- generally well answered (gaining 4 or 5 from 6 marks), but very few candidates correctly allowed for the interest on an 8% loan being entirely charged to the post-acquisition period (it was treated as accruing evenly throughout the period) when calculating the retained earnings at the date of acquisition. A significant number of candidates sitting International Standards based papers did not calculate the non-controlling interest at its (full) fair value (the 'new' method under IFRS 3), instead calculating it at the proportionate share of the fair value of the subsidiary's net assets.

- the calculation of the carrying amount of the associate was also very good, often gaining full marks. The main problems were not apportioning (by 6/12) the losses in the year of acquisition and not applying the 40% group holding percentage. Some treated the losses as profits.

The consolidated statement of profit or loss (b). Again well-prepared candidates gained good marks with most understanding the general principles. The main errors were with the more complex adjustments:

- a full year's additional depreciation of the plant was charged, but it should have been only for the post-acquisition period of six months

- many candidates incorrectly amortised the domain name; its registration was renewable indefinitely at negligible cost so it should not have been amortised

- surprisingly a number of candidates incorrectly calculated the PURP on inventory by treating the gross profit of 25% as if it were a mark up on cost of 25%

- the elimination of intra-group dividend was often ignored or the full $8 million was eliminated instead

- often the trading and impairment losses of the associate were ignored in preparing the statement of comprehensive income

- the non-controlling interest was frequently ignored and where it was calculated, many forgot to adjust for the additional depreciation on the fair value of the plant.

Despite the above, this was the best answered question and many candidates gained good marks.

182 PICANT *Walk in the footsteps of a top tutor*

Key answer tips

Part (a) required the preparation of a statement of financial position that is relatively straightforward. Ensure that you do not include the associate on a line-by-line basis and equity account instead. One of the complications in this question is the contingent consideration. The contingent consideration should be accounted for at the acquisition date regardless of its probability providing it can be reliably measured. The fair value of the consideration has then changed at the year end. Under IFRS the change in the consideration is taken via group retained earnings and the goodwill calculation is not adjusted for.

(a) **Consolidated statement of financial position of Picant as at 31 March 2010**

	$000	$000
Non-current assets:		
Property, plant and equipment (37,500 + 24,500 + 2,000 FV adj – 100 FV depn)		63,900
Goodwill (16,000 – 3,800 (W3))		12,200
Investment in associate (W6))		13,200
		89,300
Current assets		
Inventory (10,000 + 9,000 + 1,800 GIT – 600 PURP (W7)))	20,200	
Trade receivables (6,500 + 1,500 – 3,400 intra-group (W7))	4,600	24,800
Total assets		114,100
Equity and liabilities		
Equity attributable to owners of the parent		
Equity shares of $1 each		25,000
Share premium	19,800	
Retained earnings (W5))	27,500	47,300
		72,300
Non-controlling interest (W4))		8,400
Total equity		80,700
Non-current liabilities		
7% loan notes (14,500 + 2,000)		16,500
Current liabilities		
Contingent consideration	2,700	
Other current liabilities (8,300 + 7,500 – 1,600 intra-group (W7))	14,200	16,900
Total equity and liabilities		114,100

KAPLAN PUBLISHING

Workings (all figures in $ million)

(W1) Group structure

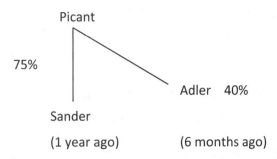

Picant

75%

Adler   40%

Sander

(1 year ago)   (6 months ago)

(W2) Net assets

Tutorial note

A net asset working really helps.

	At acquisition	At reporting date	Post acq
	$000	$000	$000
Share capital	8,000	8,000	–
Retained earnings	16,500	17,500	1,000
Fair value adjustment:			
Factory	2,000	2,000	–
Fair value depreciation		(100)	(100)
Software w/off	(500)		500
	26,000	27,400	1,400
	W3		W4/W5

Tutorial note

The effect of the software having no recoverable amount is that its write-off in the post-acquisition period should be treated as a fair value adjustment at the date of acquisition for consolidation purposes. The consequent effect is that this will increase the post-acquisition profit for consolidation purposes by $500,000.

(W3) Goodwill

Parent holding (investment) at fair value	
– Share exchange (8,000 × 75% × 3/2 × $3.20)	28,800
– Contingent consideration	4,200
	33,000
NCI value at acquisition (8,000 × 25% × $4.50)	9,000
	42,000
Less:	
Fair value of net assets at acquisition (W2)	(26,000)
Goodwill on acquisition	16,000
Impairment	(3,800)
	12,200

(W4) Non-controlling interest

NCI value at acquisition (W3)	9,000
NCI share of post-acquisition reserves ((27,400 – 26,000) × 25% (W2))	350
NCI share of impairment (3,800 × 25%)	(950)
	8,400

(W5) Group retained earnings

Picant's retained earnings	27,200
Sanders post-acquisition profits ((27,400 – 26,000) × 75% (W2))	1,050
Group share of impairment (3,800 × 25%)	(2,850)
Adler's post-acquisition profits (6,000 × 6/12 × 40%)	1,200
PURP in inventories (1,800 × 50/150)	(600)
Gain from reduction of contingent consideration (4,200 – 2,700 see below)	1,500
	27,500

Tutorial note

The adjustment to the provision for contingent consideration due to events occurring after the acquisition is reported in income (goodwill is not recalculated).

(W6) Investment in associate

Investment at cost:

Cash consideration (5,000 × 40% × $4)	8,000
7% loan notes (5,000 × 40% × $100/50)	4,000
	12,000
Adler's post-acquisition profits (6,000 × 6/12 × 40%)	1,200
	13,200

(W7) Goods in transit and unrealised profit (PURP)

The intra-group current accounts differ by the goods-in-transit sales of $1.8 million on which Picant made a profit of $600,000 (1,800 × 50/150). Thus inventory must be increased by $1.2 million (its cost), $600,000 is eliminated from Picant's profit, $3.4 million is deducted from trade receivables and $1.6 million (3,400 – 1,800) is deducted from trade payables (other current liabilities).

ACCA marking scheme		
		Marks
(a)	**Statement of financial position:**	
	property, plant and equipment	2
	goodwill	5
	investment in associate	1½
	inventory	1½
	receivables	1
	equity shares	½
	share premium	½
	retained earnings	4½
	non-controlling interest	2
	7% loan notes	½
	contingent consideration	1
	other current liabilities	1
Total		21

183 PRODIGAL

(a) (i) **Prodigal – Consolidated statement of profit or loss and other comprehensive income for the year ended 31 March 2011**

	$000
Revenue (450,000 + (240,000 × 6/12) – 40,000 intra-group sales)	530,000
Cost of sales (W1)	(278,800)
	————
Gross profit	251,200
Distribution costs (23,600 + (12,000 × 6/12))	(29,600)
Administrative expenses (27,000 + (23,000 × 6/12))	(38,500)
Finance costs (1,500 + (1,200 × 6/12))	(2,100)
	————
Profit before tax	181,000
Income tax expense (48,000 + (27,800 × 6/12))	(61,900)
	————
Profit for the year	119,100
	————
Other comprehensive income	
Gain on revaluation of land (2,500 + 1,000)	3,500
Loss on fair value of equity financial asset investments (700 + (400 × 6/12))	(900)
	————
	2,600
	————
Total comprehensive income	121,700
	————
Profit attributable to:	
Owners of the parent	111,600
Non-controlling interest (W2)	7,500
	————
	119,100
	————
Total comprehensive income attributable to:	
Owners of the parent	114,000
Non-controlling interest (W2)	7,700
	————
	121,700
	————

(ii) **Prodigal – Equity section of the consolidated statement of financial position as at 31 March 2011**

Equity attributable to owners of the parent

Share capital (250,000 + 80,000) *see below*	330,000
Share premium (100,000 + 240,000) *see below*	340,000
Revaluation reserve (land) (W6)	11,650
Other equity reserve (W7)	2,350
Retained earnings (W5)	201,600
	885,600
Non-controlling interest (W4)	107,700
Total equity	993,300

The share exchange would result in Prodigal issuing 80 million shares (160,000 × 75% × 2/3) at a value of $4 each (capital 80,000; premium 240,000).

(b) IFRS 3 allows (as an option) a non-controlling interest to be valued at its proportionate share of the acquired subsidiary's identifiable net assets; this carries forward the only allowed method in the previous version of this Standard. Its effect on the statement of financial position is that the resulting carrying value of purchased goodwill only relates to the parent's element of such goodwill and as a consequence the non-controlling interest does not reflect its share of the subsidiary's goodwill. Some commentators feel this is an anomaly as the principle of a consolidated statement of financial position is that it should disclose the whole of the subsidiary's assets that are under the control of the parent (not just the parent's share). This principle is applied to all of a subsidiary's other identifiable assets, so why not goodwill?

Any impairment of goodwill under this method would only be charged against the parent's interest, as the non-controlling interest's share of goodwill is not included in the consolidated financial statements.

The second (new) method of valuing the non-controlling interest at its fair value would (normally) increase the value of the goodwill calculated on acquisition. This increase reflects the non-controlling interest's ownership of the subsidiary's goodwill and has the effect of 'grossing up' the goodwill and the non-controlling interests in the statement of financial position (by the same amount). It is argued that this method reflects the whole of the subsidiary's goodwill/premium on acquisition and is thus consistent with the principles of consolidation.

Under this method any impairment of the subsidiary's goodwill is charged to both the controlling (parent's share) and non-controlling interests in proportion to their holding of shares in the subsidiary.

Workings (figures in brackets in $000)

(W1) **Cost of sales**

	$000
Prodigal	260,000
Sentinel (110,000 × 6/12)	55,000
Intra-group purchases	(40,000)
Unrealised profit on sale of plant	1,000
Depreciation adjustment on sale of plant (1,000/2½ years × 6/12)	(200)
Unrealised profit in inventory (12,000 × 10,000/40,000)	3,000
	278,800

(W2) **NCI (SPorL)**

NCI % ×S's post-acquisition profit (25% × (66,000 × 6/12))	8,250
Less: NCI % × PURP	(750)
	7,500

NCI (Total comprehensive income)

As above	7,500
Other comprehensive income (1,000 – (400 × 6/12) × 25%)	200
	7,700

(W3) **Net assets**

	At acquisition $000	At reporting date $000	Post acq $000
Share capital	160,000	160,000	–
Retained earnings	158,000	191,000	33,000
Other equity reserve	2,000	1,800	(200) (W7)
Revaluation surplus	–	1,000	1,000 (W6)
PURP	–	(3,000)	(3,000)
	320,00	350,800	30,800

Note: Only the post-acquisition impact on retained earnings should go to the group retained earnings. This will be the 33,000 post acquisition profits less the 3,000 PURP. Therefore P's share of post-acquisition retained earnings = 75% × 30,000 = 22,500

(W4) Non-controlling interest

NCI value at acquisition (note (iv))	100,000
NCI share of post-acquisition reserves (30,800 × 25% (W3))	7,700
	107,700

(W5) Group retained earnings

Prodigal's retained earnings (90,000 b/f + 89,900 profit for yr)	179,900
Sentinel's post-acquisition profits (30,000 (W3) × 75%)	22,500
NCA PURP	(800)
	201,600

(W6) Revaluation surplus

Prodigal's revaluation surplus (8,400 + 2,500 gain in year)	10,900
Sentinel's post-acquisition surplus (1,000 (W3) × 75%)	750
	11,650

(W7) Other equity reserve

Prodigal's equity reserve (3,200 - 700 loss in year)	2,500
Sentinel's post-acquisition surplus ((200) (W3) × 75%)	(150)
	2,350

Alternative workings for the equity section:

Prodigal – Equity section

Equity attributable to owners of the parent	
Share capital (250,000 + 80,000)	330,000
Share premium (100,000 + 240,000)	340,000
Revaluation reserve (land) (8,400 + 2,500 + (1,000 × 75%))	11,650
Other equity reserve (3,200 – 700 – (400 × 6/12 × 75%))	2,350
Retained earnings (see blow	201,600
	885,600
Non-controlling interest (see below	107,700
Total equity	993,300

Retained earnings

Prodigal at 1 April 2010	90,000
Per statement of profit or loss	111,600
	———
	201,600
	———

NCI

At acquisition	100,000
Per statement of profit or loss	7,700
	———
	107,700
	———

ACCA marking scheme				
				Marks
(a)	(i)	Statement of profit or loss and other comprehensive income		
		revenue		2
		cost of sales		5
		distribution costs and administrative expenses		1
		finance costs		1
		income tax expense		1
		non-controlling interest in profit for year		2
		other comprehensive income		2
		non-controlling interest in other comprehensive income		2
				———
			Maximum	16
				———
	(ii)	Consolidated equity		
		share capital		1½
		share premium		1½
		revaluation reserve (land)		1½
		other equity reserve		1½
		retained earnings		1½
		non-controlling interest		1½
				———
			Maximum	9
				———
(b)		1 mark per valid point		5
				———
Total				**30**
				———

184 PALADIN

Consolidated statement of financial position of Paladin as at 30 September 2011

	$000	$000
Assets		
Non-current assets:		
Property, plant and equipment (40,000 + 31,000 + 4,000 FV – 1,000 FV dep'n)		74,000
Intangible assets		
– goodwill (W3)		15,000
– other intangibles (7,500 + 3,000 FV – 500 FV amor'n)		10,000
Investment in associate (W6)		7,700
		106,700
Current assets		
Inventory (11,200 + 8,400 – 600 URP (W7)	19,000	
Trade receivables (7,400 + 5,300 – 1,300 intra-group (W8)	11,400	
Bank	3,400	33,800
Total assets		140,500
Equity and liabilities		
Equity attributable to owners of the parent		
Equity shares of $1 each		50,000
Retained earnings (W5)		35,200
		85,200
Non-controlling interest (W4)		7,900
Total equity		93,100
Non-current liabilities		
Deferred tax (15,000 + 8,000)		23,000
Current liabilities		
Bank overdraft	2,500	
Deferred consideration	5,400	
Trade payables (11,600 + 6,200 – 1,300 intra-group (W8)	16,500	24,400
Total equity and liabilities		140,500

Workings (all figures in $ million)

(W1) Group structure

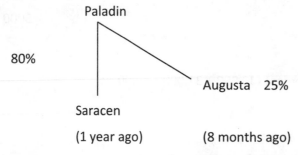

Paladin

80%

Augusta   25%

Saracen

(1 year ago)   (8 months ago)

(W2) Net assets

	At acquisition	At reporting date	Post acq
	$000	$000	$000
Share capital	10,000	10,000	–
Retained earnings	12,000	18,000	6,000
Fair value adjustment to plant	4,000	4,000	–
Fair value depreciation (4,000/4 years)		(1,000)	(1,000)
Fair value adjustment to intangible	3,000	3,000	–
Fair value amortisation (3,000/6 years)		(500)	(500)
	29,000	33,500	4,500
	W3		W4/W5

(W3) Goodwill

Immediate cash	32,000
Deferred consideration (5,400 × 100/108)	5,000
	37,000
NCI at acquisition (2,000 shares owned × $3.50)	7,000
	44,000
Less:	
Fair value of net assets at acquisition (W2)	(29,000)
Goodwill on acquisition	15,000

(W4) Non-controlling interest

Fair value on acquisition (W3)	7,000
Post-acquisition profits (4,500 (w (v)) × 20%)	900
	7,900

(W5) **Group retained earnings**

Paladin's retained earnings (25,700 + 9,200)	34,900
Saracen's post-acquisition profits (4,500 (W2) × 80%)	3,600
Augusta's post-acquisition profits (W6)	200
Augusta's impairment loss	(2,500)
PURP (W7)	(600)
Finance cost of deferred consideration (5,000 × 8%)	(400)
	35,200

(W6) **Investment in associate**

Cash consideration	10,000
Share of post-acquisition profits (1,200 × 8/12 × 25%)	200
Impairment loss	(2,500)
	7,700

(W7) **PURP**

The PURP in Saracen's inventory is $600,000 (2,600 × 30/130).

(W8) **Intra-group current accounts**

The current account balances of Paladin and Saracen should be eliminated from trade receivables and payables at the agreed amount of $1·3 million.

(b) IFRS 3 *Business Combinations* requires the purchase consideration for an acquired entity to be allocated to the fair value of the assets, liabilities and contingent liabilities acquired (henceforth referred to as net assets and ignoring contingent liabilities) with any residue being allocated to goodwill. This also means that those net assets will be recorded at fair value in the consolidated statement of financial position. This is entirely consistent with the way other net assets are recorded when first transacted (i.e. the initial cost of an asset is normally its fair value). The purpose of this process is that it ensures that individual assets and liabilities are correctly classified (and valued) in the consolidated statement of financial position. Whilst this may sound obvious, consider what would happen if say a property had a carrying amount of $5 million, but a fair value of $7 million at the date it was acquired. If the carrying amount rather than the fair value was used in the consolidation it would mean that tangible assets (property, plant and equipment) would be understated by $2 million and intangible assets (goodwill) would be overstated by the same amount.

There could also be a 'knock on' effect with incorrect depreciation charges in the years following an acquisition and incorrect calculation of any goodwill impairment. Thus the use of carrying amounts rather than fair values would not give a 'faithful representation' as required by the Framework.

The assistant's comment regarding the inconsistency of value models in the consolidated statement of financial position is a fair point, but it is really a deficiency of the historical cost concept rather than a flawed consolidation technique. Indeed the fair values of the subsidiary's net assets are the historical costs to the parent. To overcome much of the inconsistency, there would be nothing to prevent the parent company from applying the revaluation model to its property, plant and equipment.

ACCA marking scheme	
	Marks
property, plant and equipment	2½
goodwill	5
other intangibles	2½
investment in associate	2
inventory	1
receivables	1
bank	½
equity shares	½
retained earnings	5
non-controlling interest	2
deferred tax	½
bank overdraft	½
deferred consideration	1
trade payables	1
	——
	25
(b) One mark per sensible comment	5
	——
	30
	——

185 PYRAMID

(a) **Pyramid – Consolidated statement of financial position as at 31 March 2012**

	$000	$000
Assets		
Non-current assets:		
Property, plant and equipment (38,100 + 28,500 + 3,000 fair value – 600 depreciation)		69,000
Goodwill (W3)		7,400
Investments – associate (W6)	6,600	
– fair value equity investments	2,800	9,400
		——
		85,800
Current assets		
Inventory (13,900 + 10,400 + 1,500 GIT (W8) – 500 PURP (W7))	25,300	
Trade receivables (11,400 + 5,500 – 1,200 CIT – 3,200 intra group (W 8))	12,500	
Bank (900 + 600 + 1,200 CIT (W8))	2,700	40,500
		——
Total assets		126,300
		——

Equity and liabilities

Equity attributable to owners of the parent

Equity shares of $1 each		25,000
Reserves:		
Share premium	17,600	
Retained earnings (W5)	36,380	53,980
		78,980
Non-controlling interest (W4)		8,480
Total equity		87,460
Non-current liabilities		
11% loan notes (12,000 + 4,000 – 2,500 intra-group)	13,500	
Deferred tax (4,500 + 1,000)	5,500	19,000
Current liabilities		
Deferred consideration (6,400 + 640 unwinding of discount (W5))	7,040	
Other current liabilities (9,500 + 5,000 + 1,500 GIT – 3,200 intra group (W8)	12,800	19,840
Total equity and liabilities		126,300

Workings (all figures in $ million)

(W1) Group structure

Pyramid

80%

Square

(1 year ago)

(W2) **Net assets**

	At acquisition	At reporting date	Post acq
	$000	$000	$000
Share capital	10,000	10,000	–
Retained earnings	18,000	26,000	8,000
Fair value adjustment	3,000	3,000	–
Fair value depreciation		(600)	(600)
Fair value adjustment to intangible	3,000	3,000	–
Fair value adj deferred tax	(1,000)	(1,000)	–
	30,000	37,400	7,400
	W3		W4/W5

(W3) Goodwill

Shares	24,000
Deferred consideration (8,000 × 88c × 1/1.1)	6,400
	_____
	30,400
NCI at acquisition (2,000 shares owned × $3.50)	7,000
	_____
	37,400
Less:	
Fair value of net assets at acquisition (W2)	(30,000)
	_____
Goodwill on acquisition	7,400
	_____

(W4) Non-controlling interest

Fair value on acquisition (W3)	7,000
Post-acquisition profits (7,400 (W2) × 20%)	1,480
	_____
	8,480
	_____

(W5) Group retained earnings

Pyramid's retained earnings	30,200
Square's post-acquisition profits (7,400 (W2) × 80%)	5,920
Cube's post-acquisition profits (30% × $2m)	600
Gain on equity investments	800
PURP (W7)	(500)
Finance cost of deferred consideration (6,400 × 10%)	(640)
	_____
	36,380
	_____

(W6) Investment in associate

Cost	6,000
Share of post-acquisition profits (30% × $2m)	600
	_____
	6,600
	_____

(W7) PURP

The PURP in inventory is $500,000 (1,500 × 50/150).

(W8) Intra-group current accounts

The goods-in-transit and cash-in-transit need to be dealt with first.

Goods in transit: Dr Inventory 1,500, Cr Payables 1,500

Cash in transit: Dr Cash 1,200, Cr Receivables 1,200

This leaves $3,200 in receivables/payables, which can now be cancelled down.

(b) The concept of ownership is key within group accounts. In the statement of financial position, the assets and liabilities of both companies are added together in order to show that the group controls all of these. However, the shareholders of the parent do not own the entire group. As Pyramid only own 80% of Square, there is a 20% shareholding that is owned by another party, referred to as non-controlling interest. This is reflected within the equity section, separate to the other components of equity. From this, users could ascertain the value of Square which is not owned by Pyramid.

The single entity concept also underpins the construction of group accounts. This concept treats the group as if it were a single entity, despite the two companies being legally separate. As the group is treated as a single entity, any balances owed between the two companies must be removed, as if it were owed between divisions of the same entity.

In relation to Pyramid, the fact that Pyramid makes a 50% mark up on sales to Square must be removed in relation to any goods remaining in the group. This is because any goods not sold on by Square are still within the group. As the group is treated as a single entity, the profit on these goods has not been earned by the group and is deemed to be unrealised. Therefore this profit must be removed.

ACCA marking scheme	
	Marks
Statement of financial position:	
property, plant and equipment	2
Goodwill	4½
investment – associate	1
– other equity	1
inventory	2
receivables	1½
Bank	1
equity shares	½
share premium	½
retained earnings	4½
non-controlling interest	1½
11% loan notes	1½
deferred tax	1
deferred consideration	1
other current liabilities	1½
(b) One mark per sensible comment	5
	───
Total	**30**
	───

186 VIAGEM

Viagem: Consolidated statement of profit or loss for year ended 30 September 2012

	$000
Revenue (64,600 + (38,000 × 9/12) − 7,200 intra-group sales)	85,900
Cost of sales (working)	(64,250)
Gross profit	21,650
Distribution costs (1,600 + (1,800 × 9/12))	(2,950)
Administrative expenses (3,800 + (2,400 × 9/12) + 2,000 goodwill impairment)	(7,600)
Income from associate (2,000 × 40% based on underlying earnings)	800
Finance costs (420 + (14,400 × 10% × 9/12 re deferred consideration))	(1,500)
Profit before tax	10,400
Income tax expense (2,800 + (1,600 × 9/12))	(4,000)
Profit for the year	6,400
Profit for year attributable to:	
Equity holders of the parent	6,180
Non-controlling interest (W2)	220
	6,400

(W1)Cost of sales

Viagem	51,200
Greca (26,000 × 9/12)	19,500
Intra-group purchases (800 × 9 months)	(7,200)
PURP in inventory (1,500 × 25/125)	300
Additional depreciation (1,800/3 years × 9/12)	450
	64,250

(W2) NCI

NCI % ×S's post-acquisition profit (10% × (6,200 × 9/12))	465
Less: NCI % × FV depreciation (10% × 450)	(45)
Less: NCI % × impairment (10% × 2,000)	(200)
	220

ACCA marking scheme		
		Marks
(b)	consolidated statement of profit or loss	
	revenue	2
	cost of sales	3
	distribution costs	1
	administrative expenses	2
	income from associate	1½
	finance costs	2
	income tax	1
	profit for year – parent	½
	– NCI	2
		───
	Maximum	15
		───

187   PARADIGM

Paradigm – Consolidated statement of financial position as at 31 March 2013

	$000	$000
Assets		
Non-current assets:		
Property, plant and equipment (47,400 + 25,500 – 3,000 fair value + 500 depreciation)		70,400
Goodwill (W3)		8,500
Financial asset: equity investments (7,100 + 3,900)		11,000
		───────
		89,900
Current assets		
Inventory (20,400 + 8,400 – 600 PURP (W6)	28,200	
Trade receivables (14,800 + 9,000)	23,800	
Bank (2,100)	2,100	54,100
	───────	───────
Total assets		144,000
		───────
Equity and liabilities		
Equity attributable to owners of the parent		
Equity shares of $1 each (40,000 + 6,000 (W3)		46,000
Share premium (W3)	6,000	
Retained earnings (W5)	34,000	40,000
	───────	───────
		86,000
Non-controlling interest (W4)		8,800
		───────
Total equity		94,800

Non-current liabilities

10% loan notes (8,000 + 1,500 (W3)		9,500
Current liabilities		
Trade payables (17,600 + 13,000)	30,600	
Bank overdraft	9,100	39,700
Total equity and liabilities		144,000

Workings (all figures in $ million)

(W1) **Group structure**

Paradigm

75%

Strata

(6 months)

(W2) **Net assets**

	At acquisition	At reporting date	Post acq
	$000	$000	$000
Share capital	20,000	20,000	–
Retained earnings	(6,000)	4,000	10,000
Fair value adjustment	(3,000)	(3,000)	–
Fair value depreciation (3,000 × 6/36 months)		500	500
Gain on equity investment		700	700
	11,000	22,200	11,200
	W3		W4/W5

(W3) **Goodwill**

Share exchange ((20,000 × 75%) × 2/5 × $2)	12,000
10% loan notes (15,000 × 100/1,000)	1,500
Non-controlling interest (20,000 × 25% × $1`20)	6,000
	19,500
Less:	
Fair value of net assets at acquisition (W2)	(11,000)
Goodwill on acquisition	8,500

The market value of the shares issued of $12 million would be recorded: $6 million share capital and $6 million share premium as the shares have a nominal value of $1 each and their issue value was $2 each.

(W4) Non-controlling interest

Fair value on acquisition (W3)	6,000
Post-acquisition profits (11,200 (W2) × 25%)	2,800
	———
	8,800
	———

(W5) Group retained earnings

Pyramid's retained earnings	26,600
Strata's post-acquisition profit (11,200 (W2) × 75%)	8,400
PURP in inventory (W6)	(600)
Loss on equity investments (7,500 – 7,100)	(400)
	———
	34,000
	———

(W6) PURP

Strata's inventory (from Paradigm) at 31 March 2013 is $4·6 million (one month's supply). At a mark-up on cost of 15%, there would be $600,000 of URP (4,600 × 15/115) in the inventory.

ACCA marking scheme		
		Marks
(a)	Statement of financial position:	
	property, plant and equipment	1½
	goodwill	4
	equity investments	1
	inventory	½
	receivables	½
	bank	½
	equity shares	1½
	share premium	½
	retained earnings	2½
	non-controlling interest	1½
	10% loan notes	1
	trade payables	½
	bank overdraft	½
		———
Total		**15**
		———

188 POLESTAR

(a) **Polestar**

Consolidated statement of profit or loss for the year ended 30 September 2013

	$000
Revenue (110,000 + (66,000 × 6/12) − (4,000 + 9,000 intra-group sales))	130,000
Cost of sales (W6)	(109,300)
Gross profit	20,700
Distribution costs (3,000 + (2,000 × 6/12))	(4,000)
Administrative expenses (5,250 + (2,400 × 6/12) − 3,400 negative goodwill (W3)	(3,050)
Loss on equity investments	(200)
Decrease in contingent consideration (1,800 − 1,500)	300
Finance costs	(250)
Profit before tax	13,500
Income tax expense (3,500 − (1,000 × 6/12))	(3,000)
Profit for the year	10,500
Profit for year attributable to:	
Equity holders of the parent	11,250
Non-controlling interest losses (W7)	(750)
	10,500

(b) **Consolidated statement of financial position as at 30 September 2013**

	$000
Assets	
Non-current assets	
Property, plant and equipment (41,000 + 21,000 + 2,000 FV − 100 depn)	63,900
Financial asset: equity investments (16,000 − (13,500 cash consideration) − 200 loss)	2,300
	66,200
Current assets (16,500 + 4,800 − 600 PURP)	20,700
Total assets	86,900

Equity and liabilities

Equity attributable to owners of the parent

Equity shares of 50 cents each	30,000
Retained earnings (W5)	29,750
	59,750
Non-controlling interest (W4)	2,850
Total equity	62,600
Current liabilities	
Contingent consideration	1,500
Other (15,000 + 7,800)	22,800
Total equity and liabilities	86,900

Workings (all figures in $ million)

(W1) Group structure

Polestar

75%

Southstar

(6 months)

(W2) Net assets

	At acquisition	At reporting date	Post acq
	$000	$000	$000
Share capital	6,000	6,000	–
Retained earnings	14,300	12,000	(2,300)
Fair value adjustment	2,000	2,000	–
Fair value depreciation		(100)	(100)
PURP		(600)	(600)
	22,300	19,300	(3,000)
	W3		W4/W5

(W3) Goodwill

Cash consideration	13,500
Contingent consideration	1,800
Non-controlling interest	3,600
	————
	18,900
Less:	
Fair value of net assets at acquisition (W2)	(22,300)
	————
Goodwill on acquisition	(3,400)
	————

(W4) Non-controlling interest

Fair value on acquisition (W3)	3,600
Post-acquisition profits ((3000) (W2) × 25%)	(750)
	————
	2,850
	————

(W5) Group retained earnings

Pyramid's retained earnings	28,500
Strata's post-acquisition profit ((3,000) (W2) × 75%)	(2,250)
Change in contingent consideration	300
Negative goodwill	3,400
Loss on equity investments	(200)
	————
	29,750
	————

(W6) Cost of sales

	$000
Polestar	88,000
Southstar (67,200 × 6/12)	33,600
Intra-group purchases (4,000 + 9,000)	(13,000)
PURP in inventory (see below)	600
Additional depreciation on leased property (2,000/10 years × 6/12)	100
	————
	109,300
	————

The profit on the sale of the goods back to Polestar is $3·6 million (9,000 − (4,000 + 1,400)). Therefore the unrealised profit in the inventory of $1·5 million at 30 September 2013 is $600,000 (3,600 × 1,500/9,000).

(W7) **NCI (SPorL)**

NCI % ×S's post-acquisition profit (25% × ((4,600) × 6/12))	(575)
Less: NCI % × PURP (25% × 600)	(150)
Less: NCI % × FV depreciation (25% × 100)	(25)
	———
	(750)
	———

Note: IFRS 3 Business Combinations says negative goodwill should be credited to the acquirer, thus none of it relates to the non-controlling interests.

(b) The consolidated financial statements of Polestar are of little value when trying to assess the performance and financial position of its subsidiary, Southstar. Therefore the main source of information on which to base any investment decision would be Southstar's own entity financial statements. However, where a company is part of a group, there is the potential for the financial statements (of a subsidiary) to have been subject to the influence of related party transactions. In the case of Southstar, there has been a considerable amount of post-acquisition trading with Polestar and, because of the related party relationship, there is the possibility that this trading is not at arm's length (i.e. not at commercial rates).

There may be other aspects of the relationship where Polestar gives Southstar a benefit that may not have happened had Southstar not been part of the group, e.g. access to technology/research, cheap finance.

The operations of Southstar may now be centralised and run by Polestar. If Polestar doesn't allocate some of these costs to Southstar then Southstar's expenses will be understated. It could also be difficult for a purchaser to assess whether additional property would be required if Southstar share this with other group entities.

The main concern is that any information about the 'benefits' Polestar may have passed on to Southstar through related party transactions is difficult to obtain from published sources. It may be that Polestar would deliberately 'flatter' Southstar's financial statements specifically in order to obtain a high sale price and a prospective purchaser would not necessarily be able to determine that this had happened from either the consolidated or entity financial statements.

ACCA marking scheme		
		Marks
(a)	Consolidated statement of profit or loss	
	revenue	1½
	cost of sales	3
	distribution costs	½
	administrative expenses – (other than negative goodwill)	½
	– negative goodwill finance costs	5
	loss on equity investments	½
	decrease in contingent consideration	½
	finance costs	½
	income tax expense	½
	non-controlling interest	1½
		———
	Maximum	14
		———

(b)   Consolidated statement of financial position

property, plant and equipment	2
equity investments	1
current assets	1½
equity shares	½
retained earnings	3½
non-controlling interest	1½
contingent consideration	½
other current liabilities	½
Maximum	11
Total	**25**

ANALYSING FINANCIAL STATEMENTS/STATEMENTS OF CASH FLOWS

189   HARDY *Walk in the footsteps of a top tutor*

Key answer tips

This question requires an appraisal of a company that is experiencing problems as a result of a global recession, so do not be surprised when some profitability ratios produce negative results. A weak answer will simply refer to ratio movements as having increased or decreased, whereas a strong answer will refer to improvements or deteriorations in the ratios and will aim to relate it to the scenario provided by the examiner.

Note: references to 2009 and 2010 should be taken as being to the years ended 30 September 2009 and 2010 respectively.

Profitability:

Statement of profit or loss performance:

Hardy's statement of profit or loss results dramatically show the effects of the downturn in the global economy; revenues are down by 18% (6,500/36,000 × 100), gross profit has fallen by 60% and a healthy after tax profit of $3.5 million has reversed to a loss of $2.1 million. These are reflected in the profit (loss) margin ratios shown in the appendix (the 'as reported' figures for 2010). This in turn has led to a 15.2% return on equity being reversed to a negative return of 11.9%. However, a closer analysis shows that the results are not quite as bad as they seem. The downturn has directly caused several additional costs in 2010: employee severance, property impairments and losses on investments (as quantified in the appendix). These are probably all non-recurring costs and could therefore justifiably be excluded from the 2010 results to assess the company's 'underlying' performance. If this is done the results of Hardy for 2010 appear to be much better than on first sight, although still not as good as those reported for 2009. A gross margin of 27.8% in 2009 has fallen to only 23.1% (rather than the reported margin of 13.6%) and the profit for period has fallen from $3.5 million (9.7%) to only $2.3 million (7.8%). It should also be noted that as well as the fall in the value of the investments, the related investment income has also shown a sharp decline which has contributed to lower profits in 2010.

Given the economic climate in 2010 these are probably reasonably good results and may justify the Chairman's comments. It should be noted that the cost saving measures which have helped to mitigate the impact of the downturn could have some unwelcome effects should trading conditions improve; it may not be easy to re-hire employees and a lack of advertising may cause a loss of market share.

Statement of financial position:

Perhaps the most obvious aspect of the statement of financial position is the fall in value ($8.5 million) of the non-current assets, most of which is accounted for by losses of $6 million and $1.6 million respectively on the properties and investments. Ironically, because these falls are reflected in equity, this has mitigated the fall in the return of the equity (from 15.2% to 13.1% underlying) and contributed to a perhaps unexpected improvement in asset turnover from 1.6 times to 1.7 times.

Liquidity:

Despite the downturn, Hardy's liquidity ratios now seem at acceptable levels (though they should be compared to manufacturing industry norms) compared to the low ratios in 2009. The bank balance has improved by $1.1 million. This has been helped by a successful rights issue (this is in itself a sign of shareholder support and confidence in the future) raising $2 million and keeping customer's credit period under control. Some of the proceeds of the rights issue appear to have been used to reduce the bank loan which is sensible as its financing costs have increased considerably in 2010. Looking at the movement on retained earnings (6,500 − 2,100 − 3,600) it can be seen that the company paid a dividend of $800,000 during 2010. Although this is only half the dividend per share paid in 2009, it may seem unwise given the losses and the need for the rights issue. A counter view is that the payment of the dividend may be seen as a sign of confidence of a future recovery. It should also be mentioned that the worst of the costs caused by the downturn (specifically the property and investments losses) are not cash costs and have therefore not affected liquidity.

The increase in the inventory and work-in-progress holding period and the trade receivables collection period being almost unchanged appear to contradict the declining sales activity and should be investigated. Although there is insufficient information to calculate the trade payables credit period as there is no analysis of the cost of sales figures, it appears that Hardy has received extended credit which, unless it had been agreed with the suppliers, has the potential to lead to problems obtaining future supplies of goods on credit.

Gearing:

On the reported figures debt to equity shows a modest increase due to statement of profit or loss losses and the reduction of the revaluation reserve, but this has been mitigated by the repayment of part of the loan and the rights issue.

Conclusion:

Although Hardy's results have been adversely affected by the global economic situation, its underlying performance is not as bad as first impressions might suggest and supports the Chairman's comments. The company still retains a relatively strong statement of financial position and liquidity position which will help significantly should market conditions improve. Indeed the impairment of property and investments may well reverse in future. It would be a useful exercise to compare Hardy's performance during this difficult time to that of its competitors – it may well be that its 2010 results were relatively very good by comparison.

Appendix:

An important aspect of assessing the performance of Hardy for 2010 (especially in comparison with 2009) is to identify the impact that several 'one off' charges have had on the results of 2010. These charges are $1.3 million redundancy costs and a $1.5 million (6,000 – 4,500 previous surplus) property impairment, both included in cost of sales and a $1.6 million loss on the market value of investments, included in administrative expenses. Thus in calculating the 'underlying' figures for 2010 (below) the adjusted cost of sales is $22.7 million (25,500 – 1,300 – 1,500) and the administrative expenses are $3.3 million (4,900 – 1,600). These adjustments feed through to give an underlying gross profit of $6.8 million (4,000 + 1,300 + 1,500) and an underlying profit for the year of $2.3 million (– 2,100 + 1,300 + 1,500 + 1,600).

Note: it is not appropriate to revise Hardy's equity (upwards) for the one-off losses when calculating equity based underlying figures, as the losses will be a continuing part of equity (unless they reverse) even if/when future earnings recover.

	2010 underlying	2010 as reported	2009
Gross profit % (6,800/29,500 × 100)	23.1%	13.6%	27.8%
Profit (loss) for period % (2,300/29,500 × 100)	7.8%	(7.1)%	9.7%
Return on equity (2,300/17,600 × 100)	13.1%	(11.9)%	15.2%
Net asset (taken as equity) turnover (29,500/17,600)	1.7 times	same	1.6 times
Debt to equity (4,000/17,600)	22.7%	same	21.7%
Current ratio (6,200:3,400)	1.8:1	same	1.0:1
Quick ratio (4,000:3,400)	1.2:1	same	0.6:1
Receivables collection (in days) (2,200/29,500 × 365)	27 days	same	28 days
Inventory and work-in-progress holding period (2,200/25,500 × 365)	31 days	same	27 days

Note: the figures for the calculation of the 2010 'underlying' ratios have been given; those of 2010 'as reported' and 2009 are based on equivalent figures from the summarised financial statements provided.

Alternative ratios/calculations are acceptable, for example net asset turnover could be calculated using total assets less current liabilities.

ACCA marking scheme		Marks
(a)	Comments – 1 mark per valid point, up to	10
	Ratio calculations – up to	5
Total		15

190 MINSTER *Online question assistance*

Key answer tips

The question asks you to analyse the performance of the company from the statement of cash flows you have prepared and the financial statements given. There is therefore no need to calculate any ratios.

(a) **Statement of cash flows of Minster for the Year ended 30 September 20X6:**

	$000	$000
Cash flows from operating activities		
Profit before tax		142
Adjustments for:		
Depreciation of property, plant and equipment	255	
Amortization of software (180 – 135)	45	300
	———	
Investment income		(20)
Finance costs		40
		———
		462
Working capital adjustments		
Decrease in trade receivables (380 – 270)	110	
Increase in amounts due from construction contracts (80 – 55)	(25)	
Decrease in inventories (510 – 480)	30	
Decrease in trade payables (555 – 350)	(205)	(90)
	———	———
Cash generated from operations		372
Interest paid (40 – (150 × 8%) re unwinding of environmental provision)		(28)
Income taxes paid (w (ii))		(54)
		———
Net cash from operating activities		290
Cash flows from investing activities		
Purchase of – property, plant and equipment (w (i))	(410)	
– software	(180)	
– investments (150 – (15 + 125))	(10)	
Investment income received (20 – 15 gain on investments)	5	
	———	
Net cash used in investing activities		(595)

Cash flows from financing activities

Proceeds from issue of equity shares (w (iii))	265	
Proceeds from issue of 9% loan note	120	
Dividends paid (500 × 4 × 5 cents)	(100)	
Net cash from financing activities		285
Net decrease in cash and cash equivalents		(20)
Cash and cash equivalents at beginning of period (40 – 35)		(5)
Cash and cash equivalents at end of period		(25)

Note: Interest paid may be presented under financing activities and dividends paid may be presented under operating activities.

Workings (T-account format) (in $000)

(W1) **Property, plant and equipment**

	Dr			Cr
	$000			$000
b/f	940			
Provision	150			
Revaluation	35	Depreciation		255
Cash additions (Balancing fig)	**410**			
		c/f		1,280
	1,535			1,535

(W2) **Tax liabilities**

	Dr			Cr
	$000			$000
		b/f (50 + 25)		75
		SPorL charge		57
Cash paid (bal fig)	**54**			
c/f (60 + 18)	78			
	132			132

Workings (Columnar format) (in $000)

(i)   Property, plant and equipment:

Carrying amount b/f	940
Non-cash environmental provision	150
Revaluation	35
Depreciation for period	(255)
Carrying amount c/f	(1,280)
Difference is cash acquisitions	(410)

(ii)   Taxation:

Tax provision b/f	(50)
Deferred tax b/f	(25)
Statement of comprehensive income charge	(57)
Tax provision c/f	60
Deferred tax c/f	18
Difference is cash paid	(54)

(iii)   Equity shares

Balance b/f	(300)
Bonus issue (1 for 4)	(75)
Balance c/f	500
Difference is cash issue	125

Share premium

Balance b/f	(85)
Bonus issue (1 for 4)	75
Balance c/f	150
Difference is cash issue	140

Therefore the total proceeds of cash issue of shares are $265,000 (125 + 140).

191 TABBA *Walk in the footsteps of a top tutor*

Key answer tips

The statement of cash flows has the usual standard calculations but take care with the government grant and finance leases which both have balances in both current and non-current liabilities.

(a) **Statement of cash flows of Tabba for the year ended 30 September 20X5:**

Cash flows from operating activities	$000	$000
Profit before tax	50	
Adjustments for:		
Depreciation (W1)	2,200	
Amortization of government grant (W3)	(250)	
Profit on sale of factory (W1)	(4,600)	
Increase in insurance claim provision (1,500 – 1,200)	(300)	
Interest receivable	(40)	
Interest expense	260	
	_____	
	(2,680)	
Working capital adjustments:		
Increase in inventories (2,550 – 1,850)	(700)	
Increase in trade receivables (3,100 – 2,600)	(500)	
Increase in trade payables (4,050 – 2,950)	1,100	
	_____	
Cash outflow from operations	(2,780)	
Interest paid	(260)	
Income taxes paid (W4)	(1,350)	
	_____	
Net cash outflow used in operating activities		(4,390)
Cash flows from investing activities		
Sale of factory	12,000	
Purchase of non-current assets (W1)	(2,900)	
Receipt of government grant (from question)	950	
Interest received	40	
	_____	

Net cash from investing activities		10,090
Cash flows from financing activities		
Issue of 6% loan notes	800	
Redemption of 10% loan notes	(4,000)	
Repayment of finance leases (W2)	(1,100)	
Net cash used in financing activities		(4,300)
Net increase in cash and cash equivalents		1,400
Cash and cash equivalents at beginning of period		(550)
Cash and cash equivalents at end of period		850

Note: Interest paid may also be presented as a financing activity and interest received as an operating cash flow.

Workings ($000)

(W1) **Non-current assets - Cost**

	Dr		Cr
	$000		$000
b/f	20,200		
Finance lease additions	1,500	Disposals	8,600
Cash additions (Balancing fig)	**2,900**		
		c/f	16,000
	———		———
	24,600		24,600
	———		———

(W1b) **Non-current assets – Accumulated depreciation**

	Dr		Cr
	$000		$000
		b/f	4,400
Disposal	1,200	**Charge for year (Bal. Fig)**	**2,200**
c/f	5,400		
	———		———
	6,600		6,600
	———		———

(W2) **Finance lease liabilities**

	Dr		Cr
	$000		$000
		b/f (800 + 1,700)	2,500
Repaid	**1,100**	New assets to PPE	1,500
c/f (900 + 2,000)	2,900		
	———		———
	4,000		4,000
	———		———

(W3) **Government grants**

	Dr		Cr
	$000		$000
		b/f (400 + 900)	1,300
Amortisation in P/L (bal fig)	**250**	New grants	950
c/f (600 + 1,400)	2,000		
	———		———
	2,250		2,250
	———		———

(W4) **Tax liabilities**

	Dr		Cr
	$000		$000
		b/f (1,200 + 500)	1,700
SPorL credit	50		
Cash paid (bal fig)	**1,350**		
c/f (100 + 200)	300		
	———		———
	1,700		1,700
	———		———

(W5) **Retained earnings**

	Dr		Cr
	$000		$000
		b/f	850
		Profit per SPorL	100
		Transfer from revaluation reserve	1,600
c/f	2,550		
	———		———
	2,550		2,550
	———		———

(W1) **Non-current assets:**

Cost/valuation b/f	20,200
New finance leases (from question)	1,500
Disposals	(8,600)
Acquisitions – balancing figure	2,900
Cost/valuation c/f	16,000

Depreciation b/f	4,400
Disposal	(1,200)
Depreciation c/f	(5,400)
Charge for year – balancing figure	(2,200)

Sale of factory:	
Carrying value	7,400
Proceeds (from question)	(12,000)
Profit on sale	(4,600)

(W2) **Finance lease obligations:**

Balance b/f	– current	800
	– over 1 year	1,700
New leases (from question)		1,500
Balance c/f	– current	(900)
	– over 1 year	(2,000)
Cash repayments – balancing figure		1,100

(W3) **Government grant:**

Balance b/f	– current	400
	– over 1 year	900
Grants received in year (from question)		950
Balance c/f	– current	(600)
	– over 1 year	(1,400)
Difference – amortization credited to statement of comprehensive income		250

(W4) **Taxation:**

Current provision b/f	1,200
Deferred tax b/f	500
Tax credit in statement of comprehensive income	(50)
Current provision c/f	(100)
Deferred tax c/f	(200)
Tax paid – balancing figure	1,350

(W5) **Reconciliation of retained earnings**

Balance b/f	850
Transfer from revaluation reserve	1,600
Profit for period	100
	———
Balance c/f	2,550
	———

192 PINTO

Comments on the cash management of Pinto

Operating cash flows:

Pinto's operating cash inflows at $940,000 (prior to investment income, finance costs and taxation) are considerably higher than the equivalent profit before investment income, finance costs and tax of $430,000. This shows a satisfactory cash generating ability and is more than sufficient to cover finance costs, taxation (see later) and dividends. The major reasons for the cash flows being higher than the operating profit are due to the (non-cash) increases in the depreciation and warranty provisions. Working capital changes are relatively neutral; a large increase in inventory appears to be being financed by a substantial increase in trade payables and a modest reduction in trade receivables. The reduction in trade receivables is perhaps surprising as other indicators point to an increase in operating capacity which has not been matched with an increase in trade receivables. This could be indicative of good control over the cash management of the trade receivables (or a disappointing sales performance).

An unusual feature of the cash flow is that Pinto has received a tax refund of $60,000 during the current year. This would indicate that in the previous year Pinto was making losses (hence obtaining tax relief). Whilst the current year's profit performance is an obvious improvement, it should be noted that next year's cash flows are likely to suffer a tax payment (estimated at $150,000 in current liabilities at 31 March 2008) as a consequence. In any forward planning, Pinto should be aware that the tax reversal position will create an estimated total incremental outflow of $210,000 in the next period.

Investing activities:

There has been a dramatic investment/increase in property, plant and equipment. The carrying value at 31 March 2008 is substantially higher than a year earlier (admittedly $100,000 is due to revaluation rather than a purchase). It is difficult to be sure whether this represents an increase in operating capacity or is the replacement of the plant disposed of. (The voluntary disclosure encouraged by IAS 7 *Statement of cash flows* would help to assess this issue more accurately). However, judging by the level of the increase and the (apparent) overall improvement in profit position, it seems likely that there has been a successful increase in capacity. It is not unusual for there to be a time lag before increased investment reaches its full beneficial effect and in this context it could be speculated that the investment occurred early in the accounting year (because its effect is already making an impact) and that future periods may show even greater improvements.

The investment property is showing a good return which is composed of rental income (presumably) of $40,000 and a valuation gain of $20,000.

Financing activities:

It would appear that Pinto's financial structure has changed during the year. Debt of $400,000 has been redeemed (for $420,000) and there has been a share issue raising $1 million. The company is now nil geared compared to modest gearing at the end of the previous year. The share issue has covered the cost of redemption and contributed to the investment in property, plant and equipment. The remainder of the finance for the property, plant and equipment has come from the very healthy operating cash flows. If ROCE is higher than the finance cost of the loan note at 6% (nominal) it may call into question the wisdom of the early redemption especially given the penalty cost (which has been classified within financing activities) of the redemption.

Cash position:

The overall effect of the year's cash flows is that they have improved the company's cash position dramatically. A sizeable overdraft of $120,000, which may have been a consequence of the (likely) losses in the previous year, has been reversed to a modest bank balance of $10,000 even after the payment of a $150,000 dividend.

Summary

The above analysis indicates that Pinto has invested substantially in renewing and/or increasing its property, plant and equipment. This has been financed largely by operating cash flows, and appears to have brought a dramatic turnaround in the company's fortunes. All the indications are that the future financial position and performance will continue to improve.

193 HARBIN *Walk in the footsteps of a top tutor*

Key answer tip

Be aware that the examiner specifically asks you to draw your attention to the chief executives report and the purchase of Fatima – if you do not discuss this at all you will be limited in the overall marks that you can achieve. You may choose to calculate further ratios to support your analysis (marks would be awarded where relevant). The highlighted words are key phrases that markers are looking for.

Note: Figures in the calculations of the ratios are in $million

	2007	Workings	2006	2007 re Fatima (b)
Return on year end capital employed	11.2%	24/(114 + 100) × 100	7.1%	18.9%
Net asset turnover	1.2 times	250/214	1.6	0.6
Gross profit margin (given in question)	20%		16.7%	42.9%
Net profit (before tax) margin	6.4%	16/250	4.4%	31.4%
Current ratio	0.9:1	38/44	2.5	
Closing inventory holding period	46 days	25/200 × 365	37	
Trade receivables' collection period	19 days	13/250 × 365	16	
Trade payables' payment period	42 days	23/200 × 365	32	
Gearing	46.7%	100/214 × 100	Nil	

Analysis of the comparative financial performance and position of Harbin for the year ended 30 September 2007. *Note:* References to 2007 and 2006 should be taken as the years ended 30 September 2007 and 2006.

Introduction

The figures relating to the comparative performance of Harbin 'highlighted' in the Chief Executive's report may be factually correct, but they take a rather biased and one dimensional view. They focus entirely on the performance as reflected in the statement of comprehensive income without reference to other measures of performance (notably the ROCE); nor is there any reference to the purchase of Fatima at the beginning of the year which has had a favourable effect on profit for 2007. Due to this purchase, it is not consistent to compare Harbin's statement of comprehensive income results in 2007 directly with those of 2006 because it does not match like with like. Immediately before the $100 million purchase of Fatima, the carrying amount of the net assets of Harbin was $112 million. Thus the investment represented an increase of nearly 90% of Harbin's existing capital employed. The following analysis of performance will consider the position as shown in the reported financial statements (based on the ratios required by part (a) of the question) and then go on to consider the impact the purchase has had on this analysis.

Profitability

The ROCE is often considered to be the primary measure of operating performance, because it relates the profit made by an entity (return) to the capital (or net assets) invested in generating those profits. On this basis the ROCE in 2007 of 11.2% represents a 58% improvement (i.e. 4.1% on 7.1%) on the ROCE of 7.1% in 2006. Given there were no disposals of non-current assets, the ROCE on Fatima's net assets is 18.9% (22m/100m + 16.5m). **Note:** The net assets of Fatima at the year end would have increased by profit after tax of $16.5 million (i.e. 22m × 75% (at a tax rate of 25%)). Put another way, without the contribution of $22 million to profit before tax, Harbin's 'underlying' profit would have been a loss of $6 million which would give a negative ROCE. The principal reasons for the beneficial impact of Fatima's purchase is that its profit margins at 42.9% gross and 31.4% net (before tax) are far superior to the profit margins of the combined business at 20% and 6.4% respectively. It should be observed that the other contributing factor to the ROCE is the net asset turnover and in this respect Fatima's is actually inferior at 0.6 times (70m/116.5m) to that of the combined business of 1.2 times.

It could be argued that the finance costs should be allocated against Fatima's results as the proceeds of the loan note appear to be the funding for the purchase of Fatima. Even if this is accepted, Fatima's results still far exceed those of the existing business.

Thus the Chief Executive's report, already criticised for focussing on the statement of comprehensive income alone, is still highly misleading. Without the purchase of Fatima, underlying sales revenue would be flat at $180 million and the gross margin would be down to 11.1% (20m/180m) from 16.7% resulting in a loss before tax of $6 million. This sales performance is particularly poor given it is likely that there must have been an increase in spending on property plant and equipment beyond that related to the purchase of Fatima's net assets as the increase in property, plant and equipment is $120 million (after depreciation).

Liquidity

The company's liquidity position as measured by the current ratio has deteriorated dramatically during the period. A relatively healthy 2.5:1 is now only 0.9:1 which is rather less than what one would expect from the quick ratio (which excludes inventory) and is a matter of serious concern. A consideration of the component elements of the current ratio suggests that increases in the inventory holding period and trade payables payment period have largely offset each other. There is a small increase in the collection period for trade receivables (up from 16 days to 19 days) which would actually improve the current ratio. This ratio appears unrealistically low, it is very difficult to collect credit sales so quickly and may be indicative of factoring some of the receivables, or a proportion of the sales being cash sales. Factoring is sometimes seen as a consequence of declining liquidity, although if this assumption is correct it does also appear to have been present in the previous year. The changes in the above three ratios do not explain the dramatic deterioration in the current ratio, the real culprit is the cash position, Harbin has gone from having a bank balance of $14 million in 2006 to showing short-term bank borrowings of $17 million in 2007.

A statement of cash flow would give a better appreciation of the movement in the bank/short term borrowing position.

It is not possible to assess, in isolation, the impact of the purchase of Fatima on the liquidity of the company.

Dividends

A dividend of 10 cents per share in 2007 amounts to $10 million (100m × 10 cents), thus the dividend in 2006 would have been $8 million (the dividend in 2007 is 25% up on 2006). It may be that the increase in the reported profits led the Board to pay a 25% increased dividend, but the dividend cover is only 1.2 times (12m/10m) in 2007 which is very low. In 2006 the cover was only 0.75 times (6m/8m) meaning previous years' reserves were used to facilitate the dividend. The low retained earnings indicate that Harbin has historically paid a high proportion of its profits as dividends, however in times of declining liquidity, it is difficult to justify such high dividends.

Gearing

The company has gone from a position of nil gearing (i.e. no long-term borrowings) in 2006 to a relatively high gearing of 46.7% in 2007. This has been caused by the issue of the $100 million 8% loan note which would appear to be the source of the funding for the $100 million purchase of Fatima's net assets. At the time the loan note was issued, Harbin's ROCE was 7.1%, slightly less than the finance cost of the loan note. In 2007 the ROCE has increased to 11.2%, thus the manner of the funding has had a beneficial effect on the returns to the equity holders of Harbin. However, it should be noted that high gearing does not come without risk; any future downturn in the results of Harbin would expose the equity holders to much lower proportionate returns and continued poor liquidity may mean payment of the loan interest could present a problem. Harbin's gearing and liquidity position would have looked far better had some of the acquisition been funded by an issue of equity shares.

Conclusion

There is no doubt that the purchase of Fatima has been a great success and appears to have been a wise move on the part of the management of Harbin. However, it has disguised a serious deterioration of the underlying performance and position of Harbin's existing activities which the Chief Executive's report may be trying to hide. It may be that the acquisition was part of an overall plan to diversify out of what has become existing loss making activities. If such a transition can continue, then the worrying aspects of poor liquidity and high gearing may be overcome.

194 GREENWOOD

Note: IFRS 5 uses the term discontinued operation. The answer below also uses this term, but it should be realised that the assets of the discontinued operation are classed as held for sale and not yet sold. In some literature this may be described as a *discontinuing* operation.

Profitability/utilisation of assets

An important feature of the company's performance in the year to 31 March 2007 is to evaluate the effect of the discontinued operation. When using an entity's recent results as a basis for assessing how the entity may perform in the future, emphasis should be placed on the results from continuing operations as it is these that will form the basis of future results. For this reason most of the ratios calculated in the appendix are based on the results from continuing operations and ratio calculations involving net assets/capital employed generally exclude the value of the assets held for sale.

On this basis, it can be seen that the overall efficiency of Greenwood (measured by its ROCE) has declined considerably from 33.5% to 29.7% (a fall of 11.3%). The fall in the asset turnover (from 1.89 to 1.67 times) appears to be mostly responsible for the overall decline in efficiency. In effect the company's assets are generating less sales per $ invested in them. The other contributing factors to overall profitability are the company's profit margins. Greenwood has achieved an impressive increase in headline sales revenues of nearly 30% (6.3m on 21.2m) whilst being able to maintain its gross profit margin at around 29% (no significant change from 2006). This has led to a substantial increase in gross profit, but this has been eroded by an increase in operating expenses. As a percentage of sales, operating expenses were 10.5% in 2007 compared to 11.6% in 2006 (they appear to be more of a variable than a fixed cost). This has led to a modest improvement in the profit before interest and tax margin which has partially offset the deteriorating asset utilisation.

The decision to sell the activities which are classified as a discontinued operation is likely to improve the overall profitability of the company. In the year ended 31 March 2006 the discontinued operation made a modest pre tax profit of $450,000 (this would represent a return of around 7% on the activity's assets of $6.3 million).This poor return acted to reduce the company's overall profitability (the continuing operations yielded a return of 33.5%). The performance of the discontinued operation continued to deteriorate in the year ended 31 March 2007 making a pre tax operating loss of $1.4 million which creates a negative return on the relevant assets. Despite incurring losses on the measurement to fair value of the discontinued operation's assets, it seems the decision will benefit the company in the future as the discontinued operation showed no sign of recovery.

Liquidity and solvency

Superficially the current ratio of 2.11 in 2007 seems reasonable, but the improvement from the alarming current ratio in 2006 of 0.97 is more illusory than real. The ratio in the year ended 31 March 2007 has been distorted (improved) by the inclusion of assets of the discontinued operation under the heading of 'held for sale'. These have been included at fair value less cost to sell (being lower than their cost – a requirement of IFRS 5). Thus the carrying amount should be a realistic expectation of the net sale proceeds, but it is not clear whether the sale will be cash (they may be exchanged for shares or other assets) or how Greenwood intends to use the disposal proceeds. What can be deduced is that without the assets held for sale being classified as current, the company's liquidity ratio would be much worse than at present (at below 1 for both years). Against an expected norm of 1, quick ratios (acid test) calculated on the normal basis of excluding inventory (and in this case the assets held for sale) show an alarming position; a poor figure of 0.62 in 2006 has further deteriorated in 2007 to 0.44. Without the proceeds from the sale of the discontinued operation (assuming they will be for cash) it is difficult to see how Greenwood would pay its payables (and tax liability), given a year end overdraft of $1,150,000.

Further analysis of the current ratios shows some interesting changes during the year. Despite its large overdraft Greenwood appears to be settling its trade payables quicker than in 2006. At 68 days in 2006 this was rather a long time and the reduction in credit period may be at the insistence of suppliers – not a good sign. Perhaps to relieve liquidity pressure, the company appears to be pushing its customers to settle early. It may be that this has been achieved by the offer of early settlement discounts, if so the cost of this would have impacted on profit. Despite holding a higher amount of inventory at 31 March 2007 (than in 2006), the company has increased its inventory turnover; given that margins have been held, this reflects an improved performance.

Gearing

The additional borrowing of $3 million in loan notes (perhaps due to liquidity pressure) has resulted in an increase in gearing from 28.6% to 35.6% and a consequent increase in finance costs. Despite the increase in finance costs the borrowing is acting in the shareholders' favour as the overall return on capital employed (at 29.7%) is well in excess of the 5% interest cost.

Summary

Overall the company's performance has deteriorated in the year ended 31 March 2007. Management's action in respect of the discontinued operation is a welcome measure to try to halt the decline, but more needs to be done. The company's liquidity position is giving cause for serious concern and without the prospect of realising $6 million from the assets held for sale it would be difficult to envisage any easing of the company's liquidity pressures.

Appendix

	2007		2006
ROCE: continuing operations (4,500 + 400)/(14,500 + 8,000 − 6,000))	29.7%	(3,500 + 250)/(12,500 + 5,000 − 6,300)	33.5%

The return has been taken as the profit before interest (on loan notes only) and tax from continuing operations. The capital employed is the normal equity plus loan capital (as at the year end), but less the value of the assets held for sale. This is because the assets held for sale have not contributed to the return from continuing operations.

	2007		2006
Gross profit percentage (8,000/27,500)	29.1%	(6,200/21,200)	29.2%
Operating expense percentage of sales revenue (2,900/27,500)	10.5%	(2,450/21,200)	11.6%
Profit before interest and tax margin (5,100/27,500)	18.5%	(3,750/21,200)	17.7%
Asset turnover (27,500/16,500)	1.67	(21,200/11,200)	1.89
Current ratio (9,500:4,500)	2.11	(3,700:3,800)	0.97
Current ratio (excluding held for sale) (3,500:4,500)	0.77	Not applicable	
Quick ratio (excluding held for sale) (2,000:4,500)	0.44	(2,350:3,800)	0.62
Inventory (closing) turnover (19,500/1,500)	13.0	(15,000/1,350)	11.1
Receivables (in days) (2,000/27,500) × 365	26.5	(2,300/21,200) × 365	39.6
Payables/cost of sales (in days) (2,400/19,500) × 365	44.9	(2,800/15,000) × 365	68.1
Gearing (8,000/8,000 + 14,500)	35.6%	(5,000/5,000 + 12,500)	28.6%

195 VICTULAR *Walk in the footsteps of a top tutor*

Key answer tips

This style of question is naturally time consuming – ensure you answer all parts of the question and do not spend too much time calculating ratios. Part (c) offers easy marks and is independent of the rest of the question – try doing part (c) first to ensure you do not miss out on such easy marks. When interpreting the results in part (b) be wary of making generalisations – you must ensure that you relate it to the information given in the question. Presentation is also crucial in part (b) the marker cannot award you any marks if they cannot read what you have written.

(a) **Equivalent ratios from the financial statements of Merlot (workings in $000)**

Return on year end capital employed (ROCE)	20.9%	(1,400 + 590)/(2,800 + 3,200 + 500 + 3,000) × 100
Pre tax return on equity (ROE)	50%	1,400/2,800 × 100
Net asset turnover	2.3 times	20,500/(14,800 – 5,700)
Gross profit margin	12.2%	2,500/20,500 × 100
Operating profit margin	9.8%	2,000/20,500 × 100
Current ratio	1.3:1	7,300/5,700
Closing inventory holding period	73 days	3,600/18,000 × 365
Trade receivables' collection period	66 days	3,700/20,500 × 365
Trade payables' payment period	77 days	3,800/18,000 × 365
Gearing	71%	(3,200 + 500 + 3,000)/ 9,500 × 100
Interest cover	3.3 times	2,000/600
Dividend cover	1.4 times	1,000/700

As per the question, Merlot's obligations under finance leases (3,200 + 500) have been treated as debt when calculating the ROCE and gearing ratios.

(b) **Assessment of the relative performance and financial position of Grappa and Merlot for the year ended 30 September 2008**

Introduction

This report is based on the draft financial statements supplied and the ratios shown in (a) above. Although covering many aspects of performance and financial position, the report has been approached from the point of view of a prospective acquisition of the entire equity of one of the two companies.

Profitability

The ROCE of 20.9% of Merlot is far superior to the 14.8% return achieved by Grappa. ROCE is traditionally seen as a measure of management's overall efficiency in the use of the finance/assets at its disposal. More detailed analysis reveals that Merlot's superior performance is due to its efficiency in the use of its net assets; it achieved a net asset turnover of 2.3 times compared to only 1.2 times for Grappa. Put another way, Merlot makes sales of $2.30 per $1 invested in net assets compared to sales of only $1.20 per $1 invested for Grappa. The other element contributing to the ROCE is profit margins. In this area Merlot's overall performance is slightly inferior to that of Grappa, gross profit margins are almost identical, but Grappa's operating profit margin is 10.5% compared to Merlot's 9.8%. In this situation, where one company's ROCE is superior to another's it is useful to look behind the figures and consider possible reasons for the superiority other than the obvious one of greater efficiency on Merlot's part.

A major component of the ROCE is normally the carrying amount of the non-current assets. Consideration of these in this case reveals some interesting issues. Merlot does not own its premises whereas Grappa does. Such a situation would not necessarily give a ROCE advantage to either company as the increase in capital employed of a company owning its factory would be compensated by a higher return due to not having a rental expense (and *vice versa*). If Merlot's rental cost, as a percentage of the value of the related factory, was less than its overall ROCE, then it would be contributing to its higher ROCE. There is insufficient information to determine this. Another relevant point may be that Merlot's owned plant is nearing the end of its useful life (carrying amount is only 22% of its cost) and the company seems to be replacing owned plant with leased plant. Again this does not necessarily give Merlot an advantage, but the finance cost of the leased assets at only 7.5% is much lower than the overall ROCE (of either company) and therefore this does help to improve Merlot's ROCE. The other important issue within the composition of the ROCE is the valuation basis of the companies' non-current assets. From the question, it appears that Grappa's factory is at current value (there is a property revaluation reserve) and note (ii) of the question indicates the use of historical cost for plant. The use of current value for the factory (as opposed to historical cost) will be adversely impacting on Grappa's ROCE. Merlot does not suffer this deterioration as it does not own its factory.

The ROCE measures the overall efficiency of management; however, as Victular is considering buying the equity of one of the two companies, it would be useful to consider the return on equity (ROE) – as this is what Victular is buying. The ratios calculated are based on pre-tax profits; this takes into account finance costs, but does not cause taxation issues to distort the comparison. Clearly Merlot's ROE at 50% is far superior to Grappa's 19.1%. Again the issue of the revaluation of Grappa's factory is making this ratio appear comparatively worse (than it would be if there had not been a revaluation). In these circumstances it would be more meaningful if the ROE was calculated based on the asking price of each company (which has not been disclosed) as this would effectively be the carrying amount of the relevant equity for Victular.

Gearing

From the gearing ratio it can be seen that 71% of Merlot's assets are financed by borrowings (39% is attributable to Merlot's policy of leasing its plant). This is very high in absolute terms and double Grappa's level of gearing. The effect of gearing means that all of the profit after finance costs is attributable to the equity even though (in Merlot's case) the equity represents only 29% of the financing of the net assets. Whilst this may seem advantageous to the equity shareholders of Merlot, it does not come without risk. The interest cover of Merlot is only 3.3 times whereas that of Grappa is 6 times. Merlot's low interest cover is a direct consequence of its high gearing and it makes profits vulnerable to relatively small changes in operating activity. For example, small reductions in sales, profit margins or small increases in operating expenses could result in losses and mean that interest charges would not be covered.

Another observation is that Grappa has been able to take advantage of the receipt of government grants; Merlot has not. This may be due to Grappa purchasing its plant (which may then be eligible for grants) whereas Merlot leases its plant. It may be that the lessor has received any grants available on the purchase of the plant and passed some of this benefit on to Merlot via lower lease finance costs (at 7.5% per annum, this is considerably lower than Merlot has to pay on its 10% loan notes).

Liquidity

Both companies have relatively low liquid ratios of 1.2 and 1.3 for Grappa and Merlot respectively, although at least Grappa has $600,000 in the bank whereas Merlot has a $1.2 million overdraft. In this respect Merlot's policy of high dividend payouts (leading to a low dividend cover and low retained earnings) is very questionable. Looking in more depth, both companies have similar inventory days; Merlot collects its receivables one week earlier than Grappa (perhaps its credit control procedures are more active due to its large overdraft), and of notable difference is that Grappa receives (or takes) a lot longer credit period from its suppliers (108 days compared to 77 days). This may be a reflection of Grappa being able to negotiate better credit terms because it has a higher credit rating.

Summary

Although both companies may operate in a similar industry and have similar profits after tax, they would represent very different purchases. Merlot's sales revenues are over 70% more than those of Grappa, it is financed by high levels of debt, it rents rather than owns property and it chooses to lease rather than buy its replacement plant. Also its remaining owned plant is nearing the end of its life. Its replacement will either require a cash injection if it is to be purchased (Merlot's overdraft of $1.2 million already requires serious attention) or create even higher levels of gearing if it continues its policy of leasing. In short although Merlot's overall return seems more attractive than that of Grappa, it would represent a much more risky investment. Ultimately the investment decision may be determined by Victular's attitude to risk, possible synergies with its existing business activities, and not least, by the asking price for each investment (which has not been disclosed to us).

(c) The generally recognised potential problems of using ratios for comparison purposes are:

- inconsistent definitions of ratios
- financial statements may have been deliberately manipulated (creative accounting)
- different companies may adopt different accounting policies (e.g. use of historical costs compared to current values)
- different managerial policies (e.g. different companies offer customers different payment terms)
- statement of financial position figures may not be representative of average values throughout the year (this can be caused by seasonal trading or a large acquisition of non-current assets near the year end)
- the impact of price changes over time/distortion caused by inflation

When deciding whether to purchase a company, Victular should consider the following additional useful information:

–   in this case the analysis has been made on the draft financial statements; these may be unreliable or change when being finalised. Audited financial statements would add credibility and reliance to the analysis (assuming they receive an unmodified Auditors' Report).

–   forward looking information such as profit and financial position forecasts, capital expenditure and cash budgets and the level of orders on the books.

–   the current (fair) values of assets being acquired.

–   the level of risk within a business. Highly profitable companies may also be highly risky, whereas a less profitable company may have more stable 'quality' earnings

–   not least would be the expected price to acquire a company. It may be that a poorer performing business may be a more attractive purchase because it is relatively cheaper and may offer more opportunity for improving efficiencies and profit growth.

196   COALTOWN *Walk in the footsteps of a top tutor*

Key answer tips

This proved to be a relatively straightforward statement of cash flow. Watch out for the disposal, Coaltown has an unexpected COST associated with disposal that will represent a cash outflow rather than an inflow.

(a)   **Coaltown – Statement of cash flows for the year ended 31 March 2009:**

Note: Figures in brackets in $000

	$000	$000
Cash flows from operating activities		
Profit before tax		10,200
Adjustments for:		
depreciation of non-current assets (W1)	6,000	
loss on disposal of displays (W1)	1,500	
	———	
Interest expense		600
Increase in warranty provision (1,000 – 300)		700
increase in inventory (5,200 – 4,400)		(800)
increase in receivables (7,800 – 2,800)		(5,000)
decrease in payables (4,500 – 4,200)		(300)
		———
Cash generated from operations		12,900
Interest paid		(600)
Income tax paid (W2)		(5,500)
		———
Net cash from operating activities		6,800

Cash flows from investing activities (W1)		
Purchase of non-current assets	(20,500)	
Disposal cost of non-current assets	(500)	
	———	
Net cash used in investing activities		(21,000)
		———
		(14,200)
Cash flows from financing activities		
Issue of equity shares (8,600 capital + 4,300 premium)	12,900	
Issue of 10% loan notes	1,000	
Equity dividends paid	(4,000)	
	———	
Net cash from financing activities		9,900
		———
Net decrease in cash and cash equivalents		(4,300)
Cash and cash equivalents at beginning of period		700
		———
Cash and cash equivalents at end of period		(3,600)
		———

Workings	$000
(W1) Non-current assets	
Cost	
Balance b/f	80,000
Revaluation (5,000 – 2,000 depreciation)	3,000
Disposal	(10,000)
Balance c/f	(93,500)
	———
Cash flow for acquisitions	20,500
	———
Depreciation	
Balance b/f	48,000
Revaluation	(2,000)
Disposal	(9,000)
Balance c/f	(43,000)
	———
Difference – charge for year	6,000
	———
Disposal of displays	
Cost	10,000
Depreciation	(9,000)
Cost of disposal	500
	———
Loss on disposal	1,500
	———
(W2) Income tax paid:	$000
Provision b/f	(5,300)
Statement of comprehensive income tax charge	(3,200)
Provision c/f	3,000
	———
Difference – cash paid	(5,500)
	———

Workings – T account format

(W1a) Non-current assets - Cost

	Dr $000		Cr $000
b/f	80,000		
Revaluation	3,000	Disposals	10,000
Cash additions (Balancing fig)	**20,500**		
		c/f	93,500
	———		———
	103,500		103,500
	———		———

(W1b) Non-current assets – Accumulated depreciation

	Dr $000		Cr $000
Revaluation	2,000	b/f	48,000
Disposal	9,000	**Charge for year (Bal. Fig)**	**6,000**
c/f	43,000		
	———		———
	54,000		54,000
	———		———

Note: The disposal had a carrying value of $1m at disposal (cost $10m, accumulated depreciation $9m), and cost $500k to dispose, making a loss on disposal of $1,500k.

(W2) Tax Liabilities

	Dr $000		Cr $000
		b/f	5,300
Tax paid (bal fig)	**5,500**	Charge from P/L	3,200
c/f	3,000		
	———		———
	8,500		8,500
	———		———

197 QUARTILE

(a)   Below are the specified ratios for Quartile and (for comparison) those of the business sector average:

		Quartile	sector average
Return on year-end capital employed			
	$((3,400 + 800)/(26,600 + 8,000) \times 100)$	12·1%	16·8%
Net asset turnover	$(56,000/34,600)$	1·6 times	1·4 times
Gross profit margin	$(14,000/56,000 \times 100)$	25%	35%
Operating profit margin	$(4,200/56,000 \times 100)$	7·5%	12%
Current ratio	$(11,200:7,200)$	1·6:1	1·25:1
Average inventory (8,300 + 10,200/2) = 9,250) turnover	$(42,000/9,250)$	4·5 times	3 times
Trade payables' payment period	$(5,400/43,900 \times 365)$	45 days	64 days
Debt to equity	$(8,000/26,600 \times 100)$	30%	38%

(b)   **Assessment of comparative performance**

Profitability

The primary measure of profitability is the return on capital employed (ROCE) and this shows that Quartile's 12·1% is considerably underperforming the sector average of 16·8%. Measured as a percentage, this underperformance is 28% ((16·8 − 12·1)/16·8). The main cause of this seems to be a much lower gross profit margin (25% compared to 35%). A possible explanation for this is that Quartile is deliberately charging a lower mark-up in order to increase its sales by undercutting the market. There is supporting evidence for this in that Quartile's average inventory turnover at 4·5 times is 50% better than the sector average of three times. An alternative explanation could be that Quartile has had to cut its margins due to poor sales which have had a knock-on effect of having to write down closing inventory.

Quartile's lower gross profit percentage has fed through to contribute to a lower operating profit margin at 7·5% compared to the sector average of 12%. However, from the above figures, it can be deduced that Quartile's operating costs at 17·5% (25% − 7·5%) of revenue appear to be better controlled than the sector average operating costs of 23% (35% − 12%) of revenue. This may indicate that Quartile has a different classification of costs between cost of sales and operating costs than the companies in the sector average or that other companies may be spending more on advertising/selling commissions in order to support their higher margins.

The other component of ROCE is asset utilisation (measured by net asset turnover). If Quartile's business strategy is indeed to generate more sales to compensate for lower profit margins, a higher net asset turnover would be expected. At 1·6 times, Quartile's net asset turnover is only marginally better than the sector average of 1·4 times. Whilst this may indicate that Quartile's strategy was a poor choice, the ratio could be partly distorted by the property revaluation and also by whether the deferred development expenditure should be included within net assets for this purpose, as the net revenues expected from the development have yet to come on stream. If these two aspects were adjusted for, Quartile's net asset turnover would be 2·1 times (56,000/(34,600 − 5,000 − 3,000)) which is 50% better than the sector average.

In summary, Quartile's overall profitability is below that of its rival companies due to considerably lower profit margins, although this has been partly offset by generating proportionately more sales from its assets.

Liquidity

As measured by the current ratio, Quartile has a higher level of cover for its current liabilities than the sector average (1·6:1 compared to 1·25:1). Quartile's figure is nearer the 'norm' of expected liquidity ratios, often quoted as between 1·5 and 2:1, with the sector average (at 1·25:1) appearing worryingly low. The problem of this 'norm' is that it is generally accepted that it relates to manufacturing companies rather than retail companies, as applies to Quartile (and presumably also to the sector average). In particular, retail companies have very little, if any, trade receivables as is the case with Quartile. This makes a big difference to the current ratio and makes the calculation of a quick ratio largely irrelevant. Consequently, retail companies operate comfortably with much lower current ratios as their inventory is turned directly into cash. Thus, if anything, Quartile has a higher current ratio than might be expected. As Quartile has relatively low inventory levels (deduced from high inventory turnover figures), this means it must also have relatively low levels of trade payables (which can be confirmed from the calculated ratios). The low payables period of 45 days may be an indication of suppliers being cautious with the credit period they extend to Quartile, but there is no real evidence of this (e.g. the company is not struggling with an overdraft). In short, Quartile does not appear to have any liquidity issues.

Gearing

Quartile's debt to equity at 30% is lower than the sector average of 38%. Although the loan note interest rate of 10% might appear quite high, it is lower than the ROCE of 12·1% (which means shareholders are benefiting from the borrowings) and the interest cover of 5·25 times ((3,400 + 800)/800) is acceptable. Quartile also has sufficient tangible assets to give more than adequate security on the borrowings, therefore there appear to be no adverse issues in relation to gearing.

Conclusion

Quartile may be right to be concerned about its declining profitability. From the above analysis, it seems that Quartile may be addressing the wrong market (low margins with high volumes). The information provided about its rival companies would appear to suggest that the current market appears to favour a strategy of higher margins (probably associated with better quality and more expensive goods) as being more profitable. In other aspects of the appraisal, Quartile is doing well compared to other companies in its sector.

198   MONTY

Monty – Statement of cash flows for the year ended 31 March 2013:

(Note: Figures in brackets are in $000)

	$000	$000
Cash flows from operating activities:		
Profit before tax		3,000
Adjustments for:		
depreciation of non-current assets		900
amortisation of non-current assets		200
finance costs		400
decrease in inventories (3,800 – 3,300)		500
increase in receivables (2,950 – 2,200)		(750)
increase in payables (2,650 – 2,100)		550
		─────
Cash generated from operations		4,800
Finance costs paid		(400)
Income tax paid (w (i))		(425)
		─────
Net cash from operating activities		3,975
Cash flows from investing activities:		
Purchase of property, plant and equipment (w (ii))	(700)	
Deferred development expenditure (1,000 + 200)	(1,200)	
	─────	
Net cash used in investing activities		(1,900)
Cash flows from financing activities:		
Redemption of 8% loan notes (3,125 – 1,400)	(1,725)	
Repayment of finance lease obligations (w (iii))	(1,050)	
Equity dividend paid (w (iv))	(550)	
	─────	
Net cash used in financing activities		(3,325)
		─────
Net decrease in cash and cash equivalents		(1,250)
Cash and cash equivalents at beginning of period		1,300
		─────
Cash and cash equivalents at end of period		50
		─────

Workings (columnar format) | $000

(i)	Income tax paid	
	Provision b/f – current	(725)
	– deferred	(800)
	Tax charge	(1,000)
	Transfer from revaluation reserve	(650)
	Provision c/f – current	1,250
	– deferred	1,500
		———
	Balance – cash paid	(425)
		———
(ii)	Property, plant and equipment	
	Balance b/f	10,700
	Revaluation	2,000
	New finance lease	1,500
	Depreciation	(900)
	Balance c/f	(14,000)
		———
	Balance – cash purchases	(700)
		———
(iii)	Finance leases	
	Balances b/f – current	(600)
	– non-current	(900)
	New finance lease	(1,500)
	Balances c/f – current	750
	– non-current	1,200
		———
	Balance cash repayment	(1,050)
		———
(iv)	Equity dividend	$000
	Retained earnings b/f	1,750
	Profit for the year	2,000
	Retained earnings c/f	(3,200)
		———
	Balance – dividend paid	(550)
		———

Workings – T account format

(W1) Tax Liabilities

	Dr		Cr
	$000		$000
		b/f (725 + 800)	1,525
Tax paid (bal fig)	425	Charge from P/L	1,000
c/f (1,250 + 1,500)	2,750	Transfer from reval reserve	650
	———		———
	3,175		3,175
	———		———

(W2) Property, plant and equipment

	Dr		Cr
	$000		$000
b/f	10,700		
Revaluation	2,000	Depreciation	900
Finance lease additions	1,500		
Cash additions (Balancing fig)	**700**		
		c/f	14,000
	———		———
	14,900		14,900
	———		———

(W3) Finance lease liabilities

	Dr		Cr
	$000		$000
		b/f (600 + 900)	1,500
Liabilities repaid	1,050	New leases (PPE)	1,500
c/f (750 + 1,200)	1,950		
	———		———
	3,000		3,000
	———		———

Note: The disposal had a carrying value of $1m at disposal (cost $10m, accumulated depreciation $9m), and cost $500k to dispose, making a loss on disposal of $1,500k.

(W4) Retained earnings

	Dr		Cr
	$000		$000
		b/f	1,750
Dividend paid (bal fig)	550	Charge from P/L	2,000
c/f	3,200		
	———		———
	3,750		3,750
	———		———

199 KINGDOM

Kingdom – Statement of cash flows for the year ended 30 September 2013:

	$000	$000
Cash flows from operating activities:		
Profit before tax		2,400
Adjustments for:		
depreciation of property, plant and equipment		1,500
loss on sale of property, plant and equipment (2,300 – 1,800)		500
finance costs		600
investment properties – rentals received		(350)
– fair value changes		700
		─────
		5,350
decrease in inventory (3,100 – 2,300)		800
decrease in receivables (3,400 – 3,000)		400
increase in payables (4,200 – 3,900)		300
		─────
Cash generated from operations		6,850
Interest paid (600 – 100 + 50)		(550)
Income tax paid (w (i))		(1,950)
		─────
Net cash from operating activities		4,350
Cash flows from investing activities:		
Purchase of property, plant and equipment (w (ii))	(5,000)	
Sale of property, plant and equipment	1,800	
Purchase of investment property	(1,400)	
Investment property rentals received	350	
	─────	
Net cash used in investing activities		(4,250)
Cash flows from financing activities:		
Issue of equity shares (17,200 – 15,000)	2,200	
Equity dividends paid (w (iii))	(2,800)	
	─────	
Net cash used in financing activities		(600)
		─────
Net decrease in cash and cash equivalents		(500)
Cash and cash equivalents at beginning of period		300
		─────
Cash and cash equivalents at end of period		(200)
		─────

Workings – columnar format

		$000
(i)	**Income tax:**	
	Provision b/f	(1,850)
	Profit or loss charge	(600)
	Provision c/f	500
	Tax paid (= balance)	(1,950)
(ii)	**Property, plant and equipment:**	
	Balance b/f	(25,200)
	Depreciation	1,500
	Revaluation (downwards)	1,300
	Disposal (at carrying amount)	2,300
	Transfer from investment properties	(1,600)
	Balance c/f	26,700
	Acquired during year (= balance)	(5,000)
(iii)	**Equity dividends:**	
	Retained earnings b/f	8,700
	Profit for the year	1,800
	Retained earnings c/f	(7,700)
	Dividends paid (= balance)	2,800

Note: For tutorial purposes the reconciliation of the investment properties is:

	$000
Balance b/f	5,000
Acquired during year (from question)	1,400
Loss in fair value	(700)
Transfer to property, plant and equipment	(1,600)
Balance c/f	4,100

Workings – T account format

(W1) Tax Liabilities

	Dr $000		Cr $000
		b/f	1,850
Tax paid (bal fig)	**1,950**	Charge from P/L	600
c/f	500		
	2,450		2,450

(W2) Property, plant and equipment

	Dr $000		Cr $000
b/f	25,200	Revaluation	1,300
Transfer from investment properties	1,600	Depreciation	1,500
		Disposal	2,300
Cash additions (Balancing fig)	**5,000**		
		c/f	26,700
	31,800		31,800

(W3) Retained earnings

	Dr $000		Cr $000
		b/f	8,700
Dividend paid (bal fig)	**2,800**	Profit from P/L	1,800
c/f	7,700		
	10,500		10,500

(W4) Investment properties

	Dr $000		Cr $000
b/f	5,000	Transfer to PPE	1,600
Additions	1,400	FV loss	700
		c/f	4,100
	6,400		6,400

200 BENGAL

Note: references to 2011 and 2010 refer to the periods ending 31 March 2011 and 2010 respectively.

It is understandable that the shareholder's observations would cause concern. A large increase in sales revenue has not led to a proportionate increase in profit. To assess why this has happened requires consideration of several factors that could potentially explain the results. Perhaps the most obvious would be that the company has increased its sales by discounting prices (cutting profit margins). Interpreting the ratios in the appendix rules out this possible explanation as the gross profit margin has in fact increased in 2011 (up from 40% to 42%). Another potential cause of the disappointing profit could be overheads (distribution costs and administrative expenses) getting out of control, perhaps due to higher advertising costs or more generous incentives to sales staff. Again, when these expenses are expressed as a percentage of sales, this does not explain the disparity in profit as the ratio has remained at approximately 19%. What is evident is that there has been a very large increase in finance costs which is illustrated by the interest cover deteriorating from 36 times to only 9 times. The other 'culprit' is the taxation expense: expressed as a percentage of pre-tax accounting profit, the effective rate of tax has gone from 28·6% in 2010 to 42·9% in 2011. There are a number of factors that can affect a period's effective tax rate (including under- or over-provisions from the previous year), but judging from the figures involved, it would seem likely that either there was a material adjustment from an under-provision of tax in 2010 or there has been a considerable increase in the rate levied by the taxation authority.

As an illustration of the effect, if the same effective tax rate in 2010 had applied in 2011, the after-tax profit would have been $3,749,000 (5,250 × (100% − 28·6%) rounded) and, using this figure, the percentage increase in profit would be 50% ((3,749 − 2,500)/2,500 × 100) which is slightly higher than the percentage increase in revenue. Thus an increase in the tax rate and increases in finance costs due to much higher borrowings more than account for the disappointing profit commented upon by the concerned shareholder.

The other significant observation in comparing 2011 with 2010 is that the company has almost certainty acquired another business. The increased expenditure on property, plant and equipment of $6,740,000 and the newly acquired intangibles (probably goodwill) of $6·2 million are not likely to be attributable to organic or internal growth. Indeed the decrease in the bank balance of $4·2 million and the issue of $7 million loan notes closely match the increase in non-current assets. This implies that the acquisition has been financed by cash resources (which the company looks to have been building up) and issuing debt (no equity was issued).

It may be that these assets were part of the acquisition of a new business and are 'surplus to requirements', hence they have been made available for sale. They are likely to be valued at their 'fair value less cost to sell' and the prospect of their sale should be highly probable (normally within one year). That said, if the assets are not sold in the near future, it would call into question the acceptability of the company's current ratio which may cause short-term liquidity problems.

The overall performance of Bengal has deteriorated (as measured by its ROCE) from 38·9% to 31·9%. Further, it may be that the new assets were acquired part way through the year and thus the returns from this element may be greater next year when a full period's profits will be reported.

In summary, although reported performance has deteriorated, it may be that future results will benefit from the current year's investment and show considerable improvement.

Perhaps some equity should have been issued to lower the company's finance costs and if the dividend of $750,000 had been suspended for a year there would be a better liquid position.

Appendix

Calculation of ratios (figures in $000):	2011	2010
Gross profit margin (10,700/25,500 × 100)	42·0%	40·0 %
Operating expenses % (4,800/25,500 × 100)	18·8%	19·1%
Interest cover ((5,250 + 650)/650)	9 times	36 times
Effective rate of tax (2,250/5,250)	42·9%	28·6%
Return on capital employed (ROCE) ((5,250 + 650)/(9,500 + 9,000) × 100)	31·9%	38·9%
Net profit (before tax) margin (5,250/25,500 × 100)	20·6%	20·3%

The figures for the calculation of 2011's ratios are given in brackets; the figures for 2010 are derived from the equivalent figures.

Fundamentals Level – Skills Module

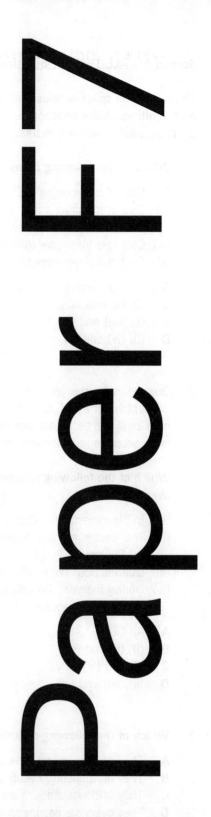

Financial Reporting

Specimen Exam applicable from
December 2014

Time allowed

Reading and planning: 15 minutes
Writing: 3 hours

This paper is divided into two sections:

Section A – ALL TWENTY questions are compulsory and MUST be
attempted

Section B – ALL THREE questions are compulsory and MUST be
attempted

Do NOT open this paper until instructed by the supervisor.

**During reading and planning time only the question paper may
be annotated. You must NOT write in your answer booklet until
instructed by the supervisor.**

This question paper must not be removed from the examination hall.

The Association of Chartered Certified Accountants

Please use the space provided on the inside cover of the Candidate Answer Booklet to indicate your chosen answer to each multiple choice question.
Each question is worth 2 marks.

1 **Which of the following items should be capitalised within the initial carrying amount of an item of plant?**

(i) Cost of transporting the plant to the factory
(ii) Cost of installing a new power supply required to operate the plant
(iii) A deduction to reflect the estimated realisable value
(iv) Cost of a three-year maintenance agreement
(v) Cost of a three-week training course for staff to operate the plant

A (i) and (ii) only
B (i), (ii) and (iii)
C (ii), (iii) and (iv)
D (i), (iv) and (v)

2 Quartile is in the jewellery retail business which can be assumed to be highly seasonal. For the year ended 30 September 2014, Quartile assessed its operating performance by comparing selected accounting ratios with those of its business sector average as provided by an agency. You may assume that the business sector used by the agency is an accurate representation of Quartile's business.

Which of the following circumstances may invalidate the comparison of Quartile's ratios with those of the sector average?

(i) In the current year, Quartile has experienced significant rising costs for its purchases
(ii) The sector average figures are complied from companies whose year end is between 1 July 2014 and 30 September 2014
(iii) Quartile does not revalue its properties, but is aware that other entities in this sector do
(iv) During the year, Quartile discovered an error relating to the inventory count at 30 September 2013. This error was correctly accounted for in the financial statements for the current year ended 30 September 2014

A All four
B (i), (ii) and (iii)
C (ii) and (iii) only
D (ii), (iii) and (iv)

3 **Which of the following criticisms does NOT apply to historical cost accounts during a period of rising prices?**

A They contain mixed values; some items are at current values, some at out of date values
B They are difficult to verify as transactions could have happened many years ago
C They understate assets and overstate profit
D They overstate gearing in the statement of financial position

4 Dempsey's year end is 30 September 2014. Dempsey commenced the development stage of a project to produce a new pharmaceutical drug on 1 January 2014. Expenditure of $40,000 per month was incurred until the project was completed on 30 June 2014 when the drug went into immediate production. The directors became confident of the project's success on 1 March 2014. The drug has an estimated life span of five years; time apportionment is used by Dempsey where applicable.

What amount will Dempsey charge to profit or loss for development costs, including any amortisation, for the year ended 30 September 2014?

A $12,000
B $98,667
C $48,000
D $88,000

5 On 1 October 2013, Fresco acquired an item of plant under a five-year finance lease agreement. The plant had a cash purchase cost of $25 million. The agreement had an implicit finance cost of 10% per annum and required an immediate deposit of $2 million and annual rentals of $6 million paid on 30 September each year for five years.

What would be the current liability for the leased plant in Fresco's statement of financial position as at 30 September 2014?

A $19,300,000
B $4,070,000
C $5,000,000
D $3,850,000

6 The following information has been taken or calculated from Fowler's financial statements for the year ended 30 September 2014.

Fowler's cash cycle at 30 September 2014 is 70 days.
Its inventory turnover is six times.
Year-end trade payables are $230,000.
Purchases on credit for the year were $2 million.
Cost of sales for the year was $1·8 million.

What is Fowler's trade receivables collection period as at 30 September 2014?

All calculations should be made to the nearest full day. The trading year is 365 days.

A 106 days
B 89 days
C 56 days
D 51 days

7 **Which of the following would be a change in accounting policy in accordance with IAS 8 *Accounting Policies, Changes in Accounting Estimates and Errors*?**

A Adjusting the financial statements of a subsidiary prior to consolidation as its accounting policies differ from those of its parent
B A change in reporting depreciation charges as cost of sales rather than as administrative expenses
C Depreciation charged on reducing balance method rather than straight line
D Reducing the value of inventory from cost to net realisable value due to a valid adjusting event after the reporting period

3

8 On 1 January 2014, Viagem acquired 80% of the equity share capital of Greca.

Extracts of their statements of profit or loss for the year ended 30 September 2014 are:

	Viagem $'000	Greca $'000
Revenue	64,600	38,000
Cost of sales	(51,200)	(26,000)

Sales from Viagem to Greca throughout the year ended 30 September 2014 had consistently been $800,000 per month. Viagem made a mark-up on cost of 25% on these sales. Greca had $1·5 million of these goods in inventory as at 30 September 2014.

What would be the cost of sales in Viagem's consolidated statement of profit or loss for the year ended 30 September 2014?

- **A** $59·9 million
- **B** $61·4 million
- **C** $63·8 million
- **D** $67·9 million

9 The objective of IAS 17 *Leases* is to prescribe the appropriate accounting treatment and required disclosures in relation to leases.

Which TWO of the following situations would normally lead to a lease being classified as a finance lease?

(i) The lease transfers ownership of the asset to the lessee by the end of the lease term
(ii) The lease term is for approximately half of the economic life of the asset
(iii) The lease assets are of a specialised nature such that only the lessee can use them without major modifications being made
(iv) At the inception of the lease, the present value of the minimum lease payments is 60% of what the leased asset would cost to purchase

- **A** (i) and (ii)
- **B** (i) and (iii)
- **C** (ii) and (iii)
- **D** (iii) and (iv)

10 **Which of the following is NOT a purpose of the IASB's Conceptual Framework?**

- **A** To assist the IASB in the preparation and review of IFRS
- **B** To assist auditors in forming an opinion on whether financial statements comply with IFRS
- **C** To assist in determining the treatment of items not covered by an existing IFRS
- **D** To be authoritative where a specific IFRS conflicts with the Conceptual Framework

11 An associate is an entity in which an investor has significant influence over the investee.

Which of the following indicate(s) the presence of significant influence?

(i) The investor owns 330,000 of the 1,500,000 equity voting shares of the investee
(ii) The investor has representation on the board of directors of the investee
(iii) The investor is able to insist that all of the sales of the investee are made to a subsidiary of the investor
(iv) The investor controls the votes of a majority of the board members

- **A** (i) and (ii) only
- **B** (i), (ii) and (iii)
- **C** (ii) and (iii) only
- **D** All four

12 Consolidated financial statements are presented on the basis that the companies within the group are treated as if they are a single (economic) entity.

Which of the following are requirements of preparing group accounts?

(i) All subsidiaries must adopt the accounting policies of the parent
(ii) Subsidiaries with activities which are substantially different to the activities of other members of the group should not be consolidated
(iii) All entity financial statements within a group should (normally) be prepared to the same accounting year end prior to consolidation
(iv) Unrealised profits within the group must be eliminated from the consolidated financial statements

A All four
B (i) and (ii) only
C (i), (iii) and (iv)
D (iii) and (iv)

13 The Caddy group acquired 240,000 of August's 800,000 equity shares for $6 per share on 1 April 2014. August's profit after tax for the year ended 30 September 2014 was $400,000 and it paid an equity dividend on 20 September 2014 of $150,000.

On the assumption that August is an associate of Caddy, what would be the carrying amount of the investment in August in the consolidated statement of financial position of Caddy as at 30 September 2014?

A $1,455,000
B $1,500,000
C $1,515,000
D $1,395,000

14 On 1 October 2013, Hoy had $2·5 million of equity shares of 50 cents each in issue.

No new shares were issued during the year ended 30 September 2014, but on that date there were outstanding share options to purchase 2 million equity shares at $1·20 each. The average market value of Hoy's equity shares during the year ended 30 September 2014 was $3 per share.

Hoy's profit after tax for the year ended 30 September 2014 was $1,550,000.

In accordance with IAS 33 *Earnings per Share*, what is Hoy's diluted earnings per share for the year ended 30 September 2014?

A 25·0 cents
B 22·1 cents
C 31·0 cents
D 41·9 cents

15 Although the objectives and purposes of not-for-profit entities are different from those of commercial entities, the accounting requirements of not-for-profit entities are moving closer to those entities to which IFRSs apply.

Which of the following IFRS requirements would NOT be relevant to a not-for-profit entity?

A Preparation of a statement of cash flows
B Requirement to capitalise a finance lease
C Disclosure of earnings per share
D Disclosure of non-adjusting events after the reporting date

16 Riley acquired a non-current asset on 1 October 2009 at a cost of $100,000 which had a useful economic life of ten years and a nil residual value. The asset had been correctly depreciated up to 30 September 2014. At that date the asset was damaged and an impairment review was performed. On 30 September 2014, the fair value of the asset less costs to sell was $30,000 and the expected future cash flows were $8,500 per annum for the next five years. The current cost of capital is 10% and a five year annuity of $1 per annum at 10% would have a present value of $3·79

What amount would be charged to profit or loss for the impairment of this asset for the year ended 30 September 2014?

A $17,785
B $20,000
C $30,000
D $32,215

17 Trent uses the formula:

(trade receivables at its year end/revenue for the year) x 365

to calculate how long on average (in days) its customers take to pay.

Which of the following would NOT affect the correctness of the above calculation of the average number of days a customer takes to pay?

A   Trent experiences considerable seasonal trading
B   Trent makes a number of cash sales through retail outlets
C   Reported revenue does not include a 15% sales tax whereas the receivables do include the tax
D   Trent factors with recourse the receivable of its largest customer

18 **Which TWO of the following events which occur after the reporting date of a company but before the financial statements are authorised for issue are classified as ADJUSTING events in accordance with IAS 10 *Events after the Reporting Period*?**

(i)   A change in tax rate announced after the reporting date, but affecting the current tax liability
(ii)   The discovery of a fraud which had occurred during the year
(iii)   The determination of the sale proceeds of an item of plant sold before the year end
(iv)   The destruction of a factory by fire

A   (i) and (ii)
B   (i) and (iii)
C   (ii) and (iii)
D   (iii) and (iv)

19 Financial statements represent transactions in words and numbers. To be useful, financial information must represent faithfully these transactions in terms of how they are reported.

Which of the following accounting treatments would be an example of faithful representation?

A   Charging the rental payments for an item of plant to the statement of profit or loss where the rental agreement meets the criteria for a finance lease
B   Including a convertible loan note in equity on the basis that the holders are likely to choose the equity option on conversion
C   Derecognising factored trade receivables sold without recourse
D   Treating redeemable preference shares as part of equity in the statement of financial position

20 Isaac is a company which buys agricultural produce from wholesale suppliers for retail to the general public. It is preparing its financial statements for the year ending 30 September 2014 and is considering its closing inventory.

In addition to IAS 2 *Inventories*, which of the following IFRSs may be relevant to determining the figure to be included in its financial statements for closing inventories?

A   IAS 10 *Events After the Reporting Period*
B   IAS 11 *Construction Contracts*
C   IAS 16 *Property, Plant and Equipment*
D   IAS 41 *Agriculture*

(40 marks)

1 Tangier's summarised financial statements for the years ended 30 September 2014 and the comparative figures are shown below.

Statements of profit or loss for the year ended 30 September:

	2014 $m	2013 $m
Revenue	2,700	1,820
Cost of sales	(1,890)	(1,092)
Gross profit	810	728
Administrative expense	(345)	(200)
Distribution costs	(230)	(130)
Finance costs	(40)	(5)
Profit before taxation	195	393
Income tax expense	(60)	(113)
Profit for the year	135	280

Statements of financial position as at 30 September:

	2014 $m	2014 $m	2013 $m	2013 $m
Non-current assets				
Property, plant and equipment		680		410
Intangible asset: manufacturing licence		300		200
Investment at cost – Raremetal		230		nil
		1,210		610
Current assets				
Inventory	200		110	
Trade receivables	195		75	
Bank	nil	395	120	305
Total assets		1,605		915
Equity and liabilities				
Equity shares of $1 each		430		250
Retained earnings		375		295
		805		545
Non-current liabilities				
5% secured loan notes	100		100	
10% secured loan notes	300	400	nil	100
Current liabilities				
Bank overdraft	110		nil	
Trade payables	210		160	
Current tax payable	80	400	110	270
Total equity and liabilities		1,605		915

The following additional information has been obtained in relation to the operations of Tangier for the year ended 30 September 2014:

(i) On 1 January 2014, Tangier won a tender for a new contract to supply Jetside with aircraft engines which Tangier manufactures under a recently acquired licence. The bidding process had been very competitive and Tangier had to increase its manufacturing capacity to fulfil the contract.

(ii) The company also decided to invest in Raremetal by buying 8% of its equity shares to secure supplies of specialised materials used in the manufacture of the engines. No dividends were received from Raremetal nor had the value of its shares increased.

On seeing the results for the first time, one of the company's non-executive directors is disappointed by the current year's performance.

Required:

Explain how the new contract and its related costs may have affected Tangier's operating performance during the year ended 30 September 2014, identifying any further information regarding the contract which may be useful to your answer.

Note: Your answer should be supported by appropriate ratios (up to 5 marks); however, ratios and analysis of working capital are not required.

(15 marks)

2 On 1 October 2013, Pyramid acquired 80% of Square's equity shares by means of a share exchange of two shares in Pyramid for every three acquired shares in Square. In addition, Pyramid would make a deferred cash payment of 88 cents per acquired share on 1 October 2014. Pyramid has not recorded any of the consideration. Pyramid's cost of capital is 10% per annum. The market value of Pyramid's shares at 1 October 2013 was $6.

The following information is available for the two companies as at 30 September 2014:

	Pyramid $'000	Square $'000
Assets		
Non-current assets		
Property, plant and equipment	38,100	28,500
Equity and liabilities		
Equity		
Equity shares of $1 each	50,000	9,000
Other components of equity	8,000	nil
Retained earnings – at 1 October 2013	16,200	19,000
– for the year ended 30 September 2014	14,000	8,000

The following information is relevant:

(i)   At the date of acquisition, Square's net assets were equal to their carrying amounts with the following exceptions:

an item of plant which had a fair value of $3 million above its carrying amount. At the date of acquisition it had a remaining life of five years (straight-line depreciation).

Square had an unrecorded deferred tax liability of $1 million, which was unchanged as at 30 September 2014.

(ii) Pyramid's policy is to value the non-controlling interest at fair value at the date of acquisition. For this purpose a share price of $3·50 each is representative of the fair value of the shares in Square held by the non-controlling interest at the acquisition date.

(iii) Consolidated goodwill has not been impaired.

Required:

Prepare extracts from Pyramid's consolidated statement of financial position as at 30 September 2014 for:

(a) Consolidated goodwill;   (5 marks)

(b) Property, plant and equipment;   (2 marks)

(c) Equity (share capital and reserves);   (6 marks)

(d) Non-controlling interests.   (2 marks)

(15 marks)

This is a blank page.
Question 3 begins on page 12.

3 The following trial balance relates to Quincy as at 30 September 2014:

	$'000	$'000
Revenue (note (i))		213,500
Cost of sales	136,800	
Distribution costs	17,500	
Administrative expenses (note (ii))	19,000	
Loan note interest paid (note (ii))	1,500	
Investment income		400
Equity shares of 25 cents each		60,000
6% loan note (note (ii))		25,000
Retained earnings at 1 October 2013		4,300
Land and buildings at cost (land element $10 million) (note (iii))	50,000	
Plant and equipment at cost (note (iii))	83,700	
Accumulated depreciation at 1 October 2013: buildings		8,000
plant and equipment		33,700
Equity financial asset investments (note (iv))	17,000	
Inventory at 30 September 2014	24,800	
Trade receivables	28,500	
Bank	2,900	
Current tax (note (v))	1,100	
Deferred tax (note (v))		1,200
Trade payables		36,700
	382,800	382,800

The following notes are relevant:

(i)   On 1 October 2013, Quincy sold one of its products for $10 million (included in revenue in the trial balance). As part of the sale agreement, Quincy is committed to the ongoing servicing of this product until 30 September 2016 (i.e. three years from the date of sale). The value of this service has been included in the selling price of $10 million. The estimated cost to Quincy of the servicing is $600,000 per annum and Quincy's normal gross profit margin on this type of servicing is 25%. Ignore discounting.

(ii) Quincy issued a $25 million 6% loan on 1 October 2013. Issue costs were $1 million and these have been charged to administrative expenses. Interest is paid annually on 30 September each year. The loan will be redeemed on 30 September 2016 at a premium which gives an effective interest rate on the loan of 8%.

(iii) Non-current assets:

Quincy had been carrying land and buildings at depreciated cost, but due to a recent rise in property prices, it decided to revalue its property on 1 October 2013 to market value. An independent valuer confirmed the value of the property at $60 million (land element $12 million) as at that date and the directors accepted this valuation. The property had a remaining life of 16 years at the date of its revaluation. Quincy will make a transfer from the revaluation reserve to retained earnings in respect of the realisation of the revaluation. Ignore deferred tax on the revaluation.

On 1 October 2013, Quincy had a processing plant installed at a cost of $10 million which is included in the trial balance figure of plant and equipment at cost. The process the plant performs will cause immediate contamination of the nearby land. Quincy will have to decontaminate (clean up) this land at the end of the plant's ten-year life (straight-line depreciation). The present value (discounted at a cost of capital of 10% per annum) of the decontamination is $6 million. Quincy has not made any accounting entries in respect of this cost.

All other plant and equipment is depreciated at 12½% per annum using the reducing balance method.

No depreciation has yet been charged on any non-current asset for the year ended 30 September 2014. All depreciation is charged to cost of sales.

Other than referred to above, there were no acquisitions or disposals of non-current assets.

(iv) The investments had a fair value of $15·7 million as at 30 September 2014. There were no acquisitions or disposals of these investments during the year ended 30 September 2014.

(v) The balance on current tax represents the under/over provision of the tax liability for the year ended 30 September 2013. A provision for income tax for the year ended 30 September 2014 of $7·4 million is required. At 30 September 2014, Quincy had taxable temporary differences of $5 million requiring a provision for deferred tax. Any deferred tax adjustment should be reported in profit or loss. The income tax rate of Quincy is 20%.

Required:

(a) Prepare the statement of profit or loss and other comprehensive income for Quincy for the year ended 30 September 2014.

(b) Prepare the statement of changes in equity for Quincy for the year ended 30 September 2014.

(c) Prepare the statement of financial position of Quincy as at 30 September 2014.

(d) Calculate the increase in the carrying amount of property, plant and equipment during the year ended 30 September 2014 from the perspective of:

    (i) the change between the opening and closing statements of financial position and;
    (ii) the statement of cash flows.

    Comment on which perspective may be more useful to users of Quincy's financial statements.

Notes to the financial statements are not required.

The following mark allocation is provided as guidance for this question:

(a) 12 marks
(b) 3 marks
(c) 12 marks
(d) 3 marks

(30 marks)

End of Question Paper

Answers

Section A

1   A

2   C

3   B

4   D

	$
Write off to 1 January 2014 to 28 February 2014 (2 x $40,000)	80,000
Amortisation 160,000 (i.e. 4 x 40,000)/5 years x 3/12 (March to June)	8,000
	88,000

5   B

$4,070,000 (19,300 – 15,230)

Workings (in $'000)

	$
Fair value 1 October 2013	25,000
Deposit	(2,000)
	23,000
Interest 10%	2,300
Payment 30 September 2014	(6,000)
Lease obligation 30 September 2014	19,300
Interest 10%	1,930
Payment 30 September 2015	(6,000)
Lease obligation 30 September 2015	15,230

6   D

Year end inventory of six times is 61 days (365/6).
Trade payables period is 42 days (230,000 x 365/2,000,000).
Therefore receivables collection period is 51 days (70 – 61 + 42).

7   B

8   C

	$
Cost of sales	
Viagem	51,200
Greca (26,000 x 9/12)	19,500
Intra-group purchases (800 x 9 months)	(7,200)
URP in inventory (1,500 x 25/125)	300
	63,800

9   B

10   D

11 A

12 D

13 A

	$'000
Cost (240,000 x $6)	1,440
Share of associate's profit (400 x 6/12 x 240/800)	60
Less dividend received (150 x 240/800)	(45)
	1,455

14 A

(1,550/((2,500 x 2 + 1,200 see below)
2 million shares at $1·20 = $2·4 million which would buy 800,000 shares at full price of $3.
Therefore, dilution element (free shares) is 1,200,000 (2,000 – 800).

15 C

16 A

	$
Cost 1 October 2009	100,000
Depreciation 1 October 2009 to 30 September 2014 (100,000 x 5/10)	(50,000)
Carrying amount	50,000

fair value less costs to sell	value in use
30,000	32,215 (8,500 x 3·79) (is higher)

the recoverable amount is therefore $32,215

	$
Carrying value	50,000
Recoverable amount	(32,215)
Impairment to income statement	17,785

17 D

Factoring with recourse means Trent still has the risk of an irrecoverable receivable and therefore would not derecognise the receivable.

18 C

19 C

20 A

IAS 10 defines adjusting events as those providing evidence of conditions existing at the end of the reporting period. In the case of inventories, it may be sales of inventory in this period indicate that the net realisable value of some items of inventory have fallen below their cost and require writing down to their net realisable value as at 30 September 2014.

Section B

1 Note: References to '2014' are in respect of the year ended 30 September 2014 and '2013' refers to the year ended 30 September 2013.

Despite an increase in revenues of 48·4% (880/1,820 x 100) in 2013, the company has suffered a dramatic fall in its profitability. This has been caused by a combination of a falling gross profit margin (from 40% in 2013 to only 30% in 2014) and markedly higher operating overheads. An eight-fold increase in finance cost caused by the increased borrowing at double the interest rate of existing borrowing and (presumably) some overdraft interest has led to the profit before tax more than halving. This is also borne out by the dramatic fall in the company's interest cover (from 79·6 in 2013 to only 5·9 in 2014).

This is all reflected in the ROCE falling from an impressive 61·7% in 2013 to only 19·5% in 2014 (though even this figure is respectable). The fall in the ROCE is attributable to a dramatic fall in profit margin at operating level (from 21·9% in 2013 to only 8·7% in 2014) which has been compounded by a reduction in the non-current asset turnover, with only $2·23 being generated from every $1 invested in non-current assets in 2014 (from $2·98 in 2013).

The information in the question points strongly to the possibility (even probability) that the new contract may be responsible for much of the deterioration in Tangier's performance. It is likely that the new contract may account for the increased revenue; however, the bidding process was 'competitive' which implies that Tangier had to cut its price (and therefore its profit margin) in order to win the contract.

The costs of fulfilling the contract have also been heavy:

Investment in property, plant and equipment has increased by $270 million (at carrying amount), representing an increase of 66%.

The increase in licence costs to manufacture the new engines has cost $100 million plus any amortisation (which is not identified in the question).

The investment in Raremetal to secure materials supplies has cost $230 million. There has been no benefit in 2014 from this investment in terms of dividends or capital growth. It is impossible to quantify the benefit of securing material supplies which was the main reason for the investment, but it has come at a high cost. It is also questionable how the investment has 'secured' the provision of materials as an 8% equity investment does not normally give any meaningful influence over the investee. An alternative (less expensive) strategy might have been to enter into a long-term supply contract with Raremetal.

The finance cost of the new $300 million 10% loan notes to partly fund the investment in non-current assets has also reduced reported profit and increased debt/equity (one form of gearing measure) from 18·3% in 2013 to 49·7% in 2014 despite issuing $180 million in new equity shares. At this level, particularly in view of its large increase from 2013, it may give debt holders (and others) cause for concern. If it could be demonstrated that the overdraft was not able to be cleared for some time, this would be an argument for including it in the calculation of debt/equity, making the gearing level even worse. It is also apparent from the movement in the retained earnings that Tangier paid a dividend during the year of $55 million (295,000 + 135,000 – 375,000) which may be a questionable policy when the company is raising additional finance through borrowings.

It could be speculated that the 73% increase of administrative expenses may be due to one-off costs associated with the tendering process (consultancy fees, etc) and the 77% higher distribution costs could be due to additional freight/packing/insurance cost of the engines, delivery distances may also be longer (even abroad).

All of this seems to indicate that the new contract has been very detrimental to Tangier's performance, but more information is needed to be certain. The contract was not signed until January 2014 and there is no information of when production/sales started, but clearly there has not been a full year's revenue from the contract. Also there is no information on the length or total value of the contract. Unless the contract is for a considerable time, the increased investment in operating assets represents a considerable risk. There are no figures for the separate revenues and costs of the contract, but from 2014's declining performance it does not seem profitable, thus even if the contract does secure work for several years, it is of doubtful benefit if the work is loss-making. An alternative scenario could be that the early costs associated with the contract are part of a 'learning curve' and that future production will be more efficient and therefore the contract may become profitable as a result.

Relevant ratios

	2014	2013
Gross profit % (810/2,700 x 100)	30·0%	40·0%
Profit margin before interest % (235/2,700 x 100)	8·7%	21·9%
ROCE (235/(805 + 400))	19·5%	61·7%
Non-current asset turnover (2,700/1210)	2·23 times	2·98 times
Debt/equity (400/805)	49·7%	18·3%
Interest cover (235/40)	5·9 times	79·6 times

2 Pyramid – as at 30 September 2014

Figures in brackets are in $'000

(a) Consolidated goodwill

Controlling interest

	$'000	$'000
Share exchange (4·8 million (w (i)) x $6)		28,800
Deferred consideration (9,000 x 80% x 0·88/1·1)		5,760
Non-controlling interest (9,000 x 20% x $3·50)		6,300
		40,860
Equity shares	9,000	
Pre-acquisition reserves	19,000	
Fair value plant	3,000	
Unrecorded deferred tax	(1,000)	(30,000)
Goodwill arising on acquisition		10,860

(b) Property, plant and equipment

	$'000
Pyramid	38,100
Square	28,500
Gross fair adjustment to plant	3,000
Additional depreciation to 30 September 2014 (3,000/5 years)	(600)
	69,000

(c) Equity

	$'000
Equity shares of $1 each (50,000 + 4,800)	54,800
Reserves	
Other components of equity (8,000 + 24,000)	32,000
Consolidated retained earnings (w (ii))	35,544

(d) Non-controlling interest

	$'000
Fair value on acquisition (from answer (a) above)	6,300
Post-acquisition profit (7,400 x 20% (w (iii)))	1,480
	7,780

Workings

(i) Pyramid acquired 7·2 million (9 million x 80%) shares in Square. On the basis of a share exchange of two for three, Pyramid would issue 4·8 million (7·2 million/3 x 2) shares. At a value of $6 each, this would amount to $28·8 million and be recorded as $4·8 million share capital and $24 million (4·8 million x $5) other components of equity.

Note: *It would be acceptable to classify the $24 million addition to other components of equity as share premium.*

(ii)

	$
Pyramid's retained earnings	30,200
Square's post-acquisition profit (7,400 x 80% see below)	5,920
Interest on deferred consideration (5,760 x 10%)	(576)
	35,544

(iii) The adjusted post-acquisition profits of Square are:

	$
As reported	8,000
Additional depreciation on plant (3,000/5 years)	(600)
	7,400

3 (a) Quincy – Statement of profit or loss and other comprehensive income for the year ended 30 September 2014

	$'000
Revenue (213,500 – 1,600 (w (i)))	211,900
Cost of sales (w (ii))	(146,400)
Gross profit	65,500
Distribution costs	(17,500)
Administrative expenses (19,000 – 1,000 loan issue costs (w (iv)))	(18,000)
Loss on fair value of equity investments (17,000 – 15,700)	(1,300)
Investment income	400
Finance costs (1,920 + 600) w (iv))	(2,520)
Profit before tax	26,580
Income tax expense (7,400 + 1,100 – 200 (w (v)))	(8,300)
Profit for the year	18,280
Other comprehensive income	
Gain on revaluation of land and buildings (w (iii))	18,000
Total comprehensive income	36,280

(b) Quincy – Statement of changes in equity for the year ended 30 September 2014

	Share capital $'000	Revaluation reserve $'000	Retained earnings $'000	Total equity $'000
Balance at 1 October 2013	60,000	nil	4,300	64,300
Total comprehensive income		18,000	18,280	36,280
Transfer to retained earnings (w (iii))		(1,000)	1,000	nil
Balance at 30 September 2014	60,000	17,000	23,580	100,580

(c) Quincy – Statement of financial position as at 30 September 2014

Assets	$'000	$'000
Non-current assets		
Property, plant and equipment (57,000 + 14,400 + 35,000 (w (iii)))		106,400
Equity financial asset investments		15,700
		122,100
Current assets		
Inventory	24,800	
Trade receivables	28,500	
Bank	2,900	56,200
Total assets		178,300
Equity and liabilities		
Equity		
Equity shares of 25 cents each		60,000
Revaluation reserve	17,000	
Retained earnings	23,580	40,580
		100,580
Non-current liabilities		
Deferred tax (w (v))	1,000	
Deferred revenue (w (i))	800	
Environmental provision (6,000 + 600 (w (iv)))	6,600	
6% loan note (2016) (w (iv))	24,420	32,820
Current liabilities		
Trade payables	36,700	
Deferred revenue (w (i))	800	
Current tax payable	7,400	44,900
Total equity and liabilities		178,300

(d) **(i)** The carrying amount of property, plant and equipment at 30 September 2014 (from (b)) is $106·4 million.

The carrying amount of property, plant and equipment at 1 October 2013 based on the trial balance figures less the acquisition of the new plant during the year is $82 million (see below). Thus the increase in property, plant and equipment from the perspective of the statement of financial position is $24·4 million.

	$'000
Land and buildings (50,000 – 8,000)	42,000
Plant and equipment (83,700 – 10,000 – 33,700)	40,000
	82,000

(ii) The increase in the carrying amount of property, plant and equipment from a cash flow perspective would be only $10,000, being the cash cost of the processing plant; the revaluation, capitalisation of the clean up costs and depreciation are not cash flows.

Thus the statement of financial position shows an increase investment in property, plant and equipment of $24·4 million whereas the cash investment is much less at $10 million. Although both figures are meaningful (but do have different meanings), in this case, users are likely to find the cash investment figure a more intuitive measure of investment as the effects of the revaluation and, particularly, the capitalisation of environmental costs are more difficult to understand. They are also (subjective) estimates, whereas the cash payment is an objective test.

Workings (figures in brackets in $'000)

(i) Sales made which include revenue for ongoing servicing work must have part of the revenue deferred. The deferred revenue must include the normal profit margin (25%) for the deferred work. At 30 September 2014, there are two more years of servicing work, thus $1·6 million ((600 x 2) x 100/75) must be treated as deferred revenue, split equally between current and non-current liabilities.

(ii) **Cost of sales**

	$
Per trial balance	136,800
Depreciation of building (w (iii))	3,000
Depreciation of plant (1,600 + 5,000 w (iii))	6,600
	146,400

(iii) **Non-current assets**

Land and buildings:

The gain on revaluation and carrying amount of the land and buildings is:

	Land		Building
Carrying amount as at 1 October 2013	10,000	(40,000 – 8,000)	32,000
Revalued amount as at this date	(12,000)	(60,000 – 12,000)	(48,000)
Gain on revaluation	2,000		16,000
Building depreciation year to 30 September 2014 (48,000/16 years)			3,000

The transfer from the revaluation reserve to retained earnings in respect of 'excess' depreciation (as the revaluation is realised) is $1 million (16,000/16 years).

The carrying amount at 30 September 2014 is $57 million (60,000 – 3,000).

Plant and equipment:

	$
Processing plant	
Cash cost	10,000
Capitalise clean up costs (environmental provision)	6,000
Initial carrying amount	16,000
Depreciation 10-year life	(1,600)
Carrying amount as at 30 September 2014	14,400
Carrying amount as at 1 October 2013 (83,700 – 10,000 – 33,700)	40,000
Depreciation at 12½% per annum	(5,000)
Carrying amount as at 30 September 2014	35,000

(iv) **Loan note and environmental provision**

The finance cost of the loan note is charged at the effective rate of 8% applied to the carrying amount of the loan. The issue costs of the loan ($1 million) should be deducted from the proceeds of the loan ($25 million) and not treated as an administrative expense. This gives an initial carrying amount of $24 million and a finance cost of $1,920,000 (24,000 x 8%). The interest actually paid is $1·5 million (25,000 x 6%) and the difference between these amounts, of $420,000 (1,920 – 1,500), is accrued and added to the carrying amount of the loan note. This gives $24·42 million (24,000 + 420) for inclusion as a non-current liability in the statement of financial position.

The unwinding of the environmental provision of $6 million at 10% will cause a finance cost of $600,000.

(v) **Deferred tax**

	$
Provision required as at 30 September 2014 (5,000 x 20%)	1,000
Less provision b/f	(1,200)
Credit to statement of profit or loss	200

This marking scheme is given as a guide in the context of the suggested answers. Scope is given to markers to award marks for alternative approaches to a question, including relevant comment, and where well-reasoned conclusions are provided. This is particularly the case for written answers where there may be more than one acceptable solution.

			Marks
Section A			
2 marks per question			**40**

Section B

1	1 mark per valid point (up to 5 marks for ratios)		15
		Total for question	**15**

2	**(a)**	goodwill	5
	(b)	property, plant and equipment	2
	(c)	equity:	
		equity shares	1½
		other equity reserves	1½
		retained earnings	3
			6
	(d)	non-controlling interest	2
		Total for question	**15**

3	**(a)**	Statement of profit or loss and other comprehensive income	
		revenue	1½
		cost of sales	2½
		distribution costs	½
		administrative expenses	1
		loss on investments	1
		investment income	½
		finance costs	2
		income tax expense	2
		gain on revaluation of land and buildings	1
			12
	(b)	Statement of changes in equity	
		balances b/f	1
		total comprehensive income	1
		transfer of revaluation surplus to retained earnings	1
			3
	(c)	Statement of financial position	
		property, plant and equipment	3
		equity investments	1
		inventory	½
		trade receivables	½
		bank	½
		deferred tax	1
		deferred revenue	1
		environmental provision	1½
		6% loan note	1½
		trade payables	½
		current tax payable	1
			12
	(d)	increase per statement of financial position	1
		increase per cash flows	1
		appropriate comment	1
			3
		Total for question	**30**

Fundamentals Level – Skills Module

Financial Reporting (International)

Wednesday 4 June 2014

Time allowed
Reading and planning: 15 minutes
Writing: 3 hours

ALL FIVE questions are compulsory and MUST be attempted.

Do NOT open this paper until instructed by the supervisor.

During reading and planning time only the question paper may be annotated. You must NOT write in your answer booklet until instructed by the supervisor.

This question paper must not be removed from the examination hall.

The Association of Chartered Certified Accountants

ALL FIVE questions are compulsory and MUST be attempted

1   On 1 October 2013, Penketh acquired 90 million of Sphere's 150 million $1 equity shares. The acquisition was achieved through a share exchange of one share in Penketh for every three shares in Sphere. At that date the stock market prices of Penketh's and Sphere's shares were $4 and $2·50 per share respectively. Additionally, Penketh will pay $1·54 cash on 30 September 2014 for each share acquired. Penketh's finance cost is 10% per annum.

The retained earnings of Sphere **brought forward** at 1 April 2013 were $120 million.

The summarised statements of profit or loss and other comprehensive income for the companies for the year ended 31 March 2014 are:

	Penketh $'000	Sphere $'000
Revenue	620,000	310,000
Cost of sales	(400,000)	(150,000)
Gross profit	220,000	160,000
Distribution costs	(40,000)	(20,000)
Administrative expenses	(36,000)	(25,000)
Investment income (note (iii))	5,000	1,600
Finance costs	(2,000)	(5,600)
Profit before tax	147,000	111,000
Income tax expense	(45,000)	(31,000)
Profit for the year	102,000	80,000
Other comprehensive income		
Gain/(loss) on revaluation of land (notes (i) and (ii))	(2,200)	3,000
Total comprehensive income for the year	99,800	83,000

The following information is relevant:

(i)   A fair value exercise conducted on 1 October 2013 concluded that the carrying amounts of Sphere's net assets were equal to their fair values with the following exceptions:

–   the fair value of Sphere's land was $2 million in excess of its carrying amount

–   an item of plant had a fair value of $6 million in excess of its carrying amount. The plant had a remaining life of two years at the date of acquisition. Plant depreciation is charged to cost of sales.

–   Penketh placed a value of $5 million on Sphere's good trading relationships with its customers. Penketh expected, on average, a customer relationship to last for a further five years. Amortisation of intangible assets is charged to administrative expenses.

(ii) Penketh's group policy is to revalue land to market value at the end of each accounting period. Prior to its acquisition, Sphere's land had been valued at historical cost, but it has adopted the group policy since its acquisition. In addition to the fair value increase in Sphere's land of $2 million (see note (i)), it had increased by a further $1 million since the acquisition.

(iii) On 1 October 2013, Penketh also acquired 30% of Ventor's equity shares. Ventor's profit after tax for the year ended 31 March 2014 was $10 million and during March 2014 Ventor paid a dividend of $6 million. Penketh uses equity accounting in its consolidated financial statements for its investment in Ventor.

Sphere did not pay any dividends in the year ended 31 March 2014.

(iv) After the acquisition Penketh sold goods to Sphere for $20 million. Sphere had one fifth of these goods still in inventory at 31 March 2014. In March 2014 Penketh sold goods to Ventor for $15 million, all of which were still in inventory at 31 March 2014. All sales to Sphere and Ventor had a mark-up on cost of 25%.

(v) Penketh's policy is to value the non-controlling interest at the date of acquisition at its fair value. For this purpose, the share price of Sphere at that date (1 October 2013) is representative of the fair value of the shares held by the non-controlling interest.

(vi) All items in the above statements of profit or loss and other comprehensive income are deemed to accrue evenly over the year unless otherwise indicated.

Required:

(a) Calculate the consolidated goodwill as at 1 October 2013.

(b) Prepare the consolidated statement of profit or loss and other comprehensive income of Penketh for the year ended 31 March 2014.

The following mark allocation is provided as guidance for this question:

(a) 6 marks
(b) 19 marks

(25 marks)

[P.T.O.

2 The following trial balance relates to Xtol at 31 March 2014:

	$'000	$'000
Revenue (note (i))		490,000
Cost of sales	290,600	
Distribution costs	33,500	
Administrative expenses	36,800	
Loan note interest and dividends paid (notes (iv) and (v))	13,380	
Bank interest	900	
20-year leased property at cost (note (ii))	100,000	
Plant and equipment at cost (note (ii))	155,500	
Accumulated amortisation/depreciation at 1 April 2013:		
leased property		25,000
plant and equipment		43,500
Inventory at 31 March 2014	61,000	
Trade receivables	63,000	
Trade payables		32,200
Bank		5,500
Equity shares of 25 cents each (note (iii))		56,000
Share premium		25,000
Retained earnings at 1 April 2013		26,080
5% convertible loan note (note (iv))		50,000
Current tax (note (vi))	3,200	
Deferred tax (note (vi))		4,600
	757,880	757,880

The following notes are relevant:

(i) Revenue includes an amount of $20 million for cash sales made through Xtol's retail outlets during the year on behalf of Francais. Xtol, acting as agent, is entitled to a commission of 10% of the selling price of these goods. By 31 March 2014, Xtol had remitted to Francais $15 million (of the $20 million sales) and recorded this amount in cost of sales.

(ii) Plant and equipment is depreciated at 12½% per annum on the reducing balance basis.

All amortisation/depreciation of non-current assets is charged to cost of sales.

(iii) On 1 August 2013, Xtol made a fully subscribed rights issue of equity share capital based on two new shares at 60 cents each for every five shares held. The market price of Xtol's shares before the issue was $1·02 each. The issue has been fully recorded in the trial balance figures.

(iv) On 1 April 2013, Xtol issued a 5% $50 million convertible loan note at par. Interest is payable annually in arrears on 31 March each year. The loan note is redeemable at par or convertible into equity shares at the option of the loan note holders on 31 March 2016. The interest on an equivalent loan note without the conversion rights would be 8% per annum.

The present values of $1 receivable at the end of each year, based on discount rates of 5% and 8%, are:

	5%	8%
End of year 1	0·95	0·93
2	0·91	0·86
3	0·86	0·79

(v) An equity dividend of 4 cents per share was paid on 30 May 2013 and, after the rights issue, a further dividend of 2 cents per share was paid on 30 November 2013.

(vi) The balance on current tax represents the under/over provision of the tax liability for the year ended 31 March 2013. A provision of $28 million is required for current tax for the year ended 31 March 2014 and at this date the deferred tax liability was assessed at $8·3 million.

4

Required:

(a) Prepare the statement of profit or loss for Xtol for the year ended 31 March 2014.

(b) Prepare the statement of changes in equity for Xtol for the year ended 31 March 2014.

(c) Prepare the statement of financial position for Xtol as at 31 March 2014.

(d) Calculate the basic earnings per share (EPS) for Xtol for the year ended 31 March 2014.

Note: Answers and workings (for parts (a) to (c)) should be presented to the nearest $1,000; notes to the financial statements are not required.

The following mark allocation is provided as guidance for this question:

(a) 8 marks
(b) 6 marks
(c) 8 marks
(d) 3 marks

(25 marks)

[P.T.O.

3 Shown below are the financial statements of Woodbank for its most recent two years:

Statements of profit or loss for the year ended 31 March:

	2014 $'000	2013 $'000
Revenue	150,000	110,000
Cost of sales	(117,000)	(85,800)
Gross profit	33,000	24,200
Distribution costs	(6,000)	(5,000)
Administrative expenses	(9,000)	(9,200)
Finance costs – loan note interest	(1,750)	(500)
Profit before tax	16,250	9,500
Income tax expense	(5,750)	(3,000)
Profit for the year	10,500	6,500

Statements of financial position as at 31 March:

	2014 $'000	2013 $'000
Assets		
Non-current assets		
Property, plant and equipment	118,000	85,000
Goodwill	30,000	nil
	148,000	85,000
Current assets		
Inventory	15,500	12,000
Trade receivables	11,000	8,000
Bank	500	5,000
	27,000	25,000
Total assets	175,000	110,000
Equity and liabilities		
Equity		
Equity shares of $1 each	80,000	80,000
Retained earnings	15,000	10,000
	95,000	90,000
Non-current liabilities		
10% loan notes	55,000	5,000
Current liabilities		
Trade payables	21,000	13,000
Current tax payable	4,000	2,000
	25,000	15,000
Total equity and liabilities	175,000	110,000

The following information is available:

(i) On 1 January 2014, Woodbank purchased the trading assets and operations of Shaw for $50 million and, on the same date, issued additional 10% loan notes to finance the purchase. Shaw was an unincorporated entity and its results (for three months from 1 January 2014 to 31 March 2014) and net assets (including goodwill not subject to any impairment) are included in Woodbank's financial statements for the year ended 31 March 2014 .There were no other purchases or sales of non-current assets during the year ended 31 March 2014.

6

(ii) Extracts of the results (for three months) of the previously separate business of Shaw, which are included in Woodbank's statement of profit or loss for the year ended 31 March 2014, are:

	$'000
Revenue	30,000
Cost of sales	(21,000)
Gross profit	9,000
Distribution costs	(2,000)
Administrative expenses	(2,000)

(iii) The following six ratios have been correctly calculated for Woodbank for the year ended 31 March 2013:

Return on capital employed (ROCE)	10·5%
(profit before interest and tax/year-end total assets less current liabilities)	
Net asset (equal to capital employed) turnover	1·16 times
Gross profit margin	22·0%
Profit before interest and tax margin	9·1%
Current ratio	1·7:1
Gearing (debt/(debt + equity))	5·3%

Required:

(a) **Calculate for the year ended 31 March 2014:**

(i) **equivalent ratios (all six) to the above for Woodbank based on its reported figures; and**
(ii) **equivalent ratios to the first FOUR only for Woodbank excluding the effects of the purchase of Shaw.**

Note: Assume the capital employed for Shaw is equal to its purchase price of $50 million.   (10 marks)

(b) **Assess the comparative financial performance and position of Woodbank for the year ended 31 March 2014. Your answer should refer to the effects of the purchase of Shaw.**   (15 marks)

          (25 marks)

[P.T.O.

4 **(a)** A director of Enca, a public listed company, has expressed concerns about the accounting treatment of some of the company's items of property, plant and equipment which have increased in value. His main concern is that the statement of financial position does not show the true value of assets which have increased in value and that this 'undervaluation' is compounded by having to charge depreciation on these assets, which also reduces reported profit. He argues that this does not make economic sense.

Required:

Respond to the director's concerns by summarising the principal requirements of IAS 16 *Property, Plant and Equipment* **in relation to the revaluation of property, plant and equipment, including its subsequent treatment.**
(5 marks)

(b) The following details relate to two items of property, plant and equipment (A and B) owned by Delta which are depreciated on a straight-line basis with no estimated residual value:

	Item A	Item B
Estimated useful life at acquisition	8 years	6 years
	$'000	$'000
Cost on 1 April 2010	240,000	120,000
Accumulated depreciation (two years)	(60,000)	(40,000)
Carrying amount at 31 March 2012	180,000	80,000
Revaluation on 1 April 2012:		
Revalued amount	160,000	112,000
Revised estimated remaining useful life	5 years	5 years
Subsequent expenditure capitalised on 1 April 2013	nil	14,400

At 31 March 2014 item A was still in use, but item B was sold (on that date) for $70 million.

Note: Delta makes an annual transfer from its revaluation surplus to retained earnings in respect of excess depreciation.

Required:

Prepare extracts from:

(i) **Delta's statements of profit or loss for the years ended 31 March 2013 and 2014 in respect of charges (expenses) related to property, plant and equipment;**

(ii) **Delta's statements of financial position as at 31 March 2013 and 2014 for the carrying amount of property, plant and equipment and the revaluation surplus.**

The following mark allocation is provided as guidance for this requirement:

(i) 5 marks
(ii) 5 marks
(10 marks)

(15 marks)

5 The following issues have arisen during the preparation of Skeptic's draft financial statements for the year ended 31 March 2014:

(i) From 1 April 2013, the directors have decided to reclassify research and amortised development costs as administrative expenses rather than its previous classification as cost of sales. They believe that the previous treatment unfairly distorted the company's gross profit margin.

(ii) Skeptic has two potential liabilities to assess. The first is an outstanding court case concerning a customer claiming damages for losses due to faulty components supplied by Skeptic. The second is the provision required for product warranty claims against 200,000 units of retail goods supplied with a one-year warranty.

The estimated outcomes of the two liabilities are:

Court case	Product warranty claims
10% chance of no damages awarded	70% of sales will have no claim
65% chance of damages of $4 million	20% of sales will require a $25 repair
25% chance of damages of $6 million	10% of sales will require a $120 repair

(iii) On 1 April 2013, Skeptic received a government grant of $8 million towards the purchase of new plant with a gross cost of $64 million. The plant has an estimated life of 10 years and is depreciated on a straight-line basis. One of the terms of the grant is that the sale of the plant before 31 March 2017 would trigger a repayment on a sliding scale as follows:

Sale in the year ended:	Amount of repayment
31 March 2014	100%
31 March 2015	75%
31 March 2016	50%
31 March 2017	25%

Accordingly, the directors propose to credit to the statement of profit or loss $2 million ($8 million x 25%) being the amount of the grant they believe has been earned in the year to 31 March 2014. Skeptic accounts for government grants as a separate item of deferred credit in its statement of financial position. Skeptic has no intention of selling the plant before the end of its economic life.

Required:

Advise, and quantify where possible, how the above items (i) to (iii) should be treated in Skeptic's financial statements for the year ended 31 March 2014.

The following mark allocation is provided as guidance for this question:

(i) 3 marks
(ii) 4 marks
(iii) 3 marks

(10 marks)

End of Question Paper